A CONSTITUTIONAL HISTORY

of the

U.S. SUPREME COURT

DATE DUE

RICHARD J. REGAN

A CONSTITUTIONAL HISTORY

of the

U.S. SUPREME COURT

THE CATHOLIC UNIVERSITY OF AMERICA PRESS
Washington, D.C.

Library of Congress Cataloging-in-Publication Data

Regan, Richard J., author.

A constitutional history of the U.S. Supreme Court / Richard J. Regan.

pages cm

Includes bibliographical references and index.

ISBN 978-0-8132-2721-4 (pbk. : alk. paper)

1. United States. Supreme Court—History.   2. Constitutional history—

United States.   3. Constitutional law—United States—History.   I. Title.

KF8742.R46 2015

342.73—dc23   2014038668

published with a grant by

Figure Foundation

for when day rule night

CONTENTS

Appendixes

PREFACE

This book is not designed for lawyers or political scientists, although I think that they will find it a good read, especially on the justices' voting. Rather, it is designed for general readers and students in courses on constitutional history and politics. The chapters deal with leading decisions of successive courts and begin with brief biographies of the justices on the courts. There are four appendices: (1) the text of the Constitution and amendments; (2) the court system (including references to important source materials); (3) a chronological list of the justices with biographical details; and (4) a chronological list of the successive membership on the courts. Readers may wish to start with the appendix on the Supreme Court system as an introduction to the work of successive courts, as may instructors in courses on the history of the court.

I devote more attention to the later courts, especially the Rehnquist and Roberts courts. There are several reasons for doing so. First, a wealth of material on earlier courts already exists. Second, decisions of the more recent courts concern developing areas of constitutional law. Third, elaborate treatment of the most recent courts gives a good picture of the current working court.

As the reader will readily perceive, many recent cases, and most of the ones reported in the text, involve decisions by a sharply divided court and the concurring and dissenting opinions of the justices. I present their arguments only summarily, but readers and students may wish to read, and I hope that they do, all the opinions in the cases, and instructors will be able to amplify presentation of the justices' arguments.

A CONSTITUTIONAL HISTORY

of the

U.S. SUPREME COURT

THE FEDERALIST COURT

(1789–1800)

The Justices

Article III, section 1 of the U.S. Constitution established the Supreme Court but did not specify the number of justices. The Judiciary Act of 1789 authorized six justices; President Washington nominated a chief justice and five associate justices on September 24, 1789, and the U.S. Senate confirmed them two days later. They were Chief Justice John Jay and Associated Justices John Rutledge, William Cushing, James Wilson, John Blair Jr., and Robert Harrison. Harrison, however, declined the appointment in January 1790 because of ill health. (He died on April 20 of that year.) On February 9, 1790, Washington nominated James Iredell as the sixth justice, and the Senate confirmed him on the next day. All six justices were members of the Federalist Party.

John Jay John Jay was born in New York City on December 12, 1745; his father was a wealthy merchant and his mother a member of the prominent Van Cortland family. He was a Calvinist Protestant, attended King's College, now Columbia University, and received an M.A. there in 1767. He was certified to practice law in 1768 after clerkship. He married Sarah Livingston, the member of another prominent family. He collaborated with Alexander Hamilton and James Madison in writing the Federalist Papers urging adoption of the Constitution.

He had a distinguished political career. He was a member of the First Continental Congress from 1774 to 1779 and its president from 1778 to 1779. He was the first chief justice of the New York Court of Appeals (New York's highest court). He served as ambassador to Spain from 1779 to 1781, helped negotiate peace with Great Britain in 1782, and was secretary for foreign affairs in the Second Continental Congress from 1784 to 1789. He served on the U.S. Supreme Court from 1789 to 1795, took a leave of absence from the court in 1794 to negotiate the treaty with Great Britain bearing his name, and resigned a year later to become governor of New York for six years. When Oliver Ellsworth resigned in the fall of 1800, he declined President Adams's offer to reappoint him to the office. He died in 1829.

John Rutledge John Rutledge was born in Charleston, South Carolina, in late September 1739. His father was a doctor. He was Protestant, was educated by private tutors, and studied law in England. He sat in the South Carolina legislature for eighteen years and was the state's attorney general for one year before the Revolution (1764–65) and governor for five years during it (1776–78, 1779–82). He was a delegate to the Stamp Act Congress (1765) and to the Continental Congresses (1774–77, 1782–83). He was a delegate to the Constitutional Convention, supported slavery and a class basis of representation, chaired its Committee on Detail, and signed the Constitution (1787).

He resigned from the court on March 5, 1791, but Washington nominated him to succeed Jay on July 1, 1795. The Senate rejected his nomination because of a speech he made opposing Jay's Treaty, but he served as interim chief justice until that date (December 15, 1795). He died on July 23, 1800.

William Cushing William Cushing was born in Scituate, Massachusetts, on March 1, 1732. He was a Congregationalist, and his father was a doctor. He attended Harvard College, studied law in England, and was admitted to the bar of Massachusetts in 1755. He was a judge on the Massachusetts Superior Court from 1772 to 1775, a judge on the Supreme Judicial Court of Massachusetts from 1775 to 1777, and chief justice of that court for twelve years, from 1777 to 1789. He served on the U.S. Supreme Court for almost twenty-one years, until his death on September 13, 1810.

James Wilson James Wilson was born on September 14, 1742, in Carskerdy (Fife), Scotland. He was a Presbyterian and the son of a poor farmer. He was educated at St. Andrew's University in Scotland and the University of Edinburgh. Emigrating to the United States in 1765, he taught Greek and rhetoric in Pennsylvania, clerked under John Dickinson, and was admitted to the bar in 1767. He married Rachel Bird in 1771 and Hannah Gray in 1793. He published a treatise on the authority of the British Parliament.

He was a delegate to the First Continental Congress and signed the Declaration of Independence. He was a delegate to the Congress under the Articles of Confederation in 1784 and from 1785 to 1786. He was an influential delegate to the Constitutional Convention in 1787 and led the fight in Pennsylvania for ratification of the Constitution. He served on the court until his death on August 21, 1798.

John Blair Jr. John Blair Jr. was born in Williamsburg, Virginia, in 1732. His father, John, was a leading figure in Virginia before the Revolution. Blair was Protestant, graduated from William and Mary College in 1754, and studied law in London at the Middle Temple, one of the Inns of Court. He was an intimate friend of George Washington.

He served in the Virginia legislature for nine years and was a judge on the Virginia General Court in 1778 and its chief justice in 1779. He was a delegate to the Constitutional Convention in 1787 and a signer of the Constitution.

He resigned from the Supreme Court on January 27, 1796, and died on August 31, 1800.

James Iredell James Iredell, a Protestant and Federalist, was born on October 5, 1751, at Ewes (Sussex), England. His father, Francis, was a Bristol merchant. The family emigrated to North Carolina. James studied law under Samuel Johnston, was admitted to the bar in 1771, and married Samuel's daughter Hannah in 1773.

At the age of seventeen he became comptroller of customs for six years (1768–74) and collector of the port of Edenton for two years (1774–76). He was a judge of the North Carolina Superior Court for a half-year (1777), attorney general of North Carolina for two years (1779–81), and a member of the council for revising statutes for three years.

He served on the U.S. Supreme Court from the date of his confirmation (February 10, 1790) until his death on October 20, 1799.

Thomas Johnson When Justice Rutledge retired in 1791, Washington nominated Thomas Johnson, a Protestant and Federalist, to the court on August 5, 1791, initially on a recess appointment. He was confirmed on November 7,

1791, but not sworn in until August 6, 1792. Johnson was born in Calvert County, Maryland, on November 4, 1732. He had only a rudimentary education, studied law under Stephen Bordley, and was admitted to the Maryland bar in 1760.

He served in the Maryland legislature for five years and was governor for two years (1777–79) and chief judge of the Maryland General Court for a year (1790–91).

He served on the court for only seven months, resigning on March 4, 1793. He died twenty-six years later, on October 26, 1819.

William Paterson On the same day that Johnson retired, Washington nominated William Paterson, a Protestant and Federalist, and the Senate immediately confirmed him. Paterson was born on December 24, 1745, in County Antrim, Ireland. His father was a manufacturer of tin plate. The family emigrated to New Jersey, and Paterson attended Princeton College, where he earned an A.B. in 1763 and an M.A. in 1766. He was married twice. He studied law under Richard Stockton, a prominent attorney in New Jersey, before the Revolution and was admitted to the bar in 1769.

He served in the New Jersey legislature for two years and was the state's attorney general for seven years. He attended the Constitutional Convention in 1787, authored the small-states federal plan, and was a signer of the Constitution. His plan was influential in leading the framers to the Great Compromise—namely, that the people would be proportionally represented in the House of Representatives and the states equally in the Senate. After the convention he served one year in the first U.S. Senate (1789–90) and was governor of New Jersey (1790–93). He continued on the court until his death on September 9, 1806.

Samuel Chase Justice Blair resigned in January 1796, and Washington on January 26 nominated Samuel Chase to replace him. Chase, a Protestant and Federalist, was born on April 17, 1741, in Somerset County, Maryland. His father, Thomas, was rector of St. Paul's Episcopal Church. He was tutored by his father, studied law in the office of Hammond and Hall, and was admitted to the bar in 1761.

He served for twenty years in the Maryland legislature, signed the Declaration of Independence after its promulgation (August 2, 1776), was a member of Congress under the Articles of Confederation for one year (1784–85), and was chief judge of the Maryland General Court for five years (1791–95).

Chase has the dubious distinction of being the only justice of the court to be impeached. He was openly political on and off the court. The House of Representatives impeached him in 1804, but the Senate acquitted him on March 1, 1805. He died on June 19, 1811.

Oliver Ellsworth The Senate in December 1795 rejected the nomination of Rutledge to be chief justice, and on March 3, 1796, Washington nominated Oliver Ellsworth to the office; the Senate confirmed him the next day. Ellsworth, a Congregationalist and Federalist, was born on April 29, 1745, in Windsor, Connecticut. His father was a ship's captain. He attended Yale but graduated from Princeton (B.A., 1766). Prior to college he studied under the Reverend Joseph Bellamy. He was admitted to the bar in 1771.

He was a member of the Continental Congress from 1777 to 1783, a member of the Governor's Council for five years (1780–85), and a judge on the Connecticut Superior Court for four years (1785–89). He was a delegate to the Constitutional Convention and coauthored with Roger Sherman the Great Compromise on representation in the House of Representatives and the Senate. He was not a signer of the Constitution. He was a U.S. senator for seven years (1789–96), where he was the chief architect of the Judiciary Act of 1789 and the chairman of the conference committee on the amendments to the Constitution that became the Bill of Rights.

On the return voyage from negotiations with France, his health suffered, and he resigned on September 30, 1800. He died on November 26, 1807.

Bushrod Washington President John Adams on September 29, 1798, three days after the death of Justice Wilson, nominated Bushrod Washington, a nephew of the former president and his future heir and literary executor, to the court. The new justice, a Protestant and Federalist, was born on June 5, 1762, in Westmoreland County, Virginia. His father, John, was a magistrate and delegate to the legislature. He graduated from William and Mary College in 1778, studied law under Wilson, and practiced law in Virginia. He served in the Virginia legislature for one year (1787–88) and on the court until his death on November 26, 1829.

Alfred Moore On the same day that Justice Iredell died, October 20, 1799, President Adams nominated Alfred Moore to the court. Moore, a Protestant and Federalist, was born on May 21, 1755, in New Hanover County, North Carolina. His father, Maurice, was a lawyer and judge. He was educated in

Boston, studied law under his father, and was admitted to the North Carolina bar in 1775.

He served in the state legislature for two years (1780–82) and was state attorney general for nine years (1782–91). As U.S. commissioner he negotiated a treaty with the Cherokee nation in 1798. He was a judge on the North Carolina Supreme Court for one year (1798–99). He resigned from the U.S. Supreme Court in March 1804 and died on October 15, 1810.

John Marshall Although the following chapter will consider the Marshall Court, it seems fitting to outline the background of Chief Justice John Marshall here. He was an active Federalist and a Unitarian, although he often attended the services of the Episcopalian church to which his wife and children belonged. He was born on September 24, 1755, in what is now Midland, Virginia. His father, Thomas, was a farmer. His early education was informal. He attended lectures in law at William and Mary College by George Whyte, a polymath, for six weeks in 1780. He was admitted to the Virginia bar in the same year. He also served for three years in the Continental Army during the Revolution.

He served seven years in the Virginia legislature (1782–86, 1789–91, 1795–97). He was envoy to France from 1797 to 1798, a U.S. congressman from 1799 to 1800, and secretary of state from 1800 to March 4, 1801. President Adams nominated him to replace Ellsworth as chief justice on January 20, 1801, and the outgoing Federalist Senate confirmed him on January 27.

He presided over the court until his death on July 6, 1835.

Summary All of the justices appointed by Presidents Washington and Adams were Federalists, and all but Marshall Protestant. They were drawn equally or nearly equally from the states north and south of the Mason-Dixon line. All were practicing lawyers. Most clerked under a practicing lawyer or judge in their state, but three (Rutledge, Cushing, and Blair) studied law in England. Three were born in the British Isles: Wilson in Scotland, Iredell in England, and Paterson in Ireland.

The fathers of five were in one of the professions: the fathers of two (Moore and Washington) were lawyers, the father of one (Cushing) a judge, the father of one (Rutledge) a doctor, and the father of one (Chase) a clergyman. The fathers of three (Iredell, Jay, and Paterson) were successful businessmen. The fathers of two (Marshall and Wilson) were modest farmers. The father of one (Blair) was a prominent landowner. Wilson and Marshall were the only justices to come from a relatively modest background.

Seven (Blair, Cushing, Ellsworth, Jay, Paterson, Washington, and Wilson) attended or graduated from college, and two (Jay and Paterson) received M.A. degrees. Eleven (Blair, Chase, Ellsworth, Jay, Johnson, Marshall, Moore, Paterson, Rutledge, Washington, and Wilson) had legislative experience. Eight (Blair, Chase, Cushing, Ellsworth, Iredell, Jay, Johnson, and Moore) had judicial experience. Seven (Iredell, Jay, Johnson, Marshall, Moore, Paterson, and Rutledge) had executive governmental experience.

Of the three chief justices before Marshall, two (Jay and Ellsworth) resigned, and the appointment of the other (Rutledge) was not confirmed. Two associate justices before Marshall became chief justice (Iredell and Wilson) died in office. Three associate justices before Marshall (Blair, Rutledge, and Johnson) resigned. Why were there so many resignations? First and probably the key factor was that contemporary aspiring politicians did not regard the office of justice or even chief justice to be as important as other offices. For example, Jay resigned to become governor of New York and would not relinquish that post when offered reappointment as chief justice by Adams. Second, since the justices needed only six weeks to decide the few Supreme Court cases submitted to them, Congress had required them to serve as judges in circuit courts, (i.e., courts chiefly assisting federal district judges in the states) when the Supreme Court was not in session. (Being a circuit judge required long journeys on horseback from one place to another in the circuit.) Third, whether in session (originally in New York City, then in Philadelphia, and finally in Washington) or riding the circuit, the justices were away from their families and estates.

When Marshall became chief justice in 1801, there were five holdover Federalist associate justices on the court: Cushing, who was the sole remaining member of the original court, Paterson, Washington, Chase, and Moore.

Leading Decisions

Jurisdiction One of the Federalist Court's early decisions, *Chisholm v. Georgia*, was a political disaster that only the Dred Scott decision surpassed. The Chisholm decision concerned the failure of Georgia to pay money owed to a South Carolinian merchant for supplies provided to Georgia during the Revolution. The merchant died, and Alexander Chisholm, another South Carolinian merchant, became his executor. Chisholm brought suit against Georgia in the U.S. Circuit Court for the district of Georgia. Georgia claimed that its sovereign and independent status under the Constitution precluded a citizen from another state suing it in federal court. The judges, Iredell, sitting as a circuit judge, and Nathaniel Pendleton, upheld Georgia's position.

In 1792 Chisholm brought the case to the Supreme Court. The case was postponed twice because Georgia failed to appear, and the court, after Georgia failed to respond to another invitation, handed down a decision on February 19, 1793. Five justices participated. The sixth, Johnson, was about to retire and did not participate. The five participating justices delivered their opinions seriatim—that is, separately. There was no opinion of the court as a whole, and one knew the outcome only by adding up the votes of individual justices. This system would persist until Marshall introduced the system of the court issuing an opinion and concurring and dissenting justices writing opinions if they so wished.

Four justices (Blair, Cushing, Jay, and Wilson) voted to reverse the circuit court for Chisholm. They cited the broad words of Article III, section 2: "The judicial power of the United Stated shall extend ... to controversies between a state and citizens of another state." There was no restrictive language to indicate that the state could not be a defendant. Moreover, as Wilson pointed out, a state obviously could be a defendant in a controversy between two states, the jurisdiction over which the same section granted to the federal courts. Iredell dissented, holding to his views in the circuit court—namely, that the words of the Constitution should not be stretched to make states defendants in suits by private citizens and that only Congress could authorize such suits.

English law had always held that the doctrine of sovereign immunity precluded private parties from bringing suits against the government under the rubric that the king as such could do no wrong. Nobody at the time of the case thought that a private citizen could sue the United States without its permission to do so, which permission it had granted with respect to contracts and torts. Nor did anyone dispute that states were sovereign within their own jurisdictions. Nor did anyone dispute that Chisholm would have been allowed to press his case in Georgia courts if that state allowed such suits. As Georgia saw the case, it concerned a private citizen of another state dragging a sovereign state into a different jurisdiction than its own.

The underlying issue in the case was a dispute about how to read the broad words of the Constitution. The majority understood them literally and logically. Iredell understood the words in the context of what he perceived to be the original intent. In the course of ratifying the Constitution, Hamilton and Madison, members of the convention, assured state legislators that a private citizen of another state could not sue a state in federal courts without its consent. Of course, those statements were made in the political context of ratification and spoke only for themselves, and Madison's notes on the convention, which had not yet been published, said nothing on the question. In view of the rapid negative reaction to the decision, however, the majority justices can hardly have been unconscious of the common public understanding that state sovereignty precluded application of the Constitution's grant of judicial power over controversies between a state and citizens of another state to suits brought *by* a private citizen against a state.

Political retribution was swift. A House resolution was filed to amend the Constitution against the decision on the very day of the decision, and a Senate resolution to that effect was filed on the next day. Congress passed the amendment, the Eleventh, overwhelmingly on March 4, 1793, two weeks after the decision, and the requisite number of states ratified it in eleven months. The amendment barred federal jurisdiction of suits against the states not only by citizens of another state but also by citizens of a foreign country. That Congress resorted to the amendment process to overturn *Chisholm* thereby implicitly recognized the power of the court to interpret the Constitution.

Taxes There were two important decisions in 1796, both involving the same individual, Daniel Hylton of Virginia. In one case (*Hylton v. U.S.*), Hylton, who was in the carriage trade and owned 125 carriages, challenged a federal law of 1794 imposing a $16 tax on each carriage. He lost in the circuit court and obtained review by the Supreme Court. Hylton claimed that Article I, section 2 required that direct taxes be apportioned to the states according to their population and that the carriage tax was a direct tax and so unconstitutional because it was not laid on the states according to population. The four participating justices (Chase, Iredell, Paterson, and Wilson) held in 1796 that the carriage tax was indirect and so did not need to be apportioned according to population. They were of the opinion that the tax was an excise tax and that only per capita and land taxes were direct taxes. Ellsworth and Cushing did not participate. Madison's notes make perfectly clear that the provision on direct taxes was inserted precisely because land-rich and population-poor states, chiefly Southern states, would be disproportionately taxed unless federal poll and land taxes were apportioned according to population. The decision suggested that federal income taxes, if laid, would be indirect taxes.

In addition to the decision's validation of federal personal property taxes, it was also important in that the court for the first time reviewed the constitutionality of an act of Congress. Although it upheld the law, the very fact that it did so implied that it could refuse to do so—that is, declare an act of Congress unconstitutional.

Debts The second case (*Ware v. Hylton*) involved a recurring thorn in post-Revolutionary relations between Great Britain and the United States: the prewar debts owed to British creditors. During the war many states sequestered British assets in the colonies. Virginia was one such state and gave its citizens the right to discharge such debts by paying the money due into the state treasury. Hylton did this in the severely depreciated Continental currency. But the Treaty of Paris at the conclusion of the war specified that creditors on either side had a legal right to collect prewar debts. Ware was a British creditor who sought repayment from Hylton. After *Chisholm*, of course, Ware had to bring his case in the courts of Virginia. He lost and obtained review by the Supreme Court.

In the same year as the other Hylton case, the four participating justices (Chase, Cushing, Paterson, and Wilson) supported the British creditor. The justices admitted that the laws of war gave Virginia the right to sequester enemy property but held that the Treaty of Paris trumped Virginia's action. In their view Article VI of the Constitution made provisions of a treaty "the supreme law of the land." Ellsworth and Iredell did not participate, although Iredell latter submitted an opinion for the record. The decision was unpopular but did not provoke the reaction that *Chisholm* did. Interestingly, Marshall was the losing attorney for Hylton on appeal to the court and argued that a treaty could not abrogate vested rights.

Ex Post Facto Laws The fourth important decision of the Federalist Court was in *Calder v. Bull* in 1798. The Connecticut legislature had passed a law granting a new hearing to Bull and his wife after their right to appeal a probate court decision had expired. At the new hearing, Bull succeeded. Calder, the rival claimant, lost his appeal to the Connecticut Supreme Court and then brought the case to the U.S. Supreme Court on a writ of error. He claimed that the Connecticut law granting the new hearing to Bull violated the prohibition in Article I, section 10 of the Constitution against states passing ex post facto laws. The four participating justices (Chase Cushing, Iredell, and Paterson) affirmed the decision of the Connecticut Supreme Court in favor of Bull. Ellsworth and Wilson did not participate.

The participating justices were agreed that the ex post facto laws prohibited in the Constitution referred only to criminal cases, not to civil cases, but they disagreed on the applicability of natural law to judicial review of state laws. Chase in particular argued that the natural law and the terms of the social contract limit the power of legislatures, whether federal or state, implying that that law alone would be sufficient to invalidate legislation, although it was not necessary in this case to invoke it. Iredell made clear his opinion that litigants have no power to invoke the natural law to invalidate legislation, although he seems to accept such a law. For him the only duty of the courts is to apply the Constitution. It should be noted that lawyers and jurists at the time almost universally acknowledged that there was a natural law, at least in the Lockean sense.

2

THE MARSHALL COURT

(1801–35)

The Justices

William Johnson Justice Moore resigned in March 1804, and President Jefferson nominated William Johnson, a Protestant and a Democrat-Republican, to the court on March 22; the Senate confirmed him two days later. Johnson was born on December 17, 1771, in Charleston, South Carolina. His father, William, was a prominent leader in South Carolina during the Revolutionary War. He attended Princeton College, studied law under Charles Pinckney, and was admitted to the bar in 1793.

He served in the South Carolina legislature for four years (1794–98), was speaker of its house for two years (1796–98), and was a justice on the South Carolina Supreme Court. He served on the U.S. Supreme Court until his death on August 4, 1834.

Brockholst Livingston Justice Paterson died in September 1806, and Jefferson nominated Brockholst Livingston, a Protestant and a Democrat-Republican, to the court on November 10; the Senate confirmed him on December 17. Livingston was born in New York City on November 25, 1757. His father, William, was a governor of New Jersey. He attended Princeton College, served as a lieutenant colonel in the Continental Army, was admitted to the bar in 1783, and was thrice married. He was a judge on a New York court for four years (1802–6) before his appointment. He served on the U.S. Supreme Court until his death on March 18, 1823.

Thomas Todd Congress added a seventh justice to the court, after which, on February 28, 1897, Jefferson nominated Thomas Todd, a Protestant and a Democrat-Republican, to the post; the Senate confirmed him on March 3. He was born on January 23, 1765, in King and Queen County, Virginia. His father, Richard, was a landholder. His education was limited, and he married twice.

From 1800 to 1806 he was a judge on the Kentucky Court of Appeals and its chief justice. He served on the U.S. Supreme Court until his death on February 7, 1826.

Joseph Story Cushing died in September 1811, and on November 15 President Madison nominated Joseph Story, originally a Congregationalist, then a Unitarian, and a Democrat-Republican, to the court; the Senate confirmed him three days later. He was born on September 18, 1779, in Marblehead, Massachusetts. His father, Elisha, was a doctor. He attended Marblehead Academy, graduated from Harvard College, read law with Samuel Sewell, and was admitted to the bar in 1801. He was married twice.

He lectured at the new Harvard Law School, served in the Massachusetts House of Representatives for five years (1805–6, 1809–10), and was its speaker in 1811. On the court he was a strong supporter of Marshall and added his legal erudition to Marshall's. He served on the court until his death on September 10, 1845.

Gabriel Duvall Chase died in June 1811, and Madison nominated Gabriel Duvall, a Protestant and Democrat-Republican, to the court on November 15; the Senate confirmed him three days later. Duvall was born on December 6, 1752, near Buena Vista, Maryland, and was married twice. He was admitted to the bar in 1778.

He was on the Council of Maryland for three years, a congressman for two years (1794–96), chief judge of the Maryland General Court for six years (1796–1802), and Comptroller of the United States for nine years (1802–11). He resigned from the court in January 1835 and died on March 6, 1844, at over ninety-one years of age.

Smith Thompson Livingston died in March 1823; on September 1, President Monroe nominated Smith Thompson, a Presbyterian and a Democrat-Republican, to the court, and the Senate confirmed him on December 19. He was born on January 17, 1768, in Amenia, New York, graduated from Princeton College in 1788, studied law under James Kent, and was admitted to the bar in 1792. He married twice, to two women of the famous Livingston family.

He served in the New York legislature for two years (1800–1802), was a judge on the New York Court of Appeals for sixteen years, the first twelve as associate justice and the last four as chief justice, and was secretary of the navy for four years (1819–23). He served on the U.S. Supreme Court until his death on December 10, 1824.

Robert Trimble Todd died in February 1826, and President John Quincy Adams nominated Robert Trimble, a Protestant and a Democrat-Republican, to the court on April 11; the Senate confirmed him on May 9. He was born in 1777 in Augusta County, Virginia. His father, William, was a landholder. He was educated in Bourbon Academy and Kentucky Academy and read law under George Nicholas and James Brown.

He was a member of the Kentucky legislature for two years (1802–4), a judge on the Kentucky Court of Appeals for two years (1807–9), U.S. attorney of Kentucky for four years (1813–17), and a U.S. district court judge for nine years (1817–26). He served on the U.S. Supreme Court until his death two years later, on August 25, 1828.

John McLean Justice Trimble died in August 1828; on March 6, 1829, President Jackson nominated John McLean, a Methodist and a Democrat who later sought nomination for the presidency on the Whig ticket (1852) and the Republican ticket (1856 and 1860), to the court, and the Senate confirmed him the next day. (Since McLean resigned as postmaster general immediately after Jackson's inauguration because of McLean's opposition to Jackson's commitment to the spoils system, it is not clear why Jackson chose to appoint McLean to the court.) McLean was born on March 11, 1785, in Morris County, New Jersey. His father, Fergus, was a weaver and farmer. He had an informal education with tutors, studied law under Arthur St. Clair, and was admitted to the Ohio bar in 1807. He married twice.

He served three years as a congressman (1813–16) and was a judge on the Ohio Supreme Court for six years (1816–22), a commissioner in the land office for one year (1822–23), and postmaster general for six years (1823–29). He served on the court until his death on April 4, 1861.

Henry Baldwin Justice Washington, the last Federalist justice besides Marshall, died in December 1829, and Jackson nominated Henry Baldwin, a Protestant and a Democrat, to the court on January 4, 1830; the Senate confirmed him two days later. He was born on January 14, 1780, in New Haven, Connecticut. He attended Yale College in 1797, studied law under Alexander Dallas, was admitted to the bar in 1801, and married twice.

He was a congressman for six years (1817–23) and engaged in private practice. He served on the court until his death on April 21, 1844.

James Wayne Justice William Johnson died on August 4, 1834; on January 7, 1835, Jackson nominated James Wayne, an Episcopalian and a Democrat, to the court, and the Senate confirmed him two days later. Wayne was born around 1790 in Savannah, Georgia. His father, Richard, was a British officer. He attended Trinity and Princeton Colleges, studied law under John Noel and Charles Chauncey, and was admitted to the bar in 1811. He was an army officer during the War of 1812, served in the Georgia legislature for two years (1815–17), and was mayor of Savannah for two years (1817–19), a judge on the Georgia Superior Court for five years (1824–29), and a congressman for six years (1829–35). He served on the court until his death on July 5, 1867.

Summary One of the Federalist carryover justices on the Marshall Court (Moore) resigned, and the others (Patterson, Cushing, Chase, and Washington) died before Marshall. Of the new justices on the Marshall Court, one resigned (Duvall), four predeceased Marshall (Johnson, Livingston, Todd, and Trimble), and five survived him on the court (Story, Thompson, McLean, Baldwin, and Wayne). All the new justices except Story were Protestants. Before the Jackson appointments, all appointees were Democrat-Republicans, and the three Jackson appointees were Democrats. Of the ten new appointees, three were from the South, four from the North, and three from Western states (two from Kentucky and one from Ohio). Four (Johnson, Livingston, Thompson, and Wayne) attended or graduated from Princeton College, Story attended Harvard College, and Baldwin attended Yale College.

Four (Duvall, Mclean, Thompson, and Wayne) had executive experience. Eight (Johnson, Story, Duvall, Thompson, Trimble, McLean, Baldwin, and Wayne) had legislative experience. Eight (Johnson, Livingston, Todd, Duvall, Thompson, Trimble, McLean, and Wayne) had judicial experience. All of the Jackson appointees (McLean, Baldwin, and Wayne) had served in the U.S. House of Representatives, as had Duvall.

Leading Decisions

Judicial Review The first major decision of the Marshall Court was *Marbury v. Madison,* on February 24, 1803. In the presidential and congressional election of 1800, President John Adams was defeated and the Federalist Party lost control of Congress. However, the new president, Thomas Jefferson, did not take office until March 4, 1801, and the new Congress did not meet until December 1801. The last session of the outgoing Federalist Congress met in December 1800. In February 1801 Congress created posts for forty-two justices of the peace in the District of Columbia. By March 3 President Adams had appointed Federalists to the judgeships, the Senate had confirmed them, and the commissions had been signed and sealed. Marshall, the outgoing secretary of state, did not deliver them to the appointees by noon, March 4, when the new administration took over.

James Madison, the new secretary of state, followed Jefferson's orders and refused to deliver the commissions. One of the designated judges, William Marbury, supported by lawyers provided by the Federalist Party, sought a writ of mandamus to Madison in an original action in the Supreme Court in December 1801. Marshall put the case off until the next court session in June 1802 and ordered Madison (i.e., the administration) to show cause why the court should not grant the writ to Marbury. (The administration sent no lawyer to argue its case against granting the writ.) Before that June the new Democrat-Republican Congress abolished the December and June terms of the court and substituted a February term, which delayed the case until February 1803.

This was evidently a politically motivated case, and Marshall faced a dilemma. If the court ruled in favor of Marbury, the administration would ignore it, and the court would be humiliated. On the other hand, if the court ruled in favor of Madison, it would hand a political victory to the administration. Marshall found a brilliant way around the horns of the dilemma. He would declare that Marbury had a right to the commission and that Madison's failure to deliver it was a dereliction of his official duty, but Marshall would refuse to issue the writ on jurisdictional grounds, in the course of which he would declare part of an act of Congress unconstitutional. But if the court had no jurisdiction to hear the case, the lecture to Jefferson was irrelevant, however much Marshall may have relished delivering it. On the court's jurisdiction Marshall could have simply declared that Marbury was neither a state nor an ambassador or other foreign representative and that Article III, section 2, clause 2 limited the court's original jurisdiction to such parties.

The argument in the lecture to the president was not airtight. The critical point of the argument was that delivery of the commission was essential to the right to the commission. But there are many examples where delivery is essential to establishing a right. I may sign a check to you or sign a contract with you, but you have no right to benefit from the signed check or signed contract until I deliver it to you.

Nor is Marshall's interpretation of section 13 of the Judiciary Act of 1789 airtight. In fact, it is implausible. The provision applicable to Marbury doesn't mention original jurisdiction and is separated from a provision referring to appellate jurisdiction only by a semicolon. Second, James Madison, the father of the Constitution, was the floor leader proposing the Judiciary Act, and Oliver Ellsworth, its author, attended the Constitutional Convention. Assuming for the moment that the act proposed to enlarge the court's original jurisdiction, is it plausible that they thought such enlargement unconstitutional? Third, George Washington, who was president of the Constitutional Convention, signed the Judiciary Act. Is it plausible that he would do so if he thought that the act unconstitutionally enlarged the court's original jurisdiction?

Nor is Marshall's argument that Article III, section 2, clause 2, by distinguishing cases falling under the court's original jurisdiction from all other cases falling under the court's appellate jurisdiction, precluded enlargement of the former cases. The clause may have intended only to specify that the cases involving states and foreign ministers fell under the court's original jurisdiction and, unlike the court's appellate jurisdiction, Congress could not *subtract* from it.

The rest of the decision consists of a disquisition on the Constitution limiting the legislative power of Congress and the executive power of the president and a declaration that it is the function of the courts to declare when legislative or executive acts contravene the Constitution. In particular, Marshall appeals to the oath of allegiance that federal judges swear to uphold it. But, of course, congressmen, senators, the president, and executive officers also take the oath, and Jefferson held that each branch of government was supreme in its sphere regarding interpretation of the Constitution. The latter position would lead to chaos, but judicial review is not the only answer to the problem of ultimate authority to interpret the Constitution. For example, under many constitutions, the parliament is the supreme authority. In defense of judicial review of congressional legislation, it should be noted that the Constitution establishes separate powers, not a unitary parliamentary system of government.

The power of judicial review concerns only the power to declare acts of Congress or parts thereof unconstitutional. Although some nineteenth-century presidents (e.g., Jackson in the Cherokee Indians case) refused to accept the finality of Supreme Court decisions about the Constitution, it is universally accepted today that, as Charles Evans Hughes said, the Constitution is what the Supreme Court says it is. That does not mean that court decisions are irreversible. Article V provides for amendments, although the process is cumbersome. More feasible is the fact that new appointments to the court may result in reversal of decisions. On average a new justice has been appointed to the court approximately every two years. In this way popular opinion can over time reverse or qualify Supreme Court decisions.

Power over State Courts *Marbury* established the power of the court regarding acts of Congress. Two subsequent decisions established the court's power over the highest state courts in cases involving constitutional questions. The first involved the confiscation of Loyalist property during the Revolutionary War. Virginia had confiscated lands belonging to a Loyalist, Lord Thomas Fairfax, and the state sold some of the confiscated land to David Hunter. When Lord Fairfax died, his claim passed to his nephew, Denny Martin. Fairfax's devisee sued for restoration of the land, but the Virginia Court of Appeals ruled in favor of Hunter's lessee. On appeal the U.S. Supreme Court in 1813 ruled in favor of Martin (*Fairfax's Devisee v. Hunter's Lessee*). Story wrote the court opinion, and Duvall and Livingston joined him. Johnson dissented, and Marshall, Todd, and Washington did not participate.

The Virginia court refused to give the decision effect, with its chief justice, Spenser Roane, arguing that section 25 of the Judiciary Act of 1789, which granted the U.S. Supreme Court jurisdiction over the final decisions of the highest state courts on federal laws or treaties, was unconstitutional. This gave rise to a second appeal to the court by Martin. This time, with Marshall alone not participating because of prior involvement in the litigation in behalf of the Fairfax claim, Story in 1816 again ruled in favor of Martin (*Martin v. Hunter's Lessee*). Four justices (Duvall, Livingston, Todd, and Washington) joined his opinion, and the other justice (Johnson) wrote a separate concurring opinion. Story rejected Roane's theory that the highest state courts had equal sovereignty with the Supreme Court and definitively affirmed federal judicial supremacy over a state court on federal questions. Scholars debate whether Martin ever got the property.

Cohens v. Virginia offered Marshall and the court another opportunity to declare federal judicial supremacy over the highest state courts, and they took it. Congress had authorized a lottery to obtain funds for the District of Columbia. Virginia had forbidden the sale of tickets on lotteries unauthorized by the state, and the Cohen brothers, Philip and Mendes, were convicted of selling the District of Columbia lottery tickets in Virginia and fined $100. The Cohens appealed to the Supreme Court, contending that their sale of lottery tickets was protected because Congress had authorized their sale. As in *Marbury*, Marshall faced the horns of a dilemma. On the one hand, if the court ruled in favor of the Cohens, Virginia would ignore the decision, and support from President Madison was at best dubious. On the other hand, if the court ruled in favor of Virginia, Roane and states-rights supporters would claim victory. Again, as in *Marbury*, Marshall escaped the horns of the dilemma by ruling in favor of Virginia while irrelevantly declaring that the decisions of state courts on federal questions were subject to review by the court.

Marshall wrote the 1821 court opinion, and all the justices except Washington, who did not participate, joined him. Marshall ruled in favor of Virginia because, in his view, Congress did not intend that the lottery tickets should be sold there, and Virginia otherwise had the right to prohibit their sale, but not before he defended the jurisdiction of the court. On that question Marshall pointed out that Article III, section 2, clause 1 declared that all cases arising under the Constitution fall within the federal judicial power and that the states thereby relinquished sovereignty to the federal government. The Eleventh Amendment prohibited individuals from *commencing* cases against the states in federal courts, but Virginia, not the Cohens, initiated the case, and the writ of error to the Supreme Court appealed the original case to the court. As to the application of federal judicial power to the judgments of state courts, the federal government is supreme, and the exercise of federal judicial power is essential to that supremacy. The federal government is not at the mercy of concurrent state jurisdiction.

Implied Powers In 1819 Marshall rendered the second of his three greatest decisions, *McCulloch v. Maryland*. Congress failed to renew the charter of the First Bank of the United States in 1811 but, in the aftermath of the War of 1812, chartered the Second Bank of the United States in 1816. The Second Bank, like the First, was a private bank in which the federal government owned 20 percent of the stock and was the functional equivalent of today's Federal Reserve System regarding control of interest rates. Initially the Second Bank pursued an inflationary policy that fueled excessive land speculation, but then changed its policy in the opposite direction. This affected state-chartered banks because the Second Bank effectively insisted on repayment of its loans in specie rather than state-bank notes. (Bank notes were the principal paper currency, and they were redeemable in specie at the banks that issued them.) As a result holders of the state-bank notes called on the state banks to redeem the notes in specie, the state banks were at risk of bankruptcy, and land speculators were at risk of foreclosure. Needless to add, the state-bank shareholders and debtors generally opposed the national bank's policy, and states-rights partisans had always opposed the idea of a national bank.

Many state legislatures sought to punish the Bank and curtail its power by taxing it. One such state was Maryland, which imposed a $15,000 annual tax on the Bank's Baltimore branch or, alternately, a tax stamp on notes issued. The cashier—that is, the manager—of the branch, James McCulloch, refused to pay the tax. When Maryland won a debt judgment in the state courts, McCulloch appealed to the Supreme Court. The attorneys on both sides of the case before the court were leading figures. Luther Martin for Maryland had attended the Constitutional Convention but left before its work was completed. Young Daniel Webster was part of the team for the Bank.

Marshall wrote the court opinion in favor of the Bank, and all the other justices joined the opinion, except Todd, who did not participate. There were two issues in the case. The first was whether Congress had the power to charter a bank. Marshall answered that question resoundingly in the affirmative. The Constitution derives from the people, not the states, and the federal government is supreme in the spheres of action granted it. It can exercise only enumerated powers, but the Constitution grants implied as well as explicit powers. It can charter a national bank because such a bank is a means to carry out powers enumerated in Article I, section 8, clauses 1–17, such as the powers to lay and collect taxes, borrow money, regulate commerce, declare and conduct war, and raise and support armies. He appealed particularly to the so-called elastic clause 18 of section 8—namely, the power to "make all laws necessary and proper to the execution of the foregoing powers" in clauses 1–17.

The second issue concerned the power of Maryland to tax the Bank. The power to create an instrument of the federal government implies a power to preserve it, and the power of a state to tax it is the power to destroy it. But is the latter proposition necessarily true? For example, would a moderate state tax on the sale of tobacco in army post exchanges in the state threaten to destroy the U.S. army? Nonetheless, the McCulloch decision has been the consistent precedent that federal instrumentalities are immune from state taxation.

Commerce Power Unlike the McCulloch decision, which was unpopular in most parts of the country, especially the South and the West, the third of Marshall's greatest decisions, *Gibbons v. Ogden*, was widely popular, especially in the Northeast. At issue in that 1824 case was the power of Congress to regulate commerce among the several states. The New York legislature had granted an exclusive right to operate steamboats in New York waters to Robert Livingston and Robert Fulton, the holders of the patents to the boats. Aaron Ogden obtained a license from the Livingston-Fulton combine to operate a steamboat service between New York and New Jersey. One of Ogden's former partners, Thomas Gibbons, ran a competing steamboat service under a federal coasting license. Ogden brought a successful action against Gibbons in the New York courts, and Gibbons appealed to the U.S. Supreme Court.

All the justices except Thompson, who did not participate, and Johnson, who wrote a separate opinion concurring in the judgment but going beyond Marshall's argument, joined Marshall's opinion. Marshall interpreted the commerce power broadly. Commerce involves more than buying and selling. It involves the intercourse leading up to buying and selling, including navigation, and presumably things resulting from buying and selling. The power to regulate is unlimited and supreme over state regulation. Commerce is among the several states if it affects more than one state—that is, affects other states— whereas internal commerce affects only one state. (The concept of purely internal commerce seems unrealistic in the context of modern economics.) In addition, state actions in the exercise of their police powers are not regulations of commerce. Marshall declined to determine whether federal power to regulate commerce among the several states is exclusive, holding only that the New York regulation conflicted with the federal legislation granting a coastal license to Gibbons. Johnson went the extra step and declared that the federal power over commerce among the several states is exclusive—that is, even when Congress has not legislated, the states cannot.

The Gibbons decision had little immediate impact regarding federal regulation of commerce, since Congress did little to regulate commerce until the

Interstate Commerce Act of 1887. While future courts always accepted the proposition that the commerce power applied to transportation, they basically ignored Marshall's broad definition of commerce and unwisely attempted to distinguish production from commerce.

Five years later, in 1829, the Marshall Court decided a commerce case involving state action affecting interstate commerce where there was no specifically contrary federal legislation (*Willson v. Blackbird Creek Marsh Co.*). Delaware had allowed a dam to be constructed across a small stream in order to drain a tidewater swamp and reclaim the land for commercial use. Willson broke the dam with his ship in order to navigate the stream, and the company sued him for damages. When Willson lost the case in state courts, he appealed to the Supreme Court on the basis of his coastal license in navigable waters. Marshall and the court ruled in favor of the state that, when Congress has not directly legislated on the subject, a state may act to promote the health, well-being, and property of its citizens. The fact that the creek was small and would have little impact on interstate commerce may have influenced him to ignore the federal coastal license.

Taxes Article I, section 10 prohibits states from taxing imports, and Marshall and the court ruled in 1827 that a state may not tax imported goods as long as they remain in their original containers and are not yet mingled with the property in the state (*Brown v. Maryland*). Maryland had imposed a license tax on wholesale dealers of imported goods, and one such dealer, Brown, appealed to the Supreme Court after losing in the state courts. Marshall held that the state tax violated both Article I, section 10 and the federal power over foreign commerce (Article I, section 8, clause 3).

Contract Clause The Marshall Court broadly interpreted the contract clause in favor of vested interests. That clause, Article I, section 10, prohibits states from passing laws impairing the obligation of contracts. In *Fletcher v. Peck*, Marshall in 1810 applied the clause to executed contracts—that is, grants or conveyances—and to public as opposed to private contracts. A bribed Georgia legislature in 1795 sold more than 35 million acres for a pittance to speculators. When the voters of Georgia became aware of the fraud, they elected a new legislature, which repealed the sale, but (presumably) innocent parties had purchased the land from the speculators. John Peck, a dealer who had purchased the lands, sold 15,000 acres to Robert Fletcher for $3,000. Fletcher later sued Peck to recover the money, alleging that the legislative repeal of the original sale invalidated the title conveyed by Peck, and Peck argued that the repeal legislation was invalid. There is some reason to believe that this was a collusive suit to establish clear title to those who bought the lands from the speculators.

Marshall, joined by Livingston, Todd, and Washington, ruled in favor of Peck, holding that the repeal legislation unconstitutionally violated the contract clause. Johnson dissented in part, and Chase and Cushing did not participate. Marshall first claimed that the repeal legislation was a violation of vested rights—that is, the natural rights of innocent parties to property that they purchased. On the contract clause Marshall included executed contracts (i.e., grants or conveyances) as one kind of contract protected by the contract clause. This was an unusual construction of the word *contract*, which lawyers then understood, and still usually understand, to be an exchange of promises, not an exchange of goods—that is, a sale. Nor did Marshall see any reason to limit the clause to *private* contracts, and so he made the clause applicable to public contracts, notwithstanding the fact that the framers' intent was to prevent states, at the behest of debtors, from repudiating the latter's debts by legislative fiat.

In 1819 the court interpreted the contract clause to cover corporate state charters (*Dartmouth College v. Woodward*). The king of England had in 1769 granted a royal charter establishing Dartmouth College in the colony of New Hampshire, and its governing board of trustees was constituted a self-perpetuating body. After the Revolution and adoption of the Constitution, a controversy developed between John Wheelock, president of the college and son of the founder, and the trustees. The trustees in 1815 removed Wheelock from office, but he secured the support of the Democrat-Republican governor and legislature of New Hampshire, newly elected in 1816, and that legislature enlarged the board with political appointees favorable to Wheelock The old trustees, who were Federalists, defied the laws and sued William Woodward, the secretary and treasurer of the college, to recover the college seal and records, which Woodward was holding in the name of the new college president and trustees. The old trustees lost in the state courts but appealed to the U.S. Supreme Court. Marshall wrote the court opinion in favor of the old trustees; Johnson and Livingston joined his opinion, Washington and Story concurred separately, Duvall dissented without opinion, and Todd did not participate. Daniel Webster delivered an eloquent speech in favor of his alma mater and its original charter.

Marshall held that Dartmouth was a private, not a public, charitable institution, that the charter was the product of a contract between the original donors and the crown, with the trustees representing the interest of the donors, and that the state, as successor to the crown, had an obligation under the contract not to amend or revoke it. He admitted that the trustees had no beneficial interest in the contract, but the corporation—that is, the board of trustees—was the assignee of the donors and the representative of their interests as well as those of the student beneficiaries. In short, the charter was a contract within the letter of the Constitution and its spirit, and New Hampshire could not impair the obligations under it. In his separate concurring opinion, Story suggested a means whereby a state might in the future amend or revoke a corporate charter—namely, by expressly reserving that right in the original charter.

While Dartmouth College was a nonprofit corporation, the decision would be equally applicable to business corporations. The doctrine of vested rights, which hitherto had to rest on principles of natural law, now had the specific protection of the contract clause. All states have followed Story's advice and have a reservation clause in their constitutions or general laws. Nevertheless, most states of the time recognized that natural law gave vested rights to individuals and corporations and that those rights limited the legislative power of the states.

Two weeks after the Dartmouth College case, the court, with Marshall writing the court opinion, rendered a decision on a New York bankruptcy law (*Sturges v. Crowninshield*). Under that law a bankrupt debtor who assigned his remaining assets to the state to be distributed to creditors was freed from liability for debts unsatisfied by distribution of the assets, and imprisonment of debtors was abolished. Marshall held that, although the Constitution gave Congress power to pass uniform bankruptcy laws (Article I, section 8, clause 4), the states might legislate in the field in the absence of federal legislation, as was then the case. Since the New York law had wiped out debtors' previously contracted liability, it had impaired the obligation of contracts and so violated the contract clause. But he upheld the statute's abolition of debtor imprisonment, arguing that debtor imprisonment concerned a remedy to enforce the obligation of contracts and its abolition did not affect the obligation itself.

Left unanswered by the Sturges decision was whether a state bankruptcy law was valid if it applied only to contracts entered into after passage of the law. In 1827 the court took up that question (*Ogden v. Saunders*). New York had revised its bankruptcy law so as to apply to contracts entered into after its passage, and the court upheld the law, since its provisions were in effect part of such contracts. Justice Washington wrote the court opinion, and Thompson, Johnson, and Trimble joined it. For the only time in his long tenure on the court, Marshall found himself in dissent on a constitutional issue, and Story and Duvall joined his dissent. Marshall argued that bankruptcy laws operating prospectively were no different from such laws operating retrospectively, since both violated natural justice in allowing debtors not to pay their debts.

The Ogden decision allowed states to shape bankruptcy laws favorable to debtors and adverse to creditors, and they did so. The state efforts to regulate bankruptcies, however, resulted in disparate results in different states, and Congress, recognizing the need of uniform law, enacted federal bankruptcy legislation in 1898.

Indian Rights Near the end of Marshall's tenure the Georgia-Cherokee crisis brought a case involving it to the Supreme Court. In 1829 President Jackson called on Congress to act to remove all Indians in the South to lands west of the Mississippi. Georgians had long resented the presence of Cherokee Indians in the northwestern part of Georgia and took their cue from Jackson to assert their jurisdiction over the tribe. Georgia convicted Samuel Worcester and another missionary of not obtaining a license that the state required any white person residing in Cherokee territory to obtain. Marshall and the court ruled in favor of the missionaries in 1832 (*Worcester v. Georgia*). He held that that the Cherokees were a distinct political community recognized by a federal treaty and that Georgia had no jurisdiction over their territory. Jackson dismissed the decision with the famous words, "John Marshall has made his decision. Now, let him enforce it." Notwithstanding the decision, the Cherokees were forcefully moved to the territory of Oklahoma.

Summary Although Chief Justice Marshall was only the first among equals, he dominated the court for thirty-five years. Successive appointments by Presidents Jefferson, Madison, Monroe, John Quincy Adams, and Jackson left him the only Federalist on the court by 1830, but he retained control. He introduced the system of court opinions and wrote half of those 1,100 opinions and two-thirds of those involving constitutional questions. There were few concurring or dissenting opinions in decisions of the Marshall Court, and he was in the minority in only one constitutional case. Marshall had established the supremacy of the court's interpretation of the Constitution both over Congress and the president and over state legislatures and courts. His court had invalidated one provision of an Act of Congress and nineteen state laws or actions. He vindicated the vested rights of creditors against state infringement and the treaty rights of the Cherokee Indians.

↶ 3 ↷

THE TANEY COURT

(1836–64)

The Justices

Justice Duvall resigned from the court in January 1835, and Chief Justice Marshall died on July 6, 1835. There remained on the court two Democrat-Republican associate justices (Story and Thompson) appointed by Presidents Madison and Monroe, respectively, and three Democrats (Baldwin, McLean, and Wayne) appointed by President Jackson. Four of the justices (Baldwin, McLean, Story, and Thompson) were from Northern states, and one (Wayne) was from the South. Only one (McLean) was from a state west of the original thirteen states (Ohio).

Roger Brook Taney To replace Marshall, Jackson picked a loyal supporter, Roger Brooke Taney. Jackson nominated him on December 28, 1835, and the Senate confirmed him on March 15, 1836. Taney was, of course, a Democrat, but he was also a Catholic, the first one appointed to the court. He was born on March 17, 1777, in Calvert County, Maryland. His father, Michael, was a planter of the landed aristocracy. He attended rural schools, had a family tutor, attended Dickinson College in 1795, and studied law under Jeremiah Chase. He married in 1806.

He was admitted to the Maryland bar in 1799, served in the Maryland legislature for seven years (1814–21), and was attorney general of Maryland for two years (1827–29). He was U.S. attorney general for two years (1831–33). Jackson made him secretary of the treasury on a recess appointment (1833–34), but the Senate rejected his permanent appointment. As secretary of the treasury he executed Jackson's order to withdraw U.S. funds from the Second Bank of the United States, thereby effectively crippling the Bank. He remained on the court through most of the Civil War, until his death on October 12, 1864. His tenure as chief justice was twenty-eight years, the second-longest tenure of any chief justice in the history of the court.

Philip Barbour To replace Duvall, Jackson, on the same day on which he nominated Taney, nominated Philip Barbour to the court, and the Senate confirmed Barbour on the same day on which it confirmed Taney. Barbour was a Democrat and a Protestant. He was born in Orange County, Virginia, on May 25, 1783. His father, Thomas, was a wealthy planter. He studied under an Episcopalian clergyman, Charles O'Neil, and attended one term at William and Mary College.

He served in the Virginia legislature for two years and in the U.S. House of Representatives for fourteen years (1814–25, 1827–30). He was a U.S. district court judge for five years (1830–35) and a judge on the General Court of Virginia until his appointment to the U.S. Supreme Court. He served on the court until his death on February 25, 1841.

John Catron The following year Congress enlarged the court to nine members; Jackson appointed one of the new justices and President Van Buren the other. Jackson nominated John Catron on March 3, 1837, and the Senate confirmed him on March 8. Catron was born around 1776 in Wythe County, Virginia. He was a Democrat and a Protestant. He had only a limited education. He was admitted to the Tennessee bar in 1815 and was a judge on the Tennessee Court of Errors and Appeals for seven years (1824–31) and chief justice of the Tennessee Supreme Court for three years (1831–34). He served on the U.S. Supreme Court until his death on May 30, 1865.

John McKinley Van Buren nominated John McKinley to be the second appointee to the enlarged court on April 22, 1837, and the Senate confirmed him on September 25. With this appointment Jackson and Van Buren had named seven of the nine justices of the court. McKinley, a Democrat and a Protestant, was born on May 1, 1780, in Culpepper County, Virginia. His father, Andrew, was a doctor. Married twice, McKinley was admitted to the Alabama bar in

1800 and served in the Alabama legislature, the U.S. House of Representatives, and the U.S. Senate. He served on the court until his death on July 19, 1852.

Peter Daniel When Barbour died on February 25, 1841, outgoing President Van Buren nominated Peter Daniel, a Democrat and a Protestant, to the court, and the Senate confirmed Daniel on March 2. Daniel was born on April 24, 1784, in Richmond, Virginia. He was tutored privately, attended Princeton without completing studies for a degree, studied law under Edmund Randolph, the first U.S. attorney general, and married twice. Daniel served in the Virginia legislature for three years (1809–12) and was a member of the privy council of Virginia for twenty-three years (1812–35) and the U.S. district court judge of Virginia for five years (1836–41). He served on the Supreme Court until his death on June 30, 1860.

Samuel Nelson When Thompson died on December 18, 1843, there was a hiatus before a successor was appointed and confirmed. On February 4, 1845, outgoing President Tyler appointed Samuel Nelson, a Democrat and a Protestant, to the court, and the Senate confirmed Nelson on February 14. Nelson was born on November 10, 1792, in Hebron, New York. His father, John, was a farmer. Nelson attended Middlebury College, studied law under a judge, and married twice.

Admitted to the bar in 1817, he was a circuit-court judge for eight years (1823–37) and chief judge of New York's highest court, the Court of Appeals, for eight years (1837–45). He retired from the U.S. Supreme Court on November 28, 1872, and died a year later, on December 13, 1873.

Levi Woodbury When Story, Marshall's scholarly ally, died on September 10, 1845, President Polk almost immediately appointed Levi Woodbury, a Democrat and a Protestant, to be Story's successor. Woodbury was appointed on September 20, and the Senate confirmed him on January 3, 1846. Woodbury was born on December 22, 1789, in Francestown, New Hampshire. His father, Peter, was a state legislator. Woodbury attended Dartmouth College and Litchfield Law School, the antecedent of Yale Law School, and studied law under Jeremiah Smith. He was admitted to the state bar in 1812.

He had an extraordinarily broad experience in government. He was clerk of the New Hampshire Senate for one year (1816), judge on the New Hampshire Supreme Court for six years (1817–23), governor of the state for two years (1823–25), and speaker of the New Hampshire House of Representatives for one year (1825). On the national level he was a U.S. senator for ten years (1825–31, 1841–45), secretary of the navy for three years (1831–34), and secretary of the treasury for seven years (1834–41). (In the latter capacity, he succeeded Taney). He was on the court for only five and a half years until his death on September 4, 1851.

Robert Grier When Baldwin died on April 21, 1844, the position was vacant for over three months; Polk nominated Robert Grier on August 3, 1846, and the Senate confirmed him on August 4. Grier, a Democrat and a Presbyterian, was born on March 5, 1794, in Cumberland County, Virginia. His father, Isaac, was a clergyman. Grier was tutored by his father, received an A.B. from Dickinson College in 1812, and studied law under Charles Hall. He was principal of an academy in 1815 and was admitted to the Pennsylvania bar in 1817.

He engaged in private practice for nineteen years and was a judge in Allegheny County for thirteen years (1833–46). He resigned from the court on January 31, 1870, and died on September 26.

Benjamin Curtis Woodbury died on September 4, 1851, and President Fillmore nominated Benjamin Curtis, a Whig and an Episcopalian, to the court on September 22; the Senate confirmed Curtis on December 29. Curtis was born on November 4, 1809, in Watertown, Massachusetts. His father, Benjamin, was a ship captain and merchant. Curtis was educated by private tutors, attended Harvard College, and married three times.

He engaged in private practice and was a member of the Massachusetts legislature for almost a year before his appointment to the court. He resigned from the court on September 30, 1857, and died on September 15, 1874.

John Campbell When McKinley died on July 19, 1852, the seat on the court was vacant until President Pierce appointed John Campbell, a Democrat and a Protestant, on March 21, 1853, and the Senate confirmed Campbell on March 25. Campbell was born on June 24, 1811, in Washington, Georgia. His father, Duncan, was a lawyer. Campbell attended the University of Georgia in 1825 and West Point from 1825 to 1828, studied law under John Clark, a former governor, was admitted to the Alabama bar in 1829, and served in the Alabama legislature.

In 1861 he resigned from the court and returned to Alabama, which had seceded from the Union, and became assistant secretary of war for the Confederate States of America from 1862 to 1865. He died on March 12, 1889.

Nathan Clifford Curtis resigned from the court on September 30, 1857, and President Buchanan nominated Nathan Clifford, a Democrat and a Protestant, to the court on December 9; the Senate confirmed Clifford on January 12, 1858. Clifford was born on August 18, 1803, in Rumney, New Hampshire. His father, Nathaniel, was a church deacon and a farmer. Clifford had little formal education; he attended Haverhill Academy in 1817 and read law in the local office of Josiah Quincy. He was admitted to the Maine bar in 1827.

He served in the Maine legislature for four years (1830–34) and was attorney general of Maine for four years (1834–38). He was a U.S. congressman for four years (1839–43), U.S. attorney general for two years (1846–48), and U.S. ambassador to Mexico for one year (1848–49). He served on the court until his death on July 25, 1881.

Two Deaths and a Resignation Lincoln, on taking office as president in 1861, faced a hostile court. There were only eight members of the court, Daniel having died in 1860 and Buchanan not having filled the post. Four (Clifford, Grier, McLean, and Nelson) were from Northern states, four (Campbell, Catron, Taney, and Wayne) from Southern states, and only McLean a Republican. Taney had written the Dred Scott decision, and Campbell, Catron, Grier, Nelson, and Wayne had separately concurred in it. Besides the vacancy, two other seats opened up when Campbell resigned at the outbreak of the Civil War and McLean died on April 4, 1861. The three justices Lincoln appointed were all Northerners and Republicans, six Northerners and three Southerners thereby comprising the court.

Noah Swayne To replace McLean, Lincoln nominated Noah Swayne on January 21, 1862, and the Senate confirmed Swayne on January 24. Swayne, a Republican and a Quaker, was born in Culpepper County, Virginia, on December 7, 1804. In addition to being tutored by his father, Joshua, he studied law in Warrenton and was admitted to the Ohio bar in 1823. He was district attorney of Coshocton County for three years (1826–29), served in the Ohio legislature for one year (1829–30), and was U.S. district attorney of Columbus for ten years (1830–40). He retired from the court on January 24, 1881, and died on June 8, 1884.

Samuel Miller To replace Daniel, Lincoln nominated Samuel Miller on July 16, 1862, and the Senate confirmed Miller on the same day. Miller, a Republican and a Protestant, was born in Richmond, Kentucky, on April 5, 1816.

His father, Frederick, was a farmer. Miller had a public school education and, uniquely for a lawyer and future judge, he received an M.D. from Transylvania University in 1838. While practicing medicine, he read law and was admitted to the Iowa bar in 1847. He held no public office before his appointment. He served on the court until his death on October 13, 1890.

David Davis To replace Campbell, Lincoln nominated David Davis of Illinois on October 17, 1862, and the Senate confirmed him on December 8. Davis, a Republican and a Protestant, was born in Cecil County, Maryland, on March 9, 1815. His father, David, was a doctor. He attended Kenyon College in 1832, read law under a judge, and attended lectures at Yale Law School in 1835. He married twice. He was admitted to the Illinois bar in 1835, served in the Illinois legislature for two years (1842–44), and was a judge on the Illinois Circuit Court for fourteen years (1848–62). On the commission to resolve the questions about disputed electors in the Hayes-Tilden election (1876), he sided with the Republicans on the commission and awarded the election to Hayes. He resigned from the court on March 4, 1877 and became a U.S. senator. He died on June 26, 1886.

Stephen Field In 1863 Congress created a tenth seat on the court. The express purpose was to create a justice for circuit duty in California, but a subsidiary purpose was undoubtedly to give the Lincoln administration another vote on the court. President Lincoln nominated Stephen Field, a Democrat and a Congregationalist, to that post on March 6, 1863, and the Senate confirmed him on March 10. (Congress during the Reconstruction period reduced the court to nine members after the death or retirement of one of the current justices, and so Field was the only tenth member in the history of the court.) He was born in Haddam, Connecticut, on November 4, 1816. His father, David, was a minister. He attended Williams College in 1837, studied law under his brother David, and was admitted to the New York bar in 1841. He moved to California in 1849 and invested in gold mining. He served in the California legislature and was an associate justice of the California Supreme Court for two years (1857–59) and its chief justice for four years (1859–63).

Field served on the court until his retirement on December 1, 1897, his term exceeding Marshall's by two months; only the terms of Douglas and Stevens exceeded his. He died on April 9, 1899.

Summary In the last year of the Taney Court, seven members (Clifford, Davis, Field, Grier, Miller, Nelson, and Swayne) were Northerners, four of whom were Lincoln appointees. Three (Catron, Taney, and Wayne) were Southerners. All were Democrats except Davis, Miller, and Swayne, who were Republicans. All were Protestants except Taney, who was Catholic. Seven (Catron, Clifford, Davis, Field, Grier, Nelson, and Wayne) had judicial experience. Five (Clifford, Davis, Swayne, Taney, and Wayne) had legislative experience. Four (Clifford, Swayne, Taney, and Wayne) had executive governmental experience. Miller had no judicial, legislative, or executive governmental experience.

Leading Decisions

Contract Clause The first important decision of the Taney Court and the first written by Taney himself was *Charles River Bridge Co. v. Warren Bridge Co.* Massachusetts had in 1785 granted a corporate charter to private investors in the Charles River Bridge Company to build and operate a bridge over the Charles River between Boston and Charlestown and to charge tolls for forty years (extended in 1792 to seventy years). Massachusetts had in 1650 granted to Harvard College an exclusive right in perpetuity to operate a ferry across the Charles River, and the college conveyed that right to the company in exchange for annual payments during the life of the bridge charter. When traffic greatly increased, Massachusetts in 1828 chartered other private investors in the Warren Bridge Company to build and operate a second bridge close to the Charles River Bridge. They were authorized to charge tolls to recover their investment, but the bridge would revert to the state when the investment and interest had been paid off and would become toll-free. Since the older bridge obviously could not compete with a soon-to-be free bridge, the Charles River Bridge Company sued in the state courts to enjoin the construction.

The Charles River Bridge Company argued that authorization of the new bridge impaired the state's contract, which implicitly gave the company an exclusive right to collect tolls. The state court ruled against the company, and the company appealed the case to the U.S. Supreme Court. The case was first argued there in 1831, but absences, illness, and deep division among the justices delayed a decision. The case was reargued in 1837 after Marshall had died and Taney replaced him. The decision was four (Baldwin, Barbour, Taney, and Wayne), all Jackson appointees, to three (McLean, Story, and Thompson) in favor of the Warren Bridge Company. Had Marshall still been on the court, the decision would almost certainly have been in favor of the Charles River Bridge Company.

Taney invoked a rule of strict construction of franchises by the public to private corporations—namely, that any ambiguities in the terms of the contract must be resolved against the company and in favor of the public, and that investors can claim only rights explicitly given them in the contract. Regarding the Charles River Bridge Company's reliance on Harvard College's exclusive franchise to operate a ferry on the site, Taney pointed out that the company's acquisition of that exclusive right, strictly construed, granted the company no exclusive right to build a bridge. Regarding the state's acts of 1785 and 1792, Taney argued that the state's police powers are vital to government, that any abandonment of its powers must be explicit, and that the acts granted the company no exclusive right. The company is allowed to keep all the franchises given to it.

All three dissenting justices wrote opinions, but Story's sixty-five-page opinion is the most important. He argued that a rational and fair construction of the charter to the Charles River Bridge Company would understand it to be exclusive, although implicitly rather than explicitly. He saw no reason to interpret public contracts against private investors where the grant imposes no burden on the public or creates any restraint injurious to the public. Moreover, allowing states to impair public contracts for a putative public good will arrest future private investment in public improvements.

It strikes this writer that Story had the better of the argument about the specific legislative intent of the act of 1785 and that Taney was right to argue that public contracts should be strictly construed. The Charles River Bridge Company had recovered its investment many times over when the state in 1828 chartered the Warren Bridge Company. One wonders what Taney would have said if Massachusetts had chartered the Warren Bridge Company in 1786. In any case, the decision had little effect on public contracts, since most states did not take advantage of it, and savvy investors made sure that the contracts spelled out their rights.

Commerce Clause Marshall, in the Gibbons decision, had left open the question of whether states, in the absence of federal legislation, could regulate matters relating to interstate or foreign commerce, while Johnson thought the power over commerce exclusively federal. The Taney Court wrestled and muddled with the question for fourteen years before it came up with a consensus. The justices were divided into three camps. The first was composed of justices who thought that the federal power over commerce was exclusive, so the states had no power over commerce, whether or not the federal government had legislated. The second was composed of justices who thought that the states had concurrent power over commerce and that states could legislate on commerce unless and until Congress legislated on the matter. The third was composed of justices who thought that the states had concurrent power over some matters of commerce but not over others in the absence of federal legislation. In addition, some justices thought that the states' police powers did not involve commerce at all.

The first decision of the Taney Court on the commerce power, *New York v. Miln*, was handed down in the same year as, but prior to, the Charles River Bridge decision. In 1824 New York passed an act that required the captains of all incoming ships to provide information about the passengers disembarking and to post a bond with New York City for passengers without means of support in order to indemnify the city for three years if the passengers became paupers dependent on public support. When William Thompson, captain of the *Emily*, and George Miln, importer of the ship's goods, refused to provide the information or post the bond for one hundred passengers, the city sued to enforce the act. Miln and Thompson lost in the state courts but appealed to the U.S. Supreme Court.

Miln contended that the law was a regulation of foreign commerce, that the Constitution granted Congress exclusive power to regulate it, and that the law was unconstitutional. The city argued that the Constitution did not explicitly make the power of Congress to regulate foreign commerce exclusive, and so the states have a concurrent power to do so in the absence of contravening federal legislation. But New York did not admit that the law was a regulation of commerce. Rather, it claimed that the law was merely an exercise of the state's internal police power.

Barbour wrote the court opinion upholding the law. He refused to examine whether Congress had exclusive power over commerce, since he held that the law was an exercise of the police power that rightfully belonged to the state, not a regulation of commerce. Barbour, a Virginian, also added gratuitous remarks to the effect that persons were not subjects of commerce, which implied that Southern states could exercise their police power to enforce slavery. Baldwin, McLean, Taney, McLean, and Wayne joined Barbour's opinion. Baldwin and Mclean, Northerners, didn't like the remarks about persons not being subjects of commerce, but they could not manifest their displeasure because the decision was delivered on the last day of the term. Thompson, who had originally been assigned to write the court opinion, concurred in the decision, holding that the New York law was an exercise of the state's police power and permissible in the absence of Congress exercising its power over commerce. Story alone dissented. While admitting that the states have police powers, he thought that the New York law was regulating foreign commerce, and this contravened the power of Congress over that commerce, which he considered exclusive.

In three cases from New England states, decided together in 1847 and called the License Cases, the court upheld taxes and regulations on the sale of alcoholic beverages imported from other states. The fact that the laws were discriminatory against out-of-state economic interests should have led the court to invalidate them as per se contrary to the commerce clause, and the court today would certainly do so. The court, however, sustained them as valid exercises of the states' police powers to protect the health and morals of their citizens. The decision was unanimous, but there was no court opinion, six justices filing separate opinions expressing different views on the commerce clause. Some of the justices argued in terms of the states' police powers, but others argued that the laws involved only intrastate commerce.

Two years later, in 1849, the court decided the Passenger Cases. New York and Massachusetts had passed laws imposing taxes on incoming ship passengers, including immigrants. The cases were argued three times over a four-year period. The laws were struck down as an interference with federal power over immigration. Each of the five justices in the majority wrote separate opinions, and three of the four dissenters also did. Two of the majority justices held that the power of Congress over foreign commerce is exclusive and so bars state regulation. Three of the majority justices held only that the state laws were in conflict with existing federal legislation.

In the context of this judicial confusion about the commerce clause and state regulations affecting interstate commerce, President Fillmore appointed Benjamin Curtis, a brilliant lawyer and the only Whig appointee, who joined the court in 1851, mediated a compromise, and resolved the muddle, at least conceptually. A Pennsylvania law of 1803 required vessels leaving the port of Philadelphia to hire a pilot or, if a pilot were not hired, to pay one half of the pilot's fee for the relief of elderly pilots and their widows and children. Cooley, who was to receive the shipments of two vessels outbound from Philadelphia, hired no pilot and refused to pay the fee. The Board of Wardens for the Society for Pilots' Relief brought suit against him in the state courts and won judgments. Cooley appealed to the U.S. Supreme Court.

Unlike the License and Passenger cases, Curtis was able to muster a majority of justices to support a court opinion (*Cooley v. Board of Wardens*). He first had to consider whether Congress had legislated on the matter. Congress in 1789 had endorsed then existing state regulations regarding port pilots, but the Pennsylvania law at issue was enacted in 1803. The 1789 federal law had also provided that states may continue to regulate pilots until Congress acts. Curtis held that Congress could not grant such discretionary power to the states if the power of Congress was exclusive, and so he arrived at the question of whether the states had concurrent power in the absence of congressional legislation. Note that Curtis could have relied on the 1789 federal law to have constituted state piloting regulations *federal* law and thereby valid, but he wanted to address the question of state power in the absence of federal legislation.

Curtis held that the commerce clause did not expressly exclude state power and proceeded to distinguish between two kinds of subject matter, one reserved exclusively to Congress and the other allowing concurrent power to the states—that is, one in which the states could legislate unless and until Congress did. Some subject matter—that is, subject matter that necessitates a uniform rule or none—is *by nature* national. This subject matter belongs exclusively to Congress. The other subject matter is local—that is, one that does not require a uniform rule but can be exercised to accommodate local peculiarities—and so the states may exercise it in the absence of federal action. The Pennsylvania law was a regulation of commerce but one regarding a local subject matter and so within the state's power.

Five justices (Catron, Grier, McKinley, Nelson, and Taney) joined Curtis's opinion. Daniel concurred only in the judgment, holding that enactment of piloting laws was an original and inherent power of the states and not one possessed by the national government. McLean and Wayne dissented, holding the view that the power over commerce belongs exclusively to the federal government.

The Cooley decision was conceptually clear and a pragmatic compromise between federal power and state interests. (Exclusive federal power would until the end of the nineteenth century have usually meant no regulation at all.)

Notwithstanding the conceptual clarity, however, the decision did not determine which subjects of commerce called for a uniform rule and which did not. Nor did it say whether Congress or the court would have the last word about when uniformity required federal action.

Political Questions Events in Rhode Island led to a decision in 1849 involving the guarantee of "a republican form of government" to each state in Article IV, section 4 (*Luther v. Borden*). In 1840 the government of Rhode Island, operating under its original charter, limited voting eligibility to freeholders and their eldest sons, which excluded half the adult males. When the charter government refused to make electoral reforms, the dissatisfied citizens held a constitutional convention and drafted a new constitution. An election organized by the dissidents adopted the new constitution and elected Thomas Dorr governor. The charter government declared the dissidents rebels and imposed martial law. Both sides appealed to President Tyler for military help to prevent domestic violence. Tyler refused but made clear his sympathy with the charter government, and the rebellion collapsed. Rhode Island adopted a new constitution with enlarged male suffrage in 1843.

During the dispute between the two governments claiming legitimacy, Luther Borden, a member of the charter government's militia, broke into the house of Martin Luther, one of the dissidents, and arrested him. Luther was convicted of the crime of insurrection. Several years later, however, Luther, having established residence in Massachusetts and thereby having created diversity of citizenship, brought a case of trespass against Borden in the federal circuit court. Borden argued that Luther had been in insurrection against the lawful government of Rhode Island, and so the entry to arrest Luther and search the house was lawful. Luther argued that the government under which Borden acted was no longer the lawful government, and so the entry was an unlawful trespass. The federal circuit court, relying on the Rhode Island court's judgment in the prosecution of Luther, ruled in favor of Borden, and Luther appealed to the Supreme Court.

Taney wrote the court opinion, and seven justices (Catron, Daniel, Grier, McKinley, Mclean, Nelson, and Wayne) joined him. Woodbury alone dissented. According to Taney, the Constitution entrusts Congress with the power to interpret the guarantee of a republican form of government when it admits representatives from the government of a state. In turn, Congress, by the act of February 28, 1795, gave the president, not the courts, the power to call out the militias of other states to suppress an insurrection. The president did not act on the request for military aid, but he did recognize the charter governor as the executive power of the state. Taney held that the federal courts in general and the Supreme Court in particular have no jurisdiction to pronounce on political questions—that is, questions entrusted to the executive and legislative branches of the federal government to decide. This judicial restraint was the federal rule until the 1962 decision in *Baker v. Carr.*

Dred Scott On March 5, 1857, the Taney Court handed down the Dred Scott decision (*Scott v. Sandford*), a catastrophic decision that, far from settling the slavery question, stimulated abolitionist sentiment in the North and opposition to slavery in the territories. The decision contributed to the election of Lincoln, secession, and the Civil War. The background to the case is complicated. Dred Scott was a black slave originally belonging to the Blair family of Virginia. The Blairs moved from Virginia to Alabama and then to St. Louis, Missouri. The Blairs in 1833 sold Scott to Dr. John Emerson, an army doctor. In 1834 Emerson took Scott with him to Rock Island, Illinois, a state that prohibited slavery. In 1836 Emerson took him to Fort Snelling in a part of the territory of Wisconsin, now Minnesota. This was part of the Louisiana Purchase territory north of 36 degrees 30 minutes, in which the Missouri Compromise had in 1820 prohibited slavery. In 1838 Emerson returned with Scott to Missouri.

After Dr. Emerson's death in 1843, Scott, apparently dissatisfied with his life under Dr. Emerson's widow, brought a suit in the Missouri courts to obtain his freedom. He claimed that he had become a freeman by reason of his residence in the state of Illinois and U.S. territory in which slavery was prohibited. The case came to trial in 1847, but a mistrial was declared. When the case was retried in 1850, the trial court ruled for Scott, but the Missouri Supreme Court reversed in 1852, holding that, whatever Scott's status was when he was in Illinois or the territory in Minnesota, he was now in Missouri and subject to its laws, which considered him a slave. No one knows what his grievances against Mrs. Emerson were, but we know that slave owners living in cities often sent their surplus male slaves to work for hire in the cities, usually at the docks. Scott may not have liked this new disposition of him. Nor do we know how or from whom he obtained the money for lawyers to bring the original case. Perhaps he complained to the Blairs, with whom he seems to have maintained a friendly relationship in St. Louis, and they helped him. In any event, there is no evidence that abolitionists were involved in the Missouri case.

In the three years' intervention between the first and second trials, Scott's wages were held in escrow until his status was adjudicated. In the meantime, Mrs. Emerson had married Charles Chaffee, a Massachusetts abolitionist. Technically, the Emerson's minor daughter was Scott's owner, and Mrs. Emerson was the custodian of Scott until the daughter reached maturity. Partially to eliminate potential conflict of interest on the part of the mother, who was now remarried, custody of Scott was transferred to Mrs. Chaffee's brother, John Sanford of New York. (The court reporter misspelled Sanford's name.) When the trial court declared Scott to be a freeman, the potential loss of his earnings held in escrow induced Sanford to appeal to the Missouri Supreme Court.

Sanford's New York citizenship provided the diversity of citizenship requisite for a federal case, and here there is clear evidence of abolitionist involvement. Chaffee arranged for Roswell Field, a prominent abolitionist lawyer in St. Louis, to bring a suit for Scott's freedom in the U.S. Circuit Court in Missouri. Scott lost in that court and appealed to the U.S. Supreme Court. The justices heard two oral arguments on the case, in February and December 1856. Each of the nine justices filed an opinion, seven against Scott (Campbell, Catron, Daniel, Grier, Nelson, Taney, and Wayne) and two in his favor (Curtis and McLean). The opinion was first assigned to Nelson, who would have decided the case on the principle that the status of slaves was a matter of state law to be determined by state courts alone, as Taney and the court had held in 1851 in *Strader v. Graham*. Taney, however, when he learned that Curtis and McLean were writing strong dissents, assumed the role of writing the court opinion, but the six concurring justices disagreed with some parts of his argument. Interestingly, Catron tipped off President Buchanan about the forthcoming decision at Buchanan's inauguration the day before, and Buchanan announced that he would cheerfully submit to the decision, which corresponded exactly with his own opinion.

First, Taney held that neither Africans who were imported into this country and sold as slaves nor their descendants, even if they had become free, could be citizens of the United States in the meaning of the Constitution, although a free black could be the citizen of a state. According to him, blacks were considered at the time of the nation's independence and the Constitution's adoption an inferior class of being and not part of the people of the United States. Were free blacks to be eligible for U.S. citizenship in the constitutional sense, the Constitution would have to be amended. Accordingly, Taney declared that

Dred Scott was not a citizen of Missouri within the meaning of the Constitution of the United States and not entitled to sue in its courts, and so the U.S. Circuit Court had no jurisdiction to hear the case. This jurisdictional point makes the rest of the opinion superfluous, but Taney wanted to settle the question of slavery in the territories.

On slavery in the continental territories of the United States, Taney basically held that the Constitution follows the flag. The territories are not colonies, and the federal power over them is to govern them according to the personal and property rights of citizens until they are ready for admission as states. Since citizens have the right to bring their property into the territories, slave owners had the right to bring their slaves into the territories. Accordingly, the Missouri Compromise's prohibition of slavery in Louisiana territory north of 36° 30' unconstitutionally deprived slave owners of their Fifth Amendment right to property. Moreover, Congress had no affirmative grant of power over slavery. And so Dred Scott did not become free by reason of residence there. This was the first time since *Marbury v. Madison* that the court had declared an act of Congress unconstitutional.

On whether residence in the free state of Illinois made Scott a freeman, Taney followed the principle established in *Strader v. Graham*—namely, that the status of blacks, whether they be slave or free, depended on the laws of the states in which they resided. Therefore, the status of Scott depended exclusively on the laws of Missouri, not those of Illinois. It is interesting to speculate what Taney would have held if Scott had brought and won a suit for freedom in the Illinois courts on the basis of the state's prohibition of slavery and his owner had been able to appeal to the Supreme Court. The logic of Taney's argument on the question of slavery in the territories suggests that a slave owner had a constitutional right to bring his slaves into any state, and so states could not prohibit them from doing so.

After the decision, Sanford manumitted Scott. Scott died a year and a half later and is buried in the Catholic cemetery of St. Louis, possibly provided for by the Blair family. One of the ironies of the decision is that Taney was personally opposed to slavery, had manumitted his slaves, and supported those emancipated slaves who were elderly or infirm for the rest of their lives.

Dissenting Justices Curtis and McLean, both of them anti-slavery, disputed Taney's arguments, but one factual point of Curtis is particularly important. Taney had argued that the people at the time of the Constitution's adoption held the view that descendants of imported African slaves could not become citizens of the United States, but Curtis fully refuted this position. He pointed out that, at the time of the ratification of the Articles of Confederation on March 1, 1781, the free native-born males of five states (Massachusetts, New Hampshire, New Jersey, New York, and North Carolina), even if they were descended from African slaves, were citizens of those states. Moreover, such of them as fulfilled the other necessary qualifications (e.g., male gender, age, residency, and property) possessed the right to vote on equal terms with other citizens. (Taney had correctly alluded to the fact that slavery was legal in every state at the time of the Declaration of Independence, but the indicated states in the late 1770s, and before March 1, 1781, legislated gradual emancipation of slaves, beginning with the children of slaves.) Curtis concluded this part of his dissent with the declaration that he could find nothing in the Constitution that deprives any class of persons who were citizens at the time of its adoption of their citizenship, and that every free person who is the citizen of a state is also a citizen of the United States.

Fugitive Slaves The Taney Court decided several cases involving federal fugitive slave laws and conflicts with state regulations. The first was *Prigg v. Pennsylvania*, decided in 1842. Edward Prigg was a professional runaway-slave hunter. He had pursued a Maryland fugitive and her children in Pennsylvania and applied to a local magistrate for a certificate to return her and her family to Maryland, but the magistrate denied the request, insisting on an affidavit by the owner. Prigg then took the runaway and her family back to Maryland. The state of Pennsylvania convicted him of violating a law that forbade abduction of runaway slaves, and he appealed his conviction to the U.S. Supreme Court.

Eight justices held the Pennsylvania law unconstitutional. Story, with Catron and McKinley, held that Article IV, section 2 of the Constitution gave the federal government exclusive power over fugitive slaves, and the Fugitive Slave Act of 1783 authorized slave owners or their agents to seize runaways in other states and required a federal or state court to order rendition on the proof or identity and ownership. Since the 1793 law was constitutional, the Pennsylvania law, by imposing higher evidentiary standards, was not. But the exclusivity of federal power over runaways had a second edge—namely, that no state can interfere with the regulations and remedies prescribed by Congress. Taney, with Baldwin, Daniel, Thompson, and Wayne, agreed that the Pennsylvania law was unconstitutional but argued that the states had concurrent power to uphold the rights of slave owners and indeed the duty to do so. The sole dissenter was the abolitionist McLean. He argued that the Pennsylvania law was only demanding proof of ownership, and that that was not interference with, or contrary to, the aim of the fugitive slave law but rather clarifying it in the interest of justice.

Two years after the Dred Scott decision, in 1859, Taney rendered a unanimous decision upholding the supremacy of the federal judiciary over a state judiciary in a case involving the Fugitive Slave Act of 1850 (*Ableman v. Booth*). Sherman Booth, an abolitionist editor in Wisconsin, had been convicted of violating the act by leading a mob to help a runaway slave escape from a federal marshal, but the Wisconsin Supreme Court intervened to free him, holding the fugitive-slave law unconstitutional. Stephen Ableman, the marshal, secured from the U.S. Supreme Court a writ of review to the Wisconsin Supreme Court, which completely ignored the writ. Taney, invoking nationalism, strongly upheld the conviction and denied the state court's power to interfere with the federal judiciary.

Note that no justice expressed any concern about the natural rights of runaway slaves, or indeed any slave. This was not true in the case of *Calder v. Bull*, in which Justice Samuel Chase strongly argued that no legislature had power to pass laws contrary to natural justice. The only justice who might have expressed such an argument was the abolitionist McLean, but he didn't. This indicates that the legal profession had come to accept that the judge's sole function was to interpret the Constitution and apply it to the law in question. For the people of the North, however, slavery was becoming a moral and political, not a legal, issue.

The Civil War When the Civil War came in 1961, Lincoln on his own authority suspended the writ of habeas corpus; the Congress later tried to legitimate the suspension. He ordered military commanders to arrest and detain any persons suspected of disloyalty or who might commit disloyal acts. Suspension of the writ was bitterly opposed by Democrats, especially those in the border states and those in the southern portions of Ohio, Indiana, and Illinois. This led to a confrontation between Lincoln and Taney.

The army had arrested John Merryman, a Maryland secessionist, on suspicion of having destroyed a railroad bridge, and he was held in Fort McHenry in Baltimore. He petitioned for a writ of habeas corpus from Taney, who was sitting as circuit-court judge in Maryland. Taney issued the writ on General George Cadwalader, the Fort's commanding officer, to bring Merryman before him and show cause why he was being detained. Lincoln ordered Cadwalader to ignore the order, and Cadwalader did. Taney then ordered Cadwalader to appear before him. Cadwalader also ignored that order. Taney as circuit-court judge issued an opinion on the issue in 1861 (*Ex parte Merryman*).

First, he held that, since the provision regarding suspension of the writ (Article I, section 9, clause 2) was in Article I, which deals with the powers of Congress, and not in Article II, which deals with the powers of the president, only Congress could exercise that power. Second, the Sixth Amendment guarantees a civilian trial in a civilian court even if the writ of habeas corpus were to have been lawfully suspended, and so military detention and trial of a civilian in a military court is illegal. Third, the president has a constitutional duty to execute the laws faithfully, and so the president has a duty to assist the judiciary to enforce its judgments.

Lincoln ignored Taney's ruling and replied in a message to Congress. He pointed out that the constitutional provision on the suspension of the writ did not specify who had the power. But the main point was that the president has the duty to see that the whole of the laws are faithfully executed and that he may fail to enforce one in order to guarantee that the rest are faithfully executed. In effect, Lincoln was claiming that he and all presidents in emergency situations have the right and the duty to take extraordinary measures to deal with the situations. Lincoln did not refer the case to the whole court for the very good reason that he would almost certainly have lost.

The whole court had an opportunity near the end of the Civil War to pass on military trial of civilians accused of disloyal acts. A military tribunal found Clement Vallandigham, a former Democratic congressman from Ohio, guilty of delivering a speech opposing the war and calling for peace with the South. He appealed to the court, arguing that the military commission had no power to try civilians, but the court in 1864 refused to hear the case on the grounds that its appellate power did not extend to military tribunals (*Ex parte Vallandigham*). As we shall see, the Chase Court would take a different position after the war.

The Supreme Court in 1863 passed on the legality of the war in regard to the blockade of Southern ports (the Prize Cases); Lincoln on his own authority as commander-in-chief had declared the blockade and informed foreign nations of its existence on April 27 and 30, 1861. Congress on July 13, 1861, authorized the blockade and retroactively legitimated Lincoln's action instituting it. Union naval forces seized several foreign ships and cargoes before the congressional action, and the owners of the confiscated vessels and cargoes sued to recover their property. The court upheld the seizures.

Grier, with Wayne and the three Lincoln appointees (Davis, Miller, and Swayne), held that a civil war requires no declaration, that the president has inherent power to suppress insurrections, and that the acts of Congress of February 28, 1795, and March 3, 1807, had authorized him to call out militias for that purpose. Moreover, Congress had retroactively legitimated Lincoln's action, although Grier did not think that action was necessary. Nelson, with Catron, Clifford, and Taney, dissented, arguing that only a prospective act of Congress signed by the president can make a conflict a war in the legal sense.

4

THE CHASE AND WAITE COURTS

(1864–88)

The Justices

Salmon Chase When Taney died on October 12, 1864, Lincoln had the opportunity to make his fifth appointment, this time the chief justice. He nominated his former secretary of the treasury, Salmon Chase, on December 6, and the Senate confirmed Chase on the same day. Chase, a Republican (formerly a Whig) and an Episcopalian, was born in Concord, New Hampshire, on January 13, 1808. His father, Ithamar, was a farmer and a tavern keeper. He attended a district grade school, was partially educated by his uncle Philander, the first Episcopalian bishop of Ohio, and attended Dartmouth College in 1826. He studied law under William Wirt, John Quincy Adams's attorney general, from 1827 to 1830 and was admitted to the bar in 1829. He was married three times, two of his wives dying within twelve years.

He was admitted to the Ohio bar in 1829 and was a lawyer for fugitive slaves and the whites aiding them. He was a U.S. senator for six years (1849–55) and the first Republican governor of Ohio (1855–59), and returned to the Senate in 1859; he was Lincoln's secretary of the treasury from 1861 to 1864. He sought the Republican nomination for the presidency in 1860 and covertly in 1864 to replace Lincoln. While serving as chief justice, he sought the Democratic nomination for the presidency in 1868 because of his opposition to the

Radical Republicans, and again in 1872. He served on the court until his death on May 7, 1873.

The Tenth Seat Eliminated After Catron died on May 30, 1865, the Radical Republican Congress progressively reduced the size of the court to seven members in order to prevent President Johnson, Lincoln's successor, from making appointments to it. Later, after Grant had replaced Johnson as president, Congress enlarged the court to nine members, which has remained the number of justices ever since. The Catron seat was thus never refilled.

Joseph Bradley When Wayne died on July 5, 1867, the seat was not technically vacant, because Congress had in 1865 reduced the Court to seven members, but the seat opened up again when Congress restored the number of justices on the court to nine. To fill the seat President Grant first appointed Edwin Stanton on December 20, 1869, but he died four days later and never sat on the court. Grant then nominated Joseph Bradley to the seat on February 7, 1870, and the Senate confirmed Bradley on March 21.

Bradley, a Republican and a Lutheran, was born in Albany, New York, on March 14, 1813. His father, Philo, was a small farmer. Bradley attended public school four months of the year, was tutored by a Lutheran pastor, and attended Rutgers College. He was admitted to the New Jersey bar in 1840 and practiced private law. He had no prior governmental experience. He served on the court until his death on January 22, 1892.

William Strong Grier resigned on January 31, 1870. He had become noticeably senile, and Justice Field in the name of the other justices asked him to resign, which he did; he died eight months later. To replace him Grant nominated William Strong on February 7, 1870, and the Senate confirmed Strong on February 18. This brought the court to nine members, the authorized number of justices. Strong, a Republican and a Presbyterian, was born in Somers, Connecticut, on May 6, 1808. His father, William, was a Congregationalist minister. William Jr. was educated in a private academy, graduated from Yale College in 1831, attended Yale Law School for six months, and clerked under Garrett Wall. He was twice married. He was admitted to the Pennsylvania bar in 1832 and was a congressman for four years (1847–51) and a judge on the Pennsylvania Supreme Court for eleven years (1857–68). He resigned from the court on December 14, 1880, and died on August 19, 1895.

Ward Hunt Nelson retired on November 28, 1872, and Grant nominated Ward Hunt to the court on December 3, 1872; the Senate confirmed Hunt on December 11. Hunt, a Republican and a Protestant, was born in Utica, New York, on June 14, 1810. His father, Montgomery, was a banker. Hunt was twice married. He took courses at private academies, attended Union College in 1828, and studied law at Litchfield Law School under James Gould. He was admitted to the New York bar in 1831. He served in the New York legislature for two years (1839–41) and was mayor of Utica for one year (1844), a judge on the New York Court of Appeals for four years (associate judge from 1865 to 1868 and chief judge from 1868 to 1869), and commissioner of appeals for four years, from 1869 until his appointment to the court. He resigned from the court on January 7, 1882, and died on March 24, 1886.

Morrison Waite Chief Justice Chase died in May 1873; Grant nominated Morrison Waite to succeed him on January 19, 1874, and the Senate confirmed him two days later. Waite, a Republican (formerly a Whig) and an Episcopalian, was born in Lyme, Connecticut, on November 29, 1816. His father, Henry, was a lawyer and served as chief justice of the Connecticut Supreme Court and as a state legislator. Waite attended Yale College and studied law under his father. He was admitted to the Connecticut bar in 1839, practiced law in the state, and served in the state legislature for two years (1844–46). Moving to Ohio, he was a lawyer in Toledo and chairman of the Ohio Constitutional Convention of 1873. He was also counsel of the arbitration commission on the *Alabama* claims. He served on the court until his death on March 25, 1888.

John Marshall Harlan (Harlan I) When Davis resigned on March 4, 1877, President Hayes nominated John Marshall Harlan to succeed him, and the Senate confirmed Harlan on March 29. Harlan, a Republican and Presbyterian, was born in Boyle County, Kentucky, on June 1, 1833. His father, James, was a lawyer, attorney general of Kentucky, and a Whig congressman. Harlan attended Centre College in 1850, studied law at the University of Pennsylvania, and was admitted to the Kentucky bar in 1853. He was a judge of the Franklin County court for one year (1858–59), served as a colonel in the Union army during part of the Civil War, and was attorney general of Kentucky for four years (1863–67). He opposed the Thirteenth Amendment and endorsed McClellan against Lincoln in 1864. He practiced law for ten years (1867–77), came to endorse the Radical Republicans' Reconstruction policies, and lost two elections as the Republican candidate for governor in 1870 and

1874. He was instrumental in Hayes's Republican nomination for the presidency in 1876. That, along with the fact that he would become the first justice from a state south of the Ohio River since Wayne's death in 1867, was a factor that undoubtedly influenced Hayes to nominate him.

Harlan had one of the longest tenures on the court, serving on it until his death on October 14, 1911. He also deserves the title *Great Dissenter* as much as Oliver Wendell Holmes Jr. As we shall see, his dissents in the Civil Rights Cases, the Income-Tax Case, *Plessey v. Ferguson,* and *Lochner v. New York* were notable.

William Woods Strong resigned on December 14, 1880, and Hayes nominated William Woods to the court on December 15; the Senate confirmed Woods on December 21. Woods, a Republican and a Protestant, was born in Newark, Ohio, on August 3, 1824. His father, Ezekiel, was a farmer and merchant. He attended Yale College and studied law under S. D. King. He was admitted to the Ohio bar in 1847, was mayor of Newark for one year (1856), served in the Ohio legislature for four years (1857–61), and rose to brevet major general in the Union army during the Civil War. After the war he went to Alabama and became a cotton planter. President Grant appointed him a judge of the U.S. Circuit Court of Georgia in 1869, and he served on that court until his appointment to the U.S. Supreme Court. He served on the Supreme Court until his death on May 14, 1887.

Stanley Matthews When Swayne retired on January 24, 1881, the seat was vacant until incoming President Garfield nominated Stanley Matthews to the court on March 14, 1881, and the Senate confirmed him on May 12. Matthews, a Republican and a Protestant, was born in Cincinnati, Ohio, on July 21, 1824. His father, Thomas, was a college professor of mathematics. Matthews attended Kenyon College in 1840, studied law in Cincinnati for several years (1840–42), and was admitted to the Ohio bar in 1842. He was clerk of the Ohio House of Representatives for one year (1848–49), judge of common pleas of Hamilton County for three years (1850–53), Ohio state senator for two years (1856–58), and U.S. attorney for the Southern District of Ohio for three years (1858–61). He was an officer in the Union army during part of the Civil War (1861–63), judge of the Cincinnati Superior Court for one year (1863–64), counsel before the electoral commission of 1876, and U.S. senator for the four years before his appointment to the U.S. Supreme Court (1877–81). He served on the court until his death on March 22, 1889.

Horace Gray Clifford died on July 25, 1881, and President Arthur nominated Horace Gray to the court on December 19; the Senate confirmed Gray the next day. Gray, a Republican and a Protestant, was born in Boston, Massachusetts, on March 24, 1828. His father, Horace, was a businessman. He attended Harvard College and Harvard Law School, read law under a judge, and was admitted to the Massachusetts bar in 1851. He was a judge on the Massachusetts Supreme Judicial Court for nine years (1864–73) and chief judge of that court for nine years (1873–81). He served on the U.S. Supreme Court until his resignation on September 15, 1902, shortly before his death.

Samuel Blatchford Hunt resigned on January 7, 1882, and Arthur nominated Samuel Blatchford to the court on March 13; the Senate confirmed Blatchford on March 27. Blatchford, a Republican and a Protestant, was born in New York City on March 9, 1820. His father, Richard, was a lawyer and legislator. Blatchford studied under William Forrest and at the grammar school of Columbia University and attended Columbia University in 1837. He was a judge of a U.S. district court for five years (1867–72) and of the U.S. Court of Appeals for ten years (1872–82). He served on the U.S. Supreme Court until his death on July 7, 1893.

Lucius Lamar Woods died on May 14, 1887, and President Cleveland nominated Lucius Lamar to the court on December 6, 1887; the Senate confirmed Lamar on January 16, 1888. Lamar, a Democrat and a Protestant, was born in Putnam County, Georgia, on September 17, 1825. His father, Lucius, was a judge. Lamar attended Emory College, was admitted to the Georgia bar in 1847, and was twice married.

He served for two years in the Georgia House of Representatives (1853–55) and in the U.S. House of Representatives from 1857 to early 1861 from a district in Mississippi. He drafted the Mississippi ordinance of secession in 1861 and served for a year (1861–62) as a lieutenant colonel in the Confederate army. After the war he was a congressman for four years (1873–77) and a senator for eight years (1877–85). He was secretary of the interior in the first Cleveland administration until his appointment to the court (1885–88). He served on the court until his death on January 23, 1893.

Summary All of the justices appointed in the twenty-four years of the Chase and Waite Courts were Protestants, and all but Lamar Republicans. As a result, Field and Lamar were the only Democrats on the court at the end of the

Waite Court. All of the eleven appointees were from Northern states except Harlan, who was from the border state of Kentucky, and Lamar, who was from Mississippi, the first Southerner since Wayne. Three of the justices (Chase, Matthews, and Waite) were from Ohio, and another (Woods) was born there. Two of the justices (Blatchford and Hunt) were from New York, and another (Bradley) was born there. Three of the justices (Strong, Waite, and Woods) attended Yale College, and one (Strong) had a master's degree from it. Seven (Blatchford, Gray, Harlan, Hunt, Matthews, Strong, and Woods) had judicial experience. Seven (Chase, Hunt, Lamar, Matthews, Strong, Waite, and Woods) had legislative experience. Six (Chase, Harlan, Hunt, Lamar, Matthews, and Woods) had executive governmental experience. Bradley had no prior governmental experience of any kind.

Leading Decisions

Military Trial of Civilians The court conveniently made no decision on the military trial of civilians during the Civil War, but it did a year after the war ended. A military court convicted Lambdin Milligan, a leading anti-war Democrat in Indiana, of conspiracy to seize arms from a federal arsenal and to free Confederate prisoners held in Northern prison camps, and the court sentenced him to be hanged. The court unanimously overturned the conviction in *Ex parte Milligan*, although the justices did so by two different lines of argument.

Davis wrote the court opinion, and Clifford, Field, Grier, and Nelson joined it. A civilian court should have indicted and tried Milligan if civilian courts were open and functioning, which they were at the time in Indiana. His military arrest and trial deprived him of his right to be indicted by a grand jury guaranteed by the Fifth Amendment and his right to be tried by a petit jury guaranteed by the Sixth Amendment. Martial law can be imposed only when there is a real invasion, which there was not in Indiana. Chase would have held for Milligan on statutory grounds, and Miller, Swayne, and Wayne joined his opinion. Chase thought that Congress had the power to suspend the writ of habeas corpus and impose martial law, even when civilian courts were open, if it judged it necessary, but that Congress had not in fact done so. Although no Congress or president in any subsequent war has suspended the writ of habeas corpus and imposed martial law, President Franklin Roosevelt ordered military internment of tens of thousands of Japanese Americans during World War II.

Reconstruction The Reconstruction period brought a different kind of war to the judgment of the court. President Johnson tried to reconstruct the South rapidly and granted amnesty liberally to most of the individuals who had supported the Confederacy. Provisional governments were set up in secessionist states under his supervision and constitutional conventions were called. These conventions were given wide latitude but were required to renounce secession, repudiate Confederate war debts, and ratify the Thirteenth Amendment. When the Radical Republican Congress elected in November 1864 convened in December 1865, Johnson announced that postwar governments had been established in every secessionist state except Texas. Most of the Johnson governments had enacted the so-called Black Codes, which denied blacks the right to vote, excluded them from juries, and restricted their entry into occupations.

The Radical Republicans had a far different program. They wanted to make social and political reforms in favor of the blacks before representatives from the secessionist states were readmitted to Congress. Congress set up military governments in the secessionist states to achieve its objectives. Several Johnson governments in the secessionist states sought injunctions against enforcement of the Reconstruction Acts.

The Johnson government in Mississippi brought an original action in the Supreme Court to enjoin the president from carrying out the acts. The court in 1867 unanimously declined to do so (*Mississippi v. Johnson*). Chase, writing the court opinion, distinguished between a ministerial duty and an executive duty. He admitted that the judicial process may in proper circumstances require the head of a department to perform a ministerial duty—that is, one in which the official has no discretion— but not the performance of executive, or discretionary, duties. As courts cannot prevent Congress from enacting unconstitutional laws, so they cannot enjoin a president from enforcing unconstitutional laws, but the acts of both when performed are subject to review as to their constitutionality. In a companion case the Johnson government in Georgia sought to enjoin Secretary of War Edwin Stanton from enforcing the Reconstruction Acts. Again, the court unanimously refused to issue the injunction, arguing that a department head was the alter ego of the president (*Georgia v. Stanton*).

Had the court issued the injunctions, it is hardly likely that Congress would have accepted the result. In fact, the justices might have faced the same fate as Johnson—namely, impeachment. The court has consistently adhered to the principle that the courts cannot force a president to execute or not to execute a law. The court, however, would subsequently develop the fiction that a suit against a department head is against the person and not the official (see *Youngstown Sheet and Tube Co. v. Sawyer*).

In another Reconstruction case a military commission, acting on the authority of the Reconstruction Acts, arrested William McCardle, a civilian newspaper editor in Mississippi, for trial on charges of publishing "incendiary and libelous" articles. His lawyer sought a writ of habeas corpus from a federal circuit court. The judge of that court heard the case but remanded him to the military authorities. Under an 1867 law granting the right of appeal from denials of the writ of habeas corpus by U.S. circuit courts, McCardle appealed to the Supreme Court. The court accepted the case and heard oral arguments on it. Meantime, the Radical Republicans in Congress were fearful that the court would hold the Reconstruction Acts unconstitutional, and so Congress at their direction and over the president's veto passed a law in 1868 repealing the 1867 act. The court in 1869 accepted the fact that it now had no jurisdiction to hear the case and dismissed the appeal (*Ex parte McCardle*).

Chase delivered the court opinion in the case, and the other seven justices (Clifford, Davis, Field, Grier, Miller, Nelson, and Swayne) joined it. Chase pointed out that Article III, section 2, clause 2, gave Congress the power to make exceptions and regulations regarding the court's appellate jurisdiction, which Congress had done in express terms in the act of 1868. He did, however, insist that the Constitution itself, not Congress, established the court's appellate jurisdiction, no doubt implying that Congress could not abolish that jurisdiction. Second, he stated that the power of Congress to make exceptions could not affect transactions of the court already finalized. Third, he pointed out that the act of 1868 did not affect other bases of appeal from denial of the writ of habeas corpus but only appeals from circuit courts under the act of 1867 (see *Ex parte Yerger*, decided in the same year as *McCardle*).

On the same day as the McCardle decision, the court handed down a decision indirectly involving the status of secessionist states during the Civil War and the Reconstruction period. Before the Civil War Congress had transferred $10 million in U.S. bonds to the state of Texas. In 1862 the Confederate Texas government authorized use of the bonds to obtain war supplies. In 1866 the provisional Johnson Reconstruction government brought an original suit in the U.S. Supreme Court to block payment of the bonds to George White and other out-of-state holders of the bonds. White and the other defendants argued that the provisional government was not a state in the constitutional sense, and so the plaintiff provisional government could not fall under the court's original jurisdiction.

In a divided court, Chase wrote the court opinion upholding the provisional government's right to bring the suit under the court's original jurisdiction (*Texas v. White*), and Clifford, Davis, Field, and Nelson joined him. Chase upheld the Lincoln view, arguing that the Constitution created an indestructible union of indestructible states. Texas's ordinance of secession and all its legislation in support of secession were null and void. At the end of the Civil War it became the duty of the national government to provide for the restoration of the state government. In the exercise of the guarantee of a republican form of government (Article IV, section 4), the president appointed a provisional governor in 1865, the people elected a governor in 1866 under a new state constitution, and the military commander of the district under the Reconstruction Acts later appointed a governor. All three exercised executive functions at different times, and each has given his sanction to prosecution of the suit. In short, Chase held that the state existed in a state of suspended animation.

Grier dissented, and Miller and Swayne joined him. For them Texas had not existed as a state since its secession in 1861, and this political fact, not a legal fiction, should determine whether the provisional government represents a state entitled to bring an original action before the court. Grier asked pointedly how there could be a valid government to bring the suit if there was no valid government to sell the bonds. In short, Grier held that Texas was a territory, and territories did not fall within the court's original jurisdiction.

The Fourteenth Amendment The same Congress that enacted the Reconstruction Acts adopted the Fourteenth Amendment in June 1866, and the requisite three-fourths of the states had ratified it by July 20, 1868. The Fourteenth Amendment had five sections. Section 1, the key part of the amendment, prohibited states from making or enforcing any law that abridged the privileges and immunities of citizens of the United States, deprived any person of life, liberty, or property without due process of law, or denied any person of the equal protection of the laws. The preceding sentence declared that all persons born or naturalized in the United States and subject to the jurisdiction thereof are citizens of the United States and of the state in which they reside. (The framers added the definition of citizenship to section 1 when they, late in the day, realized that it was necessary because the Dred Scott decision had ruled that persons of African descent imported as slaves and their descendants were not, and could not become, citizens of the United States.)

Section 2 did not grant blacks the right to vote but penalized the failure of states to do so. It provided that a state's representation in Congress would be reduced in proportion to the number of disenfranchised male inhabitants of the state over the age of twenty-one.

Section 3 disqualified from holding federal or state offices those who had engaged in insurrection or given aid to the Confederacy. Section 4 declared that the public debt of the United States should not be questioned, but that neither the United States nor any state shall assume or pay any debt or obligation incurred in aid to the Confederacy or any claim for the cost incurred by the emancipation of slaves. Section 5 gave Congress the power to enforce the other provisions of the amendment.

Section 2 had only a short-term impact, since the Fifteenth Amendment, adopted by March 30, 1870, gave blacks the right to vote if otherwise qualified. Section 3 also had a short-term impact, since it applied only to individuals who would in a few years die. Section 4 had a limited impact regarding Confederate debts, although the declaration about the validity of the public debt of the United States might have an impact on current congressional debt-limit debates. The latter arguably prohibits Congress from setting a debt limit at all once it has authorized expenditures that require borrowing money. Section 5, however, would be involved in consideration of congressional civil-rights legislation (see the Civil Rights Cases, discussed later in this chapter).

The Slaughterhouse Cases In 1869 the government of Louisiana created under the Reconstruction Acts enacted a law that confined the slaughter of livestock to one area of the city of New Orleans and granted to one company the exclusive right to operate slaughterhouses in the area. The company was obliged to license others to use the houses and slaughter their animals in them for a schedule of fees. Excluded butchers unsuccessfully sought injunctions in the state courts and appealed to the U.S. Supreme Court.

In 1873 a sharply divided court, in one of its last acts under Chase, handed down a decision in a set of cases collectively known as the Slaughterhouse Cases. Miller, speaking for himself, Clifford, Davis, Hunt, and Strong, upheld the law against challenges based on section 1 of the Fourteenth Amendment. Field wrote the principal dissent, arguing against the law and in favor of the excluded butchers. Chase, Swayne, and Bradley joined Field, and Bradley and Swayne wrote separate dissenting opinions.

Miller began with an examination of the first sentence of section 1, which defined citizenship. That sentence defined two kinds of citizenship, one of the United States and the other of the state in which a citizen of the United States resides. The second sentence of section 1 prohibited states from abridging the privileges and immunities of citizens of the *United States*, not those of citizens of the state. Miller recited some privileges and immunities of citizens of the United States (e.g., the right to come to the seat of the federal government and its agencies, to transact business with it, to call on its protection from foreign governments, and to use the navigable waters of the United States). He pointed out that, with the Fourteenth Amendment, emancipated blacks and residents of the District of Columbia enjoyed those rights as citizens of the United States. But as to the privileges and immunities of the states as such, they must rely for their security where they have hitherto relied—namely, on state governments. Miller argued forcefully and emphatically that to judge otherwise would radically alter the traditional relations between the federal government and the states.

Miller summarily answered the plaintiffs' arguments based on the due process and equal protection clauses. On the due process clause, Miller commented only that under no construction of it could the restraint imposed on the butchers' exercise of their trade by Louisiana be held to be a deprivation of property. On the equal protection clause, he doubted that it would have any other application except to discrimination against blacks.

Field argued that section 1 of the Fourteenth Amendment protects citizens of the United States against deprivation of their rights by state legislation. The amendment assumes that there are privileges and immunities that of right belong to citizens as such and ordains that state legislation shall not abridge them. If the privileges and immunities clause refers only to rights of citizens of the United States specifically designated or necessarily implied in the Constitution, it is a vain and idle enactment. With the privileges and immunities so designated or implied no state could ever have legally interfered with them, since the Constitution and the laws of the United States always controlled legislation of that character. Article IV, section 2, clause 1, guaranteed to citizens of other states the same fundamental privileges and immunities enjoyed by the citizens of a state. The privileges and immunities clause gave those rights to the citizens of a state, and the citizenship clause included blacks as citizens of the United States and of the state in which they resided.

Field then held that citizens as such had a right to engage in trade, and state legislation could not discriminate against any individual in the pursuit of the individual's trade. He admitted that states may regulate business to promote public health, secure public order, and advance the general prosperity, but every citizen should be free to engage in business within the regulations. In short, Louisiana's granting of the monopoly to one company violated the right of individual citizens to slaughter animals, although there could be regulations about where slaughterhouses would be located and how animals would be slaughtered

To analyze the decision in the Slaughterhouse Cases one needs to consider two separate questions. The first relates to the meaning of the privileges and immunities clause. On this issue Field is correct. The framers intended the clause to protect the rights of citizens as such. The phrase *citizens of the United States* in the privileges and immunities clause was drafted before the definition of citizenship in the first sentence of the clause, and that sentence was introduced to include blacks as citizens, not to restrict the meaning of the privileges and immunities protected against state infringement. Moreover, Miller was on the court in Washington during the drafting of the Fourteenth Amendment and could not have been unaware of the history of its drafting. Miller's declaration that a broad interpretation of the privileges and immunities clause would radically alter federal-state relations reveals what was his dominant consideration. His conclusion was clearly contrary to the historical and textual evidence, but later courts have consistently followed his definition of the privileges and immunities clause.

The second question to be considered is whether the right to engage in trade is so fundamental a privilege and immunity of citizens as such that states may not create a monopoly to protect public health. Here, Field is making laissez-faire economics a constitutional absolute. But, although the Louisiana statute may have resulted from bribery of the legislature, which prosecution of the malefactors could redress, there was at least a prima facie case for granting a monopoly to protect public health. Having all slaughtering of animals in one place under one company might be the most effective means to protect public health.

The Granger Cases The decision in the Slaughterhouse Cases eliminated the privileges and immunities clause as any protection of property interests against state interference. Four years later, in 1877, the court was asked to invoke the due process clause as a protection of property interests. The 1870 constitution of Illinois declared that grain elevators were public warehouses and gave the legislature power to pass laws regulating the storage of grain. The legislature in 1871, under political pressure from farmers unhappy about the rates grain warehouse owners were charging, enacted a law requiring grain warehouse owners to obtain a license, fixing the rates that they could charge, and making other regulations. Munn was convicted of operating a grain warehouse without a license and other unlawful practices, and the Illinois Supreme Court upheld the conviction. He then appealed to the U.S. Supreme Court, raising several constitutional objections to the Illinois law, one based on the due process clause and another on the commerce clause. Waite wrote the court opinion upholding the law (*Munn v. Illinois*), and six justices (Bradley, Clifford, Davis, Hunt, Miller, and Swayne) joined him. Field and Strong dissented.

On whether the Illinois law deprived Munn of property without due process, Waite appealed to the common-law principle that businesses affected with a public interest are subject to public regulation. He held that the grain warehouses were businesses affected with a public interest and so subject to regulation. Nine firms controlled the warehouses in Chicago, which control Waite called a virtual monopoly, and the warehouses were the gateway of commerce to the East. He thought that if the law considers common carriers and innkeeper businesses affected with a public interest, there is no reason not to consider Munn to be engaged in such a business. In Waite's opinion it mattered not that Munn and others had built their warehouses before the regulations were established, since the warehouses were from the beginning subject to the police powers of the state, which the owners should have understood when they went into business. The common law requires that the rates charged be reasonable, and the legislature has the power to determine what the maximum reasonable rate is. The power may be abused, but the people must resort to the polls, not to the courts, to prevent abuses.

On whether the Illinois law violated federal power over interstate commerce, Waite held that the Illinois law regulated intrastate commerce. He admitted that the law might indirectly affect interstate commerce, but held that it was valid until Congress acted. Although this case involved the power of state laws to affect interstate commerce indirectly, a future court would use the distinction between direct and indirect effects on interstate commerce to deny the *federal* government power to regulate intrastate commerce or production if it only indirectly affects interstate commerce (cf. *U.S. v. E. C. Knight Co.*).

Field wrote the principal dissent. He argued vigorously that no magic converts private property into public property. The only property affected with a public interest is property granted to a private person for a public use or property dedicated by the owner to a public use. If any property affecting the public becomes property affected with a public interest, there will be no limit to invasion of private property. The state government has no greater public interest in grain warehouses than ordinary houses. The right to private property is absolute except in cases of immediate and overwhelming necessity. The state's police power can be exercised only to interfere with individual action that affects public peace, order, health, and morals, and the Illinois law was interfering with no such action. (Note that Field omitted public welfare.)

The Contract Clause The Chase Court in the Slaughterhouse Cases denied use of the privileges and immunities clause by property interests against state regulation, and the Waite Court in the Munn case denied use of the due process clause by them against state regulation. The Waite Court also in 1880 eliminated use of the contract clause by property interests against later state regulation of public contracts. In that case Mississippi had granted a lottery charter for twenty-five years to a private company, but the state adopted a new constitution one year later that barred all lotteries. The court held that a state could not contract away future use of its police power to protect public health, safety, and morals (*Stone v. Mississippi*). Waite wrote the opinion for a unanimous court except for Hunt, who did not participate. No future courts would diverge from the decisions on the privileges and immunities clause and the contract clause, but, as we shall see, the Fuller Court would within a decade and a half adopt a substantive interpretation of the due process clause in defense of property interests.

Substantive Due Process The Waite Court took several steps after *Munn* to pave the way for the Fuller Court to adopt a substantive interpretation of the due process clause. Roscoe Conkling, a member of the Joint Committee of Fifteen that drafted the Fourteenth Amendment in 1866, had argued in *San Mateo County v. Southern Pacific Railroad* that Congress intended with the word *person* to include corporations in the protection of the due process clause. This was pure nonsense, but the court bought it in 1886. Harlan wrote the unanimous court opinion to that effect in *Santa Clara County v. Southern Pacific Railroad*.

A year and a half later, in 1887, the Waite Court struck an ominous note indicating that the court would in the future closely examine state regulation of business (*Mugler v. Kansas*). The case involved a Kansas law prohibiting the manufacture of alcoholic beverages, even for personal use. Harlan wrote the court opinion upholding the law, and all the justices joined his opinion except Field, who dissented regarding the manufacture of alcoholic beverages for export out of state. The ominous note was that the court would look behind the form of state laws regulating business and inquire whether they have a substantial relation to the objects of the state's police powers.

Civil Rights Reconstruction Congresses passed successive civil rights acts in behalf of blacks from 1866 to 1875. The purpose of section 5 of the Fourteenth Amendment was especially to empower Congress to enforce section 1. The Civil Rights Act of 1875 was the most far-reaching congressional action and the last before the middle of the twentieth century. The 1875 law made it a misdemeanor for anyone to deny to any person equal rights and privileges in inns, theaters, amusement places, and public conveyances on the basis of color or previous condition of servitude. Five cases from California, Missouri, New York, and Tennessee, collectively known as the Civil Rights Cases, involved the constitutionality of the Civil Rights Act of 1875.Those convicted of violating the act appealed to the Supreme Court. The United States claimed that the Thirteenth and Fourteenth amendments gave Congress the power to enforce their provisions, and those convicted of violating the act claimed that the Thirteenth Amendment did not affect racial discrimination and that the Fourteenth concerned only racially discriminatory *state* action.

Bradley wrote the court opinion, declaring the law unconstitutional, and all members of the court except Harlan (Blatchford, Field, Gray, Matthews, Miller, Waite, and Woods) joined him. On the Fourteenth Amendment, Bradley held that section 1 prohibits state action and that section 5 empowers Congress to take only corrective legislation to remedy state violations of section 1. Congress has no power to take the initiative with direct and primary legislation—that is, Congress has no power under section 5 to enact codes of civil conduct. The states have the right to legislate generally on the subject of race relations, and Bradley appealed to the Tenth Amendment's reserving to the states powers not delegated to the United States. On the Thirteenth Amendment Bradley held that it merely abolished slavery and that private discrimination is not a badge of slavery.

Harlan in dissent argued that racial practices by corporations or individuals in the exercise of public or quasi-public functions are badges of slavery and that section 2 of the Thirteenth Amendment empowers Congress to prevent them by appropriate legislation. As to the Fourteenth Amendment, Harlan did not attempt to resurrect the privileges and immunity clause or to relate it to the rights of citizens as such. Rather, he invoked the first sentence of the clause, which defined citizenship of the United States *and* of the state in which they reside. Blacks thereby acquire state citizenship from the nation, and the nation may protect it by direct and primary action. Section 5 empowered Congress to enforce *all* the provisions of the amendment. Rights created by the United States have always been and should be under the protection of the federal government.

The Northern press supported the decision. The *New York Times* commented approvingly that the court had served the useful purpose of undoing the work of Congress! (No democratic commentator, to my knowledge, has ever argued that it is a function of the court, much less a useful one, to undo the work of Congress.) Bradley had a plausible argument about the inapplicability of the Thirteenth Amendment to found the law at issue, but Harlan had a point about the quasi-public function of public accommodations and the like. It is the historical context of the Fourteenth Amendment that Bradley missed or deliberately ignored. The framers of the amendment fully intended that section 5 empower Congress to define and protect the rights of citizens—that is, the framers were intending to write a blank check to themselves. But the *New York Times* was undoubtedly correct about the mood of the North, which had tired of problems connected with reconstructing the South.

$\backsim$ 5 $\backsim$

THE FULLER COURT

(1888–1910)

The Justices

Melville Fuller Waite died on March 23, 1888; President Cleveland nominated Melville Fuller to be chief justice on April 30, and the Senate confirmed Fuller on July 20. Fuller, a Democrat and an Episcopalian, was born in Augusta, Maine, on February 11, 1833. His father, Frederick, was a lawyer. Fuller graduated from Bowdoin College in 1853 and received a master's degree from the college in 1856. He studied law under George Weston, his mother's brother, attended lectures at Harvard Law School, and was admitted to the bar in 1855. He was twice married. He moved to Illinois in 1856. He served in the Illinois House of Representatives for two years (1863–65) and practiced law in Chicago. He served on the court until his death on July 4, 1910.

David Brewer Matthews died on March 22, 1889; President Benjamin Harrison nominated David Brewer to the court on December 4, and the Senate confirmed Brewer on December 18. Brewer, a Republican and a Congregationalist, was born in Izmer, Turkey, on June 20, 1837. His father, Josiah, was a missionary and his mother, Emilia, a sister of Justice Field. He received a bachelor's degree from Yale in 1856, a bachelor's degree in law from Albany Law School in 1858, and a master's degree from Yale in 1859. He was twice married.

In addition to practicing law and being county attorney for two years (1869–70), he had extensive judicial experience. He was a Kansas lower-court judge for four years (1865–69), a justice on the Kansas Supreme Court for thirteen years (1871–84), and a U.S. circuit court judge for five years (1884–89). He served on the court until his death on March 28, 1910, and with his uncle for nine years, until the latter's retirement in 1897.

Henry Brown Miller died on October 13, 1890, and President Harrison nominated Henry Brown to the court on December 23; the Senate confirmed Brown on December 29. Brown, a Republican and a Protestant, was born in South Lee, Massachusetts, on March 2, 1836. His father, Billings, was a prosperous merchant and manufacturer. Brown graduated from Yale in 1856 and attended both Yale and Harvard Law Schools but received no degree from either. He was twice married.

He was admitted to the Michigan bar in 1860. He was an assistant U.S. district attorney for five years (1863–68), a judge on a Michigan circuit court, and a U.S. district court judge in Michigan for fifteen years (1875–90). He resigned from the court on May 28, 1906, and died on September 13, 1913.

George Shiras The death of Bradley on January 22, 1892, gave Harrison an opportunity to appoint his third justice to the court. Harrison nominated George Shiras on July 19, 1892, and the Senate confirmed Shiras on July 26. Shiras, a Republican and a Presbyterian, was born in Pittsburgh, Pennsylvania, on January 26, 1832. His father, George, was a brewery merchant. Shiras attended Ohio University, graduated from Yale College in 1853, attended Yale Law School, and read law under Hopewell Hepburn. He practiced private law and had no prior governmental experience. He resigned from the court on February 23, 1903, and died on August 21, 1924.

Howell Jackson The death of Lamar on January 23, 1893, gave Harrison the opportunity to appoint his fourth justice to the court. Harrison, a Republican, nominated Howell Jackson, a Democrat and a Protestant, on February 2, and the Republican Senate confirmed Jackson on February 18. Jackson was born in Paris, Tennessee, on April 8, 1832. His father, Alexander, was a doctor. Jackson attended the University of Virginia in 1850, read law under Judge H. O. W. Totten, and attended Cumberland University in 1856. Jackson, twice married, was admitted to the Tennessee bar in 1856. He served in the Tennessee legislature for one year (1880) and in the U.S. Senate for five years (1881–86), and was a judge on a U.S. court of appeals for seven years (1886–93). He served on the court until his death two years later, on August 8, 1895.

Edward White Blatchford died on July 7, 1893; President Cleveland nominated Edward White to the court on February 19, 1894, and the Senate confirmed White on the same day. White, a Democrat and a Catholic, the first Catholic since Taney, was born in Bayou La Fourche, Louisiana, on November 3, 1865. His father, Edward, was a lawyer, judge, congressman, and governor of Louisiana. He attended Mt. St. Mary's College in Maryland and studied law at Georgetown University. He was admitted to the Louisiana bar in 1868.

He served in the Louisiana legislature for four years (1874–78), was a justice on the Louisiana Supreme Court for two years (1878–80), and served in the U.S. Senate for three years (1891–94). He served as associate justice until December 12, 1910, when he was nominated and confirmed as chief justice to replace Fuller.

Rufus Peckham Jackson died on August 8, 1895, and Cleveland nominated Rufus Peckham to the court on December 3; the Senate confirmed Peckham on December 9. (The Senate had previously rejected the nomination of Peckham's brother Wheeler.) Peckham, a Democrat and a Protestant, was born in Albany, New York, on November 8, 1838. His father, Rufus, was a lawyer, congressman, and judge on a state supreme court and the New York Court of Appeals. Peckham was educated at Albany Academy and studied law in the office of his father.

He was a judge on a New York supreme court for three years (1883–86) and a judge on the New York Court of Appeals for nine years (1886–95). He served on the court until his death on October 24, 1909.

Joseph McKenna Field retired on December 1, 1897, and President McKinley nominated Joseph McKenna to the court on December 16; the Senate confirmed McKenna on January 21, 1898. McKenna, a Republican and a Catholic, was born in Philadelphia, Pennsylvania, on August 10, 1843. His father, John, was a baker. McKenna grew up in California and attended Catholic schools; he attended Benecia Collegiate Institute in 1865. He was admitted to the California bar in 1865.

He was a district attorney in California for four years (1866–70) and served in the California legislature for two years (1875–77), as a congressman for seven years (1885–92) and as a judge on the U.S. Court of Appeals for five years (1892–97). He was U.S. attorney general in 1897. He resigned from the court on January 5, 1925, and died on November 21, 1926.

Oliver Wendell Holmes Jr. Gray resigned in 1902, and President Theodore Roosevelt nominated Oliver Wendell Holmes Jr. to the court on August 11; the Senate confirmed Holmes on December 4. Holmes, a Republican and an agnostic (originally a Unitarian), was born in Boston, Massachusetts, on March 8, 1841. His father, Oliver Wendell Holmes Sr., was a doctor and essayist. Holmes Jr. was educated by a Unitarian minister and at Boston Latin School; he graduated from Harvard College in 1861 and from Harvard Law School in 1866. He served in the Union army during the Civil War, between 1861 and 1864. He was admitted to the Massachusetts bar in 1867, was a professor at Harvard Law School, and published scholarly works on the common law. He was an associate judge on the Massachusetts Supreme Judicial Court for sixteen years (1883–99) and its chief judge for three years (1899–1902). He served on the U.S. Supreme Court until his resignation on January 12, 1932. He died on March 6, 1935.

William Day Shiras wrote a letter of resignation to take effect on February 23, 1903. Roosevelt nominated William Day to the court on February 19, and the Senate confirmed Day on the date the resignation became effective. Day, a Republican and a Protestant, was born in Ravenna, Ohio, on April 17, 1849. His father, Luther, was a lawyer and judge on the Ohio Supreme Court. Day graduated from the University of Michigan in 1870 and studied law at its law school for one year (1871–72). He was admitted to the Ohio bar in 1872.

He was a judge on an Ohio court of common pleas for four years (1886–90). He was assistant U.S. secretary of state for one year (1897–98), secretary of state for a half year (1898), and chairman of the Peace Commission at the end of the Spanish-American War. He was a judge on a U.S. court of appeals for four years (1899–1903). He served on the Supreme Court until his resignation on November 13, 1922, and died on July 9, 1923.

William Moody When Brown resigned on May 28, 1906, Roosevelt appointed his third justice. Roosevelt nominated William Moody, a Republican and a Protestant, to the court on December 3, and the Senate confirmed Moody on December 12. He was born in Newbury, Massachusetts, on December 23, 1853. His father, Henry, was a farmer. Moody graduated from Phillips Andover in 1872 and from Harvard College in 1876. He studied law at Harvard Law

School under Professor Richard Dana Jr. for one semester. He was admitted to the Massachusetts bar in 1878. He was the first bachelor justice.

He was a U.S. district attorney for five years (1890–95), a congressman for seven years (1895–1902), secretary of the navy for two years (1902–4), and U.S. attorney general for two years (1904–6), He served on the court until his resignation on November 20, 1910. He died on July 2, 1917.

Horace Lurton Peckham died on October 24, 1909, and President Taft nominated Horace Lurton to the court on December 13; the Senate confirmed Lurton on December 20. Lurton, a Democrat and an Episcopalian, was born in Newport, Kentucky, on February 26, 1844. His father, Lycurgus, was a doctor and a minister. Lurton was tutored privately, attended the University of Chicago for two years (1859–61), and served in the Confederate army. After the Civil War he received a law degree from Cumberland Law School in 1867, was admitted to the Tennessee bar, and practiced private law.

Lurton was an associate justice on the Tennessee Supreme Court for seven years (1886–93) and its chief justice in 1893. He was a judge on a U.S. court of appeals for sixteen years (1893–1909) and served on that court under Taft as presiding judge for nine of those years (1893–1900). (Taft was impressed with Lurton, and that is probably the reason the former, a Republican, chose to appoint the latter, a Democrat, to the court.) Lurton was at the same time a professor of law at Vanderbilt University for seven years (1898–1905) and dean of the law school for five years (1905–10). He served on the U.S. Supreme Court until his death on July 12, 1914.

Charles Evans Hughes Brewer died on March 28, 1910, and Taft nominated Charles Evans Hughes to the court on April 25; the Senate confirmed Hughes on May 2. Hughes, a Republican and a Baptist, was born in Glens Falls, New York, on April 11, 1862. His father, David, was a minister. Hughes attended Colgate University for two years (1876–78) and graduated from Brown University in 1881 and from Columbia Law School in 1884. He engaged in private practice and was professor of law at Cornell University for two years (1891–93). He was governor of New York for five years (1905–10). He resigned from the court on June 10, 1916, in order to run as the unsuccessful Republican candidate for president in 1916.

Summary In addition to Fuller replacing Waite, four new associate justices (Brewer, Brown, Jackson, and Shiras) had by 1893 replaced Bradley, Lamar,

Matthews, and Miller of the Waite Court. By 1898 the only holdovers from the Waite Court were Gray and Harlan, White having replaced Blatchford and McKenna Field. By 1902 only Harlan remained from the Waite Court, Holmes having replaced Gray.

Including Fuller, thirteen justices were appointed between the year of his appointment, 1888, and the year of his death, 1910. Nine were Republicans and four Democrats. Ten were Protestants, two Catholics, and one an agnostic. Ten were Northerners (two from New York and two from Massachusetts), and three were Southerners (two from Tennessee). Their education was much more formal than that of earlier justices. Ten (Brewer, Brown, Day, Fuller, Holmes, Hughes, McKenna, Moody, Shiras, and White) had graduated from college, three from Yale and two from Harvard. Fuller and Brewer had master's degrees, and Lurton, Holmes, and Hughes had law degrees. All the justices besides Shiras had governmental experience. Nine (Brewer, Brown, Day, Holmes, Jackson, Lurton, McKenna, Peckham, and White) had judicial experience. Six (Brewer, Brown, Day, Hughes, McKenna, and Moody) had executive governmental experience. Five (Fuller, Jackson, McKenna, Moody, and White) had legislative experience. Only McKenna had experience in all three branches of government.

Leading Decisions

State Regulation of Commerce In 1886 the Waite Court had ruled that the states could not set the rates on the interstate shipment of goods (*Wabash, St. Louis, and Pacific Railway Co. v. Illinois*). An Illinois statute prohibited rate discrimination between long and short hauls. The railroad was charging 15 cents per pound for shipments from Peoria, Illinois, to New York City but 25 cents per pound for shipments from Gilman, Illinois, to the same city, although Gilman was eighty-six miles closer to New York than Peoria. Miller wrote the court opinion, holding that the commerce involved was national in character and that national commerce required federal regulation or none, and Blatchford, Field, Harlan, Matthews, and Woods joined him. Bradley, Strong, and Waite dissented. Since there was at that time no federal regulation of railroads, the ruling meant that there was no rate regulation at all of interstate shipments. This led Congress to pass the Interstate Commerce Act, which established the Interstate Commerce Commission (ICC) to regulate interstate rates. Eventually, with the Hepburn Act of 1906, the ICC would be empowered to *prescribe* the rates rather than merely regulate them, and, as we shall see later, the Shreveport Case would allow the Commission to regulate intrastate rates substantially related to interstate rates.

On nondiscriminatory state regulations affecting interstate commerce in the absence of congressional legislation, the Fuller Court decided two noteworthy cases. The first case, in 1890, dealt with an Iowa statute that prohibited the manufacture, sale, and dispensing of intoxicating liquors except for specified purposes, which required a permit. Leisy, an Illinois brewer, shipped beer in barrels to Iowa, and Hardin, a police officer, seized the kegs of beer while they were in the possession of Leisy's agent. The trial and lower Iowa courts held that the Iowa statute was unconstitutional as applied to beer in original packages, but the Iowa Supreme Court reversed, holding that the statute was constitutional as so applied. Leisy appealed to the U.S. Supreme Court.

The court reversed, holding that the statute as applied to intoxicating liquors in original packages was unconstitutional (*Leisy v. Hardin*). Fuller wrote the court opinion, and Blatchford, Bradley, Field, Lamar, and Miller joined him. Fuller argued that interstate commerce in commodities is national in character and that only Congress can regulate it. Therefore, since Congress had not regulated on the subject, Iowa could not regulate liquor imported from out of state as long as it remained in original packages.

Gray dissented, and Brewer and Harlan joined him. Gray pointed out that Iowa was exercising its police power to protect the public from the physical, moral, and social evils resulting from consumption of liquor, that Iowa's prohibition law did not discriminate in favor of its own industry, and that the decisions in the License Cases allowed nondiscriminatory state regulations affecting interstate commerce in the absence of congressional legislation. Moreover, the long silence of Congress indicated its approval of the License decisions. (Congress swiftly voiced its disapproval by nullifying the Leisy decision.)

Four years later, in 1894, the court reversed gears and upheld a state law prohibiting the sale of colored oleomargarine (*Plumley v. Massachusetts*). Albert Plumley, the Massachusetts agent of an Illinois company marketing colored oleomargarine, was convicted and fined for violating the law and imprisoned until he paid the fine. He petitioned the Massachusetts Supreme Judicial Court for a writ of habeas corpus, claiming that the law, as applied to interstate commerce, was unconstitutional. The writ was denied, and he appealed to the U.S. Supreme Court.

Harlan wrote the court opinion, and Brown, Gray, Jackson, Shiras, and

White joined him. Harlan held that the law was a legitimate exercise of the state's police power to prevent deception of customers. Fuller, joined by Brewer and Field, dissented, arguing that the color in oleomargarine shouldn't and wouldn't deceive customers and that Congress has exclusive power to regulate interstate commerce in commodities. Congress's nullification of *Leisy* was undoubtedly a factor in the different result, but change in the court's membership was also important and probably critical. Four members of the Leisy majority (Blatchford, Bradley, Lamar, and Miller) had died in the intervening years, and only two members of the Leisy majority (Field and Fuller) remained on the court to participate in the Plumley decision.

Substantive Due Process There remained the question about state regulation of intrastate rates. The Waite Court in its waning days sent signals that the court might not hold to the Munn interpretation of the due process clause. First, the court in the Santa Clara decision of 1886 held that corporations were persons within the meaning of the due process clause, and so corporations were entitled to whatever protection that clause afforded. Second, the court in the Mugler decision of 1887 announced that it would look behind the form of a law alleged to be an exercise of state police powers and examine whether the exercise bore a substantial relation to them.

In 1890 the Fuller Court effectively overturned the Munn interpretation of the due process clause (*Chicago, Milwaukee, and St. Paul Railway Co. v. Minnesota*). A Minnesota statute established a commission to regulate railroad rates but required no notice or hearing before the commission set rates and prohibited judicial review of the reasonableness of the rates. The court struck down the statute. Blatchford wrote the court opinion, and Brewer, Field, Fuller, and Harlan joined him. Blatchford held that the statute, by prohibiting judicial review of the reasonableness of the rates, deprived the company of due process of law. If the rates were de facto unfair, the company would lose property without due process, and courts should decide the reasonableness of the rates. Miller, who was part of the majority in *Munn*, concurred separately. Bradley, who was also part of the majority in *Munn*, dissented, and Gray and Lamar joined him. Bradley repeated the central theme of *Munn*—namely, that rate regulation is a legislative, not a judicial, function—and correctly pointed out that the decision practically overruled *Munn*.

What happened to the Waite majority? First, six members of the Waite Court (Clifford, Davis, Hunt, Strong, Swayne, and Waite) had died or resigned, and four of the six new justices (Blatchford, Brewer, Fuller, and Harlan) were in the new majority. Second, Miller, part of the *Munn* majority, became part of the new majority, although his vote was not needed for the result. If one asks why most of the new justices supported the substantive interpretation of the due process clause in support of property interests, the probable answer is that the laissez-faire political and economic philosophy had by 1890 become the dominant philosophy of legal professionals.

In 1898 the court exercised the judicial review asserted in the Chicago case to invalidate the railroad rate schedule fixed by the Nebraska legislature (*Smyth v. Ames*). Bondholders of the railroads sought and obtained an injunction in the circuit court, and the Supreme Court upheld the injunction. Specifically, the court, after a protracted analysis, held that the rates did not offer a fair return on the fair value of the assets. What is the fair value of a railroad's assets, and what is a fair return on those assets, are difficult questions to answer, and there is no reason to think that judges are better suited than legislators and administrators to estimate what is a fair return or the fair value of the assets.

The Chicago and Smyth cases involved claims by railroads and their investors that state rate regulation deprived them of property without due process of law. In 1897 the court built on the Santa Clara decision to hold that the liberty to contract was a liberty protected by the due process clause (*Allgeyer v. Louisiana*). Peckham wrote the opinion for a unanimous court. Louisiana had legislation regulating insurance companies. To force out-of-state insurance companies operating in the state to comply with the regulations, the state barred its citizens and residents from buying insurance from out-of-state companies that failed to comply—that is, from contracting with such companies. Allgeyer, a resident of Louisiana, bought insurance from a New York company that was not complying with the state's regulations, and Louisiana prosecuted him. He appealed to the U.S. Supreme Court, and the court overturned the conviction, holding that the statute violated his liberty to make a contract and that the due process clause protected his right to do so. In short, the court adopted Field's dissenting view in the Slaughterhouse Cases, although his dissent in those cases centered on the privileges and immunities clause. (The Chase Court in 1869 had unanimously held that insurance was not commerce [*Paul v. Virginia*], and so the Fuller Court, following precedent, did not consider whether the Louisiana statute unduly burdened or discriminated against interstate commerce.)

One year later (1898), the court upheld a Utah statute that limited to eight the number of hours that miners could work in the mines each day (*Holden v. Hardy*). The state's police powers to regulate public health, safety, and morals trumped liberty of contract, and the court noted the unhealthy condition of work in the mines. What about laws establishing maximum hours for workers in other employments?

The court answered that question a few years later. A New York statute limited the hours of employment in bakeries and confectionary establishments to ten hours a day and sixty hours a week. Joseph Lochner, a bakery owner in Utica, New York, was convicted of violating the law, lost in the New York Court of Appeals, and appealed to the U.S. Supreme Court. The court ruled in favor of Lochner and struck down the New York maximum-hours law as a violation of the liberty of contract protected by the due process clause (*Lochner v. New York*). Peckham wrote the court opinion, and Brewer, Brown, Fuller, and McKenna joined him. According to Peckham, the states' police powers justify interference with the liberty of contract to protect the safety, health, morals, and general welfare of the public. There was obviously no problem about public peace, and Peckham saw no involvement of public safety, morals, or welfare. The only issue concerned public health, and Peckham thought it common understanding that a baker's occupation was a healthy one. Nor did he think that there was any connection between how many hours a baker worked and the healthy quality of the bread he produced. In short, the maximum-hours law constituted meddlesome interference and was the product of unsound views—namely, views contrary to laissez-faire principles.

Four justices (Day, Harlan, Holmes, and White) dissented. Harlan, joined by Day and White, wrote one of the dissenting opinions. Harlan argued that the liberty of contract is subject to such regulations as a state may make for the common good and well-being of society and that the court should defer to state legislative judgments unless they are plainly and palpably beyond the limits of legislative power. But his most powerful argument, one that Holmes did not make, was that there is a real relation between the hours a baker works and his health. Despite Peckham's positive understanding that the working conditions of bakers were healthy, they in fact work in intense heat, and this results in profuse sweating. Holmes wrote the other dissenting opinion, one of his most eloquent. He argued that many laws infringe on the liberty of contract, that the Fourteenth Amendment did not enact Mr. Herbert Spencer's *Social Statics* (a laissez-faire tract popular with academics and legal professionals), and that the courts shouldn't invalidate laws unless they infringe on fundamental principles. The latter proposition presaged the court's later protection of civil liberties against state legislation.

Three years later, in 1908, the court faced the question of state legislation limiting the maximum hours of women workers. Oregon, a pioneer in reform legislation, had enacted a statute limiting the permissible hours of work by women to ten hours a day and six days a week. Muller, an employer, was convicted of violating the statute, lost in the state courts, and appealed to the U.S. Supreme Court. This time the court unanimously ruled in favor of the maximum-hour law (*Muller v. Oregon*). The court had the same membership as in *Lochner* except for Moody, who replaced Brown. Brewer, who wrote the court opinion, cited the contribution of the appellant's lawyer, Louis Brandeis, whose brief included a hundred pages of facts, and argued that women are weaker than men and need protection of their health and morals.

The Muller decision did not affect reform legislation regarding male workers, who constituted most of nation's workforce. In fact, in the same year as *Muller*, the court invoked liberty of contract under the due process clause of the Fifth Amendment to invalidate a congressional law outlawing the so-called "yellow-dog" contracts (*Adair v. U.S.*). Those contracts were agreements between an employer and an employee under which the employee promised not to join a union and recognized that later union membership was cause for dismissal.

Federal Taxes   The Wilson-Gorman Act of 1894 imposed taxes on income derived from various sources. Incomes above $4,000 were subject to a flat tax of 2 percent; the median income at the time was certainly less than $1,000, and probably about $500. Congress had taxed incomes on a progressive scale during the Civil War, and the Waite Court upheld it as an exercise of the war power (*Springer v. U.S.*), but shortly after the war, Congress repealed that tax. Up to the 1890s, except during the war, tariffs, excise taxes, and revenue from the sale of public land had provided enough revenue to finance the federal government's expenses, but the government by 1894, partially due to the depression of 1893, needed more revenue to finance its operations.

Charles Pollock was a shareholder in a trust company and sought to enjoin the bank from complying with the law. Since the bank had no real interest in defending the law, the federal government intervened to defend it. After losing in the lower court, Pollock appealed the case to the Supreme Court. At the first hearing in 1895 the court ruled that the taxes on income from real estate and the interest on municipal bonds were unconstitutional. One justice, Jackson, did not participate due to illness, and the other justices were evenly divided on the constitutionality of the taxes on other sources of income—namely, unearned income from personal property (i.e., investments) and earned income from business or employment (i.e., profits or wages). At the second hearing in the same year, with Jackson participating, the court held the taxes on the income from personal property, business profits, and wages unconstitutional (*Pollock v. Farmers' Loan and Trust Co.*).

Fuller wrote the court opinion, and Brewer, Field, Gray, and Shiras joined him. The issue was whether the taxes were direct or indirect. If they were direct taxes, Article I, section 2, clause 3, required that they be apportioned according to the population of each state, something disproportional and grossly inequitable. We have already seen that the early Hylton decision restricted direct taxes to head taxes and taxes on land, and this was certainly the intention of the framers of the Constitution. Fuller, however, argued that taxes on the income from land was equivalent to taxes on the land and so needed to be apportioned to the population of each state. He also held that taxes on personal property were direct taxes, although *Hylton* had explicitly held the contrary—namely, that such taxes were excise taxes and so indirect taxes. Moreover, Fuller argued that taxes on the income from personal property, like taxes on the income from land, were equivalent to taxes on personal property. Fuller did not deny that taxes on business profits and workers' salaries were indirect—that is, excise, taxes—but he argued that those taxes had to be voided, since Congress intended them as part of the whole income tax law. (On the latter point, he was undoubtedly correct. It is hardly likely that Congress would have wanted to tax business and labor without taxing the wealthy or that the country would have tolerated it.)

Harlan delivered a vigorous dissent. He pointed out that a tax on the *income* from land is not a direct tax on the land, and most lands do not bring in rents. Second, the Hylton decision held that a tax on personal property (carriages) was an excise tax and not a direct tax. Third, the majority decision would cripple the nation by preventing taxes on tangible personal property or the income derived from it. As a result, only an amendment could overturn it. (That, of course, is precisely what happened. Congress in 1909 proposed the Sixteenth Amendment, and the requisite number of states had ratified it by February 13, 1913. The amendment empowered Congress to lay and collect taxes on incomes from whatever source without apportionment or regard for population.) Brown, Jackson, and White dissented separately.

Since the court without Jackson had been evenly divided on taxing income from personal property, business profits, and employee wages in the first hearing and Jackson voted in the second hearing to uphold the constitutionality of those taxes, one of the justices supporting constitutionality in the first hearing must have changed his mind in the second. None of the justices ever said who that justice was. Shiras was the usual suspect, but Brewer and even Gray have been suggested. At any rate, most commentators cannot imagine that Fuller or Field would ever have supported the constitutionality of any of the taxes.

Almost a decade later, in 1904, the Fuller Court upheld a federal excise tax patently favoring one economic interest over another (*McCray v. U.S.*). Dairy farmers pressured Congress to levy a tax of ten cents per pound on colored oleomargarine, which looked like butter, but only a quarter of a cent per pound on uncolored oleomargarine. McCray, a retailer of oleomargarine, had purchased colored oleomargarine for resale but paid only the lower tax. He was fined $50 and appealed to the Supreme Court. White wrote the court opinion, and Brewer, Day, Harlan, Holmes, and McKenna joined him. White held that the tax on its face was a revenue measure. If Congress abused its lawful power to tax for revenue, the remedy was political—that is, citizens could pressure Congress to repeal it. If the abuse were extreme, the court could overturn it, but this tax didn't destroy any fundamental right. Brown, Fuller, and Peckham dissented without an opinion.

Federal Regulation of Commerce In 1895, the same year as the income-tax decision, the Fuller Court rendered a restrictive interpretation of congressional power under the commerce clause. The Sherman Anti-Trust Act of 1890 prohibited combinations and conspiracies in restraint of trade. In 1892 the American Sugar Refining Company, the major producer of sugar in the United States, purchased controlling stock in four other sugar-refining companies, which gave it 98 percent control of American sugar production. The federal government sought a court order canceling the American Sugar Refining Company's purchase of the four other companies, one of which was the E. C. Knight Co. The lower federal courts refused to do so, and the government appealed to the Supreme Court.

Fuller wrote the court opinion, and seven justices (Brewer, Brown, Field, Gray, Jackson, Shiras, and White) joined him (*U.S. v. E. C. Knight Co.*). Fuller drew a sharp distinction between interstate commerce and intrastate manufacture. The latter is exclusively subject to the police powers of the state to regulate and the former to the exclusive power of Congress to regulate. He admitted that monopolies over the production of goods might tend to restrain interstate commerce, but the restraint would be an indirect result. If the commerce clause empowered Congress to regulate all contracts in manufacturing that may have indirect effects on commerce, comparatively little would be left to state control. The acts of the defendant companies related exclusively to the acquisition of local refineries, and the business of refining sugar in Pennsylvania bore no direct relation to commerce among the several states. Fuller also admitted that Congress may regulate contracts to buy goods to be transported from one state to another and transportation of the goods.

Harlan was the sole dissenter. He, of course, quoted John Marshall in *Gibbons v. Ogden*. Commerce includes everything that flows into buying and selling as well as everything resulting from buying and selling. The power of Congress to regulate commerce is plenary. Commerce among the several states is commerce that affects more than one state. Moreover, Harlan pointed out that no one state can control the evils of monopolies, especially regarding products essential to the comfort of every household.

The size of the majority in the Knight case, including even White, reflected the prevalence of the laissez-faire views then dominant in the legal professional, but it also reflected the political fear that extensive federal regulation of the economy would infringe on states' rights. As to the Fuller opinion, the attempts to distinguish production from commerce and direct and indirect effects on commerce would come to haunt the court for more than forty years, climaxing in the bitter struggle over the New Deal in 1935 and 1936.

In later cases involving interpretation of the coverage of the Sherman Act, the Fuller Court gave the government a couple of important victories. In one the government sought to break up the Northern Securities Company, a holding company created by J. P. Morgan, James Hill, and E. H. Harriman. The company had acquired majority holdings in the stocks of three railroads and then operated them as a unit. The company argued that contracts to purchase stock were not part of interstate commerce and so outside the coverage of the Sherman Act. The court by the narrowest margin held in 1904 that the act was applicable to financial contracts in restraint of trade and that the application to them was constitutional (*Northern Securities Co. v. U.S.*). Harlan wrote the plurality opinion, and Brown, Day, and McKenna joined him. Brewer concurred only in the judgment, distinguishing between reasonable and unreasonable financial contracts. Fuller, Holmes, Peckham, and White dissented. White, joined by the others, argued that Congress had no power to regulate the contracts. Holmes, joined by the others, argued that Congress had not intended the act to cover financial contracts. (President Theodore Roosevelt was bitterly disappointed with Holmes's vote in the case.)

In a second case the government sought to break up a monopoly of the Chicago stockyards. The company argued that its stockyard activities were local and so not part of interstate commerce under the Knight doctrine. Holmes wrote the unanimous 1905 court opinion in favor of the government (*Swift v. U.S.*). Holmes held that the company's Chicago stockyards were local but part of a stream of commerce among the states—that is, the stockyards were only a temporary residence of cattle on their way from Nebraska to New York. The New Deal relied in part on this line of argument to support much of its legislation.

A third case involved application of the Sherman Act to a striking union's organization of a secondary boycott of the products of a hat company in Danbury, Connecticut. The national hatters union was on strike against the company and urged members of the American Federation of Labor to boycott the company's products. Loewe, the company owner, filed a civil suit under the act for treble damages, charging the union and its agent, Martin Lawler, with conspiring to restrain trade. Loewe lost in the lower courts and appealed to the Supreme Court. Fuller wrote the unanimous 1908 court opinion, holding that the union was a combination subject to the act (*Loewe v. Lawler*). The decision reflected the court's and much of the country's anti-union bias.

In 1903 the Fuller Court by the narrowest margin recognized a federal police power under the commerce clause to protect public health, safety, and morals (*Champion v. Ames*). Congress passed the Lottery Act in 1895, which prohibited the transportation of lottery tickets across state lines. Champion and others were convicted of violating the statute. They lost in the circuit court, which dismissed their petition for a writ of habeas corpus, and the defendants appealed to the Supreme Court. The court held five oral arguments on the case from 1901 to 1903. Apparently, only the appointment of Holmes to replace Gray created a decisive majority.

The technical issue in the case was whether lottery tickets, merely pieces of paper, were objects of commerce, but the underlying issue was whether the federal government had power to regulate interstate commerce for moral purposes. Harlan wrote the court opinion, and Brown, Holmes, McKenna, and White joined him. Harlan appealed to Marshall's broad definition of commerce in *Gibbons v. Ogden.* The tickets, although pieces of paper rather than goods, have potential value and so are objects of commerce subject to the power of Congress over interstate commerce; if Congress can regulate their transportation across state lines, it can prohibit the transportation altogether.

Fuller filed a vigorous dissenting opinion, and Brewer, Peckham, and Shiras joined him. In Fuller's view lottery tickets were not articles of commerce, and they did not become such by being transported over state lines. A lottery is not a business. The federal lottery law infringed on exclusively state police powers. Moreover, Fuller introduced a distinction between things in themselves causing injury and things innocent in themselves and claimed that the commerce clause empowered Congress only to prohibit transportation of the former over state lines. The court would invoke this distinction to strike down a child-labor law in the celebrated case of *Hammer v. Dagenhart.*

The lottery decision encouraged other federal laws barring the interstate transportation of things deemed harmful to public health, safety, or morals. One was the Pure Food and Drug Act of 1906, which barred the interstate transportation of adulterated or mislabeled food. Another was the Meat Inspection Act of the same year, which regulated the interstate transportation of meat. A third was the Mann Act of 1910, which barred the transportation of women across state lines for immoral purposes. The White Court upheld all of these laws on the authority of the lottery decision.

Race Possibly the most important and certainly one of the most long-enduring decisions of the Fuller Court was in the area of race relations. A Louisiana statute of 1890 mandated that railroads operating intrastate provide separate but equal accommodations for white and colored passengers, authorized train officials to enforce the law, and imposed penalties on those who disobeyed the law. (One anomaly in the law was that whites could sit in blacks' cars if there were no seats available in the whites' cars.) Blacks in New Orleans orchestrated a test case to challenge the law. In 1892 railroad officials apparently also opposed the law for economic reasons. Homer Plessy, a black, purchased a ticket to ride on an intrastate route between New Orleans and Covington. When Ferguson, a railroad conductor, arrested Plessy for violating the law, Plessy's attorney petitioned the Louisiana Supreme Court to halt the trial from proceeding. That court held that there was no conflict between the law and the Thirteenth and Fourteenth amendments. Plessy's lawyer then appealed to the U.S. Supreme Court.

Brown wrote the court opinion upholding the law, and Field, Fuller, Gray, Peckham, Shiras, and White joined him (*Plessy v. Ferguson*). Brown summarily dismissed Plessy's claim that the law violated the Thirteenth Amendment, and he argued that the aim of the Fourteenth Amendment was to enforce absolute equality before the law and that segregation as such did not imply legal inequality. Brown cited segregated public schools in the North and in the District of Columbia. The question in his view was whether segregation is arbitrary or reasonable—namely, whether social customs and the preservation of public peace and good order provide a reasonable basis for legally mandated racial segregation in public conveyances. Racial segregation, he argued, is not a badge of inferiority unless blacks wish to think it to be such. Laws cannot legislate social integration or eradicate racial instincts or abolish distinctions based on physical differences.

Harlan was the sole dissenter. (Brewer did not participate.) Harlan forcefully declared that the Constitution (as amended by the Fourteenth Amendment) is colorblind. The amendment made blacks citizens of the United States and the states in which they reside, and states were forbidden to abridge their privileges and immunities. (Harlan was vainly attempting to revive the privileges and immunities clause jettisoned in the Slaughterhouse Cases.) The Louisiana statute put the badge of servitude and degradation on blacks, and the so-called equal accommodations would deceive no one.

All of the majority justices in *Plessy* were Northerners except White, and two of them (Brown and Shiras) were Yale graduates. The North had long lost the fervor of the Radical Republicans for the civil rights of emancipated blacks. Brown's rhetoric was offensive to blacks, and Harlan, a Kentuckian and former slaveholder, was right that the judgment of the court would be as pernicious as the Dred Scott decision. Brown's reference to the fact that the Radical Republicans established segregated public schools in the District of Columbia has a point regarding the intentions of the framers of the amendment but not a completely convincing one. The framers undoubtedly did not think that the civil rights of blacks included racially integrated public schools, but the Civil Rights Act of 1875 indicates that they did think that blacks' civil rights included equal rights and privileges against discrimination in public accommodations and public conveyances.

6

THE WHITE AND TAFT COURTS

(1910–30)

The Justices

Edward White Fuller died on July 4, 1910, and President Taft nominated associate justice Edward White to be chief justice on December 12; White was the first associate justice to be named to that post. The Senate confirmed White on the same day. He served as chief justice until his death on May 19, 1921.

Willis Van Devanter To replace White as associate justice, Taft nominated Willis Van Devanter on December 12, and the Senate confirmed him on December 15. Van Devanter, a Republican and a Protestant, was born in Marion, Indiana, on April 17, 1853. His father, Isaac, was a lawyer and abolitionist. Van Devanter attended public schools in Marion, studied at De Pauw College in 1878, and received a law degree from the University of Cincinnati Law School in 1881. He was an assistant district attorney in Indiana, served in the Wyoming legislature for two years (1888–90), and was chief justice of the Wyoming Supreme Court for one year. He was assistant U.S. attorney general for six years (1897–1903) and judge on a U.S. court of appeals for seven years (1903–10). He was effectively the administrative officer of the Taft Court. He resigned from the court in June 1937, giving President Franklin Roosevelt his first appointment to the court in the midst of his fight with it, and died on February 8, 1941.

Joseph Lamar Moody resigned on November 20, 1910, and Taft had the opportunity to make another appointment to the court. On December 12, the same day on which he nominated White and Van Devanter, he nominated Joseph Lamar to replace Moody, and the Senate confirmed Lamar on December 15. Lamar, a Democrat and a member of the Disciples of Christ, was born in Elbert County, Georgia, on October 14, 1857. His father, James, was a minister. Lamar attended an academy, the University of Georgia, Bethany College, and Washington and Lee University Law School. Lamar clerked in law under Henry Foster. He was admitted to the Georgia bar in 1878, served in the Georgia legislature for four years (1886–90), was a commissioner to codify Georgia's laws, served as an associate justice of the Georgia Supreme Court for four years (1901–5), and later engaged in private practice. He served on the U.S. Supreme Court until his death on January 3, 1916.

Mahlon Pitney When Harlan died on October 4, 1911, Taft had the opportunity to make his fifth new appointment to the court. Taft nominated Mahlon Pitney, a Republican and a Protestant, to the court on February 19, 1912, and the Senate confirmed Pitney on March 13. Pitney was born in Morristown, New Jersey, on February 5, 1858. His father, Henry, was a lawyer and vice chancellor of New Jersey. (The chancellor administered the courts of equity.) Pitney attended public schools in Morristown, graduated from Princeton College, and clerked in law in his father's office. He was a congressman for four years (1895–99), served in the state senate for two years (1899–1901), was an associate justice of the New Jersey Supreme Court for seven years (1901–8), and was chancellor of New Jersey for four years (1908–12). He resigned from the court on December 31, 1922, and died on December 9, 1924.

James McReynolds Lurton died on July 12, 1914, and President Wilson nominated James McReynolds to the court on August 19, 1914; the Senate confirmed him on August 29. McReynolds, a Democrat and a Protestant, was born in Elkton, Kentucky, on February 3, 1862. His father, John, was a doctor. McReynolds was valedictorian of his graduating class at Vanderbilt University in 1882, did a year of graduate work, and graduated from the University of Virginia Law School in 1884. A lifelong bachelor, he practiced private law in Tennessee for nineteen years (1884–1903). He was assistant U.S. attorney general for nine years (1903–12) and U.S. attorney general for one year (1913).

He was a vigorous opponent of government regulation of business, anti-black, and a vitriolic anti-Semite. (He referred to his fellow justice Brandeis as "that Hebrew.") He resigned from the court on February 1, 1941, and died on August 24, 1946.

Louis Brandeis Joseph Lamar died on January 2, 1916, and President Wilson nominated Louis Brandeis, a Democrat and a Jew, to the court on January 28; the Senate confirmed Brandeis on June 1. The nomination was controversial for two reasons; Brandeis was unpopular with the legal establishment and the business community both because of his work in support of progressive legislation and, to a lesser but nonetheless real extent, because of his Jewish ethnicity. His most significant achievement was the introduction of sociological data to the legal process. He was born in Louisville, Kentucky, on November 13, 1856. He was the first Jewish appointee to the court. His father, Adolph, was a grain merchant. Brandeis attended schools in Louisville, an academy in Dresden from 1873 to 1875, and Harvard Law School, from which he received a baccalaureate. He served on the court until his resignation on February 13, 1939. He died on October 5, 1941.

John Clarke Hughes resigned from the court on June 10, 1916. To replace him, Wilson nominated John Clarke, a bachelor, on July 14, and the Senate confirmed Clarke on July 24. Clarke, a Democrat and an Episcopalian, was born in New Lisbon, Ohio, on September 18, 1857. His father, John, was a lawyer and a judge. Clarke attended public schools in New Lisbon and Western Reserve University, from which he graduated in 1877 and received a master's degree in 1880. He was admitted to the Ohio bar in 1878, twice unsuccessfully sought election to the U.S. Senate as a progressive reformer, and was a U.S. district court judge for two years (1914–16). He resigned from the court in September 1922 in order to devote himself to the cause of American entry into the League of Nations. He died on March 22, 1945.

William Howard Taft Chief Justice White died on May 19, 1921, and President Harding nominated William Howard Taft to replace him on June 30, 1921. The Senate confirmed him on the same day. Taft, a Republican and a Unitarian, was born in Cincinnati, Ohio, on September 15, 1857. His father, Alphonso, was a lawyer and judge. Taft graduated from Yale College in 1878 and the University of Cincinnati Law School in 1880, and he was admitted to the Ohio bar in that year. He was an assistant district attorney for one year (1881), U.S. collector of revenue for three years (1882–85), a state superior court judge for three years (1887–90), U.S. solicitor general for two years

(1890–92), and a judge on a U.S. court of appeals for four years (1892–96). He was dean of the University of Cincinnati Law School for four years (1896–1900). After the Spanish-American War he was governor general of the newly acquired Philippines for three years (1901–4), secretary of war for four years (1904–8), and president of the United States for one term (1909–13). After his term as president he was a professor of law at Yale Law School until his nomination to be chief justice. In fact, while riding with President Harding to Chief Justice White's funeral, he suggested to the president that he be White's successor.

Few justices of the court have had the depth of his legal expertise, and few chief justices since Marshall have been so able to unify the court and manage its personnel. He served on the court until his resignation on February 3, 1930, for reasons of health, and he died a month later, on March 8, 1930.

George Sutherland Clarke resigned, effective in September 1922, and Harding nominated George Sutherland to the court on September 5; the Senate confirmed Sutherland on the same day. Sutherland, a Republican and a Protestant (?), was born in Buckinghamshire, England, on March 25, 1862. His father, Alexander, emigrated from England to Utah and practiced law. Sutherland attended Brigham Young Academy beginning at the age of twelve and later attended the University of Michigan Law School. He was admitted to the Michigan and Utah bars in 1883.

He served in the Utah state senate for four years (1896–1900), the U.S. House of Representatives for one term (1901–3), and the U.S Senate for two terms (1905–17). In Utah politics Sutherland opposed Mormon polygamy. After the defeat of President Franklin Roosevelt's court-packing plan, he resigned on January 5, 1938. He died on July 18, 1942.

Pierce Butler Day resigned on November 13, 1922, and Harding nominated Pierce Butler to the court on November 23; the Senate confirmed Butler on December 21. His nomination was controversial because of his conservative legal views. Butler, a Republican and a Catholic, was born in Pine Bend, Minnesota, on March 17, 1866. His father, Patrick, was a farmer. Butler graduated from Carleton College in 1887 and read law in St. Paul. He was admitted to the bar in 1888, was briefly county attorney in 1893, and practiced private law, especially as an attorney for railroads. He served on the court until his death on November 16, 1939.

Edward Sanford Pitney resigned on December 31, 1922, and Harding nominated Edward Sanford, a Republican and a Protestant, to the court on January 24, 1923; the Senate confirmed Sanford on February 5. Sanford was born in Knoxville, Tennessee, on July 23, 1865. His father, Edward, was in the lumber and construction business and a millionaire. Sanford attended the University of Tennessee in 1883, graduated from Harvard College in 1885, and earned a master's degree and a law degree from Harvard University in 1889. He was admitted to the Tennessee bar in 1888, practiced private law for seventeen years (1890–1907), was special assistant to the U.S. attorney general for one year (1906), was assistant U.S. attorney general for one year (1907), and was a U.S. district court judge for fifteen years (1908–23). He served on the court until his death on March 8, 1930, a few hours before Taft.

Harlan Fiske Stone McKenna resigned on January 5, 1925, and President Coolidge nominated Harlan Fiske Stone to the court on June 12; the Senate confirmed Stone on June 23. Stone, a Republican and a Protestant, was born in Chesterfield, New Hampshire, on October 11, 1872. His father, Frederick, was a farmer. Stone graduated from Amherst College in 1894 and Columbia Law School in 1898. He was admitted to the New York bar in 1898, practiced private law, was dean of Columbia Law School for fourteen years (1910–24), and was U.S. attorney general for one year (1924). He served as an associate justice until he became chief justice in 1941.

Summary Seven of the twelve justices appointed to the White and Taft Courts (Butler, Pitney, Sanford, Stone, Sutherland, Van Devanter, and Taft) were Republicans, and five (Brandeis, Clarke, Lamar, McReynolds, and White) were Democrats, but this is a bit misleading, since there were never more than three Democrats on the court at the same time. Eight (Clarke, Lamar, McReynolds, Pitney, Sanford, Stone, Sutherland, and Van Devanter) were Protestants, two (Butler and White) Catholics, one (Brandeis) a Jew, and one (Taft) a Unitarian. Four of the appointees (Lamar, McReynolds, Sanford, and White) came from a Southern or border state.

The fathers of eight were professionals. The fathers of six (Clarke, Pitney, Sutherland, Taft, Van Devanter, and White) were lawyers, the father of one (McReynolds) a doctor, and the father of another (Lamar) a minister. The fathers of two (Butler and Stone) were farmers, and the fathers of two (Brandeis and Sanford) were businessmen. All the justices but Brandeis had some college education, and seven (Butler, Clarke, McReynolds, Pitney, Sanford, Stone, and Taft) graduated from college. (Brandeis had the functional equivalent at a German academy.) All but Pitney and Butler had some legal training at a law school, and six (Brandeis, McReynolds, Sanford, Stone, Taft, and Van Devanter) earned a law degree.

Seven of the appointees (Butler, Lamar, McReynolds, Sanford, Stone, Van Devanter, and Taft) had executive governmental experience. Five (Lamar, Pitney, Sutherland, Van Devanter, and White) had legislative experience. (Of the Taft Court appointees, only Sutherland had legislative experience.) Seven of the appointees (Clarke, Lamar, Pitney, Sanford, Taft, Van Devanter, and White) had judicial experience. (All four of those appointed by President Taft had judicial experience.) Brandeis had no governmental experience.

Leading Decisions

The White Court and Commerce The first major decision of the White Court was in *Standard Oil v. U.S.* in 1911. A lower federal court ordered the dissolution of the Standard Oil Company under the Sherman Act, and the company appealed to the Supreme Court. The case was twice argued before the court, the first time in March 1910, when Fuller was alive, and the second time in January 1911, after White became chief justice. The decision was unanimous. White wrote the court opinion, and all the justices except Harlan joined him. White upheld the dissolution order but said that the law covered only unreasonable restraints of trade and that the common law provides the standard of reasonableness. Harlan concurred separately, condemning the rule of reason as judicial legislation. The outcome was popular, but progressives and business leaders criticized it. Progressives said that the opinion undermined the Sherman Act, and business leaders said that the opinion would beget uncertainties for business. After the decision Standard Oil stock sank, but John D. Rockefeller advised a golf partner, a priest, to buy the stock. The golf partner did and became rich, since the many newly created oil companies prospered more than the one old company did.

In a complicated set of cases (the Shreveport Cases) the White Court upheld the power of the ICC over intrastate railroad rates affecting interstate commerce. Several railroads charged lower rates per mile to ship freight from Dallas and Houston to Marshal and other cities in eastern Texas, rates substantially fixed by the Texas Railroad Commission, than they did to ship freight per mile from Shreveport, Louisiana, to the cities in eastern Texas. The result was to make shipment of goods from Dallas or Houston to the cities in eastern Texas less costly than the shipment of goods from Shreveport, even though Dallas and Houston were farther from the eastern Texas markets than Shreveport was. The Louisiana Railroad Commission, at the instigation of Shreveport merchants, complained to the ICC, claiming that the higher rates from Shreveport were discriminatory against interstate commerce.

The ICC ruled that the existing interstate rates gave preference to the merchants of Dallas and Houston and discriminated against the merchants of Shreveport. To correct this discrimination, the commission ordered the carriers to desist from charging higher rates per mile from Shreveport to eastern Texas than they charged from Dallas and Houston. The railroads appealed the ruling to the federal commerce court established to hear complaints about the commission's decisions. The commerce court held that the commission order relieved the railroads from further obligation to adhere to the intrastate rates. The railroads then appealed to the Supreme Court. (The Texas Railroad Commission, which had the real interest, intervened to defend its intrastate rates against the federal commission.)

Hughes wrote the court opinion, and Day, Holmes, McKenna, Lamar, Van Devanter, and White joined him. Hughes defended the complete and paramount power of Congress to regulate commerce among the several states. Its authority to regulate interstate carriers necessarily embraced the right to control their operations in all matters that have a close and substantial relation to interstate traffic, and the railroads' lower intrastate Texas rates unfairly favored in-state localities over out-of-state localities. Lurton and Pitney dissented without opinion.

In 1917 the White Court returned to the question of maximum hours for men (*Bunting v. Oregon*). A 1913 Oregon law set a limit of ten hours a day for all workers, men as well as women, in mills and factories. It also required time-and-a-half pay for overtime. Bunting, a mill foreman, required a male employee to work thirteen hours but did not pay the overtime wage. Bunting was convicted of violating the law, and the Oregon Supreme Court affirmed his conviction. He appealed his conviction to the U.S. Supreme Court, and his lawyers (or rather his employer's lawyers) argued that state regulation of the hours of male workers deprived employer and employee of the freedom of contract protected by the due process clause, which the Lochner decision had vindicated. Brandeis was to have defended the law before the court, but he was appointed to the court in 1916. Felix Frankfurter replaced him and filed a fact-laden brief. The case was argued once in 1916 and twice in 1917.

Brandeis did not participate in the decision. The others split five-to-three in favor of the law. The maximum-hours provision was directly at issue. The sticking point was the overtime pay, which seemed to some to be a wage regulation, a stepping-stone toward minimum-wage laws. McKenna wrote the court opinion, and Clarke, Day, Holmes, and Pitney joined him. McKenna held that the maximum-hour provision was necessary or useful for preserving the health of workers, thereby effectively overruling *Lochner.* He did not think that the law violated the due process clause, because it applied only to certain workers, and determined that the overtime provision was a penalty to discourage overwork, not a wage regulation. McReynolds, Van Devanter, and White dissented without opinion.

In 1918 the White Court invalidated the 1916 Keating-Owen Child Labor Act. That act of Congress prohibited the shipment across state lines of goods produced in whole or in part by children under fourteen years of age or by children from fourteen to sixteen years of age who worked more than eight hours a day or more than six days a week or between 7:00 P.M. and 6:00 A.M. Roland Dagenhart, whose two minor sons were employed at a North Carolina textile factory, sought to enjoin William Hammer, the federal district attorney, from enforcing the act. Dagenhart was granted the injunction, and the U.S. government appealed to the Supreme Court.

The growing unionization of workers in the textile industry in New England and New York and the prohibition of child labor by Northern state legislatures induced textile manufacturers to move their production operations to the South, where there were no unions or child-labor laws. The Keating-Owen Act was an attempt to induce the textile industry in the South to eliminate child labor (and incidentally to level the economic playing field). After the Champion and successor decisions, legal experts and court watchers widely expected the law to be upheld, but the court by the narrowest margin struck it down (*Hammer v. Dagenhart*).

Day wrote the court opinion, and McReynolds, Pitney, Van Devanter, and White joined him. The power of Congress to regulate commerce deals with the means to enhance interstate commerce. The power of Congress to prohibit the shipment of goods over state lines depends on the character of the particular goods. If the goods cause social evils, Congress may prohibit their transportation over state lines, and so Congress had the power to prohibit the interstate transportation of lottery tickets and impure foods and drugs. But the textile products were good in themselves and did not cause social evil, and so

Congress may not prohibit their transportation across state lines. When the goods are shipped, the evil of child labor in producing them is over.

According to Day, the federal child-labor law attempted to regulate production, and production is not commerce, as the Knight decision held. Regulation of production is a local matter, and the power to regulate production rests with the states. Day then misrepresented the Tenth Amendment, claiming that it reserves to the states and the people thereof all the powers not *expressly* granted to the federal government (italics added). Day also claimed that the law abridged the freedom of contract protected by the due process clause of the Fifth Amendment.

Holmes wrote a powerful dissenting opinion, and Brandeis, Clarke, and McKenna joined him. The statute, in his view, acted directly on interstate commerce, and the power of Congress to regulate commerce includes the power to prohibit it. It does not matter whether the supposed evil to be suppressed precedes or follows the transportation of the prohibited goods, and civilized countries agree that premature and excessive child labor is an evil. The law did not meddle with the states' power to regulate their internal affairs and their domestic commerce. The law regulated and prohibited only the transportation of goods across state lines.

In two other cases, however, the White Court upheld governmental intervention in the marketplace. In one case, *Green v. Frazier*, the court in 1920 unanimously upheld a North Dakota statute that created an industrial commission with the power of eminent domain to conduct and manage utilities and other businesses as well as a state bank to lend money to counties and individuals. Green was a taxpayer who sought to enjoin the governor and other officials from executing the statute on the grounds that the taxes collected to carry out the statute were not expended for a public use. The lower state court denied the injunction, and the North Dakota Supreme Court affirmed. Green then appealed to the U.S. Supreme Court. Day wrote the court opinion upholding the statute, and all the other justices subscribed to it. Day accepted that the due process clause of the Fourteenth Amendment included a requirement that tax money should be expended only for public uses, although the amendment did not expressly say so, but he deferred to the state supreme court's interpretation that the expenditures for the enterprises were for the general welfare. He declared that it was not the court's duty to determine the wisdom of the expenditures.

The second case involved an act of Congress establishing rent control in the

District of Columbia (*Block v. Hirsh*). Congress passed the law after the United States entered World War I. Under the law tenants were allowed to remain in their apartments or homes at the same rent after their leases expired. Hirsh bought a house and wanted possession of it, and Block was a tenant who did not want to give up occupancy of the house. (Hirsh claimed that he wanted possession for his own occupancy, for which the rent-control law provided, and Block denied that Hirsh did.) The lower court ruled for Hirsh, holding the rent-control law unconstitutional. Block appealed to the Supreme Court, and the U.S. government filed an amicus brief in defense of the law.

The court by the narrowest margin reversed, upholding the law as constitutional. Holmes wrote a relatively short court opinion, and Brandeis, Clarke, Day, and Pitney joined him. (Note that Day and Pitney in this case were in favor of governmental intervention in the marketplace but were opposed to governmental intervention in the Hammer case.) Holmes prescinded from whether Hirsh wanted the property for his own occupancy and considered the validity of the law on its own terms. Holmes held that the law was a permissible exercise of the war power of Congress. He emphasized that it was a temporary measure in force for two years and that it was designed to protect public health and avoid burdens on wartime government officials. He further argued that rent control was effectively a tax on an owner's property, which would undoubtedly be constitutional.

McKenna filed a much longer and eloquent dissenting opinion, and White, Van Devanter, and McReynolds joined him. (Note that McKenna in this case is opposed to governmental intervention in the marketplace but favored intervention in the Hammer case.) McKenna thought that the law infringed on an owner's property and contractual rights, and its temporary character didn't alter that fact. He posed rhetorical questions about what he considered the consequences of rent control. He pointed out that rent control, by keeping one tenant in possession, kept another tenant out. Most economists consider long-term rent control counterproductive, and political pressures tend to keep rent controls in place long after the original justification for them has expired. It is, of course, another question whether courts should attempt to overturn rent-control laws.

The White Court and the War Power After Congress in 1917 declared war on Germany and the Central Powers, it passed the Selective Service Act to conscript men into military duty. Convicted violators of the act appealed to the Supreme Court (the Selective Service Cases). White wrote a unanimous court opinion upholding the law. The violators objected to the conscription law on various grounds, including the Thirteenth Amendment's prohibition of involuntary servitude and the First Amendment's prohibition of an establishment of religion in connection with the act's exemption of religious objectors to participation in all wars. But White directed most of his opinion to answering the objection that the clause empowering Congress to call out the militia (Article I, section 8, clause 15) qualified the power of Congress to raise and support armies (Article I, section 8, clause 12). White held that the two clauses were separate grants of power.

Also after the U.S. entry into World War I, Congress passed the Espionage Act of 1917. The act prohibited conspiracies to obstruct military recruitment. Charles Schenck and other Socialist party members were convicted of violating the act. They printed thousands of leaflets opposing the war and urging potential Philadelphia conscripts to assert their rights to opposition to the war and to sign an anti-war petition to Congress. After their conviction the defendants appealed to the Supreme Court, questioning the constitutionality of the Espionage Act as applied to their exercise of free speech.

Holmes in March 1919 wrote the unanimous court opinion upholding the law and the convictions under it (*Schenck v. U.S.*). Holmes enunciated the clear-and-present-danger test to limit the First Amendment protection of political speech. The question, he argued, was whether words are used in such circumstances and are of such a nature as to create a clear and present danger that they will bring about substantive evils that Congress has a right to prevent. Holmes distinguished between speech in wartime and speech in peacetime and held that the words used by Schenck and the other Socialists would bring about the substantive evil of impeding the war effort. The statute applied to conspiracies to obstruct the military, not only to actual obstruction. The problem with the decision concerns application of the clear-and-present-danger test to the facts of the case. Did Schenk and the others use the words they used with the intent to incite *acts* of obstructing the military, or were the words used in such circumstances and of such a character as to incite such acts?

Seven months later, in November 1919, the court upheld the convictions of Jacob Abrams and others for violating the Sedition Act of May 1918 (*Abrams v. U.S.*). The sedition act made it a crime willfully to publish abusive language against the U.S. form of government or to urge or advocate curtailment of things necessary or useful to prosecution of the war with an intention to hinder the government from doing so. Abrams, a Russian immigrant and anarchist, and associates in August 1918 published and distributed two leaflets, one in English and one in Yiddish, denouncing President Wilson's military intervention in Russia after the Communist revolution there in October 1917. The Yiddish leaflet also called for a general strike to protest the intervention. The defendants were convicted on counts of overt acts (the leaflets) against the U.S. form of government and interference with the war effort. They then appealed to the Supreme Court, claiming that the laws violated their right to free speech.

Clarke wrote the court opinion upholding the convictions, and Day, McKenna, McReynolds, Pitney, Van Devanter, and White joined him. Clarke followed Holmes's analysis of the free speech clause in *Schenck*. The leaflets created a clear and present danger at the supreme moment of crisis in World War I (the 1918 German offensive in France) and aimed to defeat the government's war plans. Even if the defendants' primary purpose had been to aid the Communists in Russia, the general strike they called for would have necessarily impeded prosecution of the war against Germany.

Holmes dissented, and Brandeis joined him. In *Schenck* Holmes had declared that Congress might punish speech that constituted a clear and *present* danger of producing substantive evils. In *Abrams* he declares that Congress may punish speech that constitutes a clear and *immediate* danger of producing substantive evils. He saw no immediate danger from the leaflets, which he described as silly, and he denied that the defendants had the requisite intent to disrupt war production, since their only objective was to stop American intervention in Russia. In a concluding peroration Holmes opined that the First Amendment protected the expression of all opinions "unless they so imminently threaten immediate interference with the lawful and pressing purposes of the law that an immediate check is required to save the country." One might ask whether the call for a general strike was not an imminent threat of immediate interference with war production. The pamphlets' language about the U.S. form of government may have been silly, but the call for a general strike posed a serious threat.

The White Court and the Treaty Power In 1920 the court handed down a decision that in effect held that the treaty power trumps claims against federal legislation based on the Tenth Amendment (*Missouri v. Holland*). A 1916 treaty between the United States and Great Britain, acting on behalf of Canada,

committed the two nations to the regulation and protection of birds season-
ably migrating between the United States and Canada. The Migratory Bird
Treaty Act of 1918 established seasons closed to hunters. Missouri sought to
enjoin Holland, a federal game warden, from enforcing the regulations in the
state. A federal district court declined to issue the injunction, and Missouri
appealed to the Supreme Court. Before the treaty Congress had passed an
act regulating the killing of migratory birds, claiming the power to do so under the commerce clause. Two district courts declared the law unconstitutional
on the basis of powers reserved to the states under the Tenth Amendment.
Missouri objected on the same grounds to the act of Congress enforcing
the treaty.

Holmes wrote the court opinion upholding the later regulatory act of Congress, and Brandeis, Clarke, Day, McKenna, McReynolds, and White joined
him. Article II, section 2 expressly delegated to the federal government the
power to make treaties, Article VI made all treaties the law of the land, and Ar-
ticle.I, section 8, clause 18 gave Congress the power to make all the laws necessary and proper to execute the powers of the federal government. Holmes was
careful to add that he was not implying that there were no qualifications on
the treaty power, but this treaty regarding migratory birds did not contravene
any prohibitory words in the Constitution. (He gave no example of a treaty
that would, but a treaty establishing the Church of England as the Church of
the United States surely would.) He argued that no invisible radiation from the
general terms of the Tenth Amendment forbade the treaty. Nor could Missouri
claim title to the birds because they were temporarily in the state. Pitney and
Van Devanter dissented.

The Taft Court and Commerce After the Hammer decision Congress tried
another tactic against child labor: the tax power. It imposed a 10 percent tax
on the net profit of any mining company that employed children under the age
of sixteen and of any mill or factory that employed children under the age of
fourteen or required children under the age of sixteen to work more than eight
hours a day or six days a week. The Drexel Furniture Company, which employed such children, paid the tax and sued a regional Internal Revenue Service collector, J. W. Bailey, for a refund. The company won in the tax court, but
the government appealed to the Supreme Court.

Taft wrote the 1922 court opinion invalidating the tax law, and Brandeis,
Day, Holmes, McKenna, McReynolds, Pitney, and Van Devanter joined him

(*Bailey v. Drexel Furniture Co.*). Taft held that the tax was not a revenue measure with incidental restraint and regulation but a penalty to control production, which is a matter that the Tenth Amendment reserved to the states. Taxes are sometimes imposed on commodities with the primary purpose of obtaining revenue and with the incidental purpose of discouraging their use, as in the case of the oleomargarine tax (*McCray v. U.S.*), but the child-labor taxes were purely a penalty on the use of child labor in order to control production. Nor could the case be distinguished from that of *Hammer v. Dagenhart.* Clarke dissented without opinion.

The decision was surprising in several ways. The court had hitherto allowed punitive taxes as long as the taxes were excise taxes. It is difficult to see how the tax on oleomargarine was any more for revenue than the tax on the profit of companies employing child labor. In the former case the purpose was to discourage use of oleomargarine, and in the latter case the purpose was to discourage use of child labor. The second surprising fact about the decision is that three of the dissenters in *Hammer* (Brandeis, Holmes, and McKenna) joined the court opinion. Taft's opinion in *Bailey* echoes that of Day in *Hammer,* and one might have expected all the dissenters in the latter to dissent in the former, but only Clarke did. There was strong opposition to laws against child labor, as the subsequent failure to ratify the child-labor amendment would show. Many, including some Catholic leaders, objected to the laws because they allegedly interfered with rights of parents over their children.

The Taft Court in *Bailey* limited the power of Congress to tax, but it in the same year upheld the power of Congress to regulate a local industry under the commerce clause (*Stafford v. Wallace*). Congress in 1921 passed the Packers and Stockyards Act to forbid certain unfair and discriminatory practices of the meat packers. Stafford, a meat packer, unsuccessfully sought an injunction against Henry C. Wallace, the secretary of agriculture, enforcing the act. Stafford lost in the lower court and appealed to the Supreme Court.

Taft wrote the court opinion, and Brandeis, Clarke, Holmes, McKenna, Pitney, and Van Devanter joined him. The stockyards are the throat of commerce through which the current flows. The only question was whether the business done in the stockyards between receipt of the livestock in the yards and the shipment of them out of the yards was part of interstate commerce or so associated with it as to bring the business under the power of Congress to regulate interstate commerce. The Swift decision settled the question. If Congress could punish conspiracies to restrain trade after their formation, as *Swift* held, Taft argued that it could provide regulation to prevent their formation. McReynolds dissented without opinion, and Day did not participate.

In 1923 the court declared a 1918 act of Congress fixing the minimum wages for women and minors in the District of Columbia unconstitutional (*Adkins v. Children's Hospital*). (The wages of minors were not at issue in the case.) The hospital sought to enjoin Adkins, head of the Wage Board under the act, from enforcing the minimum wages established by the board. The district court issued the injunction, and the court of appeals affirmed. Adkins appealed to the Supreme Court.

Sutherland wrote the court opinion, and Butler, McKenna, McReynolds, and Van Devanter joined him. The issue was whether the liberty of contract protected by the due process clause of the Fifth Amendment precluded establishment of minimum wages for women. Sutherland admitted that the liberty of contract might be restricted but only when necessary. He cited the Nineteenth Amendment to indicate that men and women were now equal in bargaining power over wages. Regulation of maximum hours, which *Muller* and *Bunting* upheld, does not affect the heart of the contract, but regulation of minimum wages does. The statute is vague when it asserts that the minimum wages are necessary for the health and morals of women. Granted the right to a living wage, what about fair service from the employee? Why should not the public rather than the employer have the burden of providing the living wage? The facts in the case, he argued, were only mildly persuasive. If the government can prescribe minimum wages, it may in the future prescribe maximum wages.

Holmes, Sanford, and Taft dissented. Taft pointed out that employees don't have equal bargaining power. The question is not one of the statute's wisdom. Wages are as important as hours to health. Holmes regarded the means to promote the health and welfare of citizens a matter for the legislature. The liberty of contract might be infringed in many ways (e.g., usury laws, laws against fraud, and Sunday laws). It would, in his view, take more than the Nineteenth Amendment to eliminate the difference between men and women. Brandeis did not participate, since his daughter worked for the wage board.

The Taft Court struck down 115 state laws, many involving liberty of contract. *Wolff Packing Co. v. Court of Industrial Relations* was one of the decisions that struck down a state statute under the Fourteenth Amendment's due process protection of liberty of contract. Kansas had a law requiring compulsory arbitration of labor disputes in food, clothing, fuel, and other industries declared to be affected with a public interest. Taft wrote the unanimous 1923 court opinion. He limited business affected with a public interest to public monopolies and a few other businesses historically considered to be such (e.g., inns). It was, he argued, never supposed that the government could fix a butcher's prices and wages.

In 1922 the Taft Court struck down a Pennsylvania statute (*Pennsylvania Coal Co. v. Mahon*). The Kohler Act forbade mining in such a way as to undermine surface structures. (The coal companies had sold surface land to buyers who built homes on the land. Subsurface mining weakened the foundation of the surface houses and often caused the houses to collapse.) The state courts sustained the act, and the companies appealed to the U.S. Supreme Court. Holmes wrote the court opinion, and Butler, McKenna, McReynolds, Pitney, Sutherland, Taft, and Van Devanter joined him. Holmes ruled that the statute constituted a taking of property without compensation. The homeowners had assumed the risk when they built on the land. Brandeis dissented, arguing that the statute was a legitimate exercise of the state's police power.

In 1926, however, the Taft Court sustained a zoning law (*Euclid v. Ambler Realty Co.*). The village of Euclid, Ohio, had regulated the development of land. The company sought to enjoin enforcement of the law and won in a federal district court. Euclid appealed to the Supreme Court. The case was argued and reargued before the court. Sutherland wrote the court opinion, and Brandeis, Holmes, Sanford, Stone, and Taft joined him. Butler, McReynolds, and Van Devanter dissented without opinion. That Sutherland, a strong defender of free enterprise, supported the zoning and did not vote with the dissenters was unusual.

The Taft Court was also anti-labor. Its record on labor built on one of the last decisions of the White Court (*Duplex Printing Co. v. Deering*). New York unions boycotted the products of a Michigan company whose workers were on strike. A provision of the Clayton Act forbade injunctions against unions, and the company was denied an injunction and appealed to the Supreme Court. Pitney wrote the 1921 court opinion, and Day, McKenna, McReynolds, Van Devanter, and White joined him. Pitney held that the provision of the Clayton Act applied only to the immediate parties in a dispute, not to secondary boycotts, and so an injunction could issue. Brandeis, Clarke, and Holmes dissented.

Later in 1921 the Taft Court limited peaceful union picketing in a labor dispute against employers (*American Steel Foundries v. Tri-City Trade Council*). Union members were on strike at an Illinois plant and picketing against it, arguing with nonunion workers going to and from the plant. The company sought an injunction against the union persuading or intimidating nonunion workers. The district court granted the injunction, but the court of appeals modified it to permit the union to attempt to persuade workers not to work at the plant. The company appealed to the Supreme Court against the modification. The case was argued and twice reargued before the court. Taft wrote the court opinion, and Day, Holmes, McKenna, McReynolds, Pitney, and Van Devanter joined him. Brandeis concurred separately in the decision. Taft further limited the picketing to one person at points of entry to, and regress from, the plant, since he held that picketing as such is threatening. Clarke dissented.

In the same year, the Taft Court struck down an Arizona statute that forbade injunctions against peaceful picketing (*Truax v. Corrigan*). Truax sought an injunction against union members picketing his business and accused them of causing severe loss of customer patronage. The lower state court and the Arizona Supreme Court denied injunctive relief on the basis of the statute. Taft wrote the court opinion, and four justices (Day, McKenna, McReynolds, and Van Devanter) joined him. Taft held that the statute as interpreted, by removing the legal remedy of injunction, had deprived the business owner of a property right and so denied him due process of law. (In the absence of the statute, common law permitted injunctions against conspiracies to forbid acts otherwise legal if performed severally.) Brandeis, Holmes, and Pitney dissented, and Clarke joined Pitney's dissent. Holmes stressed the importance of states' freedom to deal with problems of labor unrest and potential violence.

The Taft Court and Presidential and Congressional Powers The Taft Court handed down a ruling in 1926 enhancing presidential power over executive appointees (*Myers v. U.S.*). President Wilson, with the advice and consent of the Senate, had appointed Frank Myers postmaster of Portland, Oregon, for a four-year term. Wilson, without the advice or consent of the Senate, ordered the postmaster general to remove him, and the postmaster general did so on February 2, 1920. After expiration of his term, Myers sued in the court of claims for pay to cover the time between his removal and the end of his term. He claimed that the 1876 law establishing the postal offices specified that the consent of the Senate was required for the removal of postmasters. The court of claims ruled against him, and his estate appealed to the Supreme Court. The case was argued and reargued before the court.

Taft wrote the court opinion, and Butler, Sanford, Stone, Sutherland, and Van Devanter joined him. Taft argued that it is the duty of the president to see that the laws of the United States are faithfully executed and that the power to execute the laws implies the power to remove officials. Madison and others in the first Congress backed the power of the president to remove officers without the advice and consent of the Senate, and there is no express restriction of the removal power in the Constitution. Congress can place the power to appoint inferior offices in other hands than those of the President and establish incidental regulations regarding their removal, but where the power to appoint belongs to the president, Congress cannot limit the power to remove. Query: Is the power to remove minor officials like postmasters, unlike the power to removed major officials like members of the cabinet, critical to the power of the president to see that the laws are faithfully executed?

McReynolds, Brandeis, and Holmes dissented. McReynolds wrote a long and comprehensive critique. If Congress could place the power of appointment to inferior offices in other hands than the president's and regulate the removal of the appointees to those offices, he did not see why vesting the president with the power of appointment to inferior offices deprived Congress of the power to limit the power of removal. Brandeis stressed that the power to remove inferior officers comes from Congress. Holmes also stressed that Congress creates the power to appoint to inferior offices and so can limit the power of removal from those offices.

In 1927 the court upheld the power of Congress to subpoena witnesses and compel them to answer questions (*McGrain v. Dougherty*). The Senate was investigating the failure of President Harding's attorney general, Harry Dougherty, to prosecute those responsible for corruption in connection with the Teapot Dome oil leases. The Senate subpoenaed Dougherty's brother, Mally, who was the head of an Ohio bank holding an account of his brother, and Mally refused to answer the subpoena, claiming that the purpose of the investigation was to pillory his brother. The Senate authorized its sergeant at arms to have a deputy arrest Mally Dougherty and bring him before the Senate's select committee investigating the Teapot Dome affair. Dougherty obtained a writ of habeas corpus from a district court against the deputy, John McGrain, and the latter appealed to the Supreme Court.

Van Devanter wrote the court opinion, in which all the justices except Stone joined. (Stone was the attorney general who succeeded Harry Dougherty and so did not participate.) Van Devanter held that Congress has a right to conduct investigations as an auxiliary to its legislative functions and that investigation into whether the department of justice had properly discharged its duties regarding the corruption was an auxiliary to the functions. But Congress had no right to pry into private matters, and a witness could refuse to answer if questioned about matters not pertinent to the inquiry.

The Taft Court and Civil Liberties   In 1925 the Taft Court opened the door to incorporating most provisions of the Bill of Rights into the Fourteenth Amendment via the due process clause to bar infringement by the states. The trigger case was *Gitlow v. New York*. Benjamin Gitlow, a member of the left wing of the Socialist party—that is, in plainer language, the Communist party— was convicted of two counts of criminal anarchy. The first charged Gitlow with advocating and teaching the necessity of overthrowing organized government by force in a pamphlet entitled *The Left-Wing Manifesto*. The second count charged him with publishing and distributed a paper, *The Revolutionary Age*, which advocated the overthrow of organized government by force. He was convicted on both counts, and the New York Court of Appeals upheld his conviction. He appealed to the U.S. Supreme Court, and the case was argued and reargued before the court.

The court upheld the conviction against a claim to freedom of speech. Sanford wrote the court opinion, and Butler, McReynolds, Sutherland, Taft, and Van Devanter joined him. Sanford argued that the utterances presented a sufficient danger of substantive evil to allow legislative discretion to punish them. A single revolutionary spark may kindle a small fire that will burst into a sweeping and destructive conflagration. Holmes, joined by Brandeis, dissented on the grounds that there was no proof of any immediate danger. But the most important point of the court opinion was that the majority and minority justices assumed that the freedom of speech and the press protected by the First Amendment against infringement by Congress were among the personal rights protected by the due process clause of the Fourteenth Amendment against infringement by the states. (Since McKenna had resigned earlier in the year and his successor [Stone] had not yet been appointed, one seat was vacant.)

Two years later, in 1927, the court decided a case involving a member of the Communist Labor party, which was affiliated with the Communist International. Charlotte Whitney was convicted of violating California's 1919 criminal syndicalism act, and the California Supreme Court affirmed the conviction. She appealed to the U.S. Supreme Court.

The court unanimously sustained her conviction (*Whitney v. California*), but Brandeis wrote a concurring opinion in which Holmes joined. Sanford made the same arguments that he had made in *Gitlow*. Brandeis insisted on the necessity of a clear and imminent danger of substantive evil as the constitutional standard for the prosecution of political speech but held that Whitney had not claimed at her trial that the statute as applied to her was void because there was no clear and present danger of serious evil from her actions. Moreover, there was evidence on which the jury or the judge might have found that such a danger existed and other evidence that tended to establish the existence of a conspiracy to commit serious crimes in league with the International Workers of the World.

In another case, in 1925, the court upheld the right of private parties under the due process clause of the Fourteenth Amendment to operate schools and the correlative right of parents to send their children to them. Oregon had passed a statute requiring all children of school age to attend public schools. Some supporters of the statute wanted all children in the state to receive their education in common in order to promote civic unity, but other supporters were biased against Catholic schools, the largest group of private schools. Two schools, one operated by Catholic sisters and the other a military academy, sought an injunction in a federal district court against the governor (Pierce) before the statute took effect on September 1, 1926. The injunction was granted, and Pierce—that is, the state—appealed to the Supreme Court. Many organizations filed amici briefs in favor of the private schools.

McReynolds wrote the unanimous court opinion (*Pierce v. Society of Sisters*). He declared that the child is not the creature of the state and that parents have both the right and the duty to recognize and prepare their children for other obligations. States may regulate private schools (e.g., regulate the number of days in the school year and require secular subjects like arithmetic and reading), but they may not prohibit the schools' existence. The decision directly concerned the property right of private schools to operate in Oregon, but it clearly rested on the primary right of parents in the education of their children, a personal right. Also, insofar as one of the schools was religious, the decision was in favor of religious liberty.

In 1928 the Taft Court by the narrowest margin held government wiretapping of telephone lines without a warrant constitutional (*Olmstead v. U.S.*). Roy Olmstead and associates were convicted in a federal district court of conspiring to transport and sell alcoholic beverages in violation of the Volstead Act.

Federal prohibition agents had obtained the chief evidence against the defendants by tapping their telephone lines but without trespassing on their property. A court of appeals upheld the convictions. Olmstead and associates appealed to the Supreme Court.

Taft wrote the court opinion, ruling that the Fourth Amendment did not prohibit wiretapping if there was no trespass, and McReynolds, Sanford, Sutherland, and Van Devanter joined him. Taft argued that the Fourth Amendment concerned material things—namely, persons and things, not sounds discovered off one's premises. (The court had ruled in 1914 that evidence obtained in violation of the Fourth Amendment could not be used in a federal prosecution [*Weeks v. U.S.*].) He admitted that the government officials involved may not have engaged in the highest ethical conduct but argued that the evidence should be admissible unless and until Congress legislated otherwise. This Congress did in the Federal Communications Act of 1933 and the Crime Control and Safe Streets Act of 1968.

Four justices (Brandeis, Butler, Holmes, and Stone) dissented. Brandeis wrote the chief dissenting opinion. He argued that the Fourth and Fifth amendments guarantee to individuals a general right to privacy rather than merely protection of material things, that federal officials involved in wiretapping without a warrant were breaking the law, and that the government violated the Fifth Amendment when it introduced evidence obtained by illegal wiretapping. Brandeis also argued that the federal officials had violated a Washington state statute that made it a misdemeanor to intercept a telephone message and that this was an additional reason that the evidence should be inadmissible in a federal prosecution.

7

THE HUGHES COURT

(1930–41)

The Justices

Charles Evans Hughes Chief Justice Taft resigned on February 3, 1930, and President Hoover nominated Charles Evans Hughes to the court on the same day; the Senate confirmed Hughes on February 13 over some opposition based on his private practice with business clients. He had served as secretary of state for four years (1921–25). He served as chief justice until his retirement on January 2, 1941, and died on August 27, 1948.

Owen Roberts Sanford died on March 8, 1930; Hoover nominated John Parker, a judge on a federal court of appeals, on March 21, but the Senate rejected his nomination on May 7. The American Federation of Labor opposed the nomination because of an opinion upholding the so-called "yellow-dog" contracts, and the National Association for the Advancement of Colored People opposed his nomination because of a statement he had made during a gubernatorial campaign in 1920 objecting to black participation in politics. Two days after the nomination was rejected, on May 9, Hoover nominated Owen Roberts to the court, and the Senate confirmed Roberts on May 20.

Roberts, a Republican and an Episcopalian, was born in Germantown, Pennsylvania, on May 2, 1875. He attended Germantown Academy and graduated from the University of Pennsylvania in 1895 and from the University of

Pennsylvania Law School in 1898. He was admitted to the Pennsylvania bar in 1898 and practiced private law. He was an assistant district attorney in Philadelphia for three years (1901–3), U.S. deputy attorney general for espionage cases for one year (1918), and a special prosecutor in the Teapot Dome cases in 1924. He resigned from the court in 1945 and died on May 17, 1955.

Benjamin Cardozo Holmes resigned on January 12, 1932, and Hoover nominated Benjamin Cardozo to the court on February 15; the Senate confirmed Cardozo on March 1. Cardozo, a Democrat and a Jew, was born in New York City on May 24, 1870. His father, Albert, was a lawyer and a judge. Cardozo was tutored by Horatio Alger, received baccalaureate and master's degrees from Columbia University, and attended Columbia Law School. He was a bachelor. He was admitted to the New York bar in 1891 and was a judge on a New York supreme court for six weeks in 1913. He was also a judge on the New York Court of Appeals for thirteen years (1914–27) and its chief judge for five years (1927–32). The legal profession recognized the outstanding quality of his decisions on the New York Court of Appeals. He served on the U.S. Supreme Court until his death on July 9, 1938.

Hugo Black President Franklin Roosevelt had no opportunity to appoint a justice to the court until 1937. His New Deal legislation met a brick wall from the court in 1935 and 1936, as we shall see, and after his triumphant reelection in 1936, he proposed to enlarge the court in order to gain appointments. In the course of the debate on that proposal, the court itself changed its mind on key issues in 1937, as we also shall see, and the resignation of Van Devanter in June of that year gave Roosevelt the opportunity to appoint his first justice. Roosevelt nominated Hugo Black to the court on August 12, and the Senate confirmed Black on August 19. After his confirmation, news broke that Black had been a member of the Ku Klux Klan, and Black gave a nationwide radio address repudiating his former views.

Black, a Democrat and a Protestant, was born in Clay County, Alabama, on February 27, 1886. His father, William, was a storeowner. Black attended public schools and received a law degree from the University of Alabama in 1906. He was twice married. He was the judge of a police court for one year (1910–11), county solicitor for two years (1915–17), an army captain in World War I, and a U.S. Senator for ten years (1927–37). He served on the court until he retired on September 17, 1971. He died a week later, on September 25.

Stanley Reed Sutherland retired on January 5, 1938, and Roosevelt appointed Stanley Reed to the court on January 15; the Senate confirmed Reed on January 25. Reed, a Democrat and a Protestant, was born in Mason County, Kentucky, on December 31, 1884. His father, John, was a country doctor. Reed attended Kentucky Wesleyan College, graduated from Yale University in 1906, and studied law at the University of Virginia, Columbia University, and the University of Paris. He was admitted to the Kentucky bar in 1910, served in the Kentucky legislature for four years (1912–16), and was an army lieutenant in World War I. He was general counsel of the Federal Farm Board for three years (1929–32), general counsel of the Reconstruction Finance Corporation for three years (1932–35), and U.S. solicitor general for three years (1935–38). He served on the court until he retired on February 22, 1957. He died on April 2, 1980.

Felix Frankfurter Cardozo died on July 9, 1938, Roosevelt nominated Felix Frankfurter to the court on January 5, 1939; the Senate confirmed Frankfurter on January 17. Frankfurter, a Democrat and a Jew, was born in Vienna, Austria, on November 15, 1882. His family emigrated to the United States; his father, Leopold, was a fur merchant. Frankfurter graduated from the City College of New York in 1902 and from Harvard Law School in 1906.

He was assistant U.S. attorney for the Southern District of New York for four years (1906–10), law officer for the Bureau of Internal Affairs of the War Department for three years (1911–14), and a judge advocate of the army in 1917. He was a professor at Harvard Law School for twenty-five years (1914–39). He served on the court until he retired on August 28, 1962. He died on February 22, 1965.

William Douglas Brandeis retired on February 13, 1939, and Roosevelt nominated William Douglas to the court on March 20; the Senate confirmed Douglas on April 4. Douglas, a Democrat and a Presbyterian, was born in Maine, Minnesota, on October 16, 1898. His father, William, was a home missionary of the Presbyterian Church. Douglas graduated from Whitman College in 1920 and from Columbia Law School in 1925. He was married four times. He grew up in the state of Washington, was admitted to the New York bar, and practiced law with a Wall Street firm.

He taught law at Columbia Law School for three years, from 1925 to 1928, and at Yale Law School for three years, from 1933 to 1936. He was a member of the Securities and Exchange Commission for three years (1936–39) and its chairman for two years (1937–39). There were three attempts to impeach him because of certain judicial actions and publicly expressed opinions. After a stroke, he resigned from the court on November 12, 1975. He died on January 19, 1980.

Frank Murphy When Butler died on November 16, 1939, Roosevelt made his fifth appointment to the court. Roosevelt nominated Frank Murphy on January 4, 1940, and the Senate confirmed Murphy on January 16. Murphy, a Democrat and Catholic, was born in Harbor Beach, Michigan, on April 13, 1890. His father, John, was a lawyer. He graduated from the University of Michigan Law School in 1914 and did graduate work in Dublin and London. He was an infantry captain in France during World War I and a bachelor.

He was a judge in Detroit for seven years (1923–30), mayor of Detroit for three years (1930–33), governor general of the Philippines for two years (1933–35), governor of Michigan for two years (1937–38), and U.S. attorney general for one year (1939–40). He served on the court until his death on July 19, 1949.

Summary All of the Roosevelt appointees (Black, Frankfurter, Douglas, Murphy, and Reed) and one of the Hoover appointees (Cardozo) were Democrats. The other two Hoover appointees (Hughes and Roberts) were Republicans. Five (Black, Douglas, Hughes, Reed, and Roberts) were Protestants, two (Cardozo and Frankfurter) Jews, and one (Murphy) a Catholic. Five (Cardozo, Frankfurter, Hughes, Murphy, and Frankfurter) were from Northeastern states, two (Black and Reed) from a Southern or border state, and one (Douglas) originally from a Western state. All but Black and Murphy had college degrees, and all but Reed had law degrees. The fathers of five of the appointees (Cardozo, Douglas, Hughes, Murphy, and Reed) were in professions, and the fathers of Douglas and Hughes were ministers. The fathers of two (Black and Frankfurter) were businessmen. All but Cardozo had executive governmental experience, three of the five Roosevelt appointees (Douglas, Murphy, and Reed) had appointive posts in the president's administration, and one of the five (Frankfurter) had been a presidential adviser. Unlike the high proportion of nineteenth-century appointees who usually had legislative experience, of the Roosevelt appointees only Black and Reed had legislative experience. Five appointees (Black, Cardozo, Frankfurter, Hughes, and Murphy) had prior judicial experience, although Black and Frankfurter had very little.

Leading Decisions

Federal and State Regulation of the Economy Almost simultaneously with Hughes becoming the chief justice of the court, the Great Depression kicked in with full force, and both federal and state governments attempted to deal with its consequences. In 1934 the court decided two cases involving state measures that involved the claim of property rights against the measures. The first was *Home Building and Loan Co. v. Blaisdell.* To prevent homeowners from losing their homes by foreclosures of their mortgages, Minnesota in 1933 passed a mortgage-moratorium law. The act authorized judges to extend the period in which homeowners might redeem their property after foreclosure but in no event beyond May 1, 1935. While the mortgagor, no longer the owner of his home, was allowed to remain in the foreclosed house, he was obliged to pay the rental value of the property. The rental money was used to pay property taxes, insurance costs, and interest on the mortgage indebtedness. The mortgagee lost possession of the property. More important, he was threatened with monetary loss if the value of the property during the extended period of time declined below the nominal value of the mortgage and the mortgagor then failed to redeem the property

John Blaisdell sought and obtained a court order extending the period of redemption fixed by law at the time of the foreclosure. The Minnesota Supreme Court affirmed the judgment, and the company appealed to the U.S. Supreme Court, claiming that the law impaired the obligation of contracts contrary to Article I, section 10, clause 1 of the federal Constitution. By the narrowest of margins, the court upheld the law. Hughes wrote the court opinion, and Brandeis, Cardozo, Roberts, and Stone joined him. Emergency does not create power, he argued, but it might furnish the occasion for its exercise, in this case the police power of the state. He explicitly disavowed the idea that clauses of the Constitution should be interpreted according to the original intent of their framers.

Sutherland wrote a powerful dissent, and Butler, McReynolds, and Van Devanter joined him. While the application of a clause in the Constitution may be extended to meet conditions not envisioned by its framers, the meaning of a clause is changeless, and emergencies do not change the meaning. He argued that the contract clause was inserted in the Constitution precisely because the framers had experienced and deplored state relief of debtors before adoption of the Constitution.

Sutherland was correct, as Hughes admitted, that the framers intended to prohibit any impairment of private contracts. The larger question that Hughes's argument raises concerns to what extent judges are bound by the original intent of the framers. Hughes was correct that the impairment of the contract at issue was minimal, but is that a reason to ignore the clear meaning of the contract clause? Moreover, the mortgagee could lose money if the market declined below the nominal value of the mortgage. And one could argue that, if the public wanted to help debtors, it should have provided the money to redeem the property rather than impose risk on the mortgagee.

The second 1934 case was *Nebbia v. New York*. The New York legislature in 1933 passed a law regulating the price of milk. Dealers could buy milk from dairy farmers and deliver it at a price of ten cents a quart, and stores were required to sell milk at a minimum price of nine cents a quart (and pay eight cents a quart if they bought it from a dealer). The purpose of the law was to stabilize the dairy farming industry, in which a depressed market might cause dairy farmers to slaughter cows and thereby induce a subsequent shortage of milk. Leo Nebbia, a retailer in Rochester, was convicted of violating the law, and the New York Court of Appeals affirmed his conviction. Nebbia appealed to the U.S. Supreme Court.

By the narrowest of margins, the court upheld the New York price controls on milk against challenges based on the Fourteenth Amendment. Roberts wrote the court opinion, and Brandeis, Cardozo, Hughes, and Stone joined him. Roberts did not find the difference between the selling prices fixed for dealers and stores unequal treatment, since dealers and stores served different markets. Moreover, a storeowner might buy milk from a farmer if he so wished. On whether the milk business was one affected with a public interest and so subject to public regulation, Roberts held that any business affects the public, and so all business, not a closed class, is subject to public regulation. Of course, price controls must not be arbitrary or discriminatory, which Roberts did not think the New York milk prices were.

McReynolds dissented, and Butler, Sutherland, and Van Devanter joined him. The alleged necessity of the law arises because producers produce more than others can buy, and the distress of the producers results from their voluntary but ill-advised overproduction. The minimum-price law enriches one business class (the dairy farmers) at the expense of others (dealers, storeowners, and customers). The state may regulate the prices of businesses affected with a public interest, but the milk business is not one of these. Setting minimum prices for the retail sale of milk is an unreasonable restraint on the retail sellers of milk and so a violation of the due process clause.

These two decisions concerned state regulation of business, not New Deal legislation, but they had implications for the forthcoming cases involving the Roosevelt administration's legislative programs for the economy. On the one hand, the state regulations had been upheld. On the other hand, four members, whom the press soon dubbed the four horsemen, dissented vigorously. As the cases involving New Deal legislation wound their way to the court, there were two lines of cases involving federal power under the commerce clause. On one side were four principal cases. *Gibbons v. Ogden* had defined the congressional commerce power broadly. The Shreveport Case had held that the Interstate Commerce Commission could regulate intrastate rates that closely and substantially affected interstate commerce. The Lottery Case had upheld congressional power to prohibit goods from being transported over state lines. *Stafford v. Wallace* had upheld regulation of Chicago stockyards on a stream-of-commerce theory. On the other side were two cases in which the court drew a sharp distinction between production and commerce, the former of which was reserved to the police powers of the states: *U.S. v. E. C. Knight* and *Hammer v. Dagenhart.*

On January 7, 1935, the court handed down its first decision on New Deal legislation (*Panama Refining Co. v. Ryan*). In order to control overproduction, a provision of the 1934 National Industrial Recovery Act authorized the president to prohibit the transportation of oil produced in excess of quotas set by the oil-producing states. The refining company sought an injunction to prevent enforcement of the provision, lost in the lower court, and appealed to the Supreme Court. Hughes wrote the court opinion invalidating the provision, and all the justices but Cardozo joined him. Hughes held that the law unconstitutionally delegated legislative power to the president without establishing the primary standard to be used. Never before had the court invalidated a federal law because it illegally delegated legislative power to the executive. Cardozo defended the provision's broad delegation of power as necessary in the current national emergency.

On February 18 the court by the narrowest margin upheld one action by the Roosevelt administration and Congress (the Gold Clause Cases). In connection with the president's decision to sharply increase the dollar value of its gold reserves, Congress in 1933 abrogated the gold clauses in all private and public contracts. For example, many bonds expressly required repayment in gold. If such bondholders received repayment in the new dollar value of gold, those indebted to the bondholders, including federal and state governments, would incur a proportionately increased debt load. Conversely, if the bondholders received repayment in paper dollars, they would receive gold-devalued currency. In three cases bondholders sought to enjoin enforcement of the act and ultimately appealed to the Supreme Court.

Hughes wrote the court opinion, and Brandeis, Cardozo, Roberts, and Stone joined him. On gold clauses in private contracts, Hughes held that Congress had the power to regulate the monetary system, that the gold clauses in private contracts were merely provision for the payment of money, and that Congress could override private contracts in conflict with the monetary system it established. On gold clauses in government bonds, Hughes agreed with the bondholders that Congress had unconstitutionally impaired its obligations, but the bondholders could recover only nominal damages for breach of contract. In short, Hughes was saying that the gold-devalued dollars had the same buying power as dollars had before their devaluation. McReynolds dissented, and Butler, Sutherland, and Van Devanter joined him. McReynolds extemporaneously declared from the bench that this was Nero at his worst, alluding to Nero's reputation of chipping gold off Roman coins to pay for his extravagances.

Early in May the court turned to a minor regulatory matter unrelated to the overall New Deal program. Congress had enacted a statute that required railroad carriers to subscribe to a pension plan for senior employees. A railroad company objected to being compelled to participate in the plan and won in the lower court. The government agency established by the statute to carry out the plan appealed to the Supreme Court. By the narrowest margin, the court invalidated the law as beyond the power of Congress under the commerce clause (*Railroad Retirement Board v. Alton Railway Co.*). Roberts wrote the court opinion, and Butler, McReynolds, Sutherland, and Van Devanter joined him. Roberts ridiculed the legislation as based on the contentment-and-satisfaction-of-workers theory of social progress. The pension plan was disallowed because it was deemed to have no relation to matters of health, safety, or efficiency.

On Monday, May 27, called "Black Monday" by administration supporters, the court handed down three decisions adverse to the administration. The first was *Schechter Poultry Corp. v. U.S.* The court unanimously declared the National Industrial Relations Act (NIRA) unconstitutional. That act authorized the president to establish industry codes of prices, minimum wages, and fair trade practices, and the president in turn delegated the power to industry boards equally composed of representatives of business, labor, and the government. The Schechter brothers, owners of a kosher poultry slaughterhouse and retail market in Brooklyn, New York, were convicted of violating the code established for the poultry industry and appealed to the Supreme Court.

Hughes wrote the court opinion. First, he opined that an emergency does not change or enlarge the constitutional power to make laws—at least an attitude, if not a contradiction, at odds with the position he had espoused in the Blaisdell case the year before. Second, he held that the law delegated power to the president illegally, since the law specified no standards aside from prescribing no monopolies or restrictive memberships. (Note that redrafting the law would have cured this defect.) Third, the Schechters were not engaged in interstate commerce, nor did their business directly affect it. Most of the chickens came from New Jersey, but they had come to rest in Brooklyn. He contrasted the indirect effect that the Schechters's business had on interstate commerce with the direct effect that local conditions of the railroads had on it. Cardozo, joined by Stone, concurred separately. He agreed that the law involved what he described as delegation run riot and, without appealing to a distinction between the direct and indirect effects of local on interstate commerce, found the regulation of local matters went too far from interstate commerce.

The second case was *Louisville Bank v. Radford.* In that case the court unanimously struck down the Frazier-Lemke Emergency Farm Mortgage Act. That act allowed farmers whose farms had been foreclosed to repurchase them at reappraised lower values and provided loans to do so at 1 percent interest.

The third case was *Humphrey's Executor v. U.S.* In that case Sutherland, speaking for a unanimous court, held that President Roosevelt could not summarily remove William Humphreys, a member of the independent Federal Trade Commission. Roosevelt accused Humphreys of obstructing New Deal policies. Sutherland argued that independent commissions, unlike purely executive officers, exercised not only executive functions but also quasi-legislative and quasi-judicial functions, and Congress could for that reason constitutionally require consent of the Senate before the president was permitted to remove them. Incidentally, Roosevelt was angrier about this court decision, which he took as a personal rebuke, than he was at the Schechter decision, which invalidated a program that he probably would have dismantled anyway.

The next term was even worse for key parts of the New Deal program. On

January 6, 1936, the court invalidated the Agricultural Act of 1933 (*Butler v. U.S.*). That act attempted to limit agricultural production in order to raise the price of agricultural products. If farmers of a commodity agreed by a majority to reduce production under a quota system, they received specified payments, and the funds for the payments were raised by a tax on the first processors of the commodities (e.g., mills). Butler, the receiver for a bankrupt processor, refused to pay this tax on commodities it processed. A district court ordered payment of the tax, but a court of appeals reversed, and the government appealed to the Supreme Court.

Roberts wrote the court opinion, and Butler, Hughes McReynolds, Sutherland, and Van Devanter joined him. Critical commentators called the opinion troublesome, quixotic, and even inept. Article I, section 8, clause 1 of the Constitution grants Congress the power to levy taxes and provide for the general welfare, and Roberts accepted Hamilton's view that the provision established a general power of Congress to spend for the general welfare—that is, a power not limited to authorizations otherwise specified in the Constitution. But whatever the extent of spending for the general welfare, the purpose of the act, to which the tax was merely incidental, was to regulate agricultural production, and the Tenth Amendment reserved such regulation to the states. Moreover, the act induced farmers to participate by a form of economic coercion, and the tax in effect took money from one group (ultimately consumers) and gave it to another (farmers). Stone, joined by Brandeis and Cardozo, dissented. Stone pointed out that the spending on agricultural production, which was a national problem, was for the general welfare, that the tax raised revenue and affected localities like any other tax, and that economic inducement was proper for the general welfare.

On February 17 the court gave the New Deal a rare victory, the only other one in 1935–36 being in the Gold Clause Cases. Minority shareholders of a private utility company in the area of a dam constructed by the Tennessee Valley Authority sought to annul their board's agreement with the authority to purchase electricity generated by the dam. They lost in the lower court and appealed to the Supreme Court. Hughes wrote the court opinion upholding the sale of electricity from the dam (*Ashwander v. Tennessee Valley Authority*). Hughes held that Congress had the power to build dams for national defense and to foster interstate commerce and that the federal government could sell the electricity the dam produced as a byproduct, since Article IV, section 3 granted it the power to sell property that it lawfully acquired. Cardozo, Butler, Roberts,

Stone, Sutherland, and Van Devanter joined Hughes's opinion. Brandeis concurred separately, arguing that the constitutional issue should never have been addressed, since the case involved only an internal dispute between two factions of stockholders. McReynolds was the only dissenter.

On March 18 the court struck down another New Deal law (*Carter v. Carter Coal Co.*). Congress in 1935 passed the Bituminous Coal Act in an attempt to stabilize the depressed coal industry. It established a commission with powers over the industry. Boards were established in twenty-three districts to fix minimum coal prices at the head of the mines. National maximum hours of labor and district minimum wages became effective when producers of two-thirds of the annual tonnage and representatives of more than half of the workers agreed to the terms. Company participation in the codes was voluntary, but the remission of 90 percent of a 15 percent tax on sales at the mines was a strong incentive for the companies to do so. Carter and other shareholders sued to enjoin the company from paying the tax and participating in the program on the grounds that the act was unconstitutional. Since the shareholders' interest and the company's were substantially identical, the government intervened to defend the law. The government won in the lower court, and Carter appealed to the Supreme Court.

Sutherland wrote the court opinion, and Butler, McReynolds, Roberts, and Van Devanter joined him. The opinion held that the delegation of the power to draft codes to the producers and workers was invalid. On the commerce clause, Sutherland held that, whatever happens to the coal, the mining is local and has no direct effect on interstate commerce. (He called an effect on interstate commerce direct when there is no intervening agent between the cause and the effect, as there is none in the case of railroads transporting products across state lines.) Therefore, Congress has no power over wage and hour regulations. Citing the Knight case, Sutherland insisted that production is not commerce, and the Tenth Amendment reserved regulation of production to the states. Sutherland then threw out the price controls, not on constitutional grounds, but because he thought that Congress would not have provided for them without also providing for wage and hour regulations, although the act had expressly declared that the labor and price provisions were separable.

Brandeis, Cardozo, Hughes, and Stone dissented from different parts of the decision. Hughes agreed that the wage and hours provisions were invalid, but not that the price controls were. The coal is sold in interstate commerce, and Congress said that the provision for price controls was separable. Cardozo, joined by Brandeis and Stone, passed no judgment on the labor provisions but held that the regulation of the prices of interstate sales was valid and that the regulation of intrastate sales was also valid because of their effect on interstate commerce. The directness or indirectness of effects on interstate commerce was, in his opinion, a matter of degree. Thus the vote of the court on the labor provisions was six against and none for, with three abstaining, and the vote on the price provisions was five against and four for.

On May 25 the court by the narrowest margin invalidated the 1934 Municipal Bankruptcy Act (*Ashton v. Cameron County District*). That act authorized federal courts to readjust municipal debt burdens if 51 percent of the creditors gave consent. Cameron County, Texas, petitioned a federal district court to proceed according to the act. The district court denied the petition for want of jurisdiction on the grounds that the act invaded matters reserved to the states. The court of appeals reversed, and Ashton and fellow dissident bondholders appealed to the Supreme Court. McReynolds wrote the court opinion, and Butler, Roberts, Sutherland, and Van Devanter joined him. McReynolds held that the states had the power to control their own fiscal affairs and that Congress did not. Cardozo, dissenting with Brandeis, Hughes, and Stone, appealed to the power of Congress over bankruptcies granted in Article I, section 8, clause 4.

In two years, 1935 and 1936, the court had invalidated seven acts of Congress and ruled against the president's removal of Humphrey. Three decisions (*Schechter, Louisville Bank, and Humphrey's Executor*) were unanimous, one (*Panama Oil*) nearly unanimous, one (*Butler*) six to three, and three (*Alton, Carter, and Ashton*) five to four. (The Carter decision was 5–4 against the price provisions but 6–0 against the wage and hours provisions.) Roberts joined the four conservative justices (Butler, McReynolds, Sutherland, and Van Devanter) in all eight cases, and Hughes joined them in six. The court upheld the Roosevelt administration in two cases: the Gold Clause Cases, only narrowly, and *Ashwander.*

After his landslide reelection in November 1936, Roosevelt on February 5, 1937, proposed a court-reform bill that was quickly dubbed the "court-packing plan." The key provision authorized the president to appoint a new justice to supplement every justice on the court who was over the age of seventy. Since six justices on the court at that time were over seventy years of age, the president could appoint six justices and so enlarge the court to fifteen members. There was a storm of opposition from Republicans, prominent members of the bar, the media, and business leaders.

In the middle of this political turmoil the court itself did an about-face in a series of cases. The first, on March 29, was *West Coast Hotel Co. v. Parrish*. The case involved a 1913 Washington state law that authorized an administrative board to fix minimum wages for women and minor employees. Elsie Parrish, a chambermaid working for the hotel, was not paid the minimum wage and sued her employer for the wages required by the law. The hotel, claiming that a minimum-wage law impairs liberty of contract, as the court had held in the Adkins decision, won in the state courts, and Parrish appealed to the U.S. Supreme Court.

By the narrowest margin, the court upheld the law. Hughes wrote the court opinion, and Brandeis, Cardozo, Roberts, and Stone joined him. Hughes identified the issue as the same as that in the Adkins case: liberty of contract, although the present case involved the due process clause of the Fourteenth Amendment and the Adkins case involved the due process clause of the Fifth Amendment. He argued that the liberty of contract may be restricted in the public interest, and that the court had sustained statutes limiting the hours of work. The wages were fixed in consideration of the services rendered, and the employer was still free to hire or not hire. In particular, he pointed out that employers and employees do not have equal bargaining power and that the state has a special interest in protecting women from unscrupulous employers. The Adkins decision, therefore, was accordingly overruled.

Sutherland, who wrote the Adkins decision, dissented, and his usual associates (Butler, McReynolds, and Van Devanter) joined him. Sutherland maintained that the Constitution is the supreme law of the land and that it is the duty of justices to be faithful to it when judging the constitutionality of statutes. He argued that the Constitution does not change with the ebb and flow of economic events and that the Adkins case was rightly decided. Unlike his dissent in the Blaisdell case, where Sutherland could appeal to the literal meaning of the contract clause, he in the Parrish case could appeal to no such explicit wording regarding the extent of the liberty of contract protected by the due process clause of the Fourteenth Amendment.

The decision was contrary to a decision ten months earlier, on June 1, 1936, in which the same court had on the basis of *Adkins* invalidated a New York minimum-wage law for women and minors (*Morehead v. New York ex rel. Tipaldo*). In that decision Butler, joined by McReynolds, Roberts, Sutherland, and Van Devanter, found that the reasoning of the Adkins decision on liberty of contract was persuasive and that there was no significant factual difference between the minimum-wage law invalidated in *Adkins* and the New York minimum-wage law. Hughes dissented on the grounds that there was a significant factual difference between the Adkins case and the New York case, and Brandeis, Cardozo, and Stone joined him in that dissent. Stone also dissented on the grounds that the Adkins case was wrongly decided, and Brandeis and Cardozo, but not Hughes, joined him.

The different result in the Parrish case was evidently due to the fact that Roberts switched sides. Roberts later said that he understood the question in the New York case to be whether the New York law differed significantly from the law involved in the Adkins case. Moreover, Hughes's dissent in the New York case did not indicate that he would overrule the Adkins decision. One wag described Robert's change of position in this and subsequent cases in 1937 as the switch in time that saved nine.

On April 12 the court, by the narrowest of margins, upheld the National Labor Relations Act of 1935 (*National Labor Relations Board v. Jones and Laughlin Steel Corp.*). The act established the right of workers to organize into unions in businesses operating in interstate commerce and businesses whose activities affected interstate commerce, and it prohibited employers from dismissing or discriminating against workers because of union membership or activities. It also established a board to regulate procedures for union recognition, collective bargaining, and strikes. Workers and union associates were in 1937 attempting to unionize the workers at the steel mills, including Jones and Laughlin. The NLRB ordered the company to cease and desist from certain labor practices that the statute declared to be unfair—in this case firing ten workers for attempts to organize unions. When the company failed to comply, the NLRB asked the designated court of appeals to enforce the order. That court declined to do so, quite understandably after the Supreme Court's decision in *Carter* less than a year before. The NLRB then appealed to the Supreme Court.

Hughes wrote the court opinion, and Brandeis, Cardozo, Roberts, and Stone joined him. He cited the stream-of-commerce theory as a way to justify the labor law but did not rely on it. Rather, he relied on the argument that labor peace has a close and substantial relation to interstate commerce. Industrial strife in the steel industry would paralyze commerce. He made no attempt to distinguish the Carter decision or to distinguish between direct and indirect effects on interstate commerce.

McReynolds wrote the dissenting opinion, and Butler, Sutherland, and Van Devanter, as usual, joined him. He found the connection between the local activities and interstate commerce indirect and remote. If the federal government can regulate labor relations having such a remote connection to interstate commerce, he asked rhetorically, then could it by the same logic regulate marriage and everything else between birth and death?

On May 24 the court in a pair of cases upheld key provisions of the Social Security Act of 1935.The first concerned the unemployment compensation system. The act required employers of eight or more workers to pay an excise tax on their annual payroll. The taxpaying employer was allowed a credit of up to 90 percent of the tax for amounts contributed to a state unemployment compensation fund that met federal standards. (A state with an unemployment compensation fund meeting federal standards received federal benefits.) The Stewart Machine Company paid the tax but filed a claim for a refund with the federal administrator and sued him in a federal district court, claiming that the aim of the federal tax's credit provision was to coerce states to establish unemployment compensation funds. The company lost in the district court but appealed to the Supreme Court.

By the narrowest margin, the court upheld the tax and the unemployment compensation provisions (*Stewart Machine Co. v. Davis*). Cardozo wrote the court opinion, and Brandeis, Hughes, Roberts, and Stone joined him. First, Cardozo argued that the tax was an excise tax laid uniformly throughout the United States and could stand on its own merits independently of appropriations of the revenue collected. Second, he said that the classification was reasonably related to the general welfare. Third, he found that there was no coercion on states to create an unemployment compensation program, although there was a strong inducement. Fourth, he claimed that federal standards do not destroy state sovereignty, and thereby silently repudiated the dual federalism explicit in the Butler decision.

The four conservative justices dissented in three separate opinions. McReynolds objected to the tax on the grounds that it coerced the states to create an unemployment compensation program. Sutherland and Butler objected that the tax effectively regulated local matters and so violated the Tenth Amendment.

In a companion case, *Helvering v. Davis*, the court by a wider margin upheld the tax on employers and the old-age pension benefits to employees of the Social Security Act. Cardozo wrote the court opinion, and Brandeis, Hughes, Roberts, Stone, Sutherland, and Van Devanter joined him. Cardozo found the program constitutional under Congress's power to tax and spend for the public welfare (Article I, section 8). The provision of old-age benefits was a response to a nationwide problem that demanded a nationwide solution. Only Butler and McReynolds dissented.

On May 18, a month after the NLRB decision upholding the Wagner Act and one week before the decisions upholding key provisions of the Social Security Act, Van Devanter announced that he would retire from the court at the end of the term, on June 1. That presaged that the Roosevelt economic program would no longer face a hostile court, and so the court-packing plan died in a Senate committee in July.

In 1939 the court upheld the second Agricultural Act of 1938 (*Mulford v. Smith*). That act had set marketing quotas on tobacco farmers in order to reduce surplus production. Roberts, who had written the Butler opinion invalidating the first agricultural act, wrote the court opinion, and Black, Douglas, Frankfurter, Hughes, Reed, and Stone joined him. Roberts argued that the quotas regulated marketing, not production. He and Hughes had changed their positions from those taken in the Butler case, and Black and Reed had replaced Van Devanter and Sutherland, respectively. Roberts admitted that the Butler decision was a mistake and concluded that the commerce clause gave Congress ample power to set marketing quotas. Butler and McReynolds dissented.

On February 3, 1941, two days after McReynolds—the last of the four conservative justices to die or retire—resigned, the court put another nail into the theory of dual sovereignty and the distinction between production and commerce regarding congressional power over commerce (*U.S. v. Darby Lumber Co.*). The Fair Labor Standards Act of 1938 fixed minimum wages and maximum hours for employees in industries whose products were shipped over state lines. It also prohibited child labor. A district court quashed an indictment against the lumber company for violating the act, and the government appealed to the Supreme Court. The district court's action was understandable, given the court's relatively recent decision in the Carter case.

Stone wrote the unanimous court decision of its eight members. First, Stone pointed out that the act prohibited goods produced under substandard conditions from interstate commerce, over which congressional power is plenary. Second, as a means to this prohibition, he held that Congress could regulate the minimum wages in production of the goods and expressly overruled *Hammer v. Dagenhart.* Third, he held that Congress could do so simply to regulate commerce. The method and kind of competition were the issues. Last, he pointed out that the Tenth Amendment merely stated a truism—namely, that powers not granted to the federal government are reserved to the states and the people thereof.

Federal Power over Foreign Affairs At almost the height of the conflict between the court and the Roosevelt administration on domestic matters and before the court's dramatic reversal of its position, the court on December 21, 1936, handed down a decision endorsing the sweeping power of the federal government, specifically the president, in the conduct of foreign affairs (*U.S. v. Curtis-Wright Export Corp.*). Congress had by joint resolution authorized the president to place an embargo on arms shipments to nations at war in the Chaco region of South America, and the president had done so. Curtis-Wright was indicted for violating the embargo and claimed that Congress had unconstitutionally delegated legislative authority to the president with the issuance of the embargo at his unfettered discretion. Curtis-Wright won in the district court, not altogether unreasonably, since the court had invoked illegal delegation of power to invalidate the National Industrial Recovery Act and the Coal Act. The government appealed to the Supreme Court.

Sutherland wrote the court opinion, and Brandeis, Butler, Cardozo, Hughes, Roberts, and Van Devanter joined him. He argued that the power of sovereignty over foreign affairs did not depend on express grants in the Constitution. That sovereignty, unlike the sovereignty over domestic affairs, had passed directly from the crown to the United States—that is, the Continental Congress—upon the success of the Revolution and then by the Constitution from the Continental Congress, not the states, to the federal government. Historians have challenged Sutherland's analysis, but constitutional experts agree with his conclusion—namely, that the national government, not the states, has power over foreign affairs. Sutherland also described the president's power over foreign affairs as plenary, which suggests that the delegation question and the congressional authorization were irrelevant. McReynolds dissented, and Stone did not participate.

Civil Rights The Hughes Court invoked the due process clause of the Fourteenth Amendment to apply parts of the Bill of Rights against state infringement, a process initiated by the Gitlow decision regarding freedom of speech. In 1931 the court incorporated the freedom of the press against state infringement (*Near v. Minnesota*). Minnesota had in 1925 passed a law that permitted a judge without a jury to prohibit future publication of a newspaper in perpetuity if the judge found it was publishing obscene or malicious, scandalous, or defamatory material. A Minneapolis newspaper, the *Saturday Press,* focused flamboyantly but fairly accurately on local corruption, and a local lawyer obtained an injunction ordering the newspaper's publisher, J. M. Near, a religious and racial bigot, to cease and desist from publishing the paper. The Minnesota Supreme Court affirmed the injunction, and Near, with the legal support provided by Colonel Robert McCormick, the conservative publisher of the *Chicago Tribune,* appealed to the U.S. Supreme Court.

Hughes wrote the court opinion striking down the law, and Brandeis, Cardozo, Roberts, and Stone joined him. After declaring that the due process clause of the Fourteenth Amendment protected freedom of the press, Hughes pointed out that the law did not aim to redress a wrong, that it applied to any and all future publication, that it suppressed the newspaper, and that it constituted prior censorship. He admitted that some prior censorship might be legal and cited obscene literature as one example of permissible prior censorship. Butler wrote a dissenting opinion, and the other three conservative justices joined him. He deplored the imposition of federal regulation of state laws restricting offensive publications and insisted that the law did not involve prior censorship, since the already published writing amply evidenced malicious material.

In 1937 the court incorporated the freedom of assembly against state infringement (*DeJonge v. Oregon*). Dirk DeJonge helped to organize a meeting in Portland to protest police shooting of longshoremen on strike and raids on workers' homes and halls. DeJonge and other organizers of the meeting were Communists, but no more than 15 percent of those attending the meeting were. No one at the meeting taught criminal syndicalism or unlawful conduct, and the meeting was completely orderly. DeJonge was convicted of violating Oregon's criminal syndicalism law for helping to conduct the meeting under the auspices of the Communist Party, and the Oregon Supreme Court affirmed, holding that a person could be convicted under the statute for such a meeting even if the meeting itself did not teach criminal syndicalism.

Hughes wrote the court opinion striking down DeJonge's conviction, and all the other justices joined him except Stone, who did not participate. Hughes held that, although DeJonge was a Communist, most at the meeting were not. The assembly was for lawful purposes and peaceful. The right of assembly is related to free speech, and the due process clause of the Fourteenth Amendment protects the right against state infringement.

In 1940 the court explicitly placed peaceful picketing under the protection of the free speech clause of the First Amendment and the due process clause of the Fourteenth (*Thornhill v. Alabama*). Alabama had a statute that prohibited the picketing of businesses in a labor dispute. Byron Thornhill was convicted of violating the statute, and an appellate state court upheld the conviction. Thornhill appealed to the U.S. Supreme Court. Murphy, who had been governor of Michigan during the sit-down strike of General Motors in 1937, wrote the court opinion, and all the justices joined him except McReynolds, who dissented without opinion. Murphy held that picketing was a form of expression and so protected by the First and Fourteenth amendments. The state might prohibit methods of picketing, such as limiting the number of pickets, but not all picketing. The value of picketing is that it educates the public about economic matters.

In 1932 the court invoked the due process clause of the Fourteenth Amendment to order the retrial of eight black indigent youths (*Powell v. Alabama*). Ozie Powell and seven others had been convicted of raping two white women on a freight train in the Scottsdale area and sentenced to death. They had sporadic contact with lawyers in the pretrial process, and two lawyers appeared at the trial to represent them but had no opportunity to investigate the case and had only thirty minutes to consult with the defendants before their trials. The Alabama Supreme Court affirmed the convictions of seven but reversed the conviction of one because he was a juvenile. The Communist-dominated International Labor Defense sponsored the convicts' appeal to the U.S. Supreme Court.

Sutherland wrote the court opinion, and Brandeis, Cardozo, Hughes, Roberts, Stone, and Van Devanter joined him. Sutherland held that the due process clause required states to provide fair trials of criminal defendants and that the right to counsel in capital cases was an integral part of a fair trial. If a defendant could not afford a lawyer or was mentally incompetent to choose one, the trial court should appoint one. Accordingly, since the defendants in this case had not received effective counsel, the convictions were overturned. Note that Sutherland did not incorporate the Sixth Amendment right to counsel, as such, into the due process clause of the Fourteenth. Butler, joined by McReynolds, dissented on the grounds that the defendants had received counsel.

In December 1937, after the court's about-face on the power of Congress under the commerce clause, it declined to apply the Fifth Amendment's prohibition against placing a defendant on trial twice for the same offense to state criminal defendants (*Palko v. Connecticut*). At his first trial Palko had been convicted of murder in the second degree and sentenced to life imprisonment. The prosecution appealed to the Connecticut Supreme Court on procedural grounds, and that court ordered a new trial, at which Palko was convicted of murder in the first degree and sentenced to death. Palko appealed to the U.S. Supreme Court. Cardozo wrote the court opinion, and Black, Brandeis, Hughes, McReynolds, Roberts, Stone, and Sutherland joined him. Cardozo held that the due process clause of the Fourteenth Amendment guaranteed criminal defendants only the fundamental rights implicit in the concept of ordered liberty. Note that Black, newly appointed, joined the court opinion, although he would subsequently lead the movement to incorporate all of the rights in the first eight amendments under the due process clause. Butler dissented without opinion.

In 1940 the court held that the free exercise of religion guaranteed against the federal government in the First Amendment was guaranteed against state infringement by the due process clause of the Fourteenth (*Cantwell v. Connecticut*). Jesse Cantwell and two other Jehovah's Witnesses were engaging in proselytism on the streets of New Haven, soliciting funds, offering to play a record for listeners and to provide pamphlets. (Both the record and the pamphlets strongly attacked the Catholic religion.) The three Jehovah's Witnesses were convicted of violating a state statute that required solicitors to obtain a permit from a local official and of breaching the peace. Roberts wrote the unanimous court opinion. He held that the due process clause of the Fourteenth Amendment protected the free exercise of religion, that the free exercise of religion included two concepts—the freedom to believe, which is absolute, and the freedom to act, which is not—and that the Connecticut law laid a prior and forbidden burden on the free exercise of religion. Moreover, he found nothing in the circumstances of the case that indicated a breach of peace.

In the same year, the last of the Hughes Court, the court faced the issue of compulsory flag salutes and pledges of allegiance in the public schools. A board of education in Minersville, Pennsylvania, like many throughout the United States, had mandated a program of saluting the flag and pledging allegiance for all teachers and pupils. When two children, Lillian and William Gobitis, refused for religious reasons to salute the flag, they were expelled from the public schools of the municipality. (The Gobitises were Jehovah's Witnesses, and they believed that to salute the flag would be to worship a graven image contrary to the biblical prohibition of Exodus 10:4–5.) Since the children were of an age for which Pennsylvania compelled school attendance, the parents of the children were forced to send them to a private school. Because of the heavy financial burden thereby entailed, the father of the children sought to enjoin the local authorities from continuing to demand participation in the flag-salute ceremony as a condition of his children's attendance at the public school. The district court granted the injunction, and the court of appeals affirmed. The state then appealed to the Supreme Court.

Frankfurter wrote the court opinion overturning the lower courts' decisions and upholding the Minersville program, and Black, Douglas, Hughes, Murphy, Reed, and Roberts joined him (*Minersville v. Gobitis*). (McReynolds concurred only in the court's judgment.) Frankfurter argued that, since a free society is founded on the binding tie of cohesive sentiment in the community, it may use its educational process to inculcate that sentiment. He argued further that making an exception for conscientious objectors might interfere with school discipline and cast doubts in the minds of other children that would weaken the effect of the exercises.

Stone was the sole dissenter. He argued that the First Amendment guarantees the freedom of an individual from compulsion to express beliefs, at least if such compelled expression is contrary to the individual's religious convictions. Stone defended a searching judicial inquiry into the legislative judgment where prejudice against insular minorities may curtail the normal operations of the political process to protect them. He did not think that maintaining school discipline was justification for compelling the flag salutes.

This press and law journals sharply criticized the decision, and most commentators since have regarded the decision as one that blotted the court's civil liberties' copybook. The votes of Black, Douglas, and Murphy in favor of compulsory flag salutes were surprising in view of their known and oft-expressed civil libertarian views. As we shall see, they would change their minds. It has been suggested that the magisterial reputation of Frankfurter inclined them to support the decision. (Fellow justices reputedly referred to Frankfurter as "the professor.") It is paradoxical that, at the same time that the court rendered this decision, Nazi storm troopers were occupying France.

The Hughes Court in 1938 began the process of chipping away the separate-but-equal doctrine of the Plessy decision, ultimately culminating in *Brown v. Board of Education*. Lloyd Gaines, a black resident of Missouri, sought admission to the University of Missouri Law School. That law school was open only to whites, and the university for blacks, Lincoln University, had no law school. Canada, the registrar of the University of Missouri, denied that application, and Gaines sought a writ of mandamus from a state court. The state offered to pay Gaines's tuition at an out-of-state law school that admitted blacks. The state court denied the writ, and the Missouri Supreme Court affirmed. Gaines, supported by the NAACP, appealed to the U.S. Supreme Court.

Hughes wrote the court decision ordering Gaines's admission to the University of Missouri Law School, and Black, Brandeis, Reed, Roberts, and Stone joined him (*Missouri ex rel. Gaines v. Canada*). (Cardozo had died, and his successor had not yet been appointed and confirmed.) Hughes held that the state offer to pay Gaines's tuition at an out-of-state law school was inadequate to satisfy the requirement of the equal protection clause of the Fourteenth Amendment, since out-of-state legal education was not equal to in-state legal education in a number of intangible factors, such as social contacts for legal practice. Nor did the intention to develop a law school for blacks meet the separate-but-equal doctrine. McReynolds, joined by Butler, dissented. As for Gaines, he never enrolled in the University of Missouri Law School, and he disappeared from the pages of history.

8

THE STONE AND VINSON
COURTS

(1941–53)

The Justices

Harlan Fiske Stone Hughes retired on June 2, 1941, and President Roosevelt nominated Stone to be chief justice on June 12; the Senate confirmed Stone on June 23. He served as chief justice until his death. Stone's tenure was marked by considerable friction of the court personnel.

James Byrnes To replace McReynolds, who retired on February 1, 1941, Roosevelt nominated James Byrnes on June 12, 1941, and the Senate confirmed Byrnes on the same day. Byrnes, a Democrat and a Protestant, was born on May 2, 1879, in Charleston, South Carolina. His father, James, died before Byrnes was born; his mother was a dressmaker. Byrnes quit school at the age of fourteen and read law in a lawyer's office. He was admitted to the South Carolina bar in 1903. He worked as a court stenographer, reporter, and solicitor for ten years (1900–1910). He served as a congressman for fourteen years (1911–25) and as a U.S. senator for ten years (1931–41). He resigned from the court on October 3, 1942, in order to become director of economic stabilization during World War II. He was U.S. secretary of state for two years (1945–47) and governor of South Carolina for four years (1951–55). He died on April 9, 1972.

Robert Jackson To replace Stone as associate justice, Roosevelt nominated Robert Jackson on the same day that Roosevelt named Stone to be chief justice: June 12, 1941; the Senate confirmed Jackson on July 7, two weeks after it confirmed Stone as chief justice. With the confirmation of Jackson, the only remaining member of the Hughes Court and the only Republican was Roberts. Jackson, a Democrat and an Episcopalian, was born on February 13, 1892, in Spring Creek Township, Pennsylvania. His father, William, was a horse breeder and hotel owner. Jackson graduated from high school in Jamestown, New York, in 1910, attended Albany Law School for one year (1911), and clerked at Frank Mott's law office. He was the last justice not to have graduated from law school. He was admitted to the New York bar in 1913 and practiced private law for twenty years.

In the Roosevelt administration he was general counsel for the Bureau of Internal Revenue for two years (1934–36), assistant attorney general for two years (1936–38), solicitor general for two years (1938–40), and attorney general for one year (1940).

In May 1945, Jackson, taking a leave from the court, became chief counsel of the United States in the prosecution of Nazi war criminals at Nuremberg but returned to the court in the fall of 1946. Jackson was under consideration to become chief justice after the death of Stone, as was Black. Each threatened to resign if the other was chosen, and so neither was. Jackson served on the court until his death on October 9, 1954.

Wiley Rutledge Byrnes resigned on October 3, 1942, to become director of economic stabilization, and Roosevelt nominated Wiley Rutledge to the court on January 11, 1943; the Senate confirmed Rutledge on February 8. Rutledge was the last Roosevelt appointee to the court. Rutledge, a Democrat and a Unitarian (originally a Baptist), was born on July 20, 1894, in Cloverport, Kentucky. His father, Wiley, was a Baptist minister. Rutledge attended a Baptist theological seminary in his early years and graduated from the University of Wisconsin in 1914 and from the University of Colorado Law School in 1922. Between his graduation from college and his attendance at law school, he taught high school in Indiana, New Mexico. After graduation from law school he engaged in private practice for two years and taught law at various law schools for fifteen years. He was a judge on a U.S. court of appeals for four years (1939–43). He served on the court until his death on September 10, 1949.

Harold Burton Roberts resigned on July 31, 1945, and President Truman nominated Harold Burton, a former fellow senator, to the court on September 18; the Senate confirmed Burton on the next day. Burton, a Republican and a Unitarian, was born on June 22, 1888, in Jamaica Plain, Massachusetts. His father, Alfred, was a dean at the Massachusetts Institute of Technology. Burton graduated from Bowdoin College in 1909 and from Harvard Law School in 1912. He engaged in private practice in Ohio, served in the Ohio legislature for one year (1928–29), was mayor of Cleveland for five years (1935–40), and was a U.S. senator for four years (1941–45). He retired from the court on October 13, 1958, and died on October 22, 1964.

Frederick Vinson Stone died on April 22, 1946, and Truman named Frederick Vinson to be chief justice on June 6; the Senate confirmed Vinson on June 20. Vinson, a Democrat and a Methodist, was born on January 22, 1890, in Louise, Kentucky. His father, James, was the town jailer. Vinson graduated from Centre College in 1909 and from Centre College Law School in 1911, in which year he was admitted to the Kentucky bar. He engaged in private practice for twelve years (1911–23). He was a congressman for fifteen years (1923–38), a judge on a federal court of appeals for five years (1938–43), held administrative posts in World War II agencies for two years (1943–45), and was secretary of the treasury for one year (1945–46). He served on the court until his death on September 8, 1953.

Tom Clark When Murphy died on July 19, 1949, Truman made a fourth appointment to the court. Truman nominated Tom Clark, a member of his cabinet, on July 26, and the Senate confirmed Clark on August 18. Clark, a Democrat and a Presbyterian, was born on September 23, 1899, in Dallas, Texas. His father, William, was a lawyer. Clark graduated from Virginia Military Institute in 1918 and from the University of Texas Law School in 1922. He engaged in private practice for fifteen years (1922–37), was a civil county attorney for five years (1927–32), worked in the U.S. Justice Department for eight years (1937–45), and was Truman's attorney general for four years (1945–49). He retired from the court on June 13, 1967, and died on January 13, 1977.

Sherman Minton Rutledge died on September 10, 1949, and Truman nominated Sherman Minton, another fellow senator, to the court on September 15; the Senate confirmed Minton on October 4. Minton, a Democrat and a Protestant, was born on October 20, 1890, in Georgetown, Indiana. His father,

John, was a farmer. Minton graduated from Indiana University Law School in 1915 and received a master's law degree from Yale Law School in 1916, the same year in which he was admitted to the Indiana bar. He engaged in private practice for seventeen years (1916–33), was public counselor of Indiana for one year (1933–34), was a U.S. senator for six years (1935–41), and served on a U.S. court of appeals for eight years (1941–49). He retired from the court on October 15, 1956, and died on April 9, 1965.

Summary Six of the appointees (Byrnes, Clark, Jackson, Minton, Rutledge, and Vinson) were Democrats and one (Burton) a Republican. (This fact is hardly surprising, since Democratic presidents, Roosevelt and Truman, appointed them.) Five (Byrnes, Clark, Jackson, Minton, and Vinson) were Protestants, and two (Rutledge and Burton) Unitarians. Five (Burton, Clark, Minton, Rutledge, and Vinson) had graduated from both college and law school. Two (Byrnes and Jackson) had no college education and were the last justices to have been admitted to the bar through clerkship. Five (Burton, Clark, Jackson, Minton, and Vinson) had executive governmental experience. Four (Burton, Byrnes, Minton, and Vinson) had legislative experience. Three (Minton, Rutledge, and Vinson) had judicial experience. The fathers of three (Burton, Clark, and Rutledge) were members of a profession. Three (Byrnes, Clark, and Vinson) came from the South, three (Burton, Minton, and Rutledge) from the Midwest, one (Jackson) from New York, and none from the West.

Leading Decisions

Travel In November of the first year of the Stone tenure, 1941, the court decided a case that had first been argued in April during the Hughes tenure and was reargued in October after Stone became chief justice. California during the Depression had passed a statute that prohibited any person from bringing any nonresident indigent into the state. Many indigents were coming into the state as a result of the severe drought in the Dust Bowl. Edwards was convicted of violating the statute, and the California Supreme Court affirmed the conviction. Edwards appealed to the U.S. Supreme Court.

The court unanimously invalidated the statute (*Edwards v. California*). Byrnes wrote the court opinion, and all the justices except Jackson and Douglas joined him. Byrnes relied on the commerce clause, arguing that it established a constitutional right to travel from one state to another. Jackson wrote a concurring opinion in which Douglas joined. Jackson attempted to revive the privileges and immunities clause of the Fourteenth Amendment, arguing that the right to travel from one state to another was one of the rights of a citizen of the United States, and objected to considering persons as if purely commercial objects.

Criminal Law and the Stone Court In 1942 the court dealt with a case involving the right to counsel for a fair trial in a state noncapital felony case. Betts was indicted for robbery and requested that the trial judge appoint a counsel to defend him. The trial judge refused to do so, and Betts, representing himself at the trial, was convicted. He filed a petition for habeas corpus against Brady, the warden of the prison in which he was held, claiming that the denial of counsel in a felony case deprived him of the fair trial that the Sixth Amendment required. The lower courts denied his petition, and he obtained review by the Supreme Court.

The court upheld the conviction (*Betts v. Brady*). Roberts wrote the court opinion, and Byrnes, Frankfurter, Jackson, Reed, and Stone joined him. Roberts held that appointed counsel was not absolutely necessary for a defendant to receive a fair trial in noncapital felony cases and that the circumstances in the case did not indicate that one was necessary in Betts's case. He distinguished the case from the Powell case, where black youths were the defendants in a capital case. Black dissented, and Douglas and Murphy joined him. Black emphasized that the right to counsel was fundamental to criminal due process. As we shall see, the Gideon decision overruled the Betts decision, and Black's dissenting opinion became the law.

Interstate Commerce In the same year, the Stone Court dealt with a leftover case from the New Deal legislation regulating agricultural production. The Agricultural Adjustment Act of 1936 involved marketing quotas on a number of agricultural products, including wheat, and an amendment to the act in 1941 set penalties on farmers who produced crops in excess of the quotas. Roscoe Filburn, a small Ohio farmer, had a dairy farm and raised poultry. He planted about twelve acres of winter wheat, which he used to feed his cattle and poultry, ground into flour for family consumption, and saved for the next year's seeding. This produced 239 bushels of wheat beyond his quota, and the government imposed a penalty of forty-nine cents a bushel. Filburn sought an injunction against Claude Wickard, the secretary of agriculture, claiming that the winter wheat was not marketed. He won in the district court, and the government appealed to the Supreme Court.

Jackson wrote the opinion for a unanimous court upholding the penalty (*Wickard v. Filburn*). Jackson dispensed with language about production and marketing, explicitly rejected the dichotomy between direct and indirect effects on interstate commerce, and found that Filburn's production for home consumption had a substantial effect on interstate commerce. Filburn's home production alone might have a trivial effect on the market, but such production in combination with the home production of other farmers would have a substantial effect. Some 20 percent of the wheat produced in 1940 never left the farm. If Filburn did not produce wheat for home consumption, he would either have to buy it from the market or use part of his quota production for home consumption and so keep it out of the market.

Religious Exercise The Stone Court decided a series of cases involving Jehovah's Witnesses. In one case a Jehovah's Witness named Chaplinski was distributing religious literature on a Saturday afternoon at a busy intersection in Rochester, New Hampshire, and denouncing organized religion as a racket. When complaints were lodged with a city marshal, the latter told the complainants that Chaplinski's activities were lawful, but he also warned the Witness that the crowd was getting restless. A disturbance ensued, and the traffic officer on duty at the intersection started to escort Chaplinski to the police station but did not inform him that he was under arrest or about to be arrested. On the way to the station they met the city marshal, who had been informed that a riot was in progress and was en route to the scene. The marshal repeated his warning to Chaplinski, and the latter responded by calling the marshal a "damned racketeer" and a "damned Fascist." (Chaplinski claimed that the marshal initiated the use of invective language.) Chaplinski was then arrested and convicted of a breach of the peace under a New Hampshire statute that made it a crime to address any offensive, derisive, or annoying word to any other person who is lawfully in any street or other public place. The New Hampshire Supreme Court upheld the conviction, and Chaplinski appealed to the U.S. Supreme Court.

Murphy in 1942 wrote the unanimous court opinion upholding the conviction (*Chaplinski v. New Hampshire*). There are, he said, certain words whose use in public places the government can prohibit. These include lewd and obscene, profane, and libelous words and insulting or fighting words, whose very utterance inflicts injury or tends to incite an immediate breach of peace. Note that the court upheld the conviction solely on the basis of the words used, not their use in a context that constitutes a breach of the peace.

Two cases concerned the right of peddlers of religious tracts to be free from a license tax on persons selling or canvassing for the sale of printed matter. Such taxes varied from $15 per year in Opelika, Alabama, to $25 per month, $10 per week, and $2.50 per day in Fort Smith, Arkansas. Jones and other Jehovah's Witnesses were convicted of violating the ordinances requiring the licenses, and the state supreme courts upheld the convictions. The Witnesses appealed to the U.S. Supreme Court, claiming that application of the fees to their missionary activities violated freedom of religious exercise.

By the narrowest margin, the court upheld the convictions (*Jones v. Opelika*). Reed wrote the court opinion, and Byrnes, Frankfurter, Jackson, and Roberts joined him. Reed held that the license fee was nondiscriminatory and presumably not excessive and that the First Amendment does not require a subsidy in the form of tax exemption for the sellers of religious literature. Stone dissented, and Black, Douglas, and Murphy joined him. The flat license tax was unrelated to the defendants' activities or their receipts and tended to suppress the freedom taxed. Stone also noted the cumulative effect of such taxes on the missionary activities of itinerant evangelists. Black, Douglas, and Murphy filed a separate dissent to note that they now thought the Gobitis decision compelling flag salutes from religious objectors, a decision in which they were part of the majority, was wrongly decided.

A year later, also by the narrowest margin, the court reversed its position on license taxes on the sellers of religious literature (*Murdock v. Pennsylvania*). In a substantially identical Pennsylvania case, Douglas wrote the court opinion invalidating the taxes as applied to itinerant religious evangelists, and Black, Murphy, Rutledge, and Stone joined him. Douglas repeated Stone's arguments in the Jones case and commented that the mere fact that itinerant preachers sold rather than donated religious literature does not transform evangelism into a commercial enterprise. The appointment of Rutledge to replace Byrnes explains the court's change of position. Note that the tax exemption for the vendors of religious literature, as Reed noted in both cases, effectively gave them a subsidy. It is also interesting to note that the father of Douglas was an itinerant preacher.

On May 3, 1943, the same day that the court handed down the Murdock decision invalidating flat license taxes on the incidental sale of religious literature by itinerant evangelist Jehovah's Witnesses, the court affirmed their right to visit homes to distribute handbills advertising a meeting (*Martin v. Struthers*). Struthers, Ohio, had an ordinance that forbade knocking on the door or ringing the doorbell of a private residence to deliver a handbill. The city argued that the ordinance was designed in part to prevent crime but principally to assure privacy in an industrial community where many citizens worked on night shifts and slept during the day. The court, however, held that these reasons were insufficient to justify the ordinance.

Black wrote the court opinion, and Douglas, Murphy, Rutledge, and Stone joined him. Black thought that the ordinance curtailed the freedoms of speech and press too broadly. He pointed out that the law of trespass protected householders who posted notices against uninvited solicitors and that a requirement that solicitors register with local authorities could control against the risk of crime. Murphy, joined by Douglas and Rutledge, argued further that freedom of religion has higher constitutional weight than personal convenience. Frankfurter concurred only on the grounds that the ordinance involved invidious discrimination against ordinary vendors. Reed, joined by Jackson and Roberts, dissented, arguing that the ordinance did not prohibit the distribution of literature, only handbills, and that the distribution of handbills might be judged a more serious problem than the distribution of other materials.

Three years after the first flag-salute decision, the court on June 14, 1943, reversed itself (*West Virginia Board of Education v. Barnette*). That board of education had ordered that a daily flag-salute ceremony become a regular part of the program of activities in its public schools and that all teachers and pupils participate in the salute. Some Jehovah's Witness pupils were expelled from the schools and others were threatened with expulsion for failing to participate in the ceremonies. Officials also threatened to send the children to reformatories, and their parents were prosecuted or threatened with prosecution for causing delinquency. Walter Barnette and other Jehovah's Witness parents sought in a federal district court to enjoin enforcement of the statute against themselves and their children. The district court issued the injunction, and the board of education appealed directly to the U.S. Supreme Court.

The court ruled for the Jehovah Witnesses and overruled the Gobitis decision; Jackson wrote the memorable court opinion, and Black, Douglas, Murphy, Rutledge, and Stone joined him. The action of the local authorities compelling flag salutes, Jackson argued, invades the sphere of intellect and spirit that it is the purpose of the First Amendment to reserve from all official control. Note that Jackson did not say that the state might not *sponsor* the flag-salute ceremony.

Jackson thus restated the issue in the flag-salute cases as one of freedom from the compulsion to affirm a belief or attitude of mind—that is, freedom of speech—rather than freedom of religious exercise. But Black and Douglas, in a separate concurrence, stressed the claim of conscience—that compelling children to participate in a ceremony culminates in a fear of spiritual condemnation. Frankfurter, joined by Reed and Roberts, dissented, repeating his view that the only issue was whether the legislators could reasonably prescribe the flag salute at all.

Japanese Relocation The tenure of the Stone Court coincided with American entry into World War II, and the West Coast was thought to be in danger of invasion by Japan. Approximately 112,000 persons of Japanese ancestry (70,000 of whom were American citizens) lived on the West Coast. Fearful that these Japanese Americans and Japanese aliens would commit espionage and assist the Japanese armed forces in the case of invasion, President Roosevelt, on February 19, 1942, signed an executive order that empowered the secretary of war to establish military areas from which civilians might be excluded. The president on March 18 established the War Relocation Authority to oversee the internment of all West Coast persons of Japanese ancestry, and Congress unanimously passed legislation to implement the executive orders. General John DeWitt in May imposed a curfew from 8:00 P.M. to 6:00 A.M. on all those persons and required them after May 9 to report to assembly centers from which they would be evacuated to relocation centers, where most remained until 1945. Gordon Hirabayashi, an American-born citizen of Japanese ancestry and a senior at the University of Washington, was convicted of violating the curfew and the order to report to an assembly center and sentenced to concurrent three-month sentences. He then appealed to the Supreme Court.

The court in 1943 unanimously upheld the conviction for violating the curfew but, because of the concurrent sentences, declined to consider the conviction for violating the order to report to an assembly center (*Hirabayashi v. U.S.*). Stone wrote the court opinion, and all but Douglas and Murphy subscribed to it. The curfew fell within the power of Congress to wage war, and there were, in Stone's opinion, reasons to suspect persons of Japanese ancestry of loyalty to Japan rather than to the United States. The court could not reject as unfounded the military and congressional judgment that there were disloyal members of the Japanese race in the United States, whose number could not be precisely and quickly ascertained. Note that the decision regarded only the curfew issue. Although the decision was unanimous, three justices (Douglas, Murphy, and Rutledge) wrote separate concurring opinions. Douglas and

Murphy concurred in the opinion, but Rutledge concurred only in the result. Murphy, though concurring, railed against the internment policy, saying that it bore a melancholic resemblance to the Nazi policy against the Jews.

On December 18, 1944, more than two years after the executive orders, the court returned to the issue of the internment. Fred Korematsu, an American-born citizen of Japanese ancestry, was convicted of remaining in San Leandro, California, an officially designated military area, contrary to DeWitt's executive order directing that all such persons be excluded from the area. Korematsu had moved to a nearby town and had not reported to an assembly center for relocation to an internment camp. No question was raised about Korematsu's loyalty. In fact, there couldn't be any. He had tried to enlist in the U.S. army but was rejected because of ill health, and he then obtained work in a defense industry. A court of appeals affirmed his conviction, and he appealed to the Supreme Court.

The court upheld the conviction (*Korematsu v. U.S.*). Black wrote the court opinion, Douglas, Reed, Rutledge, and Stone joined him, and Frankfurter concurred separately. Black repeated the argument of Stone in the Hirabayashi case—namely, that the impossibility of readily distinguishing the disloyal from the loyal justified the temporary exclusion of the whole group. Jackson, Murphy, and Roberts dissented. Jackson disapproved of the court giving any approval to the exclusion order, although that order might be a military necessity. Murphy bluntly declared that the exclusion order fell into the ugly abyss of racism, and did not think suspicion of the loyalty of Japanese Americans as a group was at all warranted. He admitted the necessity to give wide berth to military judgment, but there are definite individual rights and constitutional limits to military discretion, especially since Congress had not imposed martial law or suspended the writ of habeas corpus. In the same year the court ruled that a Japanese-American woman who had clearly established her loyalty to the United States was entitled to a writ of habeas corpus releasing her from a relocation center (*Ex parte Endo*).

Korematsu was sentenced to five years' imprisonment, paroled, and immediately interned in Utah until the end of the war. In 1983, however, the Justice Department asked the district court in San Francisco to remove Korematsu's conviction, admitting that the government had exaggerated the security risks at his trial. Korematsu and other Japanese Americans then sued the government for damages but were not successful because of the statute of limitations. Congress then authorized token payments of $20,000 to surviving internees.

State Regulation of Commerce Near the end of his tenure Stone wrote a significant opinion in a case involving the power of states to regulate things affecting interstate commerce, on which power he was a recognized expert. Arizona had a train-limit law, a law passed in 1912. The law forbade railroads from running trains of more than fourteen passenger or seventy freight cars in the state. The avowed safety reason was to avoid the slack movement or whiplash effect on employees when large trains started or stopped suddenly. (There was evidence that local railroad workers, a sizeable percentage of the state's voting population at the time, supported the legislation because it created more jobs for Arizonans.) In 1940 Arizona sought to collect penalties from Southern Pacific Company for violations of the act. A trial court ruled in favor of the company, but the Arizona Supreme Court overturned that decision, and the company appealed to the U.S. Supreme Court.

Stone held that the Arizona law unduly burdened interstate commerce (*Southern Pacific Co. v. Arizona*), and Frankfurter, Jackson, Murphy, Reed, and Roberts joined him. Rutledge joined only in the result. In the absence of congressional legislation, Stone argued, the court should weigh the burdens on interstate commerce against the putative benefits for local interests—in this case, safety. Regarding the burden on interstate commerce, Stone indicated that interstate trains would need to be broken up when entering the state and reconstituted when exiting the state and that this constituted a serious economic burden on interstate commerce. Regarding the putative local safety benefits, he cited the trial court's finding that safety risks to the public from an increased number of trains would offset whatever safety benefits accrued to railroad employees from limiting the number of cars per train. Therefore, on balance, the Arizona statute constituted an undue burden on interstate commerce.

The Cooley decision held that, in the absence of congressional legislation, states and localities might regulate local matters affecting interstate commerce unless such matters required a national standard. That rule left open the question of whether or when a national standard was required. Stone attempted to fill that lacuna with a balancing test between the burdens of local regulations on interstate commerce and the benefits to local residents. The balancing test has its own weakness—namely, how to determine when the local regulations impose an *undue* burden on interstate commerce. Black and Douglas dissented precisely on that point and would have deferred to the state legislative judgment on the wisdom of safety regulations, and left it to Congress to legislate otherwise. Future courts will return to the issue.

Criminal Law and the Vinson Court In 1947 the Vinson Court reaffirmed the Palko principle regarding the fairness of state criminal trials protected by the due process clause of the Fourteenth Amendment—namely, that the clause does not draw all the rights of the federal Bill of Rights under its protection. California had convicted Adamson of murder, and the prosecutor and judge commented to the jury on the fact that he had failed to take the stand in his own defense. (He had a record of three previous felony convictions, which the prosecution could have elicited from him in cross-examination.) In federal and most state prosecutions, prosecutors and judges were prohibited from commenting on the failure of the defendant to take the stand. The California Supreme Court affirmed, and Adamson appealed to the U.S. Supreme Court, claiming that the comments violated his privilege against self-incrimination.

By the narrowest margin the court upheld the conviction, despite the comments (*Adamson v. California*). Reed wrote the court opinion, and Burton, Frankfurter, Jackson, and Vinson joined him. (Frankfurter wrote a concurring opinion.) The privilege against self-incrimination is not fundamental to a fair trial, Reed argued, and California only slightly infringed the principle. Black, joined by Douglas, dissented. Black pointed out, correctly, that the framers of the Fourteenth Amendment wanted to incorporate the Bill of Rights against state infringement and also argued that an attempt to distinguish fundamental from other rights was to endow the court with endless power under a sort of natural law to expand and contract constitutional standards. Murphy, joined by Rutledge, also dissented. As we shall see, Black's views regarding the Fourteenth Amendment incorporating the Bill of Rights, at least most of it, against state infringement via the due process clause of the Fourteenth Amendment would subsequently prevail.

Two years later, in 1949, the court decided an important case involving the Fourth Amendment and state officials. Wolf, a doctor in Colorado, was convicted of conspiring to commit abortion. The Colorado Supreme Court affirmed the conviction. Colorado officials had obtained evidence used at the trial without a warrant or exigent circumstances, and a court decision had interpreted the amendment to require federal officials to obtain one (*Weeks v. U.S.*). Wolf asked for and obtained court review of whether the federal rule applied to the states.

The court upheld the conviction (*Wolf v. Colorado*). Frankfurter wrote the court opinion, and Burton, Jackson, Reed, and Vinson joined him. There were two questions to answer. The first question concerned whether the Fourteenth

Amendment incorporated the rights of citizens against searches and seizures without a warrant or exigent circumstances. Frankfurter, following the Palko principle, held that Fourth Amendment rights were fundamental to the concept of ordered liberty, and so the Fourteenth Amendment incorporated the protections of the Fourth Amendment. The second question concerned the use of the evidence at the trial, about which the Fourth Amendment said nothing. Frankfurter claimed that there was no fundamental liberty involved and suggested that other means were available to prevent state officials from violating the amendment. Black in a separate opinion concurred with the decision, but only because incorporation of the Fourth Amendment did not require the application of the judicially created rule of evidence for the federal courts to state courts.

There were two dissenting opinions. Douglas argued that Fourth Amendment rights are rendered ineffective without the exclusion of evidence obtained in violation of it. Murphy, joined by Rutledge, argued that few states would voluntarily devise effective means to prevent police and prosecutorial violations.

Speech During the Cold War with the Soviet Union, there were investigations about Communists and Communist sympathizers in the government, the film industry, and labor unions. The most serious case involved the trial of eleven Communist Party leaders. In 1948 the government put the leaders on trial for violations of the Smith Act. That act, passed in 1940, made it a crime to advocate or teach overthrow of the government by force, to publish or distribute printed material advocating or teaching overthrow of the government by force, to organize or be the member of a group advocating or teaching the overthrow of the government by force, or to conspire or commit any of the aforementioned acts. The defendants were convicted, and a court of appeals upheld the convictions. The defendants appealed to the Supreme Court to review the decisions on both procedural and constitutional issues, and the court granted review only on the constitutional questions raised.

The court upheld the convictions (*Dennis v. U.S.*). Vinson wrote the court opinion, and Burton, Minton, and Reed joined him. Vinson adopted a modified version of the clear-and-present danger test used by Judge Learned Hand in the court-of-appeals decision—namely, whether the gravity of the evil, discounted by its improbability, justifies such invasion of free speech as is necessary to avoid the danger. (Note that Hand had dispensed with the immediacy of the danger.) Vinson then emphasized the gravity of the threat and said that the government did not need to wait until the threat was imminent.

Two justices concurred only in the result. Frankfurter concurred because of judicial deference to legislative determination. Jackson concurred because the clear-and-present danger test of speech was inapplicable to conspiracies to commit overt acts against the government, and that is what the defendants had been convicted of, for which conspiracy their speech and printed material were evidence. Black and Douglas dissented. Black saw the issues as ones involving individuals attempting to organize the Communist Party and to use speech and press to advocate overthrow of the government at a later date. This constituted prior censorship. Douglas thought that the Communists posed no real threat in the United States at the moment, being miserable merchants of unwanted ideas, their wares unsold.

Religious Establishment The Vinson Court handed down three significant decisions on the religious establishment clause. The first was *Everson v. Board of Education* in 1947. A New Jersey statute authorized local boards of education to reimburse parents of students attending public and church-related schools for the costs of bus transportation to and from the schools. The nonpublic schools were obliged to meet the educational standards set by the state. Ewing Township had such a program, and a resident taxpayer in the township, Arch Everson, objected to the reimbursement of the parents of pupils attending parochial schools. His objections were twofold: such reimbursements were for a private, not a public, purpose, and they violated the establishment clause. Everson lost in the state courts and petitioned for review by the U.S. Supreme Court.

The court by the narrowest margin upheld the reimbursements. Black wrote the court opinion, and Douglas, Murphy, Reed, and Vinson joined him. Black found that the reimbursements served a public purpose—namely, the safe transportation of children to and from school. On the religious establishment issue, Black incorporated the clause into the due process clause of the Fourteenth Amendment and said that the clause precluded the expenditure of any public money for one or all religions. Nonetheless, he held that financial support for the transportation of the parochial-school children extended the benefits of public-welfare legislation to parochial-school children and safeguarded them from traffic hazards in the school areas. In short, the reimbursement of parents for the bus transportation of their children to and from parochial schools was a child benefit, not a church-related school benefit.

Four justices (Burton, Frankfurter, Jackson, and Rutledge) dissented. Jackson argued that the reimbursement served no public purpose, that Catholic schools are religious schools, and that the tax money for the reimbursements indirectly aided the schools. Rutledge's dissent is most memorable for its analysis of what he considered the historical setting of the religious establishment clause. He cited the struggle in Virginia after independence and before adoption of the Constitution over Patrick Henry's proposal to support all Christian religions and the ensuing adoption of Thomas Jefferson's Statute of Religious Liberty, which disallowed any support of religion. According to Rutledge, Madison's views in that debate indicated his views on the religious establishment clause in the first Congress. The situations, however, were very different. As floor leader in the House of Representatives Madison went to great lengths to assure the representatives from Connecticut and Massachusetts, in which the Congregational Church was established, that the clause would not affect those establishments and that it would guarantee that the federal government would prefer no religion over another. The Virginia debate undoubtedly shows much about Madison's personal views but is of dubious value in interpreting the federal religious establishment clause.

One year later, in 1948, the court decided a case involving the teaching of religion in the public schools. The board of education of Champaign, Illinois, allowed public-school pupils to receive religious instruction (Protestant, Catholic, or Jewish) in public-school classrooms for one period of thirty to forty-five minutes each week. The instructors received no pay but needed the approval of the superintendent of the schools. (There was no evidence that the superintendent used his authority in any other than an administrative way.) Students whose parents requested that their children attend one of the religious-instruction classes were then assigned to the class requested. Reports on the presence or absence of the students at the religious-instruction classes were made to the students' secular teachers. Students whose parents did not request that their children attend one of the religious-instruction classes were assigned to another location for a study period. Vashti McCollum, the mother of Terry, a student not participating in the religious-instruction program, sought an injunction against the program. The Illinois courts denied the injunction, and Mrs. McCollum appealed to the U.S. Supreme Court.

A nearly unanimous court held that the Illinois released-time program violated the religious establishment clause (*Illinois ex rel. McCollum v. Board of Education*). Black wrote the court opinion, and all the other justices except

Reed joined him. Black invoked a principle of absolute separation of church and state and said that the use of public school buildings for religious instruction and the state's compulsory public-school machinery violated separation of church and state. Frankfurter filed a concurring opinion, and Burton, Jackson, and Rutledge joined him. Frankfurter claimed that the Illinois program exercised social pressure on students to participate and sharpened consciousness of religious differences. Reed admitted that the religious establishment clause has a broader meaning than it did when it was written but argued that it should not be interpreted to preclude incidental advantages that religious bodies, with other groups similarly situated, obtain as a byproduct of organized society.

Religious groups, especially but not exclusively Protestant groups, strongly objected to the McCollum decision, and the court, four years later, in 1952, qualified it. The New York City Board of Education had a released-time religious instruction program similar to the Illinois program except that the instruction was conducted off the public-school premises. Mrs. Zorach, a city resident and taxpayer, sought to enjoin the program, but the New York courts denied her suit. She then brought the case to the U.S. Supreme Court.

The court upheld the New York program (*Zorach v. Clausen*). Douglas wrote the court opinion, and Burton, Clark, Minton, Reed, and Vinson joined him. (Minton and Clark had replaced Rutledge and Murphy, respectively.) Douglas interpreted the establishment clause to allow accommodation of religion in the public square and the McCollum decision to rest on the fact that the religious instruction took place within the public school. (Douglas in every subsequent religious establishment case endorsed the principle of absolute separation of church and state.) Black, Frankfurter, and Jackson dissented. Black, who had written the court opinion in the McCollum case, objected to the majority's interpretation of that decision. So did Frankfurter and Jackson. They argued that the central objection to released-time religious instruction programs was that they put the coercive power of the compulsory education laws behind religious instruction, requiring students released for the instruction to attend the classes and students not attending the classes to stay in confinement at the school.

Race   In 1950 the Vinson Court handed down two landmark cases in the history of race relations in the United States. Herman Sweatt, a black mail carrier in Houston, Texas, applied for admission to the University of Texas Law School in 1946. He was denied admission solely on the basis of color.

Sweatt sought and got the assistance of the NAACP and its chief legal counsel, Thurgood Marshall. In the meantime, Texas established a state law school for blacks, which Sweatt claimed was not equal to the education he would receive at the whites-only law school. He sought a court order to admit him to the University of Texas Law School. After losing an entangled legal battle, Sweatt appealed to the U.S. Supreme Court.

Speaking for a unanimous court, Vinson held that the equal protection clause of the Fourteenth Amendment required that Sweatt be admitted to the previously all-white state law school (*Sweatt v. Painter*). The newly created law school for blacks was in no tangible way equal to the University of Texas Law School. Even if it were, it would still lack the intangible elements that constitute a distinguished law school, such as faculty reputation, alumni prestige, and business contacts.

In a companion case, *McLaurin v. Oklahoma State Regents,* the court unanimously ordered the full integration of George McLaurin, a black state resident, into the doctoral program in education at the whites-only Oklahoma University at Norman. A federal district court had ordered the university to admit McLaurin, but the university separated him from white students in class, library, and cafeteria. Vinson wrote a brief and blunt opinion insisting that the treatment deprived McLaurin of the equal protection of the laws.

Steel Seizure Case One of the last decisions of the Vinson Court was also one of its most important. During the Korean War the United Steel Workers, after failing to reach an accord, went on strike against the steel companies. President Truman in May 1952 issued an executive order directing Secretary of Commerce Charles Sawyer to seize the plants. The president did so on the basis of his duty as president and commander-in-chief of the armed forces, not any statutory mandate. He reported his action to Congress, but Congress took no action. The workers returned to work, and the companies continued to manage the plants. (Note that the workers were obliged to do so because it is illegal to strike against the government.) The companies, however, objected to their loss of control over collective bargaining and obtained an injunction from a district court judge. The government immediately appealed to the Supreme Court. The court immediately held oral arguments on the case on May 12 and 13 and handed down a decision on June 2. The short time span of the case from the seizure to the trial court to the decision of the Supreme Court was one of the shortest in history.

The court ruled against the president's action and upheld the injunction (*Youngstown Sheet and Tube Co. v. Sawyer*). Black wrote the court opinion, and only Douglas subscribed to it. Black held that the president had no inherent power to seize private property without authorization from Congress. Burton, Clark, Frankfurter, and Jackson concurred separately. They agreed that the president had no power in the instant case to seize the mills but tried to nuance whether the president ever had inherent power to seize private property. Burton alone hit the nail on the head. He argued that the president had no inherent power to seize private property in this case because the Taft-Hartley Act of 1947 specified the use of an injunction for eighty days in the case of an emergency, and Congress in the course of passing that law specifically rejected authorizing the president to seize private property. Vinson dissented, and Minton and Reed joined him. Vinson argued that the president has inherent power to seize private property in emergency situations and that the need for weapons to wage the Korean War justified the president's action in this case.

There are two ways to read the decision. First, the court voted 6–3 that Truman in the instant case had no inherent power as president and commander-in-chief to seize the mills. Second, seven justices thought that the president might have inherent power to seize private property: the four separately concurring justices thought that the president might have inherent power to seize private property in other situations, and the three dissenters obviously thought that the president not only could have inherent power to do so in other situations but also actually did in the instant case. After the decision Truman complied with the decision but did not invoke the Taft-Hartley Act, which had been passed over his veto. The workers went on a short-lived strike that posed no hindrance to the production of war material.

$\backsim$ 9 $\backsim$

THE WARREN COURT

(1953–69)

The Justices

Earl Warren Vinson died on September 8, 1953, and President Eisenhower appointed Earl Warren to be chief justice by a recess appointment on October 2 and nominated him to the permanent post on January 11, 1954; the Senate confirmed Warren on March 1. Warren, a Republican and a Protestant, was born on March 19, 1891, in Los Angeles, California. His father, Mathias, was a workman for the Southern Pacific Railroad. Warren graduated from the University of California at Berkeley in 1912 and from its law school in 1914. He was admitted to the California bar in 1914 and served as a first lieutenant in the U.S. Army during World War I (1917–18).

He was a deputy district attorney for three years (1920–23), chief deputy for two years (1923–25), district attorney for fourteen years (1925–39), attorney general of California for four years (1939–43), and governor of California for ten years (1943–53). He served on the court until his retirement on June 23, 1969. He died on July 9, 1974.

John Marshall Harlan II Jackson died on October 9, 1954, and Eisenhower nominated John Marshall Harlan II on November 8, but the Senate took no action. Eisenhower again nominated him on January 10, 1955, and the Senate confirmed Harlan on March 16. Harlan, a grandson of the first John Marshall Harlan, was born on May 20, 1899, in Chicago, Illinois. He was a Republican and a Presbyterian. His father, John Maynard Harlan, was a lawyer. Harlan graduated from Princeton in 1920, attended Oxford as a Rhodes Scholar, receiving a master's degree from that university, and completed a two-year program in one year at New York Law School. He was admitted to the New York bar in 1924.

He principally engaged in private practice, but he held several governmental posts. He was an assistant U.S. attorney for two years (1925–27), an assistant attorney general of New York for two years (1928–30), and chief counsel of a state crime commission for two years (1951–53). He was a judge on a U.S. court of appeals for one year before his appointment to the Supreme Court (1954–55). He retired on September 23, 1971, and died on December 29.

William Brennan When Minton retired on October 15, 1956, Eisenhower appointed William Brennan by a recess appointment on the same day. Eisenhower nominated Brennan for the permanent post on January 14, 1957, and the Senate confirmed Brennan on March 19. Brennan, a Democrat and a Catholic, was born on April 25, 1905, in Newark, New Jersey. His father, William, was a labor leader. He graduated from the Wharton School of the University of Pennsylvania in 1928 and from Harvard Law School in 1931. After the death of his first wife, he married his secretary.

He engaged in private practice and served in the army during World War II. He was a New Jersey lower-court judge for three years (1949–52) and a justice on the New Jersey Supreme Court for four years (1952–56). He served on the U.S. Supreme Court until he resigned on July 20, 1990. He died on July 24, 1997.

Charles Whittaker Reed retired on February 22, 1957, and Eisenhower nominated Charles Whittaker to the court on March 7; the Senate confirmed Whittaker on March 19. Whittaker, a Republican and a Methodist, was born on February 22, 1901, in Doliphan, Kansas. His father, John, was a farmer. He did not finish high school but graduated from Kansas City Law School in 1924. He was admitted to the Kansas bar in 1923 and engaged in private practice for twenty-six years (1928–54). He was a U.S. district court judge for two years (1954–56) and a judge for one year on a U.S. court of appeals (1956–57). He resigned on April 1, 1962, and died on November 26, 1973.

Potter Stewart When Burton retired on October 13, 1958, Eisenhower nominated Potter Stewart to the court the next day, and the Senate confirmed

Stewart on May 5. Stewart, a Republican and an Episcopalian, was born on January 23, 1915, in Cincinnati, Ohio. His father, James, was a judge. Stewart attended Hotchkiss School and graduated from Yale College in 1937 and from Yale Law School in 1941. Between college and law school, he attended Cambridge University on a fellowship. He was admitted to the New York bar in 1941. He served in the navy during World War II (1942–45). After the war he returned to a Wall Street firm but soon left to practice in Cincinnati. He was twice elected to the city council and served as vice mayor. He was a judge on a U.S. court of appeals for four years (1954–58). He retired from the court on July 3, 1981, and died on December 7, 1985.

Byron White Whittaker resigned on April 1, 1962, and President Kennedy nominated Byron White to the court on April 3; the Senate confirmed White on April 11. White, a Democrat and an Episcopalian, was born on June 8, 1917, in Fort Collins, Colorado. His father, Alpha, was the branch manager of a lumber supply company. He attended local schools in Wellington, Colorado, graduated from the University of Colorado in 1938, played professional football for a season, and was accepted as a Rhodes Scholar at Oxford in 1939 but was forced to abandon study there because of the outbreak of World War II. He served in the navy during World War II (1942–45). After the war he attended Yale Law School, completing his studies in 1946. He was admitted to the Colorado bar in the same year. He was law clerk to Chief Justice Vinson for one year (1946–47) and engaged in private practice for thirteen years (1947–60). He was deputy U.S. attorney general from 1961 to 1962. He resigned from the court on June 28, 1993, and died on April 15, 2002.

Arthur Goldberg Frankfurter resigned on August 28, 1962, and Kennedy nominated Arthur Goldberg to the court on August 29; the Senate confirmed Goldberg on September 25. Goldberg, a Democrat and Jewish, the son of Russian immigrants, was born in Chicago, Illinois, on August 8, 1908. His father, Joseph, delivered produce. Goldberg attended Chicago public schools and Crane Junior College and graduated from Northwestern University Law School in 1929. He was admitted to the Illinois bar in the same year.

He engaged in private practice for nineteen years (1929–48), except for his service in the army during World War II (1942–44), and worked as counsel for labor organizations for thirteen years (1948–61). He was U.S. secretary of labor for one and a half years (1961–62). He resigned from the court on July 25, 1965, in order to accept President Johnson's request that he become the U.S. representative to the United Nations. He served in that post for three years (1965–68). He died on January 19, 1990.

Abraham Fortas To replace Goldberg, Johnson nominated Abraham Fortas to the court on July 28, 1965, and the Senate confirmed Fortas on August 11. Fortas, a Democrat and a Jew, was born on June 19, 1910, in Memphis, Tennessee. His father, William, was a cabinetmaker. Fortas graduated from Southwestern College in 1930 and from Yale Law School in 1933.

He worked in the agricultural adjustment administration during the New Deal and was undersecretary of the interior for four years (1942–46). He was in private law practice in the District of Columbia for nineteen years (1946–65). He was an adviser to President Johnson before and after his appointment to the court.

In June 1968 Warren indicated to Johnson that he would retire when a successor was nominated and confirmed. On June 26 Johnson nominated Fortas to succeed Warren. Republicans in the Senate opposed the nomination, and financial irregularities by Fortas were alleged. As a result, Johnson on October 4 withdrew the nomination at Fortas's request. More reports of alleged financial irregularities circulated in the next six months, and Fortas resigned on May 14, 1969. He died on April 5, 1982.

Thurgood Marshall When Clark retired from the court on June 12, 1967, Johnson on the next day nominated Thurgood Marshall, a black man and great-grandson of a slave, to succeed him, and the Senate confirmed Marshall on August 30. Marshall, a Democrat and an Episcopalian, was born on July 2, 1908, in Baltimore, Maryland. His father, William, was a dining-car waiter. Marshall attended the public schools of Baltimore and graduated from college at Lincoln University in 1930 and from law school at Howard University in 1933. He was twice married.

He engaged in private legal practice for four years (1933–37). He was a counsel for the NAACP for fourteen years (1936–50) and counsel, then director of the association's legal defense and educational fund for twenty-one years (1940–61). He was a judge on a federal court of appeals for four years (1961–65) and U.S. solicitor general from 1965 to 1967. He retired from the court on October 1, 1991, and died on January 24, 1993.

Summary Four of the appointees (Harlan, Stewart, White, and Whittaker), all appointed by Eisenhower, were Republicans; and five (Brennan, Fortas,

Goldberg, Marshall, and White) were Democrats, one (Brennan) appointed by Eisenhower and the other four by Kennedy and Johnson. Six (Harlan, Marshall, Stewart, Warren, White, and Whittaker) were Protestants, three (Marshall, Stewart, and White) Episcopalians, two (Fortas and Goldberg) Jews, and one (Brennan) a Catholic. Four (Brennan, Goldberg, Harlan, and Stewart) were from the Northeast, three (Warren, White, and Whittaker) from west of the Mississippi, and two (Fortas and Marshall) from the South. The fathers of two appointees (Harlan and Stewart) were lawyers, the father of one (Whittaker) a farmer, and the fathers of the others managers or workers.

All but Whittaker were college graduates, and all, for the first time in the history of the court, held law degrees, three (Fortas, Stewart, and White) from Yale and one (Brennan) from Harvard. All but Brennan had executive governmental experience, and all of the Kennedy-Johnson appointees (Fortas, Goldberg, Marshall, and White) had served in the federal executive branch. In contrast to previous courts, only one appointee (Stewart) had legislative experience, and his experience was limited to the city council. All of the Eisenhower appointees but Warren (Brennan, Harlan, Stewart, and Whittaker) had judicial experience, but only Marshall of the Kennedy-Johnson appointees did. Warren served in the army during World War I, and Goldberg, Stewart, and White served in the army or navy during World War II.

Leading Decisions

Segregation In the first year of the Warren Court, on May 17, 1954, it handed down a unanimous decision declaring racial segregation in public schools unconstitutional (*Brown v. Board of Education I*). The NAACP had sponsored cases challenging the racial segregation in four states (Delaware, Kansas, South Carolina, and Virginia) and a fifth case challenging racial segregation in the District of Columbia. The cases were first argued in December 1952 under Chief Justice Vinson, but the court, while fundamentally in agreement that legally imposed racial segregation in public schools was unconstitutional, could not agree on the immediacy or scope of the remedy. The court ordered the case to be reargued in December 1953 and asked the parties to file briefs answering a series of questions. The principal questions concerned the framers' intentions about the Fourteenth Amendment's effect on segregation in public schools and the scope of a remedy if the court ordered desegregation. Vinson, who was reluctant to order immediate massive desegregation, died on

September 8, 1953, and Warren succeeded him. Warren persuaded all justices to subscribe to one opinion and to delay a ruling on the remedy. (Jackson had been disposed to write a separate concurring opinion and Reed to write a dissenting opinion.)

Warren wrote the unanimous court opinion, about ten pages long. He began by addressing the question of the intentions of the framers of the Fourteenth Amendment. He found the evidence inconclusive and noted that public education was just beginning. In view of the fact that the same Congress that approved the amendment also voted to fund segregated public schools in the District of Columbia, Warren's position on this question was at best disingenuous. A better argument would have been that the words in the amendment, not the framers' specific intentions, should be determinative.

He concluded that the segregated public schools in Kansas were tangibly equal or in the process of being tangibly equalized, but that the country could not go back to 1868 or 1896. Education is the foundation of good citizenship, and intangible factors are especially important for pupils in grade and high schools. He specifically cited the sociologist Kenneth Clark on the detrimental effect of segregated schools on colored children. He concluded his opinion on the constitutionality of segregated public schools with the judgment that racially separate facilities are inherently unequal—that is, irrational. That is where the opinion should have begun and rested. His citation of sociological date weakened rather than strengthened the basic argument.

In the companion case involving segregated public schools in the District of Columbia (*Bolling v. Sharpe*), Warren observed that there was no equal protection clause in the Fifth Amendment but thought the concept of due process closely related. He held that racial segregation was irrational and so denied blacks due process of law, adding that it would be unthinkable to allow segregation in the nation's capitol and disallow it in the states.

Brown I reserved questions about the remedy for decision the following year, 1955. Warren again wrote the unanimous court opinion (*Brown v. Board of Education II*). He held that the district courts supervising the integration of public schools should rely on principles of equity. The courts should require the defendants to make a prompt and reasonable start to comply with *Brown I*. To that end, courts could consider problems arising from the physical condition of the school plant, the school transportation system, personnel, and revision of school districts into compact units. District courts should enter orders and decrees to integrate segregated public schools with all deliberate speed.

Brown II left it up to the plaintiffs—that is, the NAACP—to pursue implementation of *Brown I*. The court gave no precise guidelines to the district courts. It could have imposed a time frame for complete integration. For example, it could have required a grade-by-grade yearly model or a grade-school-first model. By 1964, ten years after *Brown I*, less than 2 percent of formerly segregated school districts had achieved *any* desegregation. Southern white activists had used legal obstruction to block integration and promised defiance. But Congress passed the Civil Rights Act of 1964, one provision of which enabled the U.S. Department of Health, Education, and Welfare to cut off federal funds to segregated school districts. The department did so in 1969, and this broke the back of Southern white opposition to any integration. In short, money accomplished what *Brown II* declined to do by judicial fiat.

Another section of the Civil Rights Act of 1964 (Title II) barred racial segregation in public accommodations. Two 1964 cases tested the constitutionality of that title. In one case a motel in Atlanta, Georgia, refused to serve blacks. It was located near an interstate highway, and three-quarters of its patrons were transient travelers from out of state. The court unanimously upheld the judgment of a three-judge district court in favor of the title's prohibition as applied to the motel (*Heart of Atlanta Motel v. U.S.*). Clark wrote the court opinion. He cited the Gibbons decision and a long line of cases to show that Congress had plenary power to regulate interstate commerce and intrastate commerce that affects more than one state.

The companion case was *Katzenbach v. McClung*. McClung operated a small restaurant, Ollie's Barbeque, in Birmingham, Alabama. The restaurant was remote from any interstate highway and served only local customers. A three-judge district court had held that the act could not be applied to the restaurant, and Nicholas Katzenbach, the U.S. attorney general, appealed to the Supreme Court. The court unanimously reversed the district court and held that the act could be applied to Ollie's restaurant. Clark again wrote the majority opinion. Although most of the restaurant's customers were local, it purchased much of its food and supplies through interstate commerce, and so Congress could determine that segregation in the public facility would adversely affect interstate commerce. (Interestingly, McClung claimed that he would lose business if he served blacks, and so his serving them would *adversely* affect interstate commerce.)

Douglas and Goldberg each concurred separately in both decisions but argued further that Congress had the power to bar segregation in public accommodations under section 5 of the Fourteenth Amendment as well as under the commerce clause.

Criminal If the Brown case was the most notable of the Warren Court decisions in the 1950s, its decisions on criminal procedure in the states were the most notable in the 1960s. The first was in *Mapp v. Ohio.* An informant had told police in Cleveland, Ohio, that a bombing suspect and gambling equipment were in Dolly Mapp's house. Seven police officers forcibly entered her house and searched it. (The officers claimed that they had a warrant and that Dolly snatched it and tucked it into her bosom. In any event, no warrant or record of the warrant's existence was in evidence.) The officers did not find the suspect or the equipment, but they did find allegedly obscene material. Dolly was tried and convicted of possessing obscene literature, and the Ohio Supreme Court affirmed the conviction, concluding that the evidence, although unlawfully obtained, was admissible. Mapp's lawyers appealed the conviction on two grounds—namely, that the obscenity statute was unconstitutionally vague and that the police behavior violated due process of law—but did not argue that the due process clause requires exclusion of evidence obtained in violation of Fourth Amendment guarantees against unreasonable searches. An amicus brief by the American Civil Liberties Union (ACLU), however, did tepidly request that the court reexamine the Wolf decision on the applicability of the exclusionary rule to state criminal prosecutions.

The court by the narrowest margin ruled that the due process clause required the states to exclude evidence obtained in violation of Fourth Amendment guarantees. Clark wrote the plurality court opinion, and Brennan, Douglas, and Warren joined him. Clark argued that without the exclusionary rule the Fourth Amendment guarantees of privacy would be mere words and that other means to effectuate the guarantees (e.g., civil suits against the police violating the guarantees or prosecutors bringing criminal charges against such police) were futile. Black concurred on different grounds. Since he had in the Wolf decision agreed with the majority in the case that the due process clause did not require that the states follow the federal exclusionary rule, he had some explaining to do for reversing his position. He explained that the *combination* of the Fourth Amendment guarantees against unreasonable searches and the Fifth Amendment guarantee against compulsory self-incrimination mandated application of the exclusionary rule to the states.

Harlan dissented, and Frankfurter and Whittaker joined him. Harlan rejected the idea that the due process clause incorporated the Fourth Amendment as such and held that the clause protected only the principle of privacy, which he considered the core of the Fourth Amendment. Accordingly, he saw no reason to apply the exclusionary rule to state criminal prosecutions. Stewart simply opted out of deciding the exclusionary-rule question. He correctly pointed out that none of the parties' briefs in the case had addressed it. The decision was a surprise to the legal profession, but the ensuing negative reaction of conservative legal professionals and public officials was not. Many agreed with the observation of Cardozo in a New York Court of Appeals decision that the criminal should not go free because the constable blundered.

Two years later, in 1963, the court again faced the question of whether the due process clause required that the states provide counsel to an indigent defendant charged with a noncapital felony. As we have seen, the court in the 1942 Betts case held that, in the absence of special circumstances, the due process clause did not. In 1963 the court overruled *Betts* and held that the Sixth Amendment right to counsel, at least in felony cases, was fundamental to a fair trial and so binding on the states (*Gideon v. Wainwright*). Florida had charged Clarence Gideon with the felony of breaking and entering a poolroom with the intent to commit a crime. At his trial, Gideon, who was indigent, requested that the judge appoint a counsel for him, but the judge refused, and Gideon conducted his own defense. He was convicted and filed a habeas corpus petition against Wainwright, the prison warden, in the Florida Supreme Court. That court refused to grant the petition, and Gideon appealed to the U.S. Supreme Court *in forma pauperis* (i.e., as a petitioner too indigent to pay the court costs). The court accepted the case, appointed the future justice Abe Fortas to represent Gideon, and asked Fortas and Florida to address the question of whether the Betts decision should be overruled.

The Gideon decision was unanimous. Black, who had dissented in *Betts*, wrote the court opinion, and Douglas, Clark, and Harlan wrote separate concurring opinions. Harlan concurred only in the decision. He approved the Betts principle but thought that, since the court had since 1960 given only lip-service to it, it was best to set it aside in favor of an unqualified right to counsel in at least felony cases. The Burger Court later extended the right to counsel to misdemeanor cases that involved prison sentences (*Argensinger v. Hamlin*).

In 1964 the court recognized more rights of criminal suspects and defendants. One, the first, involved Winston Massiah, who was indicted for federal narcotics violations. He retained counsel, pled not guilty, and was released on bail. A codefendant, Jesse Colson, who was also released on bail, invited Massiah to discuss the case. Although Massiah did not know it, Colson had agreed to become a government agent and had a radio transmitter in his car, in which they met. The radio transmitter broadcast their conversation to a federal agent, and Massiah made incriminating statements. The statements were admitted into evidence at his trial, and he was convicted. Messiah then appealed to the Supreme Court, claiming that his Sixth Amendment right to counsel had been violated, and so the incriminating statements should not have been admitted into evidence (the exclusionary rule).

The court ruled for Massiah (*Massiah v. U.S.*). Stewart wrote the court opinion, and Black, Brennan, Douglas, Goldberg, and Warren joined him. Stewart held that once adversary judicial proceedings, whether by indictment or information, preliminary hearing, or arraignment, had begun, the Sixth Amendment guaranteed the defendant the right to the presence of counsel as a medium during police interrogation. Thus, once adversary judicial proceedings have begun, the government may not deliberately elicit statements from the defendant in the absence of counsel. Stewart was careful to point out that the government could use a government agent to elicit statements about other crimes of which the defendant was not formally accused. White, joined by Harlan and Clark, dissented. As the dissenters pointed out, Massiah was not in custody, nor was he being subjected to *police* interrogation.

The principle behind the Massiah decision is reasonable, but the facts of the case made it a poor instrument to endorse the principle. Massiah was freely talking to someone that he thought was his friend, and one confides things to a putative friend at one's own risk. Nonetheless, the Massiah principle did extend the right to counsel to the very beginning of the judicial process, and the principle would be involved in the question of government plants in prisons or jails, as we shall see when we consider the Burger Court. The Massiah decision did not touch the problem of custodial police interrogation *before* the beginning of the judicial process, nor did it give any guidance about what constitutes deliberate eliciting of statements from a defendant.

Another 1964 case, however, the third in time, did involve stationhouse interrogation. Danny Escobedo, who was suspected of having committed a Chicago murder, was taken by the police to the stationhouse and interrogated there. He repeatedly asked to speak to his retained lawyer, and the lawyer asked to speak with Escobedo when the lawyer arrived at the stationhouse. The police did not allow Escobedo and his lawyer to meet, nor did they advise

Escobedo that he had a right to remain silent. In response to a police accusation, Escobedo made incriminating statements that he was present at the time and place of the murder. He then confessed that he committed the murder, and the confession was used in the trial in which he was convicted of the murder. The Illinois Supreme Court upheld his conviction and admission of the signed confession, and he appealed to the U.S. Supreme Court.

By the narrowest margin, the court held the confession inadmissible and overturned his conviction (*Escobedo v. Illinois*). Goldberg wrote the court opinion, and Black, Brennan, Douglas, and Warren joined him. The decision rested on the suspect's Sixth Amendment right to counsel and so extended the reach of the Massiah decision from the courthouse to the stationhouse. But the opinion was less clear on what was the precise reason Escobedo had a right to counsel. Was it because he requested to see his retained lawyer? Was it because his lawyer asked to see him? Was it simply because he had become the police's prime suspect and the focus on him had shifted from the investigatory stage to the accusatorial stage? If the latter was the rationale, then many officials and conservative legal scholars were concerned that the decision would make meaningful legal interrogation of suspects virtually impossible. The four dissenters (Clark, Harlan, Stewart, and White) raised these questions. (Note that Stewart, who wrote the *Massiah* opinion, dissented in the Escobedo case.) Two years later the Miranda decision would basically make the Escobedo decision irrelevant.

One week before the Escobedo decision the court decided a case that paved the way for the Miranda decision. Malloy had pleaded guilty to participating in an unlawful gambling operation. A Connecticut trial court sentenced him to a year in prison, but he was released on probation for two years after serving ninety days of his prison term. A state inquiry into gambling and related crimes called him to testify during his probation. He refused to answer questions related to his earlier conviction and cited what he claimed was his Fifth Amendment privilege against self-incrimination. The inquiry held him in criminal contempt for refusing to answer the questions, and he was thereby imprisoned until he was willing to answer them. The Connecticut state courts denied his applications for a writ of habeas corpus against his warden, Hogan. Malloy then appealed his case to the U.S. Supreme Court.

The court ruled in Malloy's favor (*Malloy v. Hogan*). The decision involved two issues. The first concerned whether the due process clause of the Fourteenth Amendment, in the matter of self-incrimination, incorporated the full protection against the states that the Fifth Amendment afforded persons against the federal government. As we saw in connection with the Adamson case, the court majority of five in that case took the position that the due process clause did not incorporate the full protection that the Fifth Amendment provision afforded against self-incrimination, and Black and three others took the position of full incorporation. In the Malloy case Brennan wrote the court opinion fully incorporating the privilege against self-incrimination and so effectively overruled the Adamson decision, and Black, Douglas, Goldberg, Stewart, Warren, and White joined him. The time had come, Brennan said, to recognize that the American system of criminal prosecution is accusatory, not inquisitorial, and that the Fifth Amendment privilege is essential to maintaining justice in the system.

On this issue Clark and Harlan dissented. They argued that the due process clause required only the basic principles of justice, and that these principles should be derived from accepted notions of decency in a civilized society. Such discriminatory approach would allow the states a measure of flexibility in the matter of local law enforcement.

The second issue concerned the applicability of the incorporated privilege against self-incrimination to the facts of the case—that is, whether requiring Malloy to answer the questions asked would compel him to incriminate himself. On this issue Brennan spoke only for himself and four other justices (Black, Douglas, Goldberg, and Warren). White and Stewart dissented. They thought that Malloy was in no danger of incriminating himself if he answered the questions asked. (Clark and Harlan, having rejected the incorporation theory, had no need to pass on application of the theory to the facts of the case.)

The Warren Court in the 1950s faced many challenges to the stationhouse confessions used to convict defendants. Confessions were a shortcut for police and prosecutors. They were a shortcut for police because police would not have to do any further investigation for evidence. They were a shortcut for prosecutors because a signed confession assured conviction without further effort. Legal authorities over centuries held that coerced confessions should not be admissible as evidence for two reasons. Coercing confession was regarded as uncivilized behavior—that is, it violated rights implicit in the concept of ordered liberty, to express the reason in technical terms. Second, coerced confessions were unreliable, since suspects are likely to say anything to avoid physical abuse. The court wrestled with the problem of defining coercion or undue influence and applying the definition to the facts of a particular case. Physical abuse (e.g., rubber-hosing suspects) was clearly coercion, but what, if any, degree of psychological pressure should be considered undue influence on the free will of the suspect?

The Escobedo decision articulated a suspect's right to counsel in the stationhouse under certain circumstances, although the court was not clear, even to legal experts, about which circumstances were decisive. The Malloy decision established the right of a subject to remain silent when interrogated in an official inquiry. This was the traditional understanding of the privilege against self-incrimination—namely, that an individual could not be *legally* compelled to incriminate self. Dicta in the Malloy opinion indicated that the Fifth Amendment privilege should govern whether the confessions of suspects made during police interrogation were admissible in federal and state criminal prosecutions.

Two years later, in 1966, the court reviewed four state cases that involved the key question—namely, whether the police before stationhouse or other extrajudicial interrogation had an affirmative obligation to advise suspects about their rights to remain silent and consult with counsel. None of the cases involved police using violence or threatening to use violence. In the chief case, the Phoenix, Arizona, police in 1963 arrested Ernesto Miranda, a twenty-three-year-old indigent who had not finished the ninth grade, at his home on rape and kidnapping charges. He was immediately taken to a police station, and the victim identified him as the perpetrator. He was taken to an interrogation room and questioned. Although he at first professed his innocence of the crimes, he admitted his guilt and signed a confession. At the top of the statement was a typed paragraph declaring that the statement was made voluntarily and "with the full knowledge of my legal rights, understanding that any statement I make may be used against me." (An officer testified that he had read this paragraph to Miranda but apparently only after Miranda's oral confession.) At Miranda's trial the written confession was admitted into evidence, and he was convicted. The Arizona Supreme Court affirmed the conviction, and Miranda appealed to the U.S. Supreme Court.

By the narrowest margin, the court overturned Miranda's conviction (*Miranda v. Arizona*). Warren wrote the court opinion, and Black, Brennan, Douglas, and Fortas joined him. Warren held that a suspect in police custody has a right to remain silent and a right to have counsel during the interrogation if the suspect so wishes. To insure these rights, the police must, unless other procedural safeguards are devised, warn the suspect that he may remain silent, that anything he says can and will be used against him, that he has a right to counsel before and during the interrogation, and that if he cannot afford a counsel, one will be provided. Any evidence obtained by interrogation without these warnings is inadmissible at a federal or state criminal trial. Warren stressed the psychological pressure on the suspect under custodial police interrogation and cited police manuals instructing police how to use psychological pressure to induce a confession. Warren added that a suspect in custody could knowingly and freely waive his rights to silence and counsel, although he did not indicate how this was even possible under the psychologically compelling conditions he ascribed to police custody.

Clark dissented for himself. Harlan dissented for himself and Stewart and White, and White dissented for himself and Harlan and Stewart. The dissents stressed two points: that the decision stretched the rights to silence and counsel beyond traditional concepts and that the decision would cripple law enforcement. Prosecutors and police officials echoed those points, and much of the public was alarmed about what they perceived to be coddling criminals. The Miranda decision had no such consequences. Almost all empirical studies show that most criminal suspects in the years after the decision continued frequently to make incriminating statements, possibly to relieve conscience. (In about three-quarters of homicides, the victim and the perpetrator are relatives or friends.) Moreover, police quickly adjusted to the decision (e.g., they carried a printed card to read to persons they took into custody). Why then was there such a public outcry against *Miranda?* One explanation is that the Miranda decision coincided with a large rise of street crime, of which the public was keenly aware.

The Miranda decision left to the Burger Court to answer many questions. Aside from arrest, when is a suspect in custody? When is police conversation with a suspect in custody interrogation? How exactly do the police have to articulate the warnings? If a suspect has invoked his rights, can he reopen the subject or change his mind? Did the suspect in a custodial situation knowingly and willingly waive his rights? Has a suspect in custody "volunteered" an incriminating statement to the police after he has invoked his rights?

In the same year the court interpreted the privilege against self-incrimination not to apply to evidence considered to be nontestimonial. California convicted Schmerber of drunken driving on the basis of a blood sample taken without his permission, and the California Supreme Court affirmed. Schmerber appealed to the U.S. Supreme Court, and the court ruled that a blood sample was not testimony and so not protected by the privilege against self-incrimination (*Schmerber v. California*). Brennan wrote the court opinion, and Clark, Harlan, Stewart, and White joined him. (This may be the only time that Brennan joined those four justices to form a narrow majority in favor of the prosecution in a criminal case.) Four justices (Black, Douglas, Fortas, and Warren) vigorously dissented.

In 1967 the court radically revised the standard for what constitutes a search for which police need probable cause and usually a warrant. Charles Katz, a professional gambler, habitually transmitted gambling information from an enclosed public telephone booth in Los Angeles to Boston and Miami in violation of federal law. Federal agents, without obtaining a search warrant, attached an electronic recording device to the exterior of the booth and obtained evidence of Katz's activities. Katz was tried and convicted. The trial held that there had been no search within the meaning of the Fourth Amendment because there had been no physical penetration of the wall of the booth. Katz petitioned the court to review the case, and it did.

The court almost unanimously overturned the conviction and ruled that the evidence obtained from the recording device violated the Fourth Amendment (*Katz v. U.S.*). Stewart wrote the court opinion, and Brennan, Douglas, Fortas, Harlan, White, and Warren joined him. As we have seen, the Olmstead decision held that a federal government wiretap of Olmstead's property did not constitute a search and so did not need a warrant. Stewart rejected that standard and substituted one based on an individual's expectation of privacy. Where there is such an expectation, the Fourth Amendment requires that police obtain a warrant to search the constitutionally protected area in the absence of exigent circumstances. Katz had entered the glass telephone booth and closed the door. He could expect privacy regarding electronic ears overhearing his conversations, although he could not expect privacy regarding others seeing him or even reading his lips.

Three justices who joined Stewart's opinion also wrote concurring opinions. Harlan interpreted the new rule to have two requirements: an actual expectation of privacy and an expectation that society regards as objectively reasonable. The second requirement—namely, that an area is constitutionally protected from a government search only where there is an objectively *reasonable* expectation of privacy—became the crucial one in later cases, and the Burger Court especially would have to wrestle with it. White thought that there should be an exception from the warrant requirement in national security investigations, and Douglas, with Brennan, thought that there shouldn't.

Marshall did not participate, presumably because of his role as solicitor general in the preparation of the government's brief in the case.

Black was the sole dissenter. His objection was twofold. He argued first that the words of the Fourth Amendment preclude extending its protection beyond tangible things. The first clause of the amendment protected "persons, houses, papers, and effects" against unreasonable searches and seizures, and the second clause provided that no warrants shall issue but those "particularly describing the place to be searched and the person or things to be seized." In short, the framers of the amendment did not intend it to apply to eavesdropping, which is what an electronic recording device effectively does. Second, he did not believe that it was the proper role of the court to rewrite the amendment to bring it into harmony with the times. Legal historians uniformly agree with Black about the original understanding of the reach of the Fourth Amendment, but many would argue that words about the right of persons to be secure against unreasonable searches and seizures allows for a more extensive reach than the original understanding.

After *Katz*, Congress in 1968 enacted the Omnibus Crime Control and Safe Streets Act, which authorized federal and state wiretapping and electronic surveillance with a warrant in a broad range of cases. The act plays an important role in fighting crime, with up to 1,000 or more federal and state warrants issued each year.

In the following year, 1968, the court ruled on the constitutionality of police stopping and frisking a suspect. Detective police officer Martin McFadden, while on patrol in plain clothes in downtown Cleveland at around 2:30 P.M., noticed two men, John Terry and Richard Chilton, standing on a street corner. Officer McFadden saw one of the men leave the other and walk past some stores. The man paused for a moment and looked into the store window, then walked on a short distance, turned around and walked back, and rejoined his companion at the corner, and the two conferred briefly. Then the second man went through the same series of motions. Each of the two men alternately repeated this ritual five or six times. A third man approached the two, engaged them in conversation, and then walked away. Chilton and Terry resumed previous movements to and from the stores. After this had gone on for ten to twelve minutes, the two men walked off together. McFadden, suspicious that the men were casing the stores for a robbery, followed the two men and saw them stop in front of a store to talk to the third man. The officer approached the men, identified himself, and asked for their names. When the men mumbled in response, McFadden grabbed Terry, spun him around, patted down his clothing, and felt a pistol inside the overcoat pocket. McFadden removed a .38 caliber revolver from the overcoat pocket and another revolver from the overcoat pocket of Chilton. Terry and Chilton were convicted of the crime of carrying hidden weapons, and the Ohio Supreme Court upheld the convictions. The two appealed to the U.S. Supreme Court, contending that McFadden had violated their Fourth Amendment rights.

The court upheld the convictions (*Terry v. Ohio*). Warren wrote the court opinion, in which all the other justices except Douglas joined. Warren held that there was both a seizure of the men, however limited, and a search of their property, however limited, subject to protection of the Fourth Amendment. Nonetheless, under the particular circumstances, which Warren stressed, the actions of McFadden were reasonable. McFadden, an experienced officer, had reason to suspect that a crime was afoot and that, if it was, he was in physical danger if the suspects were armed. While Warren seems to suggest that the officer needed only reasonable suspicion rather than the probable cause required to issuance of a warrant, it is probably better to interpret Warren's position to mean that reasonable suspicion is sufficient probable cause for the seizure and search involved. Harlan and White wrote concurring opinions. Douglas was the sole dissenter. He would require strict probable cause to think that a crime has been committed, is being committed, or is about to be committed.

In the same year the court completed incorporation of the Sixth Amendment into the due process clause of the Fourteenth. Louisiana prosecuted Gary Duncan on a charge of simple battery, a misdemeanor punishable for up to two years' imprisonment and a $300 fine. He requested a jury trial, but the judge denied the request because the state constitution restricted trial by jury to capital crimes and those punishable by hard labor. He was convicted by the judge and sentenced to sixty days in jail and fined $150. The Louisiana Supreme Court affirmed the conviction, and Duncan appealed to the U.S. Supreme Court.

The court held that the Fourteenth Amendment incorporated the Sixth Amendment requirement of trial by jury in federal criminal prosecutions "bag and baggage" as a requirement on criminal prosecutions by the states (*Duncan v. Louisiana*). White wrote the court opinion, in which Black, Brennan, Douglas, Fortas, Marshall, and Warren joined. White stressed that the right to trial by jury had a long historical foundation. Black, joined by Douglas, wrote a concurring opinion to celebrate the triumph of his Adamson dissent. Fortas wrote a concurring opinion warning about imposing all the federal rules on the states. Harlan, joined by Stewart, dissented, arguing that due process required only that criminal trials be fundamentally fair and that there be no evidence that the magistrate unfairly convicted Duncan.

In 1969, its last year, the Warren Court decided a case involving the area of permissible search without a warrant in the course of a lawful felony arrest. Police officers arrested Ted Chimel in his home for burglary of a coin shop. They conducted a warrantless search of his entire home, garage, workshop, and furniture drawers. Some of the items discovered were used to convict him, and the California Supreme Court affirmed the conviction, holding that the search had been incidental to a lawful arrest.

The court held that the evidence was inadmissible and overturned the conviction (*Chimel v. California*). Stewart wrote the court opinion, and Brennan, Douglas, Harlan, Marshall, and Warren joined him. Stewart held that the police may without a warrant legally search the person lawfully arrested but only the area under the arrestee's immediate control—that is, the area that he might quickly reach. The reason that justifies such a search is so that the arrestee cannot obtain a weapon or destroy evidence. The reader can readily surmise that just how large the area under the arrestee's immediate control is would be contested in future cases.

Harlan wrote a separate concurring opinion. White, joined by Black, dissented. White saw no reason to impose on the police the need to obtain a warrant if they had solid probable cause to believe that there was evidence of the crime in the parts of the premises they searched. Moreover, White pointed out that Chimel's wife was in the house at the time of the arrest and could have removed the evidence, or a collaborator could have.

It is, of course, true that the police in this case had plenty of time to get a search warrant before they made the arrest. But it is also true that, not having done so, they would have needed to leave one officer on the premises while another took the arrestee to the station house and obtained a search warrant. In any case, the police officers in this case were operating on the basis of previous court decisions (*Harris v. U.S.* and *U.S. v. Rabinowitz*), decisions that the officers could not possibly know would be explicitly overruled in the instant case.

In the foregoing ten criminal-justice Supreme Court decisions from 1962 to 1969, the defendant won in all but two (*Schmerber* and *Terry*). Warren, Black, Brennan, Douglas, and Goldberg-Fortas voted together in all those cases except *Katz*. (Black voted for the government in *Katz*.) Harlan and White dissented in five of the eight pro-defendant decisions (not always in the same cases). Stewart dissented in four out of the eight pro-defendant decisions and Clark in four out of the five pro-defendant decisions in which they participated.

Apportionment In addition to the quasi-revolutionary decisions in the areas of racial segregation in public facilities and criminal procedure, the Warren Court rendered quasi-revolutionary decisions in the area of federal congressional and state legislative apportionments. Although states had in the nineteenth century regularly reapportioned congressional and legislative districts, many states were failing to reapportion them after 1900. Legislators were naturally reluctant to reapportion themselves out of existence, and the worse the existing apportionments became, the less likely that legislatures on their own initiative would do so. Reformers looked to the federal courts and invoked the equal protection clause of the Fourteenth Amendment.

Federal district courts in the 1950s dismissed the petitioners for what they described as lack of jurisdiction. That phrase in context meant that the petitioners were raising questions outside the competence of courts to resolve. In particular, the district courts relied on the 1946 case of *Colegrove v. Green.* William Colegrove, a professor of political science, and other qualified Illinois voters had sought an injunction against Green, the governor, to prevent holding the 1946 congressional elections in the existing districts, some of which Colegrove claimed were grossly overrepresented, others grossly underrepresented, and many not compact. A three-judge district court panel dismissed the suit, and Colegrove appealed to the Supreme Court.

Only seven justices participated in the court decision. Stone had died, and Jackson was the U.S. prosecutor at the Nuremberg war-crimes trials. The court by the narrowest margin affirmed the dismissal, but only two other members (Burton and Reed) subscribed to the plurality court opinion of Frankfurter. Frankfurter held that the federal courts lacked jurisdiction because the issue was a political question and that the remedy of injunction would result in statewide congressional elections, which would be worse than the existence of unequal districts. Rutledge concurred only in the result, arguing that the shortness of time until the 1946 elections made it almost impossible to devise a fitting equitable remedy. Black, joined by Douglas and Murphy, dissented. Black argued that the unequal districts deprived voters of the equal protection of the laws and that Article I guaranteed the right to vote in congressional elections.

In this context a case involving legislative districting came to the Warren

Court. Baker and other plaintiffs from Knoxville, Nashville, and Memphis sought under the Civil Rights Act of 1875 an injunction against Joseph Carr, the secretary of state of Tennessee, holding legislative elections under the existing apportionment. They claimed that the unrevised 1901 legislative apportionment debased their votes and so deprived them of the equal protection of the laws. A three-judge district court dismissed the suit, and the plaintiffs appealed to the Supreme Court.

The court held oral arguments twice before deciding the case in 1962. There were six opinions taking up 163 pages in the official reports, Frankfurter's alone taking up sixty-four pages. The court ruled in favor of the plaintiffs (*Baker v. Carr*). Brennan wrote the masterfully crafted court opinion, and Black, Clark, Douglas, Stewart, and Warren joined him. Brennan's opinion decided only the threshold questions—namely, that the plaintiffs had standing—that is, a tangible interest; that the federal courts had jurisdiction to hear the case—that is, that the case dealt with a constitutional question; and that the case was justiciable—that is, that the case was amenable to judicial standards and remedies. The last threshold question was the difficult one because of the political-question doctrine. Brennan disposed of that doctrine by restricting it to cases involving issues that are by the text of the Constitution committed to a coordinate branch of the *federal* government, and he interpreted the clause guaranteeing to each state a republican form of government such a case. The instant case potentially involved a conflict with a state government but none with a political branch of the federal government.

Brennan decided nothing about the merits of the case or equitable remedies if the plaintiffs prevailed on the merits. He, Black, Douglas, and Warren would presumably have supported the one-person, one-vote rule, as they later did, but he didn't have a fifth vote. Whittaker's nonparticipation left only eight voting justices. Frankfurter and Harlan dissented, and two concurring justices indicated that they were unwilling to subscribe to the one-person, one-vote rule. Clark was willing only to condemn what he called a crazy-quilt apportionment without any rational basis, and Stewart stressed that the decision settled only threshold questions. Douglas also wrote a concurring opinion that indicated his view that the case involved voting rights, which have long been under the protection of the federal courts.

Frankfurter wrote a long dissenting opinion, his last before his resignation in August, in effect his swansong, and Harlan joined it. He repeated his views in the Colegrove decision: that the courts should not get into conflicts between political forces and that the issue was not the right to vote but the weight of the right to vote, a matter of political philosophy. Harlan, joined by Frankfurter, also dissented. Harlan went to the merits of the question and held that, even if the courts had jurisdiction, there was no constitutional requirement that state legislatures be structured so as to reflect the mathematical equality of each voter. In an appendix he indicated ways in which geographical and economic factors could be relevant to representation.

Officials favored by existing legislative apportionments and conservative legal scholars condemned the decision as judicial usurpation and contrary to states' rights. On the other hand, disfavored politicians and liberal legal scholars endorsed the decision. In view of the longstanding stalemate on reapportionment in most states, the public generally supported the decision. For the moment, the political opposition was relatively mute, but not for long.

The court in 1964 turned its attention to congressional districting and the failure of states to reapportion the districts after the decennial census. Wesberry and other qualified voters in one of Georgia's congressional districts whose population was twice or thrice larger than that of some other districts challenged the apportionment of the districts. They claimed that the failure of Georgia's legislature to revise congressional districts according to the decennial census had debased their vote and sued in a federal district court to have the present apportionment declared unconstitutional and the governor, Sanders, and other officials enjoined from conducting elections under it. The three-judge district court dismissed the complaint for want of jurisdiction, basically relying on *Colegrove v. Green*. Wesberry appealed to the Supreme Court.

Article I, section 2 provides that "the House of Representatives shall be composed of members chosen every second year by the people of the several states." Section 2 of the Fourteenth Amendment provides that "representatives shall be apportioned among the several states according to their respective numbers," but this did not in any way suggest how representatives should be apportioned *within* the states having more than one representative or even that they should be in separate districts. Beginning in 1929 Congress dropped the requirement that the congressional districts created by state legislatures should be compact, contiguous, and equal in population.

The court ruled in favor of Wesberry, holding both that the federal courts have jurisdiction and that the Constitution required representation by equal numbers of people (*Wesberry v. Sanders*). Since Goldberg had replaced Frankfurter and White had replaced Whittaker, this result was never in doubt. Black wrote the court opinion, and Brennan, Douglas, Goldberg, Stewart, Warren, and White joined him. Black dispensed summarily with the political-question problem. The right to vote, he said, is simply too important to be stripped of judicial protection. On the merits, he argued that the word *people* in Article I meant that the article commanded that one man's vote in a congressional election should be worth as much as another's as much as practicable. Black admitted that it might not be possible to apportion congressional districts with mathematical precision.

Harlan in dissent pointed out that Article I specified that the people chose representatives to distinguish the mode of electing representatives from the mode of electing senators—namely, by state legislatures. Moreover, Congress had since 1929 not required that congressional districts be equal in population, and the decision thus was in conflict with a political branch of the *federal* government. Clark concurred in the court's judgment that federal courts had jurisdiction but dissented from the holding that congressional districts should be as equal in population as practicable.

Five years later, in 1969, the court narrowed the level of permissible population deviations permissible under the Wesberry standard. A federal district court had rejected Missouri's 1967 congressional redistricting. That redistricting resulted in population disparities ranging from 3.13 percent above to 2.83 percent below the statewide mean, based on the 1960 census. The Supreme Court affirmed (*Kirkpatrick v. Preisler*). Brennan wrote the court opinion, and Black, Douglas, Marshall, and Warren joined him. Brennan insisted that the Wesberry requirement that congressional districts be as nearly equal as practicable requires a state to make a good-faith effort to achieve precise mathematical equality and that a state must justify each variance, no matter how small. Thus mathematically precise equality became the constitutionally mandated norm for congressional districting.

Fortas concurred in the result but objected to a quest for mathematical precision based on inexact and obsolete census data. Harlan and White wrote separate dissents. They additionally decried judicial intrusion on legislative practical judgments and the minimizing of the constraints of local geography. Stewart also dissented.

After the 1962 decision in *Baker v. Carr*, many suits were instituted in district courts against state legislative apportionments. Cases involving apportionments in six states (Alabama, Colorado, Delaware, Maryland, New York, and Virginia) had by 1964 wended their way to the Supreme Court. In each case a district court had invalidated an existing apportionment. The Supreme Court, not unexpectedly, affirmed the district court decisions, but the breadth of the court decisions surprised legal scholars and political officeholders (*Reynolds v. Sims*).

The leading decision concerned the Alabama apportionment. Alabama had not reapportioned legislative districts since after the 1900 decennial census. As a result, the ratios between the most populous district and the least populous district were 41 to 1 in the state's senate and 16 to 1 in the state's lower house. Warren wrote the court opinion, and Black, Brennan, Douglas, Goldberg, and White joined him. Clark and Stewart concurred only in the judgment. Warren declared in sweeping terms that legislative districts should be substantially equal in population and as nearly equal in population as practicable. This principle applied to both the upper and lower houses of the state legislature. Warren rejected the analogy of unequal popular representation in the U.S. Senate to unequal popular and weighted representation of counties in state senates, since states, unlike counties, are legally recognized units in the federal union. Harlan alone dissented in this case and also dissented in the other five cases in which state legislative apportionments were challenged. He reiterated his view that historical, geographical, and economic factors could make weighted voting in the makeup of the state legislature rational and so compatible with the equal protection of the laws and that courts should not intrude into political processes.

The Reynolds decision set forth a comprehensive principle that reached beyond the Alabama apportionment. The decision in the companion case from Colorado indicated its breadth. Colorado had by the process of initiative and referendum in 1962 approved weighted voting in the upper house of the state legislature. In the referendum, every county voted for the plan. Warren wrote the court opinion invalidating it (*Lucas v. Forty-Fourth General Assembly of Colorado*), and the same justices who joined his Reynolds opinion joined the Lucas opinion. He held that popular majorities could not debase the right of individuals to cast an equally weighted vote.

Harlan dissented for the same reasons he gave against the Reynolds decision. In the Lucas case Stewart, joined by Clark, also dissented. They held that the equal protection clause allows the states considerable leeway to design legislative constituencies, provided that the districts are rational on the basis of the state's composition and needs and that they do not systematically prevent ultimate majority rule.

After these decisions Senator Everett Dirksen of Illinois proposed a constitutional amendment allowing one house of a state legislature to be apportioned on the basis of factors other than equal population. Using the second and untried method of amending the Constitution in Article V, many state legislatures petitioned Congress to call a convention to consider such an amendment. (One of the questions about an Article V convention was whether it would be open to consider other amendments.) The number of petitioning state legislatures came close to the required two-thirds, but many legislatures had by the early 1970s been reapportioned, and the newly constituted legislatures were indisposed to change the result.

Despite the misgivings of Frankfurter and Harlan and later of Harlan alone, the district courts achieved realignment of legislative districts proportionate to the number of voters relatively effectively and rapidly. Within a period of two years the map of legislative districts had changed dramatically in almost all states. There was still the problem of how much deviation from the norm of equal population was permissible, and the Berger Court would wrestle with it. More importantly, there remains the problem of gerrymandering—that is, manipulating the constituencies of equally populated districts to party advantage by concentrating opposition votes in a minority of districts. It is also important to note that the only way to assure absolutely equal weight to all voters is to have representatives elected in multi-member districts by proportional representation.

Welfare The court, in three cases argued and reargued before it, invalidated a one-year residency requirement for welfare eligibility (*Shapiro v. Thompson*). Welfare laws in Connecticut, Pennsylvania, and the District of Columbia required the residency. The leading case concerned Vivian Thompson, a nineteen-year-old unwed mother of one child and pregnant with another. She had moved in June 1966 from Dorchester, Massachusetts, to Hartford, Connecticut, to live with her mother. She moved to her own apartment in August when her mother could no longer support her and her infant son and applied for welfare assistance, which was denied because of the residency requirement. A three-judge district court struck down the requirement, as did district courts in the other two cases, and the respective governments appealed to the U.S. Supreme Court.

Brennan wrote the court opinion, and Douglas, Fortas, Marshall, Stewart, and White joined him. Brennan agreed with the district courts that the freedom to travel was among the fundamental personal liberties guaranteed by the Fourteenth Amendment against infringement and that the residency requirement lacked a compelling public interest to justify it in relation to the equal protection clause. Warren, joined by Black, dissented, arguing that the residency requirement was not a restriction on the right to travel. Harlan dissented, arguing against declaring the right to travel so fundamental that a compelling public interest was needed to justify it. Whatever the merits of Brennan's linking the residency requirement to the right to travel and calling for a compelling public interest to justify the requirement, there is no doubt that the decision imposed fiscal costs on local governments. The decision served as a precedent for striking down residency requirements for voting.

Privacy The court in 1965 struck down a Connecticut statute that prohibited the use of contraceptives as applied to married couples and advising or prescribing their use except for medicinal purposes (*Griswold v. Connecticut*). Estelle Griswold, executive director of the Planned Parenthood association in the state, was convicted of violating the statute, and a higher state court upheld the conviction.

Douglas wrote the court opinion, and Brennan, Clark, Goldberg, and White joined him. Douglas held that the law operated directly on a fundamental right—namely, the intimate relation of husband and wife and a physician's role in one aspect of that relation. Although none of the Bill of Rights specifically guarantees this right of privacy, various penumbras, said Douglas, emanate from the amendments, and these penumbras support the right to privacy of married couples. Goldberg, joined by Brennan and Warren, although joining the court opinion, concurred separately to stress the importance of the Ninth Amendment to show that the Fourteenth Amendment guarantees more than the rights enumerated in the first eight amendments. Harlan, concurring separately only in the judgment, rejected yet again the incorporation theory and relied on the basic values implicit in the concept of ordered liberty. White also concurred separately only in the judgment, stressing the requirement of a compelling public interest to justify infringement on fundamental rights. Black and Stewart dissented separately and concurred in each other's dissent. Black objected to stretching the due process clause beyond incorporating the first eight amendments and to judges further determining which rights are fundamental. Stewart objected to judges determining the wisdom of legislation, although he thought the Connecticut law silly.

The Connecticut statute as applied to married couples was indeed a silly law, and there was no indication that the law so applied was being enforced or could be enforced. The statute as applied to unmarried persons, however, might have a rational purpose, and the Berger Court would consider that question. Moreover, the Griswold decision, by establishing a constitutionally protected right to privacy in the intimate relationship of married couples, paved the way for the landmark decision of *Roe v. Wade*, which invoked the right to privacy as the basis for invalidating state laws prohibiting abortions.

Religion   The Warren Court decided several important cases involving the religious establishment and religious exercise clauses. Four cases from three states (Maryland, Massachusetts, and Pennsylvania) concerned the so-called Sunday laws, which forbade many or most work or sales on Sundays. Entrepreneurs and others in some of the cases challenged the laws as an establishment of religion because the laws officially established the Christian holy day as the day of rest. In 1961 the court held that the Sunday laws at issue in the three states were not religious establishments (*McGowan v. Maryland*). Warren wrote the court opinion, and all the justices except Douglas (Black, Brennan, Clark, Frankfurter, Harlan, Stewart, and Whittaker) joined him. Warren conceded that the laws were originally designed to establish the Christian day of rest but argued that the laws were currently designed to establish salutary conditions of employment and competition and to establish a day of rest and recreation. Moreover, the laws' purpose was not only to provide a day of no work but also to set a common day on which members of the family and the community have the opportunity to spend and enjoy together, and it would be unrealistic to require a state to choose a common day of rest other than the one most persons would prefer. Douglas, dissenting, thought the laws religious establishments and put a penalty on those who observed Saturday rather than Sunday as their holy day.

The court was more divided on the question of whether the laws should exempt Sabbatarian entrepreneurs from the Sunday closing laws. In one of the cases the court held that the religious exercise clause did not require that Sunday laws exempt entrepreneurs who close on another day of the week for religious reasons—principally Orthodox Jews, who observe Saturday as their religious holy day (*Braunfeld v. Brown* and *Gallagher v. Crown Kosher Supermarket*). Warren again wrote the court opinion, and Black, Clark, Frankfurter, Harlan, and Whittaker joined him. Warren noted that the laws did not make any religious practice unlawful but simply regulated a secular activity and made the practice of Sabbatarian religious beliefs more expensive. He was unwilling to strike down legislation that imposed only an indirect burden on the exercise of religion without the most critical scrutiny. To the objection of Sabbatarians that the state could achieve the secular goals of Sunday laws with exemptions for conscientious Sabbatarians, Warren raised practical problems regarding enforcement and the potential competitive advantage that would be accorded Sabbatarian entrepreneurs, but, more importantly, he stressed the importance of a *common* day of rest.

Douglas, of course, dissented in all four cases, but Brennan and Stewart also dissented separately in the two cases involving the burden of Sunday closings without exemptions for conscientious Sabbatarians. Brennan admitted the practical difficulties if Sabbatarian entrepreneurs were exempted from Sunday closings and the potential competitive advantage to them, but did not think that the mere convenience of having everyone rest on the same day justified making some religious practices more expensive. The free exercise of religion is a preferred freedom and can be infringed, even indirectly, only to prevent crime or substantive evils. Stewart echoed those views, calling the interest in a common day of rest the interest of enforced Sunday togetherness. The problem of what the religious exercise clause requires of public laws indirectly affecting religious minorities would weigh on the court for more than the next three decades.

In fact, two years later, in 1963, the court had to decide a kindred case involving a government regulation and a petitioner claiming that the regulation indirectly burdened her religious exercise contrary to the guarantee of the First Amendment. Adell Sherbert, a Seventh-Day Adventist, would not accept work on Saturday, a day on which her religion prohibited labor, and she failed to find employment involving no work on Saturday. She then applied for unemployment compensation, but the South Carolina unemployment compensation commission denied the application because she failed to accept suitable work—that is, work on Saturdays. The South Carolina Supreme Court upheld the commission, and Sherbert appealed to the U.S. Supreme Court. Sherbert claimed that the denial of benefits penalized her if she followed her religious beliefs, and the state argued that granting Sherbert benefits would open the workers' fund to fraud.

The court ruled for Sherbert (*Sherbert v. Verner*). Brennan wrote the court opinion, and Black, Clark, Douglas, Goldberg, Stewart, and Warren joined him. Brennan held that the state needed to have a compelling public interest in order to deny her benefits and that none of the state's interests were such. The state's claim of a public interest in preventing fraudulent access to the workers' fund came down to mere administrative convenience and so was not a compelling public interest. Stewart wrote a separate concurring opinion to insist that the Sherbert decision was inconsistent with the Braunfeld decision. Harlan, joined by White, thought that the state regulation was rational and that the decision gave applicants unwilling to work on Saturdays for religious reasons a standing superior to others unwilling to work on Saturdays for other reasons. Note that religious exemption cases involve two issues: the standard to apply (compelling public interest or mere rationality) and application of the standard to the facts of the case.

The court decided two important cases regarding the public schools and the religious establishment clause. The New York State Board of Regents had in 1951 recommended that the following prayer be recited at the beginning of each school day: "Almighty God, we acknowledge our dependence upon Thee, and we beg Thy blessings upon us, our parents, our teachers, and our country." The North Hempstead board of education adopted the regents' prayer in 1958, and Engel and four other local taxpayers and parents sought to enjoin recitation of the prayer as a violation of the religious establishment clause. The plaintiffs lost in the trial court, and the New York Court of Appeals affirmed. The plaintiffs then appealed to the U.S. Supreme Court. Many amicus briefs, both for and against the regents' prayer, were filed with the court.

The court in 1962 struck down the Regents' prayer (*Engel v. Vitale*). Black wrote the court opinion, and Brennan, Clark, Frankfurter, Harlan, and Warren joined him. Government officials composed the prayer as part of a governmental program to further religious beliefs. Moreover, laws officially prescribing a particular form of religious worship indirectly coerce religious minorities to participate. A significant footnote dissociated the religious exercise of the New York program from patriotic or ceremonial occasions in which school pupils are officially encouraged to recite historical documents or sing traditional anthems that contain the composer's profession of religious faith. Douglas concurred separately, arguing that governments may not finance a religious exercise, including prayers at the opening of court or congressional sessions. White did not participate. The sole dissent was that of Stewart, in whose view the local school board had merely provided an opportunity for willing pupils to join in a brief prayer at the beginning of the school day, and so there was no establishment of an official religion.

The decision stirred up a storm of criticism. Indeed, several amendments to overrule the decision were introduced into Congress. But it is difficult to see how the court could have ruled otherwise. The prayer professed belief in the existence of God, his providence over human persons and affairs, and the relevance of prayer to him. There was no doubt that the prayer was a religious exercise and that public authorities were sponsoring it. While no one was forced to participate, a nonparticipating student had to petition to be absent from recitation of the prayer or remain noticeably silent while others prayed.

The next year, 1963, two cases before the court involved Bible reading, and one case recitation of the Lord's Prayer, in public schools. In one case a Pennsylvania law required that ten verses of the Hebrew Bible be read in classrooms at the opening of each school day. The Schempps were a family sponsored by the American Civil Liberties Union to bring suit against the practice in Abington Township. A three-judge district court struck down the Pennsylvania statute, and the township appealed to the Supreme Court. In the other case, an ordinance of Baltimore, Maryland, required the reading without comment of a chapter of the Bible and/or the recitation of the Lord's Prayer at the opening exercises of the city's schools. Madalyn Murray and her son William, professed atheists, brought suit in state courts in enjoin the practice. The Maryland Court of Appeals refused to hold the Baltimore practice unconstitutional, and the Murrays petitioned to the U.S. Supreme Court. Many amicus briefs supporting and opposing the religious practices were filed.

The court ruled in favor of the Schempps and the Murrays (*Abington School District v. Schempp*). Clark wrote the court opinion, and all the justices but Stewart (Black, Douglas, Brennan, Goldberg, Harlan, White, and Warren) joined him. Clark proposed a neutrality test for government involvement with religion, the first time a court opinion had attempted to distinguish between acceptable and unacceptable accommodations to religious activities and public institutions. He held that there must be a secular legislative purpose and a primary effect that neither advances nor inhibits religion in order for a governmental action to withstand the strictures of the establishment clause. Applying this two-pronged test, he found that the Bible reading and recitation of the Lord's Prayer were religious exercises—that is, their purpose was religious, and their primary effect advanced religion. The exercises might have the secular effect of promoting good moral behavior (e.g., respecting others), but that effect was secondary—that is, the result of the primary religious effect. This test, supplemented by a third prong regarding excessive entanglement a few years later, would become the standard test in establishment cases.

Douglas wrote a concurring opinion to argue in favor of his view that the establishment clause prohibited any public expenditure for religious activity. Goldberg, joined by Harlan, concurred separately, arguing that the court was not disallowing all connection between government and religion and specifically indicating support for military chaplaincies. The most notable concurring opinion was Brennan's, which ran seventy-four pages. Brennan gave a nuanced historical analysis of the relations between government and religion, especially regarding the public schools. Stewart, the sole dissenter, thought that the government programs at issue might provide the opportunity of religious exercises for those who so wished and without coercion on those not so wishing, and he would have remanded the cases to the trial courts to determine whether that was the case.

Obscenity Prosecutions of persons selling obscene material had been common in the United States since colonial times. In 1957 the Warren Court passed on the constitutionality of such prosecutions in a pair of cases. One involved a federal prosecution and the other a state prosecution. The court upheld both prosecutions (*Roth v. U.S.; Alberts v. California*). Brennan wrote the court opinion, and Frankfurter, Burton, Clark, Warren, and Whittaker joined him. Brennan held that the First Amendment did not protect obscene material. Although he did not give a precise test, he did say that a work would be considered obscene only if the dominant theme of the material, taken as a whole and according to contemporary community standards, appealed to the prurient interest of the average person. Harlan concurred in the judgment in the Alberts case but not in the judgment in the Roth case. Black and Douglas dissented. Subsequent courts would have to specify further the definition of obscenity, but it became clearer and clearer that the attempt to define obscenity was an attempt to define the indefinable. Eventually the focus of obscenity prosecutions would be on pornography, especially child pornography.

Press The court decided a major case involving freedom of the press. L. B. Sullivan, an elected commissioner of Montgomery, Alabama, whose duties included supervision of the police department, brought a civil libel suit against the *New York Times* and four black clergymen in a local court. He alleged that a full-page advertisement in the *New York Times* contained libelous statements and that the names of the clergymen were in it. The advertisement described alleged Montgomery police maltreatment of students protesting against racial segregation and contained minor factual errors. The trial judge in the case instructed the jury that, if the statements about the Montgomery police were false, they were libelous per se—that is, the plaintiff did not have to prove monetary loss or malice on the part of the defendants. The jury returned a verdict against the defendants and awarded the plaintiff $500,000 damages from each defendant. The Alabama Supreme Court affirmed the verdict and the damages awarded. The defendants appealed to the U.S. Supreme Court.

The court in 1964 unanimously overturned the verdicts against the defendants (*New York Times Co. v. Sullivan*). Brennan wrote the court opinion, and Clark, Harlan, Stewart, White, and Warren joined him without qualification. Brennan held that the First Amendment guarantee of freedom of the press requires a federal rule that prohibits a public official from recovering damages for a defamatory falsehood relating to his official conduct unless the official proves that that the statement was made with actual malice—that is, with knowledge that it was false or with reckless disregard of whether it was true or false. Black, Douglas, and Goldberg qualified their concurrence with an assertion of their view that citizens have an absolute, unconditional privilege to criticize official conduct, and Goldberg, with Douglas, added that even the imposition of newspaper liability for malicious defamation of private individuals would abridge freedom of the press.

The *New York Times* decision limited the liability of newspapers for alleged defamatory statements about public officials. Later decisions extended that limitation to all public figures (e.g., movie stars and athletes) but allowed private individuals to sue newspapers for defamatory statements, even regarding matters of public concern.

Symbolic Speech When U.S. participation in the war in South Vietnam escalated after 1964, there were frequent antiwar demonstrations, especially by young men liable to be drafted. In one demonstration David O'Brien and three companions in 1966 burned their Selective Service registration cards on the steps of a Boston federal courthouse to protest participation in the war. O'Brien was convicted of knowingly destroying the draft card; the court of appeals reversed, holding that the law criminalizing destruction of a draft card violated the free speech clause of the First Amendment, but that O'Brien could be sentenced to prison for violating a regulation that required registrants to possess their draft cards. The government appealed to the Supreme Court.

The court vacated the judgment of the court of appeals and reinstated the judgment and sentence of the district court (*U.S. v. O'Brien*). Warren wrote the court opinion, and Black, Brennan, Fortas, Harlan, Stewart, and White joined him. Warren set down the test for determining whether a government regulation was justified in cases involving symbolic speech. The test required that the government have an important or substantial interest unrelated to the suppression of free speech and that the restriction on expression be no greater than necessary in furthering that interest. The statute, he argued, met those requirements. Congress has power to raise and support armies. The registration card served governmental interests in connection with raising and supporting armies, such as being proof of registration and communication between the registrant and the local board. Those interests are unrelated to the suppression of free expression. No alternate means would secure the smooth running of the Selective Service system. Harlan concurred separately. Douglas dissented on the grounds that conscription is impermissible in the absence of a congressional declaration of war. Marshall did not participate. The significance of the case is that the court held that some external action is the functional equivalent of speech; future courts would have to consider cases in which defendants would claim that prohibited actions (e.g., burning the flag) were symbolic speech.

$\backsim$ 10 $\backsim$

THE BURGER COURT

(1969–86)

The Justices

Warren Burger After President Johnson, on October 4, 1968, withdrew the nomination of Fortas to be chief justice, the president made no new nomination and left the appointment to his successor, President Nixon. Nixon nominated Warren Burger to the post on May 21, 1969, and the Senate confirmed him on June 9. Burger, a Republican and a Protestant, was born on September 17, 1907, in St. Paul, Minnesota. His father, Charles, was a rail cargo inspector and traveling salesman. Burger attended college at the University of Minnesota for two years (1925–27) and graduated from Mitchell College of Law in 1931. He was admitted to the Minnesota bar in the same year and engaged in private practice for twenty-two years (1931–53). He was an assistant U.S attorney general for three years (1953–56) and the judge on a U.S. court of appeals for thirteen years (1956–69). He resigned from the court on September 26, 1986, and died on July 25, 1995.

Harry Blackmun When Fortas resigned on May 4, 1969, Nixon successively nominated two men to the court, Clement Haynesworth and G. Harrold Carswell, but the Senate rejected both. Nixon then nominated Harry Blackmun on April 14, 1970, and the Senate confirmed Blackmun on May 12. Blackmun, a Republican and a Methodist, was born on November 12, 1908, in Nashville,

Illinois. He grew up in St. Paul, Minnesota, where his father, Corwin, was a fruit wholesaler, bank official, and insurance salesman. Blackmun graduated from Harvard College in 1929 and Harvard Law School in 1932. He was admitted to the Minnesota bar in the same year. He was resident counsel of the Mayo Clinic for ten years (1950–59) and a judge on a U.S. court of appeals for eleven years (1959–70). He resigned from the court on August 3, 1994, and died on March 4, 1999.

Lewis Powell Black resigned on September 17, 1971, and Nixon nominated Lewis Powell to the court on October 21; the Senate confirmed Powell on December 6. Powell, a Democrat, a Presbyterian, and a descendant of distinguished Virginia families, was born on September 19, 1907, in Suffolk, Virginia. His father, Lewis, was the managerial employee of a furniture company. Powell graduated from college at Washington and Lee University and from the same university's law school in 1931. He was admitted to the Virginia bar in that year and received a master's of law degree from Harvard Law School in 1932.

He engaged in private practice for thirty-nine years (1932–71). He held the presidencies of three legal associations: the American Bar Association (1964–65), the American College of Trial Lawyers (1969–70), and the American Bar Foundation (1969–71). He served on the Virginia State Board of Education and the Richmond school board, of which he was the chairman from 1952 to 1961 and responsible for racially integrating the city's public schools. He resigned from the court on June 26, 1987, and died on August 25, 1998.

William Rehnquist Harlan II resigned on September 23, 1971, and Nixon nominated William Rehnquist to the court on October 21, 1970; the Senate confirmed Rehnquist on December 10. Rehnquist, a Republican and a Lutheran, was born on October 1, 1924, in Milwaukee, Wisconsin. His father was a paper salesman. Rehnquist was educated in the Milwaukee public schools, graduated from college at Stanford University in 1948, received one master's degree in political science from Stanford in 1949 and another from Harvard University in 1950, and graduated from Stanford Law School in 1951. He clerked for Justice Jackson in the 1952 and 1953 court terms. He engaged in private practice in Phoenix, Arizona, for sixteen years (1953–69). He was a special state prosecutor in 1958 and an assistant U.S. attorney general for two years (1969–71).

John Paul Stevens Douglas resigned on November 12, 1975, and President Ford nominated John Paul Stevens to the court on November 28; the Senate confirmed Stevens on December 17. Stevens, a Republican, a Baptist, and the member of a prominent local family, was born on April 20, 1920, in Chicago, Illinois. He graduated from the University of Chicago in 1941 and served in the navy during World War II from 1942 to1945. He was twice married. He graduated from Northwestern University Law School in 1947 and was admitted to the Illinois bar in the same year. He was a law clerk for Justice Rutledge for one year (1947–48). He engaged in private practice for twenty years, from 1948 to 1950 and from 1952 to 1970. In between, in 1951, he was associate counsel to a subcommittee of the U.S. House of Representatives. He was a judge on a U.S. court of appeals for five years (1970–75). He resigned from the court on June 30, 2010.

Sandra Day O'Connor Stewart resigned on July 3, 1981, and President Reagan nominated Sandra Day O'Connor to the court on July 7; the Senate confirmed her on September 21. O'Connor, a Republican and a Protestant, was born on March 26, 1930, in El Paso, Texas. Her father, Harry, was a wealthy rancher. She attended a convent school and graduated from college and law school at Stanford University in 1952. Practicing in Arizona, she was deputy county attorney (1952–53), an assistant state attorney general (1965–69), a state senator (1969–75), a state trial judge (1975–79), and an intermediate appellate state judge (1979–81). On July 1, 2005, she tendered her resignation, to be effective on the confirmation of her successor.

Summary Republican presidents Nixon, Ford, and Reagan appointed all of these justices, and all except Powell were Republicans. All were Protestants. One (O'Connor) was the first woman appointed to the court. The fathers of all the appointees were middle-class employees or wealthy, and Powell and Stevens came from prominent families. Only one (Burger) was not a college graduate, although he attended college for two years. Rehnquist and O'Connor graduated from college at Stanford, Blackmun from Harvard, and Stevens from the University of Chicago. Rehnquist had master's degrees from Stanford and Harvard. All graduated from law school; two (Rehnquist and O'Connor) graduated from Stanford Law School and one (Blackmun) from Harvard Law School, and one (Powell) had a master's degree from Harvard Law School. All but Blackmun had executive governmental experience, all but Powell and Rehnquist judicial experience, and only one (O'Connor) legislative experience.

Leading Decisions

Regime The Burger court decided a number of important cases regarding regime principles. The first (*Oregon v. Mitchell*) involved the constitutional right of eighteen-year-olds to vote in national, state, and local elections. Supreme Court decisions rarely provoke an amendment to the Constitution, and never has an amendment followed a decision so swiftly as in *Mitchell*. Congress in 1970 amended the 1965 Voting Rights Act to lower the voting age for participating in all elections. Article I, section 4 specified that the legislature of each state shall prescribe the time, manner, and place of holding elections, but that Congress may alter such regulations. Four justices (Brennan, Douglas, Marshall, and White) thought that this provision gave Congress power to regulate the age of voters in federal elections and that the enforcement provisions of the Fourteenth and Fifteenth amendments (sections 5 and 2, respectively) gave Congress power to regulate the age of voters in state and local elections. Four justices (Blackmun, Burger, Harlan, and Stewart) thought that neither Article I nor the Fourteenth and Fifteenth Amendments empowered Congress to establish the age of voters. Black supported the grant of voting rights to eighteen-year-olds in federal elections but not the grant of voting rights to them in state and local elections.

Obviously, Black's vote was decisive, but the split decision promised administrative chaos whenever national elections coincided with state and local elections. The decision was rendered on December 21, 1970. When the new Congress came into session in January 1971, it immediately passed an amendment giving eighteen-year-olds the vote, and the requisite number of states had ratified the Twenty-Sixth Amendment by July 1.

In another case the court was asked to rule on whether a state had a duty to equalize the funding of public schools. In 1968 Demetrio Rodriguez and other parents living in a poor school district filed suit in a federal district court to have the court declare Texas's school financing system in violation of the equal protection clause and order the state to ensure that the schools were equally financed. There was a large discrepancy between the funds spent on public schools in property-poor districts and in property-rich districts. Property-poor districts taxed more and spent less per student than property-rich districts, and property-poor districts had larger student populations. In 1971 a three-judge district court ruled that public education is a fundamental right and that the Texas funding system did not meet the strict-scrutiny test regarding governmental impediments to fundamental rights. It ordered the state to adopt a new system of school financing to insure that the wealth of a district would not determine the amount spent per pupil in each district. The state became the defendant in the case and appealed to the Supreme Court.

In 1972 the court, by the narrowest margin, reversed the decision and ruled for Texas (*San Antonio Independent School District v. Rodriguez*). Powell wrote the court opinion, and Blackmun, Burger, Rehnquist, and Stewart) joined him. Powell held that public education is not a fundamental right and so there was no need to apply the strict-scrutiny test to the state funding of it. Applying the mere rationality test, Powell found the choice of local funding fostered local participation in public education. Four justices (Brennan, Douglas, Marshall, and White) dissented in three opinions. White argued that the Texas funding system was not even minimally rational, since the property-poor districts had no enhancement options open to them. Brennan argued that public education is a fundamental right and that the Texas funding system failed the strict-scrutiny test. Marshall, joined by Brennan and Douglas, would have employed a sliding scale of strictness regarding the distribution of government funds according to the importance of the class disadvantaged.

The result reflected the views of the four justices appointed by Nixon in favor of the traditional decentralized local control of education, and precise judicial remedies would be difficult to fashion. Nonetheless, the large discrepancies in the funding of school districts are disadvantageous to the poor. It is satisfying to note that the Texas Supreme Court in 1989 ruled that the unequal Texas school funding system violated the *Texas* constitution, and many state courts have declared their school funding laws in violation of state constitutions.

In 1972 burglars invaded the Democratic headquarters in the Watergate complex in Washington. White House officials were implicated, and seven were indicted for conspiracy to obstruct justice. Nixon in 1974 appointed a special prosecutor, Archibald Cox, to head an investigation and promised not to interfere with it. When congressional investigations established that Nixon had a voice-activated recorder in his office, Cox sought to obtain the tapes. Nixon ordered Cox to desist, but Cox refused. Nixon ordered the attorney general, Elliot Richardson, to fire Cox, but Richardson and his deputy resigned. Solicitor General Robert Bork became acting attorney general and carried out the order. There was a public outcry; Nixon was in effect forced to appoint a new special prosecutor, Leon Jaworski, and Nixon assured congressional leaders that he would not interfere. Jaworski reinstated the request for a subpoena on Nixon to deliver certain tapes, and the trial judge, John Sirica, so ordered. Nixon produced some of the sought materials but not others, claiming that executive privilege placed confidential presidential documents beyond judicial reach. Sirica denied Nixon's claim and refused to quash the subpoena, and Nixon appealed to the court of appeals. Jaworski then asked the Supreme Court to review the case immediately. The court agreed, heard arguments on July 8, and decided the case on July 24.

Burger wrote the unanimous court opinion upholding the subpoena, and all the justices, including the Nixon appointees except Rehnquist, who did not participate, joined him (*U.S. v. Nixon*). As a threshold question, Nixon challenged the special prosecutor's standing to seek an injunction against him and the justiciability of the courts over a dispute within the executive branch of the government. He claimed that he was by the Constitution the *chief* executive, that a subordinate executive officer could not request a court to subpoena him, and that a court could not issue the subpoena. Burger rejected that contention, citing the attorney general's delegation of authority to the special prosecutor, with the power to contest the invocation of executive privilege. Burger admitted that it was theoretically possible for the attorney general to amend or revoke the authority of the special prosecutor but emphasized that the attorney general had not done so. (Unsaid was the fact that Nixon himself could have fired Jaworski. Absolutely speaking, Nixon could have, but the impeachment process would have precipitously accelerated.)

On the substantive question Burger rejected Nixon's claim to an absolute presidential executive privilege, analyzing two arguments. One was the need for the confidentiality of communications between the president and his advisers, since the president would be unlikely to receive completely candid advice if the contents could become public knowledge to the political disadvantage of the adviser. Burger conceded that this was an important consideration justifying a presumptive privilege but denied that it would justify an absolute privilege. The second argument was that disclosure of confidential communications between the president and his advisers would violate separation of powers—that is, the power of the president to carry out his constitutional duties. Burger, without committing himself or the court, asserted that presidential communications relating to military, diplomatic, or national security secrets might be absolutely privileged but was only willing to grant a presumptive privilege regarding other matters.

In the matter of the challenged subpoena, Burger declined to recognize an executive privilege. He cited the fact that the prosecutor sought the subpoena in the process of prosecuting the seven indicted officials and that the cause of criminal justice trumped the president's presumptive privilege. He also cited the fact that Sirica had ordered that the materials be screened in camera—that is, in the secrecy of his chambers—to remove irrelevant and inadmissible material before the materials were transferred to the special prosecutor.

Nixon complied with the subpoena and released the documents to the public. The House Judiciary Committee voted to impeach Nixon, but his resignation in July, three weeks later, ended the impeachment proceedings. The court decision hastened Nixon's departure by resignation, and this undoubtedly spared the country the agony of a lengthy impeachment trial in the Senate. But in addition to the opinion's rather rambling and repetitious prose, scholars raised questions about the court's treatment of the legal issues.

On the threshold question one might argue that, although Nixon had not fired Jaworski or revoked the agreement at the time of his appointment, he had effectively indicated his will as chief executive. Should not the will of the chief executive govern the activities of subordinate officials? The Rehnquist Court would return to this question—namely, whether an autonomous special prosecutor is compatible with presidential executive authority. And when another special prosecutor, Kenneth Starr, precipitated the impeachment of another president, William Clinton, Congress and the public would reconsider the wisdom of empowering special prosecutors.

On the substantive question of executive privilege one might ask whether the court's distinction of military, diplomatic, and national security communications from other communications implies that the president enjoys an absolute privilege regarding the former. If so, what if Nixon had alleged that the materials subpoenaed concerned such matters? If not, should an in-camera proceeding be held to determine whether or not they were such? In the actual case, would in-camera inspection of the materials guarantee that irrelevant information would not become public? For example, the judge or his secretary playing the recording might make comments to friends or reporters. The judge would decide whether material is relevant or irrelevant. Would the opposing attorneys be present at the playing of the recordings? Would they be able to object? If so, would that be part of the court record?

A decision in 1974 expanded the reach of the Eleventh Amendment, which prohibits citizens of other states or, by judicial interpretation, citizens of the same state from suing states in federal courts. The court had allowed citizens to sue in federal courts to enjoin state officials from enforcing allegedly unconstitutional state laws. John Jordan filed a class-action lawsuit in federal courts against Illinois officials for payments in arrears under federal-aid programs administered by the state. The district court ruled in favor of the plaintiffs and ordered the state to make retroactive payments. The court of appeals reversed, and the plaintiffs took the case on appeal to the Supreme Court.

The court by the narrowest margin ruled that the Eleventh Amendment barred the plaintiffs from initiating suits in federal courts (*Edelman v. Jordan*). Rehnquist wrote the court opinion, and Burger, Powell, Stewart, and White joined him. Rehnquist argued that the participation of Illinois in the federal programs did not constitute a waiver of its Eleventh Amendment immunity from suits in federal courts and that mandating states to make retroactive payments was fundamentally different from enjoining state officials from performing unconstitutional acts. Blackmun, Brennan, Douglas, and Marshall dissented, disputing both of Rehnquist's contentions. Later decisions limited the impact of the decision by allowing Congress to overcome the immunity of states from suits through its powers to enforce the Fourteenth Amendment and regulate commerce.

The decision in a 1976 case seemed to resurrect the Tenth Amendment after its demise in *U.S. v. Darby*. The Fair Labor and Standards Act of 1938 originally required private employers covered by the act to pay their employees a minimum hourly wage and time-and-a-half wages for work in excess of forty hours but excluded the employees of states and their political subdivisions from its coverage. Congress amended the act in 1974 to remove the exemption from almost all employees of states and their political subdivisions. The National League of Cities and many individual cities and states sued against William Usery, the secretary of labor, in the district court of the District of Columbia to have the amendments declared unconstitutional. (Since most states and their political subdivisions already paid at least the prescribed minimum wage, the suit was aimed at the prescription of time-and-a-half wages for overtime.) A three-judge court refused to do so, and the plaintiffs appealed to the Supreme Court.

The court by the narrowest majority reversed the decision of the lower court and held that the amendments were unconstitutional (*National League of Cities v. Usery*). (The case was argued twice, due to the fact that Douglas had a stroke and resigned after the first argument.) Rehnquist wrote the court opinion, and the other Nixon appointees (Burger, Blackmun, and Powell) and Stewart joined him. Rehnquist held that the imposition of wage requirements on states invaded their sovereign capacity to govern. He distinguished essential or integral functions of state governments, which the federal government may not regulate, from nonessential ones, which they may. Of traditional or essential governmental functions he listed police, fire, sanitation, health, and parks departments. Blackmun concurred to stress that the court opinion was flexible in construing which governmental functions were essential. Brennan, whom Marshall and White joined, strongly dissented, stressing the plenary power of Congress to regulate commerce. Stevens also filed a dissenting opinion.

The National League decision had a short lifespan. After almost a decade of trying to distinguish between essential and nonessential governmental functions, the court gave up. The San Antonio Metropolitan Transit Authority, which runs the transit system in San Antonio, Texas, informed its employees after the National League decision that it was no longer obligated to pay the overtime wages prescribed by the federal law. Joseph Garcia and several other employees of the authority filed suit in a federal district court against it for overtime pay under the federal law. In 1981 the district court ruled in favor of the transit authority on the basis of the National League rule. The plaintiffs and the Department of Labor appealed to the Supreme Court.

The court was expected to render another decision based on whether a majority considered the transit authority to exercise an essential governmental function, and the case was argued and reargued before the court. Instead, the court in 1985 by the narrowest margin overruled *National League of Cities v. Usery* and held that the fair-labor federal law applied to *all* employees of states and their political subdivisions (*Garcia v. San Antonio Metropolitan Transit Authority*). Blackmun wrote the court opinion, and the dissenters in *National League of Cities* joined him. Blackmun pronounced the essential-governmental-function test unsound in principle and unworkable in practice. He considered the test unsound in principle because the Constitution relies on a federal system of governance in which the states have equal representation in the U.S. Senate. Burger, Powell, Rehnquist, and O'Connor (a new justice) dissented. They stressed their view that the Tenth Amendment imposed a substantive limitation on federal power, and Rehnquist predicted that a future majority would return to that view. As we shall see, he was right and would as chief justice, supported by a strong neoconservative legal movement, lead the way, but not in the area of federal labor law.

In 1979 the court for the first time since the Warren Court declared a controversy a political question and declined to consider it. President James Carter had terminated the mutual defense treaty with Taiwan without consulting or obtaining the approval of the Senate, a subject on which the Constitution is silent. Senator Barry Goldwater and other members of Congress sought to enjoin that action unless and until the Senate approved. A court of appeals held on the merits that the president did have the authority to terminate the treaty without the consent of the Senate, and the Supreme Court granted review.

The court summarily reversed the court of appeals but not on the merits, with the plurality opinion ruling that the issue was a political question (*Goldwater v. Carter*). Rehnquist wrote the plurality opinion, and Burger, Stewart, and Stevens joined him. Marshall and Powell concurred separately. Rehnquist argued that this was a nonjusticiable political question because it involved the authority of the president to conduct foreign affairs and that the court was being asked to settle a dispute between coequal branches of the federal government. Powell concurred separately, arguing that the issue, although justiciable, was not ripe for judicial decision, since Congress had collectively not yet taken any action. Marshall, without giving his own opinion, concurred only in the result. Brennan, joined by Blackmun and White, dissented, arguing that the court was asked only to decide whether the Constitution makes the president the sole repository of the power to terminate a treaty and that the case should be set for full argument. On the merits, Brennan argued that the president alone has the power to terminate treaties, since the treaty at issue was related to the presidential decision to recognize mainline China, and the president alone has the power to recognize foreign governments.

A case involving one individual (and four others) led to a sweeping decision in 1983 on the separation of powers and the so-called legislative veto. Jagdish Chadha, an East Indian born in Kenya, was admitted to the United States on a student visa in 1966. His visa expired in 1972, and he was ordered deported. Since neither Kenya nor Great Britain would allow Chadha to return, he applied for a suspension of the deportation order and permanent-resident status. A section of the Immigration and Naturalization Act authorized the attorney general at his discretion to suspend the deportation of an alien, and an immigration judge in the Department of Justice, acting for the attorney general, in 1974 ordered the suspension and granted Chadha permanent-resident status. The same section of the act required the attorney general to report such suspension to Congress, which he did, and authorized either the House or the

Senate to invalidate the suspension by a simple resolution to that effect. On December 16, 1975, three days before the adjournment of Congress and the last day on which a house of Congress could exercise its veto, the House of Representatives vetoed suspension of Chadha's deportation. Anti-immigrant sentiment presumably prompted the House action, although business and other special interests were the usual beneficiaries of the legislative veto.

The immigration judge held that he had no authority to question the legislative veto and ordered Chadha's deportation, and the Board of Immigration Appeals upheld the judge's order. Chadha appealed to the court of appeals in San Francisco. Ralph Nader's consumer organization took over Chadha's case as an instrument to challenge the legislative veto, which it regarded as an obstacle to consumer interests, and the Immigration and Naturalization Service supported Chadha. The court of appeals invited both the House and the Senate, the only parties with a real interest in defending the legislative veto, to submit amicus briefs, which they did. The court of appeals ruled in 1981 that the House had no constitutional authority to order Chadha's deportation. Congress formally intervened to defend the veto in the name of the immigration service and appealed the case to the Supreme Court.

The court, after two sessions of oral argument, held that a legislative veto by one or both houses of Congress violated the constitutional process of making law (*Immigration and Naturalization Service v. Chadha*). Burger wrote the court opinion, and Blackmun, Brennan, Marshall, O'Connor, and Stevens joined him. Powell concurred in the judgment. Burger argued that the House's action made law contrary to the process prescribed by the Constitution—namely, that both houses pass a bill and present it to the president for his signature or veto. Powell concurred but insisted that the House action was adjudicatory rather than legislative—that is, the House made its own determination about application of the statutory criteria for suspending the deportation to Chadha (and four other individuals).

White wrote a powerful dissent. He pointed out the central problem of the modern capitalist state—namely, how to give the executive enough flexibility to deal with the complexity of state capitalism and simultaneously retain legislative control over the exercise of executive power. The legislative veto was designed as a means of reserving ultimate legislative power and included in nearly two hundred statutes. (The War Powers Resolution has such a feature.) Moreover, the power to exercise the veto is not the power to write a *new* law without bicameral approval or presidential consideration. The veto has been authorized by statute and may negate only what an executive department or administrative agency proposed. The attorney general had proposed suspension of Chadha's deportation, and the House refused to approve it. Nor does the legislative veto infringe on judicial power, White argued, since Congress by the legislative veto had reserved its own judgment as part of the *statutory* process. Rehnquist, joined by White, also dissented. Rehnquist thought that the legislative veto at stake in the case was inseparable from the congressional grant of power to the attorney general to suspend deportations, and so the suspension itself was void.

The court, by deciding that Congress may not use the legislative veto to control exercise of delegated power, forces it to fish or cut bait. Congress must either delegate with exacting standards or modify the delegated power by new legislation. Whatever the theoretical merits of the court's constitutional exegesis, its holding will not help solve the central weakness of congressional legislation over the last half-century—namely, delegation of broad powers to executive agencies without exacting standards to guide administrators. The decision just might force Congress to make the harder decisions that it is supposed to make. In any case, given Congress's other powers (e.g., over appropriations), it is unlikely that the decision will seriously erode democratic control over executive agencies.

As a result of the Warren Court's Wesberry and Reynolds decisions, the Burger Court faced challenges as to whether congressional and state legislative districts accorded closely enough with the one-person, one-vote standard. In 1983 a five-man majority (Brennan, with Blackmun, Marshall, O'Connor, and Stevens) invalidated a New Jersey congressional plan with less than 1 percent difference in the population of districts (*Karcher v. Daggett*). The majority found that, despite the fact that the population deviations were small, the state had not demonstrated a good-faith effort to achieve population equality. The odd shapes of the districts were undoubtedly a factor in the decision. In a concurring opinion, Stevens objected to the quest for absolute precision in the population of districts and strongly hinted that the districting at issue involved judicially remedial political gerrymandering. Burger, Powell, Rehnquist, and White dissented on the grounds that the decision required more precision than the Constitution required.

A case from Indiana in 1986 presented the court with an opportunity to consider the constitutionality of political gerrymandering of legislative districts—namely, drawing their lines for partisan advantage. The state legislature in 1981 reapportioned districts to conform to the 1980 decennial census. Bandemer and other Indiana Democrats filed suit in a federal district court, claiming that the apportionment plan was an intentional political gerrymander against Democrats and so a violation of the equal protection clause. Before the case was heard, elections under the plan were held in 1982. In the Indiana Senate Democrats received 53.1 percent of the votes statewide and elected a proportional number of senators (13 out of 25). In the Indiana House, Democrats received 51.9 percent of the votes statewide but elected only 43 percent of the House seats (43 out of 100). In two counties divided into multi-member districts, Democratic candidates received 46.6 percent of the vote but elected only three out of 21 seats at stake. The disproportionate results in the House districts, particularly in the two multi-member districts, were evidently the product of political gerrymandering, and the district court invalidated the 1981 apportionment and ordered the state legislature to adopt a new plan. Indiana, represented by Davis, appealed to the Supreme Court.

The court overturned the district court ruling and upheld the 1981 apportionment (*Davis v. Bandemer*), but the court split into three opinions on two questions. The first question was whether political gerrymandering was justiciable—that is, subject matter for judicial determination. White wrote the plurality opinion holding that it was, and Blackmun, Brennan, and Marshall joined him. White found the case justiciable and held that there would be unconstitutional discrimination only when an electoral system was so arranged as consistently to degrade the influence of an individual voter or a group of voters on the political process as a whole. Powell, joined by Stevens, objected to the indefinite standard proposed by White. Powell argued that, if Democratic voters in a number of critical districts were discriminated against, the effect would be felt over the political process of the state as a whole. Thus there were six votes for the justiciability of political gerrymandering. O'Connor, joined by Burger and Rehnquist, dissented on this question. She thought political gerrymandering not justiciable, and judicial intervention into the partisan political thicket of apportioning equally populated districts would lead inevitably to a system of proportional representation.

The second question was whether the 1981 Indiana legislative apportionment violated the equal protection clause. On this question White and the plurality held that the findings of the district court did not add up to a discriminatory effect on the political process of the state as a whole. O'Connor and her two associates, since they did not think the case justiciable at all, concurred in White's judgment. Powell and Stevens dissented on this question, since they held the findings of discrimination in critical districts enough. Thus seven justices upheld the Indiana apportionment. Given that White and Powell could not agree on what threshold of political gerrymandering was permissible, perhaps O'Connor's view was better that, as long as districts are equal in population, districting should be left to legislators (and politicians).

In the same year, 1986, the court passed on the Balanced Budget and Emergency Deficit Control Act, which President Reagan had signed into law in December 1985. To reduce and eliminate the annual budget deficit, the act set a maximum deficit for each fiscal year from1986 through 1991. If the annual federal budget exceeded that maximum, the act provided for across-the-board cuts in spending to meet the deficit goal. Each year the directors of the Office of Budget and Management and the Congressional Budget Office were independently to estimate the annual budget deficit and to calculate any program budget cuts necessary to meet the deficit goal. They were to report their estimates and calculations to the comptroller general. He would report his conclusions about them to the president, who was then required to mandate the reductions. Representative Mike Synar and other members of Congress filed suit against Charles Bowsher, the comptroller general, to enjoin enforcement of the act, principally arguing that Congress was impermissibly delegating its authority over appropriations to government bureaucrats. Synar won in the district court, and Bowsher appealed to the Supreme Court.

The court affirmed the lower-court decision and held the essential part of the act giving discretionary power to the comptroller general unconstitutional (*Bowsher v. Synar*). Burger wrote the court opinion, his last, and Brennan, O'Connor, Powell, and Rehnquist joined him. Burger argued that the comptroller general was an officer of Congress, and his powers under the act were executive. The comptroller general was a legislative agent because Congress by joint resolution had the sole power to initiate his removal, and his powers under the act were an exercise of executive power applying the general legislative standards to specific circumstances. Thus entrusting the comptroller general with executive power invaded presidential power and so violated the separation of powers. Stevens, joined by Marshall, concurred in the judgment but for a radically different reason. Stevens thought that the constitutional flaw in the act was that it attempted to delegate *legislative* power to a single individual, the comptroller general. White and Blackmun dissented. White argued that the court opinion was formalistic. The president had signed the act, and the congressional role in initiating removal of a comptroller general did not render the latter a congressional agent incapable of executing the act.

The Burger opinion applied the separation-of-powers principle rigidly, but the Constitution allows considerable interaction between the powers. For example, the president's veto power gives him a powerful voice in the legislative power, and the Senate's power to approve or disapprove the appointment of executive officers gives it a powerful voice in the executive power. Congress could have revised the deficit act to put ultimate power in the hands of the director of the budget and management, but it didn't, presumably much to the relief of interest groups that would be affected by budget cuts. The budget crisis, however, passed away by the end of the century, thanks to large-scale, prosperity-generated increase of tax revenues. Ten years later prospective annual deficits of more than a trillion dollars would confront the country. From this perspective the Bowsher decision may be an obstacle to the legality of the 2012 sequestering act, which is similar to the 1985 act.

Campaign Financing In 1976 the court in a per curiam opinion ruled on provisions of the 1971 Federal Election Campaign Act, as amended in 1974 (*Buckley v. Valeo*). Only three justices (Brennan, Powell, and Stewart) subscribed to the whole opinion. Five justices (Blackmun, Burger, Marshall, Rehnquist, and White) dissented to parts of the opinion. (Newly appointed Stevens did not participate.) The court opinion and the opinions of individual justices filled almost three hundred pages of the official reports. The opinion distinguished between limits on expenditures and contributions. The opinion held that the First Amendment prohibited the limits on a candidate's use of his own money or that of the candidate's immediate family. Nor could the government limit campaign expenditures by individuals and political action committees. The court, however, upheld limits on the contributions that individuals and groups could make to candidates for federal office.

Race *Brown II* left the process of desegregating public schools in the South to district courts. In rural areas and small towns, desegregating the schools posed administrative problems (integrating faculties of previously all-white and all-black schools and equalizing facilities) but no problem about integrating white and black students, since whites and blacks there lived in checkerboard proximity and bus transportation was already necessary. Desegregating public schools in Southern urban areas posed a special problem because urban neighborhoods were racially disparate, and so the neighborhood schools also were. In 1973 the Burger Court handed down a unanimous decision approving the use of busing to achieve integration of formerly segregated schools in the South (*Swann v. Charlotte-Mecklenburg Board of Education*).

The school district was partially urban and partially rural, covered 550 square miles, and enrolled 84,000 pupils in 101 schools. The school population was 29 percent black, and those pupils were mostly in one-quarter of the city of Charlotte. The original plan of the district court focused on zoning and free transfers of blacks to previously all-white schools, but, under that plan, more than half of the black pupils attended schools without any white student or teacher. The district court later adopted a sweeping plan to disperse the concentrated black student population to formerly all-white schools. The goal was to achieve a 71-white-to-29-black pupil ratio in specified schools. This involved the district school system transporting 13,000 more students, buying or renting 100 new buses, and spending more than $500,000 annually after a $1,000,000 startup cost.

Burger wrote the court opinion upholding the plan. He explained that, once a constitutional violation has been found, the scope of the remedy becomes a routine exercise of the principles of equity. He maintained that, although the Constitution did not require that every school in a previously segregated district must reflect the racial composition of system as a whole, mathematical ratios were used sparingly and were within remedial discretion of the district court. He further held that, since freedom-of-choice systems were not and would not eliminate the dual system, busing and such other remedies as redrawing school zones were within the district court's remedial power. *Swann* is most notable because it approved large-scale busing to achieve desegregation of public schools.

In the 1970s the court's attention shifted from desegregation of public schools in the South to desegregation of public schools in the North. By 1974, twenty years after *Brown I*, public schools in the South were either de jure desegregated or well on the way to becoming such. On the other hand, public schools in the North were becoming increasingly de facto segregated. In some cases school district administrators had intentionally manipulated school zones to exclude black students from predominantly white schools, which, of course, was constitutionally impermissible.

The Detroit school district, the fifth-largest in the nation, was one such district guilty of de jure segregation. The district covered 140 square miles and had a school population of almost 290,000 in 1970, 65 percent of which was black and 35 percent white. White flight to the suburbs resulted in a ratio of three whites to one black in the whole metropolitan area (Detroit and the suburbs). A group of citizens in Detroit in 1970 brought a class-action suit in a federal district court against the Detroit board of education and state officials and sought an order desegregating the city's public schools. The district court, finding desegregation of Detroit's schools impossible without combining them with those in the whole metropolitan district, ordered the defendant officials to submit desegregation plans for the city proper and the three-county metropolitan area. The fifty-three suburban school districts were not defendants in the case, and there was no claim that they had ever pursued a policy of segregation. The federal court of appeals affirmed, and the state officials appealed to the Supreme Court.

The court by the narrowest margin in 1974 reversed and remanded the case to the district court to formulate a desegregation decree that did not include the suburban school districts in the metropolitan district (*Milliken v. Bradley*). Burger wrote the court opinion, and all the other Republican justices (Blackmun, Powell, Rehnquist, and Stewart) joined him. For Burger, the federal judiciary should not impose desegregation of public schools on school districts that had never discriminated against blacks, and so the district court should limit its decree to desegregating the public schools within the city limits of Detroit. All four Democratic justices (Brennan, Douglas, Marshall, and White) dissented. Marshall argued that the state had a duty to eliminate all vestiges of racial discrimination and that desegregation of Detroit's public school could be achieved only by involving the whole metropolitan district's schools.

The Milliken case posed not only a difficult legal but also a difficult political problem. Suburban whites overwhelmingly opposed integrating their local schools, and they had some reasons for their opposition that were not due to racial bias. In the plan devised by the district court in the Milliken case, some whites would be bused into inner-city schools, which might be located in dangerous neighborhoods and not have so favorable an educational environment as the suburban schools. Indeed, whites within the city limits of Detroit might raise similar objections to desegregating the city's public schools. Moreover, busing students over long distances twice a day takes up a lot of time that students might otherwise use to greater educational or recreational benefit.

The Burger Court faced the first challenges to affirmative-action programs. The University of California in 1968 opened a medical school at Davis and admitted one hundred applicants annually. It in 1970 established a special admissions program for African Americans, Hispanics, Asians, and American Indians, reserving sixteen of the hundred admissions for them. Allan Bakke, a white male, applied for admission to the medical school in 1973 and 1974 and was rejected both times. Bakke then sued in a superior court of California for admission, claiming that, since he had higher entrance examination scores and scholastic grades than those admitted under the special admissions program, the medical school had violated federal law and the equal protection clause. The trial court and the California Supreme Court held that the program was unconstitutional and ordered the medical school to admit Bakke. The University of California appealed to the U.S. Supreme Court.

The court in 1978 affirmed the decision of the California Supreme Court invalidating the special admissions program and ordering the admission of Bakke (*Regents v. Bakke*). Powell wrote the court opinion, but no other justice joined him in all of it. Powell applied the standard of strict scrutiny regarding racial classifications and held that fixed quotas could not meet that standard. Stevens, joined by Burger, Rehnquist, and Stewart, concurred with Powell's judgment that Bakke should be admitted to the medical school but on the basis on Title VI of the 1964 Civil Rights Act, which prohibited racial discrimination in any federally funded activity. Blackmun, Brennan, Marshall, and White dissented from Powell's opinion about the standard to be applied. Brennan opted for a standard of heightened scrutiny in between strict scrutiny and mere rationality, a standard under which race-conscious remedies to help minorities that had been discriminated against would be constitutional. Powell also concluded that a special admissions program that took race or ethnicity into account as a factor in admissions was constitutionally permissible, since diversity in the student body was a permissible educational objective. This, of course, was pure dictum regarding the Bakke case itself, but, because Blackmun, Brennan, Marshall, and White concurred, it enjoys the status of legal precedent.

If 1978 was the year of Allan Bakke in the 1977 Supreme Court term and newspaper headlines, 1979 was the year of Bakke's blue-collar cousin, Brian Weber, in the 1978 Supreme Court term. As part of a collective bargaining agreement, Kaiser Aluminum Company established craft job training programs for unskilled production workers, both black and white. Admission to the programs was based on seniority, but 50 percent of the openings were to go to blacks. Weber, an unskilled white worker at the Kaiser plant in Louisiana, had more service than some of the black workers selected for the program but less than any of the white workers selected. He sued the company and union and won in the district court. The company and the union appealed to the Supreme Court.

The court ruled in favor of the company and the union (*United Steelworkers v. Weber*). Brennan wrote the court opinion, and Blackmun, Marshall, and White joined him. So did Stewart, who in *Bakke* had opposed the racial quotas there at issue. The central issue involved Title VII of the 1964 Civil Rights Act, which prohibited racial discrimination in employment. Brennan interpreted that title to permit voluntary private affirmative-action programs and took judicial notice of prior exclusion of blacks from craft jobs. Powell, who had not participated in the oral argument, and Stevens, who had done legal work with Kaiser, did not participate. Burger and Rehnquist vigorously dissented. Rehnquist thoroughly reviewed the title's legislative history and demonstrated that congressional spokesmen in the House and Senate repeatedly reassured colleagues that the title prohibited discrimination against white workers as well as discrimination against black workers. Voluntary private affirmative-action programs may be good public policy, as Burger observed, but the law is the law, and this hard case led to the bad interpretation of a law.

If the Weber decision indicated wide tolerance for purely voluntary affirmative-action programs under Title VII, a case in 1986 involved a court order on affirmative action to remedy past discrimination. A sheet metal workers' local union in New York City had discriminated against blacks in violation of Title VII, and a district court ordered it to set a minority membership goal of 29 percent to be achieved by a specified date and to fund increased nonwhite participation in apprenticeship training and union membership. The court of appeals affirmed, and the union appealed to the Supreme Court.

The court by the narrowest margin upheld the order (*Local 28 v. Equal Economic Opportunity Commission*). Brennan wrote the court opinion, and Blackmun, Marshall, Powell, and Stevens joined him. Brennan argued that the court-ordered racial quotas were permissible to remedy past discrimination by the union and that the beneficiaries of remedial racial goals need not themselves have been victims of the past discrimination. Powell wrote separately to emphasize that the union had in the past practiced racial discrimination and that the remedy did not burden innocent whites. Burger and Rehnquist dissented, arguing that courts may order racial quotas only to benefit actual victims of past discrimination. White dissented because he judged the displacement effect on whites excessive, and O'Connor dissented because she objected to rigid racial quotas.

In the same year, in another case, the court considered preferential treat-ment of blacks in the layoff of teachers in a public-school system. A local board of education had a collective bargaining agreement providing for the reten-tion of the most senior teachers during layoffs, except that at no time during the layoffs would there be a greater percentage of minority personnel laid off than the current percentage of minority personnel employed at the time of the layoffs. In other words, the most recently hired minority personnel were pro-tected against being laid off. A laid-off white teacher brought suit against the board of education in a district court and lost. The teacher appealed to the Su-preme Court.

The court by the narrowest margin struck down the preferential treatment of blacks in the layoffs (*Wygant v. Jackson Board of Education*). Powell, with Burg-er, O'Connor, and Rehnquist, thought that "societal" discrimination was too amorphous to justify the preferences, and the allegations of past discrimina-tion were unproven. Powell, with Burger and Rehnquist, also contended that, even if past discrimination had been established, the preferential treatment of blacks in layoffs was not satisfactorily tailored to remedy the wrong. O'Connor similarly judged the means unrelated to providing a remedy for the past dis-crimination. White concurred separately, arguing bluntly that it was not con-stitutionally permissible to fire whites to make room for blacks. Marshall, with Blackmun, Brennan, and Stevens, dissented, maintaining that there was a prima facie case of prior discrimination by the board of education, that there was a public interest in an integrated faculty, and that the teachers' union had voluntarily agreed to preferential layoffs. Thus the court held that, although voluntary race-based *hiring* is constitutionally permissible in the absence of proven discrimination, race-based *firings* would be constitutionally acceptable only to remedy past discrimination.

The year after the Weber decision, 1980, the court decided the first case on another kind of affirmative action, setting aside a percentage of government contracts for minority businesses. In the 1977 Public Works Employment Act, Congress provided for setting aside 10 percent of public works contracts for minority business enterprises. Fullilove and a group of majority contractors sued Klutznick, the federal administrator, claiming that the provision violated the equal protection component of the Fifth Amendment's due process clause. The district court and the court of appeals ruled against him, and he appealed to the Supreme Court.

The court upheld the provision (*Fullilove v. Klutznick*). There was, however, no court opinion. Burger, with Powell and White, found the objectives of the provision within the power of Congress to enforce the equal protection guarantees of the Fourteenth Amendment. Although there had been no specific legislative hearings, Burger held that Congress had ample evidence that existing construction procurement practices were perpetuating the effects of past discrimination against the access of minority contractors to public works contracts. He then argued that limited use of racial quotas was a constitutionally permissible means to achieve remedial objectives and so didn't violate the equal protection clause. Powell, concurring separately, emphasized the role of Congress in identifying the past discrimination against minorities to be remedied by the racial quota. Marshall, with Blackmun and Brennan, applying a heightened but not strict scrutiny, was satisfied that the substantial and chronic underrepresentation of minority contractors in public works was reasonably attributable to past discrimination without reliance on congressional findings and that racial quotas were a reasonable means to remedy that underrepresentation.

Three justices dissented. Stewart, with Rehnquist, insisted that the Constitution was color-blind and that the racial quotas of the minority business set-aside provision penalized innocent majority entrepreneurs. In a separate dissent Stevens thought that Congress had not demonstrated justification of its statutory preference of minority contractors simply on the basis of their racial profile. Where Stewart was concerned that the minority set-aside provision penalized innocent majority contractors, Stevens was concerned that the provision benefited minority entrepreneurs who had not been victimized. Interestingly, none of the justices seemed concerned about the added cost to the taxpayer when the government did not award contracts to the lowest bidder.

In 1972 the court decided a case involving whether and when racial discrimination by private individuals and groups can be equivalent to action by the state and so be a violation of the equal protection clause. A white member of a private club took a black man, Leroy Irvis, as his guest to the dining room of the Harrisburg Moose Lodge and requested food and beverage. Irvis was refused service because he was black. Membership in the national organization of Moose was restricted to whites, but the national organization had no bylaw in this regard about guests. After the district court decision restricted guest eligibility to whites, Irvis brought action to enjoin the liquor authority from licensing Moose Lodge until it ceased its discriminatory policy. The district court ordered the state liquor board to revoke the lodge's license if the lodge did not discontinue its discriminatory practices. (After the decision, the national organization amended its bylaws so as to state explicitly that guest eligibility was restricted to whites.) The lodge appealed to the Supreme Court.

The court ruled for the lodge (*Moose Lodge v. Irvis*). Rehnquist wrote the court opinion, and Blackmun, Burger, Powell, Stewart, and White joined him. Rehnquist argued that the lodge was a private social club in a private building and that the limited number of licenses could not be said to foster or encourage racial discrimination. Douglas, joined by Marshall, dissented, arguing that the state-imposed scarcity of liquor licenses in Harrisburg restricted the ability of blacks to obtain liquor, since liquor was commercially available only at private clubs when the state liquor stores were closed. Brennan, with Marshall, also dissented, arguing more generally that the whole liquor regulatory system involved the state in the lodge's discriminatory practices.

Privacy Perhaps the most well-known decision of the Burger Court is the abortion decision, *Roe v. Wade*. In 1970 Norma McCorvey (Jane Roe) of Dallas, Texas, wanted to have an abortion to terminate her pregnancy, but Texas prohibited abortions except by a physician to save the life of the mother. She sued in a district court against Henry Wade, the district attorney of Dallas County, to have the law declared unconstitutional and have him enjoined from enforcing it. The district court declared the law unconstitutional but refused to enjoin its enforcement. Roe appealed to the Supreme Court, and the court heard arguments twice, in 1971 and 1972.

The court in January 1973 ruled in favor of Roe. Blackmun wrote the court opinion, and Brennan, Burger, Douglas, Marshall, Powell, and Stewart joined him. Blackmun began with a discourse on the relatively recent origin of anti-abortion statutes in the nineteenth century. He argued that the right to privacy is founded on the concept of fundamental liberty in the due process clause of the Fourteenth Amendment and encompasses a woman's decision whether to terminate her pregnancy. But if the government has a compelling public interest, it can regulate exercise of the right. The state has a compelling public interest in the health of the mother only at the end of the first trimester of pregnancy, a compelling public interest in the life of the fetus only at the point of viability, the third trimester, and none in the first trimester. Even in the third trimester, the state must permit abortions to save the life of the mother. Burger, Douglas, and Stewart wrote separate concurring opinions.

Rehnquist and White vigorously dissented. Rehnquist conceded that the due process clause of the Fourteenth Amendment protected the right of individuals to be free from arbitrary state regulation of consensual transactions but objected to the introduction of a compelling-public-interest standard to test the validity of government regulations in due process cases. Using a simple rationality test, he argued that the state had a rational interest in the life of the fetus from the moment of its conception, although it would be irrational to prohibit abortions necessary to save the life of the mother, since one life saved is better than two lives dead. He pointed out that in 1868, the year the Fourteenth Amendment was adopted, thirty-six states and territories had statutes limiting abortion. Many of those states ratified the amendment, which they were hardly likely to have done if they thought the amendment nullified their anti-abortion laws.

Although the decision had its champions and considerable positive support from relevant interest groups, it also unleashed harsh negative criticism from those who regarded it as judicially usurping the legislative function and violating the right of a fetus to life. This negative backlash led to efforts to restrict the decision's scope—that is, to make procurement of an abortion more difficult. As long as the Burger Court flourished, it frustrated those efforts. But the critics were able to prevent the funding of abortions, and this the court approved. The Hyde amendment prohibited the use of federal Medicaid funds for abortions except where the life of the mother was at risk or in cases of rape or incest. In 1980 the court by the narrowest margin upheld the ban (*Harris v. McRae*). Stewart wrote the court opinion, and Burger, Powell, Rehnquist, and White joined him. Stewart argued that the Roe decision protected the right of women to choose abortion but did not require the government to subsidize the choice. If the latter were the case, individuals could claim a right to support for the exercise of other fundamental rights. Brennan, joined by Blackmun, Marshall, and Stevens, dissented. Brennan argued that the government burdened a woman's choice regarding abortion because it provided funded medical assistance for childbirth.

Another case involved the claim to a right of privacy regarding consensual homosexual acts. The case arose when police officers came to Michael Hardwick's home in Atlanta, Georgia, to serve a summons on him in another case. A third party admitted the officers and directed them to a bedroom. Hardwick and another man were engaged in oral sex, which the state included in the definition of the crime of sodomy, and the officers arrested him on that charge. State officials declined to prosecute, but Hardwick brought a civil action in federal district court against Michael Bowers, the attorney general of

Georgia, to have the sodomy statute declared unconstitutional. Bowers won in the district court, but the court of appeals reversed, ruling in favor of Hardwick. Bowers then appealed to the Supreme Court.

In 1986 the court by the narrowest margin upheld the Georgia statute (*Bowers v. Hardwick*). White wrote the court opinion, and Burger, O'Connor, Powell, and Rehnquist joined him. White refused to recognize a fundamental right of privacy for consenting homosexual adults to practice sodomy, since there are no roots in tradition for recognizing such a right. Blackmun, joined by Brennan, Marshall, and Stevens, dissented. Blackmun charged that the decision authorized the state to invade the homes of homosexual citizens and that there are many right ways of relating sexually to others. Thus we have the anomaly that the Burger Court failed to find a constitutionally protected right to privacy here, where no third party was directly affected, and did find a constitutionally protected right for women to choose abortions, where third parties (of whatever legal status) were surely affected. The dissenters were perfectly consistent, as were White and Rehnquist. Burger had expressed misgivings about the Roe decision earlier that year, and O'Connor was new to the court. Powell was influenced by the fact that Hardwick was not prosecuted, although the felony charge against him remained on the books.

Criminal A large part of the Burger Court case workload concerned criminal justice. This was partially due to the influx of habeas corpus petitions, which the court curtailed, but it was also due to the doors that landmark decisions of the Warren court had opened. For example, the Katz decision had redefined the place protected by the Fourth Amendment to mean a place where one has a reasonable expectation of privacy rather than a place to which one has a proprietary right. This invited questions about when a person has a reasonable expectation of privacy. In 1983 the court unanimously disallowed detaining the luggage of a deplaning suspect for ninety minutes before a trained police dog could sniff the luggage for the presence of narcotics (*U.S. v. Place*). Six justices (O'Connor with Burger, Powell, Rehnquist, Stevens, and White), however, specifically approved limited detention of luggage reasonably *suspected* of containing narcotics and exposure of the luggage to dog sniffs. Brennan and Marshall insisted that there needed to be *probable cause* to detain the luggage and expose it to dog sniffs. Blackmun did not commit himself on that issue.

In 1984 the court reaffirmed the doctrine that the Fourth Amendment does not protect "open fields" (*Oliver v. U.S.*). Powell wrote the court opinion, and

Blackmun, Burger, O'Connor, and Rehnquist joined him. The opinion upheld the warrantless search of open fields by police officers looking for marijuana. White concurred in the result, but Marshall, joined by Brennan and Stevens, dissented. In the same year, the court ruled that the police did not need a search warrant before they attached an electronic beeper to a can of ether used to extract cocaine residue from clothing (*U.S. v. Karo*). Police traced the can to a house in New Mexico, obtained a search warrant, and found cocaine and a drug laboratory there. The same majority as in the Oliver case held that Karo's legitimate expectation of privacy extended only to his home, not to the can, and the same dissenters reached the opposite conclusion regarding the can.

In 1985 a similarly divided court affirmed the warrantless search of a fully mobile motor home in a public parking lot in the absence of exigent circumstances, relying on the automobile exception to the warrant requirement of the Fourth Amendment (*California v. Carney*).

In 1986 the court heard arguments on two cases involving aerial surveillance of property without a warrant by local police and federal inspectors. In one, police flew over the fenced-in backyard of a suspect and observed marijuana plants growing there. In the other, federal inspectors took aerial photos of company operations without a warrant. The court by the narrowest margin (Burger with O'Connor, Rehnquist, Stevens, and White) held both surveillances not to be searches within the meaning of the Fourth Amendment (*California v. Ciraolo*). Four justices (Powell, with Blackmun, Brennan, and Marshall) dissented. Note that the court did not rule on the use of more sophisticated aerial surveillance.

In 1983 the court radically revised the standard for a judge to issue a search warrant on the basis of testimony from an anonymous informant ("Old Reliable"). The facts of the case are as follows: Police in Illinois received an anonymous letter accusing a married couple (Lance and Sue Gates) of drug dealing and describing details of how the couple purchased drugs in Florida and transported them to their home in Illinois. Police in Illinois and Florida verified the movement of Gates as detailed in the letter, and the police in Illinois then obtained search warrants for the Gates's home and car while the Gateses were driving back from Florida to Illinois. The searches uncovered drugs, and the Gateses were convicted.

Previous decisions had required police applying for search warrants to set forth the circumstances on which the informant based his conclusions and the reasons the police thought the informant credible or his information reliable. In *Illinois v. Gates*, however, the court (Rehnquist with Blackmun, Burger, O'Connor, and Powell) scrapped that test of the probable cause required by the Fourth Amendment and substituted one deriving from the totality of circumstances. Rehnquist then concluded that verification of details in the letter provided enough evidence to satisfy the new test. White, concurring, argued that the Illinois police had satisfied the previous test. Brennan, joined by Marshall, argued that the previous test should be retained and that the Illinois police had not satisfied that test. Stevens also dissented, arguing that the Illinois police had not even satisfied the totality-of-circumstances test.

From the days of Prohibition the court had recognized an automobile exception to the warrant requirements of the Fourth Amendment—namely, that police with probable cause may stop and search an automobile. In the late 1970s and the early 1980s the Burger Court became embroiled in a series of cases involving police searches of closed compartments or containers of legally stopped automobiles. In 1979 the court held that the police needed a warrant to search a suitcase that they had probable cause to believe contained marijuana (*Arkansas v. Sanders*), with only Blackmun and Rehnquist in dissent. In 1981 the court held that police need a search warrant before they may legally open closed containers found in the passenger compartments of automobiles detained for traffic violations (*Robbins v. California*). Three justices (Brennan, Marshall, and White) would have required warrants for all police searches of automobiles in the absence of exigent circumstances (risk of injury to officers, destruction of evidence). Three justices (Blackmun, Rehnquist, and Stevens) would have allowed police with probable cause to open and examine any container found in a lawfully detained automobile without obtaining a warrant. Three justices (Burger, Powell, and Stewart) held middle positions, Powell arguing for a reasonable-expectation-of-privacy test, Stewart arguing for custodial arrest as the bright line, and Burger keeping the reason for his vote to himself.

The next year, 1982, the court spectacularly reversed gears on the issue in *U.S. v. Ross.* A hitherto reliable informant had reported to the police that he had observed a man selling narcotics and that the narcotics were kept in the trunk of the man's car. The informant fully described the man and specifically indicated the location of the car. When the police spotted the car in motion they stopped it, and the man driving it, Ross, answered the informant's description. The officers arrested Ross and opened the trunk of his car. They found in the trunk a closed paper bag. Inside the bag they found glassine bags containing white powder later identified as heroin. At the police station the officers conducted a more thorough search of the trunk and found a zippered leather pouch containing cash. Partially on the basis of the heroin and cash discovered in these warrantless searches, Ross was convicted of illegal possession of heroin and the intention to sell it.

Stevens wrote the court opinion, and not only Blackmun and Rehnquist, his fellow dissenters in *Robbins*, but also Burger, Powell, and O'Connor joined him. Stevens held that the mobility of automobiles makes warrantless search of them reasonable on probable cause and that the legal scope of such a search should be defined by the probable cause to search a part of the automobile rather than the characteristic of the parts searched. Powell concurred in Stevens's opinion only in order to settle the question. Marshall, joined by Brennan and White, dissented, repeating his view that warrants should be required for all police searches of automobiles in the absence of exigent circumstances. Note that warrantless searches of an automobile still required the police to have probable cause to search where they searched. The Rehnquist Court would expand the right of police to search the interior of automobiles lawfully stopped.

Earlier, in 1973, the court had ruled on the extent of a permissible search of a person under custodial arrest. Police officer Richard Jenks of the District of Columbia had observed Willie Robinson driving a car in Washington, and because of a prior investigation, Jenks had good reason to believe that Robinson's driver's license had been revoked. Jenks stopped Robinson and informed him that he was under arrest for driving without a license. After Robinson got out of the car, Jenks searched him. While patting the arrestee down, Jenks felt an object in the pocket of Robinson's coat and removed it. It was a crimpled cigarette package, and Jenks opened it, finding fourteen gelatin capsules of white powder, which turned out to be heroin. Robinson was convicted of possessing heroin, but the court of appeals reversed. The court reinstated the conviction (*U.S. v. Robinson*).

Rehnquist wrote the court opinion, and Blackmun, Burger, Powell, Stewart, and White joined him. Rehnquist held that the very fact of custodial arrest gives rise to authority to search the arrestee and anything on his person, including a package of cigarettes. Marshall, joined by Brennan and Stevens, dissented, arguing that the search of Robinson by Jenks involved more than a search of his person—namely, a search of the effects found on his person. In 1981 the court, over the dissents of Brennan, Marshall, and White, held that the police may after the custodial arrest of an automobile's occupant open any closed container in the passenger compartment and examine its contents without a search warrant (*New York v. Belton*). And in *Michigan v. Summers*, over the dissents of Brennan, Marshall, and Stewart, the court ruled that police executing a warrant to search a home for contraband are automatically authorized to detain the occupants during the search.

In 1984 the court carved out an exception to the exclusionary rule (*U.S. v. Leon*). Police had obtained a defective search warrant, which they executed, and the evidence obtained was admitted in the conviction of Leon. White wrote the court opinion, and Blackmun, Burger, O'Connor, Powell, and Rehnquist joined him. White saw no point in excluding the evidence, since to do so would not deter police from executing what they assumed to be a valid warrant, nor should the police be expected to know the fine points of criminal law. Brennan, joined by Marshall and Stevens, dissented, arguing that the decision would erode deterrence of illegal police action. Civil libertarians shared Brennan's concerns, but the decision does not seem to have caused the feared results.

In the same year the court also made two exceptions to the admission of evidence obtained from a defendant without giving him the Miranda warnings. One case, *New York v. Quarles*, involved the public-safety exception. A woman reported to the police that she had been raped at gunpoint. In a neighborhood supermarket police apprehended a man, later identified as Quarles, who fitted the woman's description. One officer noticed that Quarles had an empty shoulder holster, and the officer asked him where the gun was. Quarles nodded toward a pile of boxes and said, "The gun is over there." Police went to the boxes and found a loaded .38 caliber revolver. The officer then arrested Quarles on a weapons charge. Quarles's lawyer moved successfully in the trial court to prevent the statement and the gun from being admitted into evidence on the grounds that the police had not given Quarles the required Miranda warning before questioning him.

Rehnquist, joined by Blackmun, Burger, Powell, and White, held that a public-safety factor justified an exception here to the Miranda requirement that police advise suspects of their rights to silence and counsel before police question them. Although the police were themselves in no danger from Quarles, then in handcuffs, the discarded gun was concealed in the supermarket and so accessible to an accomplice, a customer, or an employee. Marshall, joined by Brennan and Stevens, dissented, deploring any departure from *Miranda* and holding that absolutely no coerced statements or their fruits should be admissible in criminal prosecutions. O'Connor would exclude the responses of suspects in custody but admit nontestimonial evidence like the gun. The decision seems to have exaggerated the public-safety factor. The suspect was in handcuffs. There was no reason to believe that there was an accomplice in the rape. Employees were unlikely to appropriate the gun. A criminally minded customer might find and appropriate the gun for criminal uses, but the police, with the help of employees, could search the store for the gun.

Precisely because the gun would have been discovered anyway, it might have been admissible on the grounds of inevitable discovery. This was the reasoning of the court in another case that year (*Nix v. Williams*). The "inevitable discovery" rule is even more apposite in the Quarles case than in the Williams case. In the Quarles case the police needed to search only the narrow confines of the store, but in the Williams case, the police were searching a wide area for a murder victim's body, and the body was discovered in a remote culvert.

The Burger Court was concerned with a number of issues relating to a suspect's right to silence and a defendant's right to counsel. In 1980 the court upheld a murder conviction based on evidence discovered when an accused under arrest led officers to the murder weapon as a result of officers' comments on the way to the police station (*Rhode Island v. Innis*). The accused had been arrested and advised of his Miranda rights to silence and counsel. On the trip to the station, one of the three officers accompanying him commented that there was a school for handicapped children in the area and expressed fear that a handicapped child would discover the loaded weapon. The accused thereupon took the police to the gun.

Stewart wrote the court opinion, and Blackmun, Powell, Rehnquist, and White joined him. (Burger concurred only in the judgment.) Stewart argued that *Miranda* forbade express questioning of the accused by the police or its functional equivalent, that the police had not expressly questioned Innis, and that the police had not equivalently questioned him because they had no reason to know that Innis was susceptible to this kind of psychological pressure. Marshall, joined by Brennan, dissented on the facts—that is, they thought the police *did* have reason to know that this psychological pressure might elicit a response from Innis. Stevens dissented on principle—that is, he thought the test should be what was likely to happen as a result of the police comments, not what the police had reason to think would happen.

In a 1981 case (*Edwards v. Arizona*), police had initially informed the accused, Edwards, of his rights to remain silent and to have counsel present during interrogation, and he refused to talk. Later, the police told Edwards that he "had to" talk but repeated the Miranda warnings. The accused then implicated himself in the crime and was convicted. The court unanimously overturned the conviction. All the justices agreed that Edwards had not waived his Miranda rights simply by responding to the police questioning. Six justices categorically rejected the right of the police to question an accused once he has invoked his Miranda rights unless the accused initiates the questioning. Burger, Powell, and Rehnquist would not limit voluntary waiver of previously invoked Miranda rights to the initiation of questioning by the accused.

In 1985 the court ruled that because a defendant had been indicted and the Sixth Amendment right to counsel had attached to the defendant, Perley Moulton, police use of a codefendant as a jail-plant to engage in conversation with him, even about other suspected crimes, violated his right to counsel (*Maine v. Moulton*). The codefendant agreed to become an undercover agent for the police investigating the other crimes, and conversations between the defendant and the codefendant were recorded. Moulton initiated conversations about the crime for which both had been indicted and made incriminating statements that were used as evidence to convict him. Brennan wrote the court opinion, citing the Massiah decision, and Blackmun, Marshall, Powell, and Stevens joined him. Burger, joined by Rehnquist and White, dissented from the holding, citing the good faith of the police. O'Connor dissented only on the decision to exclude the evidence.

In 1986 the court upheld the admission of a confession into evidence despite the fact that the accused was not informed of the efforts of an attorney to reach him and despite the fact that that the police had assured the attorney that they would not question the accused (*Moran v. Burbine*). Police had arrested Moran for burglary but suspected him of an unrelated murder. Moran's sister had retained a lawyer to represent him on the burglary charge. The police did not tell the attorney that they suspected Moran of the murder and reassured the attorney that they would not question Moran. The police also did not tell Moran that his sister had retained the attorney. Moran, after the police read him his Miranda rights, waived them and confessed to the murder. O'Connor wrote the court opinion, and Blackmun, Burger, Powell, Rehnquist, and White joined her. She argued that the Sixth Amendment right to counsel did not attach until after the first formal hearing, that Moran had knowingly and freely waived his right to silence, and that the police questioning him after assuring the attorney that they would not do so did not violate due process. Stevens, joined by Brennan and Marshall, dissented, arguing that Moran did have a right to counsel from the attorney hired by his sister, that the police lying offended fundamental fairness, and that its fruits should not be admitted in a court of justice.

Religion The Warren Court, in the decision on Bible reading in public schools (*Abington School District v. Schempp*), set down a twofold test of the religious establishment clause. The government activity must have a secular purpose, and its primary activity must neither advance nor inhibit religion. Many plaintiffs invoked this test to challenge traditional practices involving government and religion, and so the Burger Court considered a large number of such cases.

In 1970 the court upheld tax exemptions for the property of religious and charitable organizations, even property used for religious worship (*Walz v. Tax Commission*). Burger wrote the court opinion, and all the other justices except Douglas joined him. Burger did not apply the Schempp test but substituted an excessive-entanglement test. He held that the tax exemption of church property avoided what he regarded as excessive entanglement between government and religion and that the government in this way showed benevolent neutrality toward religion when the tax exemption was coupled with a like exemption for charitable organizations. Brennan, concurring separately, stressed the fact that the tax exemptions of churches and other fraternal organizations fostered freedom of association. Douglas, the sole dissenter, raised his usual objection to any financial support of religion. Note that Burger did not find any secular purpose other than avoiding excessive entanglement of government with religion, and Brennan filled that lacuna by linking the tax exemption to freedom of association and freedom of religious exercise. No doubt the court was also well aware that the tax exemption of church property enjoyed widespread public support.

The following year, 1971, the court heard two cases involving governmental aid to church-related schools. Pennsylvania directly reimbursed private nonprofit, including church-related, schools for the costs of the salaries of teachers of secular subjects, and Rhode Island supplemented the salaries of the teachers of secular subjects in private, including church-related, schools. The court combined the cases and ruled the financial aid in both cases a violation of the religious establishment clause (*Lemon v. Kurzman*).

Burger wrote the court opinion, and Black, Blackmun, Brennan, Douglas, Harlan, and Stewart joined him. (Marshall concurred in the Rhode Island decision but did not participate in the Pennsylvania case.) Burger again used the excessive entanglement religious-establishment test. He conceded the secular purpose and did not deny the secular effect—namely, the learning of secular subjects—but thought that the state would become administratively involved because it would need to insure that the teachers excluded religion from their instruction, which he did not think the teachers would be able to do spontaneously. Burger also cited a further entanglement—namely, that state aid to church-related schools would cause political divisiveness between those favored and those who opposed the aid. White dissented, arguing that he would presume in the absence of contrary evidence that religion was not being taught or would not be taught in state-funded courses and that enforcement measures would not be so extensive as to border on a violation of the free religious exercise.

In 1973 the court invalidated a New York program that provided tuition grants to low-income parents and tax deductions to middle-income parents of children attending private nonprofit, including church-related, schools (*Committee for Public Education v. Nyquist*). Ten years later, in 1983, the court by the narrowest margin upheld the constitutionality of a Minnesota program that permitted taxpayers to deduct from taxable income $500 to $700 of actual expenses for tuition, textbooks, and transportation of dependents to any primary or secondary school (*Mueller v. Allen*). Rehnquist wrote the court opinion, and Burger, O'Connor, Powell, and White joined him. Rehnquist feebly attempted to distinguish *Mueller* from *Nyquist* but did make the substantive point that the Minnesota program channeled aid to parochial schools through the private choice of individual parents. Marshall, joined by Blackmun, Brennan, and Stevens, dissented. Marshall saw no difference between the Mueller case and the Nyquist case, since both in his view had the direct and immediate effect of advancing religion.

In his dissents in *Lemon* and *Nyquist*, White argued that the ultimate judgment about whether the primary effect of governmental financial aid is secular or religious depends on whether the aid supports a separable secular function. If it does, then any financial benefit to religious organizations is secondary. If it does not, then the aid subsidizes religion.

In 1985 the court decided two cases involving public assistance to church-related schools. In one case a Michigan school district had adopted two programs in which classes for nonpublic, principally parochial, school pupils were taught by teachers hired by the public school system but conducted in nonpublic-school classrooms. One was a shared-time program in mathematics, reading, art, music, and physical education and the other a community education program for children and adults after regular school hours in arts, crafts, home economics, Spanish, gymnastics, drama, and the humanities. (The community education teachers were part-time employees of the public school system, but almost all were also full-time employees of the nonpublic schools in which the classes were held.) The court struck down both programs (*Grand Rapids v. Ball*). Brennan wrote the court opinion, and Blackmun, Marshall, Powell, and Stevens joined him. Brennan for various reasons, among which was what he described as the persuasively sectarian nature of the religious schools, found the primary effects of the programs religious. Burger and O'Connor concurred regarding the community education program and dissented regarding the shared-time program. Rehnquist and White dissented in favor of both programs.

The other case involved a federal program of remedial instruction for poor children administered by New York City. Title I of the 1965 Elementary and Secondary Education Act required that local school districts receiving federal funds provide the same remedial instruction for nonpublic-school students as for public-school students. The New York City program covered 300,000 students, including 183,000 in church-related schools. Public-school teachers taught the classes to parochial school students in parochial-school classrooms, religious symbols were removed from the classrooms during the instruction, and supervisors, unannounced, visited the classes once a month.

The court struck down the New York City program as an unconstitutional violation of the establishment clause (*Aguilar v. Felton*). Brennan wrote the court opinion, and the same four justices that joined him in the Grand Rapids decision joined him in this one. Here, Brennan argued that the program involved an excessive entanglement of government with religion, since the presence of public-school teachers in pervasively sectarian schools necessitated constant monitoring to prevent religious indoctrination. O'Connor, joined by Burger, Rehnquist, and White, dissented, directly questioning the utility of the excessive-entanglement test. O'Connor would have the privilege of laying the Aguilar decision to rest twelve years later in *Agostini v. Felton*.

In 1985 the court struck down a 1981 Alabama statute that authorized a period of silence in public schools for "meditation or voluntary prayer" (*Wallace v. Jaffree*). Stevens wrote the court opinion, and Blackmun, Brennan, Marshall, and Stevens joined him. Stevens argued that the establishment clause today prohibits governmental preference of religious belief over unbelief, although the framers probably intended only to prohibit preference of one religious belief over another. Applying the Schempp-Lemon test, he held that the statute lacked a secular legislative purpose and cited the pro-religious statements by its sponsors. Moreover, a 1978 statute, which authorized a minute of silence for meditation without mentioning prayer, fully served any secular purpose of a period of silence. O'Connor concurred in the judgment because she interpreted the 1981 statute to endorse prayer but suggested a different test than the Schempp-Lemon test—namely, whether the government in a given context is endorsing religion.

Three justices dissented. Rehnquist bluntly rejected the proposition that the establishment clause requires government to be strictly neutral between religion and nonreligion or that it prohibits government from endorsing prayer generally. Burger objected to the court's contention that the Alabama statute endorsed prayer by specifying voluntary prayer as one permissible mental activity during the period of silence. White argued that the statute did no more than answer a likely student question, "May students pray during the period of silence?" The decision had no consequence, since the 1978 statute authorizing a minute of silence for meditation was unobjectionable.

In 1984 the court by the narrowest margin upheld the constitutionality of a Christmas display that included a crèche and nativity scene (*Lynch v. Donnelly*). Each year the city of Pawtucket, Rhode Island, in cooperation with its downtown retail merchant association, erected a display during the Christmas season in a park owned by a nonprofit group and located in the heart of the shopping district. The display included both secular figures like Santa Claus and the figures of Mary, Joseph, and the infant Jesus. The district court enjoined the practice, and the court of appeals affirmed.

Burger wrote the court opinion, and O'Connor, Powell, Rehnquist, and White joined him. Burger held that the Constitution, by guaranteeing religious freedom, positively mandates that the government accommodate religion, and he applied the Schempp-Lemon test. He concluded that the crèche display had the secular purpose of celebrating a traditional public holiday, conferred no substantial or impermissible benefit on religion, and created no deep political division along religious lines. O'Connor concurred separately, arguing that the constitutional test of religious establishment is whether the government is endorsing religion. Brennan, joined by Blackmun, Marshall, and Stevens, dissented. Brennan applied the Schempp-Lemon test and reached a conclusion diametrically contrary to Burger's. The sectarian exclusivity of the nativity scene indicates a religious purpose beyond celebrating a holiday season, and inclusion of the scene in the municipal display put a government imprimatur on Christian beliefs, which would be offensive to non-Christians.

In 1985 the court struck down a Connecticut statute that forbade employers from requiring work of employees on the employees' religious day of rest and held that the statute was an unconstitutional establishment of religion (*Thornton v. Caldor*). Burger wrote the court opinion, and all the justices but Rehnquist joined him. Burger focused on the primary effect of the statute, which he said armed religious observers with an absolute and unqualified right not to work on whichever day they designated as a day of rest, and so religious concerns automatically dominated over the secular interests of employers and fellow employees. O'Connor, concurring separately, argued that the statute conveyed a message that endorsed religion and advanced it in that way. Rehnquist dissented without opinion.

The above decisions on the establishment clause by the Burger Court were not the only such decisions, especially regarding various aids to church-related schools or their patrons. If the reader feels confused by the decisions, he or she is not alone. First, the justices often disagreed on the test to apply. Second, they often disagreed on application of the two prongs of the Schempp test. Third, the excessiveness of governmental involvement with religion is obviously in the eye of the beholder. If one looks at the votes of the justices from 1981, when O'Connor joined the court, to 1986, when Burger retired, four (Blackmun, Brennan, Marshall, and Stevens) were almost always opposed to the governmental activity, three (O'Connor, Rehnquist, White) generally favorable, and two (Burger, Powell) unpredictable.

The Warren Court's decision in the Sherbert case spawned cases in the Burger Court and would continue to do so in the Rehnquist Court. In 1972 the court decided a case involving a conflict between the Amish Mennonites, whose religion prohibits attending school beyond the eighth grade, and Wisconsin, which required school attendance until the age of sixteen. The court ruled in favor of the Amish parents (*Wisconsin v. Yoder*). Burger wrote the court opinion, and Blackmun, Brennan, Marshall, Stewart, and White joined him. (Newly appointed Powell and Rehnquist, who had not heard the oral argument, did not participate.) Burger argued that ordinary secondary education contravened the basic tenets and practice of the Amish faith and that the state had the burden of demonstrating that the loss of one or two years of secondary education would impair the physical or mental health of the children or render them unable to support themselves as adults and be responsible citizens. He pointed out that the Amish parents had indicated their willingness to provide a few hours of vocational training each week, including a few hours of formal study. In short, the state had to show a substantial public interest against exempting Amish children from the compulsory-education law.

Stewart, joined by Brennan, added that the decision involved no question about the rights of Amish children to attend high schools if they wished to do so against the will of their parents. White, joined by Brennan and Stewart, added that the state had not demonstrated the inability of Amish children who leave school after the eighth grade to acquire further skills if they later abandon their parents' faith. Douglas dissented in the cases in which the children had not testified and would have remanded those cases for hearings on the children's views.

The court decided a number of cases involving government regulations that imposed indirect but severe financial burdens on the exercise of religious beliefs. One such case in 1981 (*Thomas v. Review Board*) was a carbon copy of the Sherbert case. Thomas, a Jehovah's Witness pacifist, terminated his employment at a roll factory producing sheet steel when he was assigned to work on armaments, and the Indiana board denied his application for unemployment compensation. The Indiana Supreme Court sustained the board, but the U.S. Supreme Court upheld Thomas's eligibility for unemployment compensation.

Burger wrote the court opinion, and all the justices but Rehnquist joined him. The religious beliefs of Jehovah's Witnesses forbid participation in war, and Thomas held the honest conviction that those beliefs extended to armament production. Indiana, by conditioning receipt of unemployment compensation upon conduct proscribed by Thomas's faith, imposed a severe, though indirect, burden on his exercise of religion. Burger held that that burden could only be justified if it was the least restrictive means to achieve a compelling public interest. Indiana advanced two justifications for the burden it imposed on workers like Thomas: the financial integrity of the unemployment compensation fund and the social undesirability of probing the religious beliefs of employees. Burger summarily dismissed both. Burger found no violation of the establishment clause for Thomas to receive the benefit of unemployment compensation precisely because of his religious beliefs, since the government has an obligation to be neutral in the face of religious differences.

Rehnquist was the sole dissenter. Rehnquist did not read the free exercise clause to ban indirect financial burdens on religious exercise to achieve minimally rational public interests. Applying that standard, he concluded that the free exercise clause did not require Indiana to recognize Thomas's eligibility for unemployment compensation. On the other hand, Rehnquist would not read the establishment clause to ban aid to religion involving no support for proselytizing activities. Applying that standard, he concluded that the establishment clause would not prohibit Indiana from recognizing Thomas's eligibility if it chose to do so. In a decade, Rehnquist's position on indirect financial burdens on religious exercise would become the court's.

The court decided two cases in 1986 that involved different kinds of indirect effects on religious exercise. One involved Goldman, an Orthodox Jewish rabbi and clinical psychologist serving as an officer in the U.S. Air Force. The air force dress code prohibits the wearing of any headgear indoors and unauthorized headgear outdoors. Goldman sought to enjoin application of the regulation to him on the grounds that he had a religious duty to wear a yarmulke and that the free exercise clause guaranteed him the right to do so. After he lost in the lower court, he appealed to the Supreme Court.

The court by the narrowest margin ruled against him (*Goldman v. Weinberger*). Rehnquist wrote the court opinion, and Burger, Powell, Stevens, and White joined him. Rehnquist declined to use the compelling-public-interest standard. Since the military has a special need for discipline, he argued that courts should be more deferential to military than to civilian decisions, and so it was a matter for military authorities to decide whether exception for Goldman and other Orthodox Jews to wear yarmulkes while on duty was compatible with military discipline. Stevens, joined by Powell and White, concurred, expressing concern about what an exception for the headgear of Orthodox Jews would imply regarding other religious claims to exemption (e.g., Sikhs to wear turbans).

Brennan, joined by Marshall, dissented, criticizing deference to military authorities in matters of constitutional right, foreseeing no discipline problem if Orthodox Jewish personnel were permitted to wear yarmulkes, and challenging the need for uniformity when military personnel were permitted to wear rings. Blackmun in dissent argued that the government had failed to demonstrate any significant cost to discipline if Goldman and possibly a few others were permitted to wear yarmulkes. O'Connor, joined by Marshall, would require the government to demonstrate that regulations serve important governmental interests and that exceptions for religious reasons would substantially harm those interests, which she thought the government had failed to do. Note that the conflict in this case was between a conditional command of the government—namely, don't wear a yarmulke on duty if you wish to serve in the air force—and the claim of Goldman to a right to serve in the military without being required to doff his yarmulke.

In the second case the court ruled against an American Indian who objected to a requirement that his daughter have a Social Security number in order for him to be eligible for aid to families with dependent children and for food stamps (*Bowen v. Roy*). Roy claimed that use of the number would cause evil to befall his daughter. Burger and all the other members of the court except White agreed that governmental use of the number did not affect Roy's beliefs or his actions and that Roy could not claim a denial of freedom of religious exercise because the government failed to act according to his religious beliefs. Whether the government could or would attempt to force Roy to provide the number on an application form is unclear; nor is it clear how the court would have decided if the issue had been clearly presented to them.

Press The Burger Court rendered several important decisions in the area of freedom of the press. On June 30, 1971, the court decided the Pentagon Papers case fifteen days after the government had initiated it in the New York federal district court (*New York Times Co. v. U.S.*). The district court on June 15 granted a temporary restraining order against the *Times* printing the papers, which dealt with administrative deliberations on the Vietnam War, and which the *Times* had begun to publish on June 13; the court of appeals affirmed the order pending the outcome of the government's case. On June 25 the Supreme Court expedited review, with oral arguments scheduled the next day.

The government claimed that publication of the papers would endanger lives, the release of war prisoners, and the Vietnam peace negotiations. On June 30 the court, by a six-to-three vote, dismissed these claims and issued a brief per curiam opinion holding that the government had not met the heavy burden of justifying prior restraint of the papers' publication, with each justice delivering a separate opinion. Three justices (Black, Brennan, and Douglas) held that *any* injunction against publication constituted a prior restraint, and none should ever be issued. Three justices (Marshall, Stewart, and White) held that no prior restraint was necessary in this case but rejected the absolutist position of the other majority justices. Three justices (Blackmun, Burger, and Harlan) dissented, objecting to the haste in reaching the decision. Note that the court did not say that the *Times* could not be prosecuted for violation of security laws after publication. Most observers later agreed that the published papers contained no material substantially injurious to national interests.

Almost exactly one year later, on June 29, 1972, the court decided three cases involving media personnel claiming a First Amendment privilege to protect the confidentiality of sources. Paul Branzburg, a Kentucky reporter, moved to quash a grand jury subpoena to provide additional material on his story about the production of hashish. Paul Pappas, a television journalist, refused to answer a grand jury's questions about his coverage of the Black Panthers. A federal grand jury held Earl Caldwell, a reporter for the *New York Times*, in contempt for refusing to appear before it to answer questions about his reporting on the Black Panthers. The U.S. Supreme Court consolidated the cases and by the narrowest margin held that there was no special privilege for the press in the matter of protecting the confidentiality of sources (*Branzburg v. Hayes*).

White wrote the court opinion, and Blackmun, Burger, Powell, and Rehnquist joined him. White cited common law and case law to hold that reporters had the same duty to answer questions before a grand jury as any other citizen. Stewart, joined by Brennan and Marshall, dissented, arguing that confidentiality of sources was essential to newsgathering and that a compelling public interest was required before a grand jury could gain information about a reporter's sources. Douglas dissented even more vigorously. Many states subsequently passed shield laws to protect the confidentiality of reporters' sources, but Congress has not done so.

In 1978 the court decided a case involving a warrant to search the offices of a college newspaper. In 1971 police in Palo Alto, California, were attempting to control demonstrators at Stanford University Hospital, during which violence and physical injuries resulted. The police then obtained a warrant to search the offices of the Stanford students' newspaper. The police found a photograph of the incident and in the course of the search read a number of confidential files. The *Stanford Daily* brought civil charges against the police and contended that the search violated the guarantee of freedom of the press and the Fourth Amendment's guarantee against unreasonable searches. The federal district court and the court of appeals ruled for the newspaper, and the government appealed to the Supreme Court.

The court ruled for the government (*Zurcher v. Stanford Daily*). White wrote the court opinion, and Blackmun, Burger, Powell, and Rehnquist joined him. (Brennan did not participate.) White argued that the Fourth Amendment made no special provision regarding the search of press offices, that such searches would not have a chilling effect on reporting news, and that a subpoena would not be an adequate substitute. White pointed out that, after issuance of a subpoena, someone friendly to the suspects could destroy the photographic evidence. Stewart, joined by Marshall, dissented, arguing that the search threatened physical disruption of newspaper activities and might lead to revelation of confidential sources. Stevens also dissented, arguing that the search did not meet the reasonableness standard, since the newspaper was not itself under suspicion. The decision led to the Privacy Protection Act of 1980, which limited the use of warrants to search newspapers when neither the newspaper nor its staff was suspected of wrongdoing.

Summary The Burger Court was an active court. It had a docket of more than 5,000 cases by its last year, the 1985 term. By comparison, the Hughes Court's docket in its last year, the 1940 term, was only slightly over 1,000 cases, and the docket in the Burger Court's first year was 4,000 cases. Moreover, the Burger Court decided more cases with a signed or per curiam opinion in the 1979 term (155) than the Warren Court did in the 1959 term (126). The Burger Court also invalidated more laws than the Warren Court had. The Warren Court struck down 23 federal statutes or parts thereof and 188 state statutes or local ordinances, but the Burger Court struck down 32 federal statutes or parts thereof and 308 state statutes or local ordinances. In regime decisions, the Burger Court strongly supported separation of powers. In racial desegregation cases, the Burger Court continued and even expanded the policies of the Warren Court. In split criminal justice decisions, the Burger Court overwhelmingly favored the government over the defendant but did not overturn any of the Warren Court rulings. In the area of privacy, the outstanding case, of course, was on the right of women to choose to have an abortion. In religious-establishment decisions, there was a radical division of the justices, four (Blackmun, Brennan, Marshall, and Stevens) generally opposed to the government activity at issue, two (Rehnquist and White) generally in favor of the activity, and three (Burger, Powell, and Stewart) sometimes opposed and sometimes in favor. Moreover, those decisions collectively seem to lack consistency.

11

THE REHNQUIST COURT

(1986–2005)

The Justices

William Rehnquist When Burger indicated that he would resign after his successor was confirmed, President Reagan nominated Associate Justice William Rehnquist to be chief justice on June 17, 1986, and the Senate confirmed Rehnquist on September 17. Burger formally resigned on September 26, and Rehnquist was sworn in as chief justice. He served in that capacity until his death on September 3, 2005.

Antonin Scalia To replace Rehnquist as associate justice, Reagan, also on June 17, 1986, nominated Antonin Scalia, and the Senate confirmed Scalia on September 17. Scalia, a Republican and a Catholic, was born on March 11, 1936, in Trenton, New Jersey. His father, Eugene, was an Italian immigrant and teacher of Romance languages at Brooklyn College. Scalia attended Xavier High School in Manhattan and graduated from Georgetown University in 1956 and from Harvard Law School in 1960. After graduation from college he spent a year as a student at the University of Fribourg, Switzerland. He was in private practice in Cleveland, Ohio, for seven years (1960–67). He taught at the University of Virginia Law School for four years (1967–71), served in the Nixon and Ford administrations for six years (1971–77), and taught at the

University of Chicago Law School for five years (1977–82). He served on a U.S. court of appeals for four years (1982–86).

Anthony Kennedy When Powell resigned on June 26, 1987, Reagan successively nominated Robert Bork and Douglas Ginsburg to the post, but the Senate rejected both nominees. Reagan then nominated Anthony Kennedy on November 24, and the Senate confirmed Kennedy on February 3, 1988. Kennedy, a Republican and a Catholic, was born on July 23, 1936, in Sacramento, California. His parents were middle-class professionals. He graduated from Stanford University in 1958, and his undergraduate work included study at the London School of Economics. He graduated from Harvard Law School in 1961. He engaged in private practice for thirteen years (1961–70, 1972–75). In 1971 he was a judge on the U.S. Tax Court, and he was a judge on the U.S. Ninth Circuit Court of Appeals for more than twelve years (1975–88). From 1965 to 1988, he taught at the University of the Pacific Law School.

David Souter Brennan resigned on July 20, 1990, and President George H. W. Bush nominated David Souter to the court on July 25; the Senate confirmed Souter on October 2. Souter, a Republican and a Protestant, was born on September 17, 1939, in Melrose, Massachusetts. He graduated from Harvard College in 1961, was a Rhodes Scholar for two years (1961–63), and graduated from Harvard Law School in 1966. He is a bachelor. In New Hampshire he was an assistant district attorney for eight years (1968–76), attorney general for two years (1976–78), a trial judge for five years (1978–83), and a justice on the Supreme Court of New Hampshire for seven years (1983–90). Shortly before his appointment to the court, he served on a federal court of appeals in 1990. He resigned from the court on July 29, 2009.

Clarence Thomas Marshall indicated his intention to resign on October 1, 1991, and Bush nominated Clarence Thomas to the post on July 1; the Senate narrowly (52–48) confirmed Thomas on October 15. A former aide and law professor, Anita Hill, had in October made sensational accusations of sexual harassment against Thomas, and the Senate Judiciary Committee held a second hearing on his nomination. Thomas, black, Republican, and Catholic, was born in relative poverty on June 23, 1948, in Savannah, Georgia. He graduated from Holy Cross College in 1971 and from Yale Law School in 1974. He was admitted to the Missouri bar and was assistant attorney general of the state for three years (1974–77). He was an assistant U.S. secretary of education for a year (1981–82) and chairman of the Equal Educational Opportunity Commission for eight years (1982–90). He served for one year on a federal court of appeals (1990–91).

Ruth Bader Ginsburg White indicated that he would resign on June 28, 1993, and President Clinton nominated Ruth Bader Ginsburg to the court on June 22; the Senate confirmed Ginsburg on August 3. Ginsburg, a woman, a Democrat, and Jewish, was born on March 15, 1933, in Brooklyn, New York. She graduated from Cornell College, attended Harvard Law School, and graduated from Columbia Law School in 1959. She was a research associate at Columbia Law School and taught at Rutgers Law School and Columbia Law School.

Stephen Breyer When Blackmun indicated his intention to resign after a successor had been chosen, Clinton nominated Stephen Breyer to the post on May 17, 1994, and the Senate confirmed Breyer on July 29. Blackmun resigned on August 3, and Breyer was sworn in. Breyer, a Democrat and a Jew, was born on August 15, 1938, in San Francisco, California. He graduated from Stanford University in 1959, attended Oxford University for two years (1959–61), and graduated from Harvard Law School in 1964. He was an assistant U.S. attorney general for two years (1965–67), assistant special prosecutor investigating the Watergate scandal in 1973, and special counsel to the Senate Judiciary Committee in 1974 and 1975 and its chief counsel in 1979 and 1980. He was a member of a sentencing commission for four years (1985–89) and at the same time taught at Harvard Law School. He was a judge on a federal court of appeals for the four years before his appointment to the Supreme Court (1990–94).

Summary Two Republican presidents (Reagan and Bush I) appointed four Republicans to the Rehnquist Court (Kennedy, Scalia, Souter, and Thomas), and a Democratic president (Clinton) appointed two Democrats (Breyer and Ginsburg). Three appointees (Kennedy, Scalia, and Thomas) were Catholics, two (Breyer and Ginsburg) Jewish, and one (Souter) a Protestant. All were graduates from elite colleges and elite law schools. Four (Breyer, Kennedy, Scalia, and Souter) graduated from Harvard Law School, and one (Souter) was a Rhodes Scholar. Four (Breyer, Scalia, Souter, and Thomas) had executive governmental experience, five (Breyer, Kennedy, Scalia, Souter, and Thomas) had judicial experience, and *none* had legislative experience. It is also interesting to note that all but Souter and Thomas had taught full-time or part-time in law schools before their appointment. The education of these appointees indicates the higher academic standards now prevalent in the legal professions.

Leading Decisions

Regime In its early years the Rehnquist Court decided several cases involving the separation of powers. The first case concerned the constitutionality of independent counsels. Title VI of the 1978 Ethics in Government Act provided for appointment of an independent counsel, whom the president could remove only for good cause—that is, misconduct—to investigate and possibly prosecute high-ranking executive officials for violations of federal criminal laws. The House Judiciary Committee requested that the attorney general, Edwin Meese, have an independent counsel appointed to investigate an assistant attorney general, Theodore Olson, whom the committee accused of making false and misleading statements to it. Meese applied to the special division of the Court of Appeals of the District of Columbia to appoint an independent counsel to investigate Olson. The special division appointed Alexia Morrison. When a grand jury under Morrison's guidance issued a subpoena to Olson, he moved to quash it on the grounds that the act providing for independent counsels violated the separation of powers. Olson lost in the district court but won in the court of appeals. Morrison appealed to the Supreme Court.

The court ruled that the act establishing independent counsels did not unconstitutionally abridge the executive power of the president (*Morrison v. Olson*). Rehnquist wrote the court opinion, and Blackmun, Brennan, Marshall, O'Connor, Stevens, and White joined him. (Newly appointed Kennedy did not participate.) Rehnquist held that an independent counsel is an inferior officer of the United States and so can be appointed by the court of appeals under Article II, section 2, clause 2 and that the assignment of the appointive power to the judiciary did not exceed the limitations implied by Article III, section 2, clause 1. He also thought that the limitation of the president's removal power to good cause did not impermissibly limit the president's executive authority.

Scalia was the vigorous sole dissenter. He argued that an independent counsel exercises executive functions, and Article II, section 3 clearly commits to the president the duty to see that the laws are faithfully executed. He ridiculed the court's argument that the president retained some control because he could fire the independent counsel for cause. Finally, Scalia denied that an independent counsel is an inferior officer of the United States, since he or she (in this case) is not subordinate to any executive officer, including the president. This provision of the Ethics in Government Act was later repealed, but Kenneth Starr would shine as the last independent counsel. Most commentators think that Scalia has been proved right.

The following year the court decided another separation-of-powers case, this time involving the delegation of legislative authority to an independent body of judges. Congress in 1984 passed the Sentencing Reform Act, which, among other things, established a sentencing commission of judges to promulgate mandatory sentencing guidelines. John Mistretta was at the end of 1987 indicted on counts of selling cocaine. He pled guilty to one count and was sentenced under the guidelines to a $1,000 fine, an eighteen-month imprisonment, and a subsequent three-year term of supervised release. Mistretta and the government petitioned the Supreme Court for immediate review, which the court accepted because of chaos resulting from contrary rulings by district courts on the constitutionality of the guidelines.

The court upheld the power of the sentencing commission to draft guidelines for sentencing (*Mistretta v. U.S.*). Blackmun wrote the court opinion, and the majority justices in *Morrison*, plus Kennedy, joined him. Blackmun argued that Congress had established sufficiently specific and detailed standards for the sentencing power it delegated to the commission and that the separation of powers is flexible. Scalia again dissented vigorously. He argued that Congress had granted the judicial commission the power to *make* laws. There is, however, one difference between the law at stake in the Morrison case and the one at stake in the Mistretta case. In the former, Congress was attempting to *limit* presidential power, but in the latter, Congress was attempting to *enlarge* judicial power, since the Sentencing Reform Act allowed the judges to determine collectively what they already had the power to determine severally.

In its last decade the Rehnquist decided a spate of cases involving regime principles. One involved the term limits of congressmen and senators. In 1992 the voters of Arkansas approved an amendment to the state's constitution that prohibited the listing of otherwise eligible candidates on the general election ballot for congressmen if the candidate had served in the House for three or more terms and for senators if the candidate had served in the Senate for two or more terms. Two advocacy groups immediately instituted suits in state courts challenging the constitutionality of the term-limits amendment. One won, and the other lost, in the state courts, and the losers petitioned to the

U.S. Supreme Court for review. The cases were combined and decided in 1995 under the name of one, *U.S. Term Limits, Inc. v. Thornton.*

The court by the narrowest margin declared the term-limits amendment unconstitutional. Stevens wrote the court opinion, and Breyer, Ginsberg, Kennedy, and Souter joined him. Stevens contended that the states could not add to the qualifications specified in the Constitution for congressmen (Article I, section 2, clause 2) and for senators (Article I, section 3, clause 3)—namely, age, length of citizenship, and state residency. He reached this conclusion because he thought term limits contrary to a fundamental principle embedded in the Constitution—namely, that the people should choose whom they please to govern them. He cited a strong precedent (*Powell v. McCormick*), in which the court in 1969 held that the House of Representatives could not add to the qualifications for congressmen specified in the Constitution. He also dismissed the argument that the Tenth Amendment reserves to the states the power of adding qualifications for congressmen and senators, since there were no rights to elect congressmen and senators to be reserved to the states before the adoption of the Constitution, a point the separate concurring opinion of Kennedy stressed.

Thomas, joined by O'Connor, Rehnquist, and Scalia, wrote an eighty-eight-page dissent. Thomas argued that the qualification clause specified the age, length of citizenship, and state residency required of congressmen and senators, and the states may not alter those requirements. But the Constitution does not specify that the states may not add qualifications, and so the Tenth Amendment becomes operative. The Constitution derives its authority from the consent of the people of the states, and so it is incoherent to say that the people of the states could not reserve any power that they did not previously control. The Tenth Amendment uses the word *reserves* to specify that all powers not prohibited to the states are reserved to them or the people. He pointed out the anomaly that follows from the court's opinion—namely, that the states may prohibit convicted felons from voting in congressional elections but not from running for Congress.

In 1985 Congress passed amendments to the Radioactive Waste Act of 1980 that provided incentives for the states to act. One of the "incentives" was that states that did not enter into regional compacts would have to take possession of waste and assume liability for the damages incurred by those who produced the waste. New York did not join a compact but created disposal sites within its own borders. When residents of counties in which the sites would be located brought suit against the amendments on the grounds that they violated the Tenth Amendment, the state joined their suit and became the principal plaintiff. New York lost in the district court and the court of appeals and appealed the case to the Supreme Court.

The court in 1992 ruled that the "take-title" incentive violated the Tenth Amendment (*New York v. U.S.*). O'Connor wrote the court opinion, and Kennedy, Rehnquist, Scalia, Souter, and Thomas joined her. Admitting that Congress may use incentives to win state compliance with regulations that it wishes to accomplish, she held that the "take-title" incentive crossed the line between encouragement and coercion and so violated state sovereignty. Unlike reliance on financial incentives, the "take-title" incentive gave the state a choice between regulating waste disposal as Congress wished or having the ownership of and liability for waste, neither of which Congress would have power to order a state to do.

White, joined by Blackmun and Stevens, dissented. White did not think the "take-title" provision was unconstitutional, in part because Congress could adopt a similar measure conditioning the payment of funds on the state's willingness to take title if it has not already provided a waste disposal facility and because Congress has the power under the commerce clause to regulate the producers of waste directly.

Congress in 1990 enacted a statute that banned the possession of guns within 1,000 feet of any school. In 1992 federal officials charged Antonio Lopez with knowing possession of a gun and bullets at a high school in San Antonio, Texas. The district court found him guilty of violating the statute, but the court of appeals reversed the conviction, holding the statute an unconstitutional invasion of states' rights. The government appealed to the Supreme Court.

In a landmark decision, the court by the narrowest margin affirmed the decision of the court of appeals (*U.S. v. Lopez*). This was one of the rare times since the New Deal days that the court denied the power of Congress to legislate under the commerce clause. Rehnquist wrote the court opinion, and all the Reagan appointees (Kennedy, O'Connor, and Scalia) and Thomas joined him. Rehnquist thought that the statute had nothing to do with any economic enterprise and that it could be sustained under the commerce power only if the possession of guns near schools *substantially* affected commerce. The government argued that the possession of guns in school zones might result in violent crime and that this would affect commerce in many ways and handicap the education of commercially productive citizens. Rehnquist rejected this line of arguments because it would convert congressional authority under the commerce clause to a general police power, which is the prerogative of the states and guaranteed to them by the Tenth Amendment.

Breyer, Ginsburg, Souter, and Stevens dissented. Breyer wrote the principal dissent, in which all the others joined. Breyer cited the links between an educational environment free of the threat of violence and economic commerce. Moreover, he did not understand how the majority could reconcile its decision denying Congress's power under the commerce clause to regulate a school environment by banning the possession of guns with the court's other decisions upholding Congress's power to regulate that environment by banning drugs, alcohol, and asbestos. He further compared the court's reasoning on the commerce clause to the court's previous use of substantive due process to invalidate state regulation.

Rehnquist argued that Congress had under the commerce clause power to regulate local things only if the intrastate activities had a *substantial* effect on interstate commerce. This sounds rather like the argument of the conservatives on the Hughes Court that Congress had under the commerce clause the power to regulate local things only if the intrastate activities had a *direct* effect on interstate commerce. Sutherland, the chief spokesman of the conservatives on the Hughes Court, tried to distinguish such effects on the basis of whether they result from proximate or remote causes. Rehnquist distinguished such effects on the basis of whether they are substantial, but what seems substantial or important depends on the beholder. Breyer, for example, reviewing the same facts, thought that the effects of possessing guns in school zones on commerce, although remote, *were* substantial.

Two years later, in 1997, the court ruled on a provision in the Brady Act that required local law enforcement officials to conduct background checks on handgun purchasers, and local governments bore the financial burden of implementing the federal regulatory program. (This provision was to be operative only for an interim before the federal program was fully implemented.) Two local law enforcement officials, Jay Printz of Montana and Richard Mack of Arizona, brought separate suits to enjoin enforcement of the provision as an infringement on state sovereignty but lost in the district courts. They appealed the case to the Supreme Court, and the court by the narrowest margin ruled in their favor (*Printz v. U.S.*).

Scalia wrote the court opinion, and Kennedy, O'Connor, Rehnquist, and

Thomas joined him. Stevens wrote the dissenting opinion, and Breyer, Ginsburg, and Souter joined him. Scalia admitted that the Constitution said nothing about the federal government conscripting local officials to enforce federal laws but argued that Congress had not in the past relied on state officials to enforce federal laws. He admitted that Congress had relied on state judges to process naturalizations and aliens, but that was compatible with the duty of the judges. Stevens read the same history as allowing the use of local officials to enforce federal laws. Note that Scalia mentioned the financial burden imposed on local governments by the Brady Act but did not make it an essential part of his argument.

In 2000 the court decided a case very similar to the Lopez case. Christy Brzonkala accused Antonio Morrison and James Crawford of rape and brought a civil suit in a federal court for damages under the 1994 Violence against Women Act. Morrison and Crawford moved to dismiss the complaint on the grounds that the statute's civil remedy was unconstitutional. The United States intervened to defend the statute. Morrison and Crawford won in the district court, and the government appealed to the Supreme Court.

As in the Lopez case, the court by the narrowest margin ruled that the statute at issue unconstitutionally infringed on states' rights (*U.S. v. Morrison*). Rehnquist wrote the court opinion, and Kennedy, O'Connor, Scalia, and Thomas joined him. Rehnquist made the same arguments that he had made in the Lopez case—namely, that violence against women, like possession of handguns, is not an economic activity and had no substantial effect on interstate commerce. He dismissed the congressional findings of a linkage, declaring that it was the judicial function to determine whether the linkage was substantial. This time, Souter wrote the dissenting opinion, in which Breyer, Ginsburg, and Stevens joined. Souter stressed the congressional findings and deference to the legislative judgment as long as it was minimally rational. Moreover, he deplored the lack of a workable definition of the New Federalism—that is, reactivation of the Tenth Amendment and reliance on ad hoc decisions.

In the last year of the Rehnquist Court, 2005, the court seemed to retreat from, or at least temper, the Lopez and Morrison decisions. The case involved the use of marijuana for medical reasons as permitted by a 1996 California statute but prohibited by the federal Controlled Substances Act. California doctors prescribed the use of marijuana for Angel Raich and Diane Monson. Raich received her supply from "caregivers" who grew it, and Monson cultivated her own supply. Federal and county officials came to Monson's home and found cannabis. The federal agents seized and destroyed the cannabis. Raich and Monson sought to enjoin the attorney general, Alberto Gonzales, from enforcing the Controlled Substances Act against them. The district court refused to issue a temporary injunction, but the court of appeals reversed on the grounds that Congress had no police power under the commerce clause to regulate a local activity. The federal government, in the name of Gonzales, appealed to the Supreme Court. The only issue before the court was the reach of the commerce power. In the early years of the twentieth century Congress had used the commerce clause to exercise police powers, and the court had sustained the laws, but the Lopez and Morrison decisions cast doubt on such exercises of federal police power.

The court held that the power of Congress over interstate commerce extended to any local activity that had a substantial effect on commerce and that the individual use of marijuana did (*Gonzales v. Raich*). Stevens wrote the court opinion, and Breyer, Ginsburg, Kennedy Scalia, and Souter joined him. Stevens argued that, while individual use of marijuana is a local activity, such activity in the aggregate would have a substantial effect on drug trafficking, an interstate commercial activity. Scalia concurred but contended that application of the drug law to individual local users was a necessary and proper means to deal with the problem of drug trafficking. O'Connor, Rehnquist, and Thomas dissented. O'Connor argued that controlled individual use would have no substantial effect on interstate commerce. Thomas argued that prohibition of individual use was not a necessary and proper means to regulate interstate commerce. This decision illustrates the intrinsic difficulty of determining when local activity has a substantial effect on interstate commerce. Indeed, the New Federalist justices themselves split on the issue, Kennedy and Scalia finding a substantial effect and O'Connor, Rehnquist, and Thomas not finding one.

In the twilight of the twentieth century and at the dawn of the twenty-first, the Rehnquist Court expanded states' sovereign immunity from suits by Indian tribes and private individuals. Congress in 1988 passed the Indian Gaming Regulatory Act, which permitted tribes to operate gambling casinos and required states to negotiate in good faith about opening casinos. It also allowed tribes to sue in federal courts if states failed to do so. In Florida Governor Lawton Chiles refused to negotiate with the Seminole tribe over casino gambling, and the tribe sued Florida in the federal district court. Ultimately, the court of appeals held that Congress had no authority to force states to negotiate and appealed to the Eleventh Amendment, which denied federal jurisdiction to hear suits by private parties against the states. The case then went to the Supreme Court.

In 1996 the court by the narrowest margin upheld the decision of the court of appeals (*Seminole Tribe v. Florida*). Rehnquist wrote the court opinion, and Kennedy, Rehnquist, Scalia, and Thomas joined him. Rehnquist argued that the Eleventh Amendment restricted federal judicial power over suits by private parties against the states and that Congress cannot use its other constitutional powers, such as the power to regulate commerce with the Indian tribes (Article I, section 8, clause 3) to circumvent that amendment. Souter, joined by Breyer, Ginsburg, and Stevens, dissented. Souter insisted that the Constitution always intended that the states should be subject to the jurisdiction of the federal courts when an individual claims a federal right and that the Seminole tribe was asserting a federal right on the basis of the Indian gaming act. Ironically, with the act voided, the tribe could seek and obtain authorization to open a casino from the federal Department of the Interior.

In 1992 a group of probation officers filed suit against their employer, the state of Maine, in the district court. They alleged that the state had violated the overtime provisions of the 1938 Fair Labor Standards Act, as later amended. The district court dismissed the action on the basis of the Eleventh Amendment and the Seminole Tribe decision, which the court handed down while the instant case was pending. Petitioners then filed the same action in a state court, which the act authorized. The state trial court dismissed the action on the basis of sovereign immunity, and the Maine Supreme Judicial Court affirmed. That court's decision challenged the constitutionality of the act's authorization of suits against the states in their courts without their consent, and the plaintiffs successfully petitioned the U.S. Supreme Court for review.

In 1999 the court by the narrowest margin affirmed the Maine court's decision holding the act's authorization of private suits against nonconsenting states in state courts unconstitutional (*Alden v. Maine*). The same five conservative justices in favor of state sovereignty formed the majority, and Kennedy this time wrote the majority opinion. The original Constitution said nothing on this subject, and the Eleventh Amendment concerned only federal judicial power. Nonetheless, Kennedy emphasized that, after the Chisholm decision in 1793, Congress immediately proposed the Eleventh Amendment, and the requisite number of states had ratified it by 1798. He thought that action indicated a broad-based consensus on a state sovereignty that precluded private individuals bringing suits against them without the states' consent. He was also concerned that private suits might threaten the financial integrity of the states. In the light of history, congressional practice, and the dual-sovereignty structure of the Constitution, the court held that states retain immunity from private suits in their own courts and that it is beyond congressional power to abrogate the immunity by Article I legislation.

Souter, joined by Breyer, Ginsburg, and Stevens, dissented. Souter argued that Kennedy's conception of sovereign immunity lacked support in the thinking of the founding era. (Souter did not consider contemporary newspaper comments on the Chisholm decision, which support Kennedy's position.) Maine has advanced no valid excuse for its courts' refusal to hear federal claims in which the state is the defendant, and sovereign immunity cannot be such an excuse, since the state is not sovereign with respect to the subject of the federal claim against it.

The next year, 2000, the court further expanded the doctrine of state immunity from private suits. The Age Discrimination Act of 1967, as amended in 1974, forbade discrimination against any employee, including any employee of a state. Plaintiffs, one of whom was J. Daniel Kimel, filed a federal suit under the act seeking money damages for alleged age discrimination by their state employers. They claimed that section 5 of the Fourteenth Amendment abrogated the state immunity of the Eleventh Amendment and that Congress exercised its enforcement power under section 5 against age discrimination, which violates the equal protection clause of section 1. They lost in both the district court and the court of appeals but took their case to the Supreme Court.

The court upheld the decision of the court of appeals and ruled that the attempted abrogation of state immunity exceeded Congress's authority under section 5 of the Fourteenth Amendment (*Kimel v. Florida Board of Regents*). O'Connor wrote the court opinion, and the four other New Federalist justices (Kennedy, Rehnquist, Scalia, and Thomas) agreed with the judgment and Rehnquist and Scalia with the whole opinion. O'Connor acknowledged that section 5 of the Fourteenth Amendment authorized Congress to override the sovereign immunity of states but held that, in light of the indiscriminate scope of the act's substantive requirements and the lack of widespread and unconstitutional age discrimination by states, the act's purported abrogation of state immunity was invalid. (O'Connor's argument about the congressional enforcement power under section 5 reflects the reasoning in *Boerne v. Flores*, which we shall consider later.)

Stevens, joined by Breyer, Ginsburg, and Souter, dissented from the court's judgment and most of its opinion. Stevens argued that the framers originally gave the states as such representation in the Senate; the states' representatives in Congress, all now directly elected by the people, are quite capable of representing the states' interests. Congress has power under the commerce clause to prohibit age discrimination by any employer, and Congress has made a policy choice to allow private parties to sue state employers in federal courts. Besides, the Eleventh Amendment declares that the federal judicial power shall not extend to suits by citizens of different states or foreign citizens, while the plaintiffs in the instant case were citizens of the same state.

One year later, in 2001, the court by the same five-to-four split reached a similar conclusion about the Americans with Disabilities Act insofar as the statute gave a right to disabled state employees to sue for damages in federal courts if a state failed to provide reasonable accommodation of their disabilities (*Board of Trustees of the University of Alabama v. Garrett*). Although the valid exercise of Congress's power to enforce the equal protection clause of the Fourteenth Amendment would abrogate a state's Eleventh Amendment immunity, application of the act to state employees was not a valid exercise of section 5. It was entirely rational and so constitutional, in the court's view, for a state employer to conserve scarce financial resources by hiring employees who were able to use existing facilities.

Regarding the Tenth Amendment–related cases, the Lopez and Morrison decisions have no large practical import for either the federal or state governments, and Congress can surmount the obstacles that the New York and Printz decisions placed in the way of federal regulatory programs by using incentives to induce state cooperation. But, had the Eleventh Amendment–related cases (*Alden, Kimel*) gone the other way, plaintiff tort lawyers in overdrive might indeed have threatened the finances of the states.

In 2002 the court by the narrowest margin extended state immunity to include immunity from the proceedings of federal administrative agencies (*Federal Maritime Commission v. South Carolina State Ports Authority*). The federal 1984 Shipping Act prohibited marine terminal operators from discriminating against terminal users and authorized the federal maritime commission to enforce it. The South Carolina Maritime Services Company complained to the commission that the state port authority had discriminated against it by denying it berthing space for a cruise ship in Charleston. An administrative law judge ruled that the state authority enjoyed immunity from proceedings of the commission. The commission reversed that holding, but the court of appeals reversed the commission's decision, and the commission appealed to the Supreme Court.

The court reversed the decision of the court of appeals and ruled that the state's sovereign immunity barred the commission from adjudicating a private party's complaint against a nonconsenting state. Thomas wrote the court opinion, and Kennedy, O'Connor, Rehnquist, and Scalia joined him. Although the Eleventh Amendment limits only the judicial power, not the executive power, of the federal government, Thomas understood state sovereign immunity to be a structural principle that extends to federal administrative agencies and argued that administrative decisions were the functional equivalent of judicial decisions. Breyer, Ginsburg, Souter, and Stevens dissented. They argued that the commission was a federal executive agency whose officials were appointed by the president and confirmed by the Senate and so represented the United States.

In 1990 the court handed down a sweeping decision against party patronage in public employment. In Illinois, a Republican governor issued an order prohibiting state hiring without his express consent, an order that in effect limited hiring to Republicans. Cynthia Rutan, a woman seeking promotion, and others brought suit against the Republican party of Illinois, claiming that the order violated the right of association guaranteed by the First Amendment. The district court dismissed the complaint, and the court of appeals affirmed. Rutan appealed to the Supreme Court.

The court by the narrowest margin ruled in favor of Rutan and the other plaintiffs, holding that party tests for promotions, transfers, recalls from layoffs, and even hiring of public employees in low-level jobs involving no policymaking were unconstitutional (*Rutan v. Republican Party of Illinois*). Brennan wrote the court opinion, and Blackmun, Marshall, Stevens, and White joined him. Brennan argued that to deny individuals low-level government jobs for partisan reasons would abridge their First Amendment rights to associate politically as they wished, and to do so would serve no vital government interest. Scalia, joined by Kennedy, O'Connor, and Rehnquist, dissented. Scalia's dissent was longer than the court's and blunt. He detailed the benefits of a party patronage system without endorsing such a system and argued that a legislative body, not the court, should be allowed to weigh the benefits of patronage against other values.

In 1996 the court struck down an amendment to the Colorado constitution

(*Romer v. Evans*). A statewide referendum adopted an amendment that prohibited all legislative, executive, or judicial actions at any level of state or local governments to protect the status of persons regarding their sexual orientation. Richard Evans, a gay activist, and a coalition of groups sued in Colorado courts to enjoin enforcement of the amendment. The trial court did so, and the Colorado Supreme Court affirmed. Colorado, in the name of the governor, Roy Romer, then appealed to the U.S. Supreme Court. The state argued that the amendment did not discriminate against gays, but only removed special rights for them, and that the court should respect the people's judgment and states' rights. Counsel for Evans argued that the amendment had no legitimate purpose.

The court affirmed the decision striking down the amendment. Kennedy wrote the court opinion, and Breyer, Ginsburg, O'Connor, Souter, and Stevens joined him. Kennedy argued that the amendment had no rational purpose but instead made gays unequal to everybody else. Rehnquist, Scalia, and Thomas dissented. They argued that the people of Colorado were within their constitutional rights to preserve traditional sexual mores and that they had adopted a reasonable provision that does not even discriminate against homosexuals.

In 1997 the court decided whether a sitting president, during his term of office, could be subject to a civil trial for unofficial conduct. Paula Jones sought to recover damages from President Clinton for actions by him before he became president—namely, improper sexual advances, punitive actions against her while he was governor of Arkansas, and authorizing various persons to brand her a liar while president. The district court deferred trial until the end of Clinton's term. The Supreme Court granted review.

The court unanimously reversed and ordered the civil judicial process to continue (*Clinton v. Jones*). Stevens wrote the court opinion, and all the justices except Breyer concurred in it. Stevens argued that there was no constitutional necessity to delay the judicial process, that the case was unlikely to prevent the president from carrying out his presidential duties, and that judges could control infrequent vexatious suits. Breyer concurred in the judgment but thought that civil suits against a president while he was in office, especially if there were many, could interfere with presidential functions, and that the court should have been more explicit on the point. Ironically, allowing the Jones suit to continue led to the discovery of a scandal (the Lewinski affair) and the impeachment of Clinton.

A very important regime question decided by the Rehnquist Court concerned the constitutionality of the 1996 Line-Item Veto Act. That act gave the president the power to cancel specified types of provisions in larger bills authorizing spending or conferring tax benefits. President Clinton exercised this power on two items, and the affected recipient parties, one of which was New York City, challenged his veto of the items. They won in the lower court, and the president appealed to the Supreme Court.

The court in 1998 upheld the lower court decision and ruled the Line-Item Veto Act unconstitutional (*Clinton v. City of New York*). Stevens wrote the court opinion, and Ginsburg, Kennedy, Rehnquist, Souter, and Thomas joined him. Stevens argued that the power to make line-item vetoes made law—that is, it repealed the original authorization, contrary to the mode specified by Article I, section 7. That article specifies that a law must be passed by Congress and presented to the president for his signature or veto. In short, the act gave the president alone the power to make law.

Three justices (Breyer, O'Connor, and Scalia) dissented. Breyer argued that the act conveyed executive, not legislative, power to the president. It did not violate any textual constitutional prescription, and it closely resembled congressional delegation of authority to the president to spend or not to spend appropriations, to change or not to change tariff rates, authority that Congress has frequently granted to the president. Moreover, Congress could specify that the act not apply to a subsequent authorization, and the president was permitted to act only in accord with the terms set by Congress.

The presidential election of 2000 was a cliffhanger, and the Supreme Court effectively decided it. Although the Democratic candidate, Albert Gore, narrowly won the popular vote by four-tenths of 1 percent, the electoral vote hinged on the outcome in the state of Florida. The returns on election night showed George W. Bush the winner of the state by 1,784 votes out of the nearly six million cast. Two days later a recount showed Bush still the winner but only by 327 votes. Gore asked for a recount. Katherine Harris, Florida's secretary of state, refused to waive the statutory deadline so that the manual recount could be completed, but the Florida Supreme Court voted unanimously to extend the deadline twelve days. This led to a chaotic scene to determine the validity of individual votes. The counties applied different standards in making their decisions. At the expiration of that deadline, November 26, the secretary of state certified the results on that date as official, with Bush the winner by 537 votes. Gore contested the certification, and the trial judge held on December 4 that Gore's lawyers had not shown that enough legal votes were rejected in order to challenge the result. Gore appealed to the Florida Supreme Court, and that court by a vote of four to three on December 8 overruled the trial court and ordered a manual recount of 45,000 unrecorded votes. The trial court allowed each of the sixty-seven county boards to set its own standards for judging the voter's intent.

Bush then filed an emergency petition to the U.S. Supreme Court to halt the manual recount, and the court issued a temporary injunction on December 9. It heard oral argument on December 11 and issued its decision late in the evening of December 12 (*Bush v. Gore*). The per curiam opinion held that the recount ordered by the Florida Supreme Court violated the equal protection clause of the Fourteenth Amendment because it failed to provide a uniform standard to govern the manual recount. Seven justices (Breyer, Kennedy, O'Connor, Rehnquist, Scalia, Souter, and Thomas) joined this holding of the court opinion. Stevens with Ginsburg dissented from it, finding no violation of equal protection or due process in the lack of uniform standards. Rehnquist, joined by Scalia and Thomas, argued in a concurring opinion that the Florida Supreme Court by ordering the manual recount and moving the date for certification had violated Article I, section 1, which says that the state legislature, not the state judiciary, should decide the manner of choosing electors. In short, the legislature should determine the electors according to existing state laws.

The per curiam opinion, supported by only five justices (Kennedy, O'Connor, Rehnquist, Scalia, and Thomas) voted to reverse the Florida Supreme Court's order for the manual recount. The opinion argued that there was no chance that the recount could be accomplished in compliance with the requirements of equal protection and due process before December 12, the last day federal law allowed the state legislature to appoint presidential electors if a valid slate had not been determined. This was, of course, the very day of the court's decision. In addition to Ginsburg and Stevens, Breyer and Souter dissented specifically from this holding and argued for remanding the case to the Florida Supreme Court, instructing it to establish uniform standards for the manual recount. They would have allowed five days to accomplish this— that is, until December 18, the day the electors were to meet, admittedly a tall order.

Whatever the merits of the legal arguments, the decision as a practical matter resolved a question that was otherwise unlikely to be settled expeditiously. In fact, it was probably impossible to determine the validity of disputed ballots in any principled way. The acceptance of the decision was a testimonial to the acceptance of the rule of law and the role of the Supreme Court in defining it. Kennedy and O'Connor provided the key votes on ending the manual recount.

In 2002 the court reviewed a canon of judicial conduct by the Minnesota Supreme Court that forbade candidates for elective state judgeships from announcing their views on legal, political, or social issues. Gregory Wersel, a past and potential future candidate, sued in a federal court against White, the chairperson of the board of judicial standards, to have the rule declared unconstitutional and to enjoin its enforcement. The Republican party of Minnesota joined his suit. The district court and the court of appeals upheld the rule, and the plaintiffs took the case to the Supreme Court.

The court by the narrowest margin declared that the rule violated the First Amendment (*Republican Party of Minnesota v. White*). Scalia wrote the court opinion, and Kennedy, O'Connor, Rehnquist, and Thomas joined him. Scalia argued that the rule did not survive the strict-scrutiny test because it was not narrowly tailored to promote a compelling public interest—namely, the goal of electing impartial judges. Moreover, judicial codes were only a relatively recent phenomenon, having been first advanced by the American Bar Association in the 1920s. States may not mandate judicial elections and simultaneously prohibit candidates from discussing issues. Breyer, Ginsburg, Souter, and Stevens dissented. They argued that states could restrict speech by judicial candidates in the interest of electing impartial judges.

Campaign Financing In 2002 Congress enacted the Bipartisan Campaign Reform (McCain-Feingold) Act. The statute contained five titles, two of which were key. Title I regulated the contribution of national parties to state and local party candidates. Title II limited the amount of money and the timing of ads by groups (chiefly corporations and unions) to influence elections. Mitchell McConnell, Republican leader in the Senate, and others brought suit in the district court of the District of Columbia against the Federal Elections Commission (FEC), claiming that the law was unconstitutional and seeking to have its enforcement enjoined. The district court upheld some provisions and disallowed others. Both opposing parties appealed the ruling to the Supreme Court.

The court heard oral arguments on the case on September 8, 2003, and handed down its decision on December 10 (*McConnell v. Federal Elections Commission*). The opinions of the justices covered 251 pages of the official reports, and the syllabus by the court clerk summarized the decision in seventy-three pages. Different coalitions of justices determined the outcome of particular provisions, upholding most of the law. Stevens and O'Connor wrote the court opinion upholding Title I and Title II by the narrowest margin, and Breyer, Ginsburg, and Souter joined them. Stevens and O'Connor adopted what they called a close-scrutiny test, a test in between strict scrutiny and minimum rationality. They argued that the contribution limits of Title I marginally restricted free speech and association and that congressional findings demonstrated the influence of money on policymaking. By the same standard and for the same reason, the court opinion upheld Title II's limits on the spending and timing of "electioneering" ads. Kennedy, Rehnquist, Scalia, and Thomas dissented from the court opinion on the two titles. They would have adopted a strict-scrutiny test and sustained the First Amendment challenges. The McConnell decision would not be the court's last word on campaign financing.

Race The Rehnquist Court decided a number of cases involving so-called racial gerrymandering. Two cases involved the same racial-minority congressional districting. After the 1990 census the North Carolina legislature, in order to comply with the 1965 Voting Rights Act, created one such district, the twelfth, which ran about 160 miles down Interstate 85 and was in some places no wider than the highway. The Department of Justice insisted that North Carolina create another racial-minority district, which the state did. Ruth Shaw, a white Democrat and resident of the twelfth district, sued the U.S. government in the person of Attorney General Janet Reno to enjoin the racial districting, but the district court dismissed the complaint. Shaw and the other plaintiffs then appealed to the Supreme Court.

In 1993 the court by the narrowest margin rejected the redistricting plan and the district-court ruling (*Shaw v. Reno*). O'Connor wrote the court opinion, and Kennedy, Rehnquist, Scalia, and Thomas joined her. O'Connor applied the strict-scrutiny test to the racial discrimination involved in the redistricting, which test requires a compelling public interest to justify the racial discrimination, and remanded the case to the district court for further proceedings consistent with that test. Blackmun, Stevens, Souter, and White dissented. White argued that the use of race in districting did not deny anyone access to the political process or equal protection of the laws.

On remand, the district court ruled that the redistricting plan was constitutional because it helped to remedy past discrimination. On appeal, the Supreme Court in 1996 again overruled the district court by the same narrow margin

(*Shaw v. Hunt*). Rehnquist wrote the court opinion, and Kennedy, O'Connor, Scalia, and Thomas joined him. Rehnquist stressed that the twelfth district lacked compactness and so was not narrowly tailored to meet the objective of remedying past discrimination. Breyer, Ginsburg, Souter, and Stevens dissented. They argued that the court should not use the strict-scrutiny test regarding state efforts to remedy past racial discrimination.

On the same day the court decided another race-conscious redistricting case. After the 1990 census the Texas legislature had redrawn three congressional districts in accordance with the 1965 Voting Rights Act, and the newly redrawn districts were more compact and regularly sized than those in the North Carolina redistricting. Two of the districts were predominantly black and one predominately Hispanic. The court, again by the narrowest margin, declared the racial gerrymandering unconstitutional (*Bush v. Vera*). There was no court opinion, but O'Connor wrote the plurality opinion, in which Kennedy and Rehnquist joined. O'Connor acknowledged that race had not been the only factor in creating the new districts, but that the other factors were subordinated to race. Scalia and Thomas agreed that the Texas redistricting plan was unconstitutional but refused to join O'Connor's opinion because they thought that it accepted the possibility that race might under some circumstances be used to draw district lines. Breyer, Ginsburg, Souter, and Stevens dissented. They thought the court's principle unworkable and that the states should have greater latitude to remedy the underrepresentation of minorities in Congress and to meet requirements of the Voting Rights Act.

The court in 1995 entered the thicket of another state's racial gerrymandering, this time concerning congressional redistricting in Georgia after the 1990 census, which showed blacks to constitute 27 percent of the state's population. In 1991 the Georgia legislature redrew its congressional districts, creating two majority black districts, the second of which was in response to demands by the Department of Justice. The department rejected even the revised plan, and the legislature in 1992 added a third majority-black district. Johnson and four other white voters in the new eleventh district filed suit in a district court to have the plan declared unconstitutional. The district court held for the plaintiffs, and the state in the name of Miller, the governor, appealed to the Supreme Court.

The court by the narrowest margin upheld the district court (*Miller v. Johnson*). Kennedy wrote the court opinion, and O'Connor, Rehnquist, Scalia, and Thomas joined him. Kennedy held that the burden was on the plaintiffs in racial gerrymandering cases to show that race was the predominant feature and that the plaintiffs had met that burden. Subjecting the plan to strict scrutiny, the court found it unconstitutional. Breyer, Ginsburg, Souter, and Stevens dissented. They thought that the court was applying a vague standard to review routine redistricting plans.

The Georgia legislature deadlocked on redistricting, and the district court overseeing the case created only one black-majority district. The Department of Justice and black voters headed by Lucius Abrams filed suit, claiming that the district court should have retained at least the two black-majority districts that the legislature proposed in 1991.

In 1997 the court by the narrowest margin upheld the decision of the district court (*Abrams v. Johnson*). Kennedy wrote the relatively brief court opinion, and the other conservative justices (O'Connor, Rehnquist, Scalia, and Thomas) joined him. Kennedy found the original 1991 plan, the legislature's, itself invalid because it was the result of pressure by the Department of Justice, and so the district court did not need to adhere to it. Second, he denied that the failure of the district court to create a second black-majority district was contrary to the Voting Rights Act. Breyer, joined by Ginsburg, Souter, and Stevens, dissented. Breyer argued that the majority paid too much attention to race and so threw the court into the political thicket of reapportionment, which the court should avoid. The 1991 plan, he argued, was a response to many pressures, not only to that by the Department of Justice. The decision reaffirmed the position of a narrow majority that race can be a factor in redistricting but cannot be the predominant factor.

Another case concerned the single-member commission form of government in Bleckly County, Georgia, since 1912. Hall and other black voters in the county brought suit in the federal district court against Jackie Holder, the single commissioner, and Robert Johns, the superintendent of elections. The black voters claimed that they were effectively disenfranchised because no black candidate could win office in an at-large election and that the court should establish five single-member districts, in one of which they would be able to do so. The district court ruled against Hall, but the court of appeals reversed on the basis of section 2 of the 1965 Voting Rights Act, which prohibits any practice that abridges voting rights on the basis of race.

The court by the narrowest margin in 1994 reversed (*Holder v. Hall*). Kennedy wrote the majority opinion, holding that the vote-dilution claim against the size of the commission under section 2 lacked a reasonable alternative practice to use as a benchmark and denying that section 2 must cover the same matter as section 5 (the pre-clearance requirement). Rehnquist agreed with both points. O'Connor agreed only with the first. Thomas, joined by Scalia, wrote a long concurrence (fifty-five pages of the official reports), calling for a major revision of the court's decisions on voting rights. Thomas read section 2 to protect only individual access to the ballot, not a minority group's right to influence election results. Blackmun, Ginsburg, Souter, and Stevens dissented. Blackmun, joined by the other three, argued that section 2 should be read broadly in order to implement its remedial purpose to eradicate racial discrimination in the electoral process. Stevens, joined by the other three, rejected Thomas's narrow reading of section 2.

The Rehnquist Court decided a few cases involving set-aside provisions for minority businesses. In 1983 the Richmond, Virginia, City Council adopted a five-year minority business plan requiring prime contractors with the city to subcontract at least 30 percent of the dollar amount of the contract to minority businesses. The plan contained waiver provisions for cases where every feasible attempt to comply failed. The council did not rely on any past discrimination by the city or prime contractors. J. A. Croson Company, a plumbing supplier, was denied a waiver and lost a contract. He sued in a federal district court to have the plan declared unconstitutional. Ultimately the court of appeals ruled that the plan failed the strict-scrutiny test and so violated the equal protection clause. Richmond appealed to the Supreme Court.

In 1989 the court affirmed the decision of the court of appeals, holding that the plan violated the equal protection clause (*Richmond v. J. A. Croson Co.*). O'Connor wrote the court opinion, and Kennedy, Rehnquist, Scalia, Stevens, and White joined her. O'Connor distinguished the case from that in *Fullilove* on the grounds that the latter case involved the federal government and that section 5 of the Fourteenth Amendment gave Congress a unique mandate to enforce the amendment's equal protection clause. To survive the strict-scrutiny test, the decision required that state and local governments rely on past discrimination in business contracts to justify affirmative action. Scalia's concurring opinion went further, arguing that the Constitution is colorblind and implying that all race-conscious plans, including those by the federal government, are unconstitutional in the absence of remedial action for past discrimination. Blackmun, Brennan, and Marshall dissented. In addition to the issue of merit, affirmative-action programs of set-asides for minority businesses raise the issue of probable extra costs for governments and ultimately taxpayers.

A year later, 1990, the court by the narrowest margin upheld two federal affirmative-action programs intended to increase minority ownership of broadcast licenses (*Metro Broadcasting v. Federal Communications Commission*). (The specific minority groups were African Americans, Hispanics, Eskimos, Aleuts, American Indians, and Asians.) Brennan wrote the court opinion, and Blackmun, Marshall, Stevens, and White joined him. Brennan held that congressional and commission findings supported the conclusion that diversity of ownership would promote diversity of programming. Kennedy, O'Connor, Rehnquist, and Scalia dissented. They doubted that Congress had sufficiently expressed such a legislative intent and that an individual minority station owner would program differently than a majority owner. Note that the decision sustained the minority affirmative-action program without reference to past or present discrimination.

In 1995 the court decided another federal set-aside program. The program provided financial incentives to government contractors who gave at least 10 percent of their business to minority subcontractors. Adarand Construction Company made the lowest bid for a national forest project, but the contract went to a Hispanic-owned company. Adarand then brought suit against the Department of Transportation and its head, Federico Pena, claiming that the set-aside subcontracting policy violated the due process clause of the Fifth Amendment. The federal district court and the court of appeals held that federal affirmative-action programs were not subject to strict scrutiny and that the set-aside program was constitutional.

The court by the narrowest margin overruled the Metro Broadcasting decision and remanded the case back to the lower court for reconsideration in terms of the strict-scrutiny test (*Adarand Construction Co. v. Pena*). O'Connor wrote the court opinion, and Kennedy, Rehnquist, Scalia, and Thomas joined her. (Thomas, Ginsburg, and Breyer had replaced Marshall, White, and Blackmun, respectively, and the advent of Thomas was the key to the reversal of position from *Metro Broadcasting*). O'Connor held that federal affirmative-action programs, like state and local programs, need to satisfy the strict-standard test and remitted the case to the lower court. Scalia went further, noting his belief that the program at issue could not withstand that test. Thomas, in another concurring opinion, described affirmative-action programs as patronizing and paternalist. Breyer, Ginsburg, Souter, and Stevens dissented. Stevens urged that the history of race relations required the federal government to take remedial action. Ginsburg argued against Scalia and Thomas that a carefully crafted affirmative-action program could satisfy the equal-protection requirement of the Fifth Amendment. The net effect of the decision was that any affirmative-action program had to be narrowly tailored and apply to victims of past discrimination.

In 2003 the court for the first time in twenty-five years since the Bakke decision heard and decided two cases on affirmative-action programs for the admission of minority students to public colleges and universities. In one, Barbara Grutter, a white applicant and resident of the state, was denied admission to the University of Michigan Law School in 1996 and contended in a federal lawsuit in December 1997 that the school's affirmative-action program had deprived her of the equal protection of the laws. She sought compensatory and punitive damages. That school's policy required individual evaluation of each applicant based on undergraduate grades, the law school admission test, letters of recommendation, and an essay on how the applicant would contribute to the law school. Admissions officials were to ensure that the applicant was well-qualified and to assess the applicant's contribution to the school. Special attention was to be given to inclusion of students from traditionally discriminated-against groups like African Americans, Hispanics, and American Indians. The district court ruled in her favor, but the court of appeals reversed. She appealed to the Supreme Court.

The court by the narrowest margin upheld the law school's affirmative-action program (*Grutter v. Bollinger*). O'Connor wrote the court opinion, and Breyer, Ginsburg, Souter, and Stevens joined her. She applied the strict-scrutiny test and found that the programs served a compelling public interest—namely, the benefits flowing from a diverse student body—and that it was narrowly tailored to consideration of race without imposing quotas. Kennedy, Rehnquist, Scalia, and Thomas dissented. Kennedy and Rehnquist argued that the program was not narrowly tailored to achieve racial diversity but rather a subterfuge for achieving racially proportionate admissions. Scalia and Thomas argued that the equal protection clause prohibits any consideration of race in admissions.

In the other case, Jennifer Gratz and Patrick Hamacher, white Michigan residents, unsuccessfully sought admission to the undergraduate program of the University of Michigan's College of Literature, Science, and Arts They contended in a federal lawsuit that the undergraduate affirmative-action admissions program deprived them and others similarly situated of the equal protection of the laws and sought compensatory and punitive damages. That program automatically assigned twenty points to every applicant from an underrepresented minority group. Every applicant for admission needed to reach one hundred points to achieve admission, and the twenty points assigned by the program to minorities was larger than the points assigned to any other factor. The district court rendered summary judgment for the plaintiffs regarding the program from 1995 to 1998 but upheld the current program. While the court of appeals was reviewing the district court decision, the plaintiffs appealed the case to the Supreme Court, which accepted review along with the Grutter case.

The court upheld the district court decision regarding the undergraduate affirmative-action program in 1995 to 1998 but rejected the part upholding the present guidelines (*Gratz v. Bollinger*). Rehnquist wrote the court opinion, and Kennedy, O'Connor, Scalia, and Thomas joined him. Breyer concurred only in the judgment. Rehnquist followed the strict-scrutiny test and held that the undergraduate program was not narrowly tailored to the compelling interest of a diverse student body. The automatic assignment of twenty points to each applicant from a minority group was a quota system and provided for no individualized consideration. In fact, the automatic assignment made the race factor virtually decisive for every minimally qualified minority applicant. Ginsburg, Souter, and Stevens dissented. Stevens, with Souter, would have dismissed the case on the grounds that the plaintiffs lacked proper standing, since they had already enrolled in other schools before they filed their action. Souter, with Ginsburg, also dissented on the merits. Ginsburg, joined in part by Breyer, argued that the court should distinguish between official policies using racial classifications for exclusion, which are unconstitutional, and official policies using racial classifications for inclusion. Given the history of racial discrimination, she held that racial classification might be constitutional if it is benign and does not unduly trample on the opportunities of others.

Gender-Based Affirmative Action In 1987 the court decided a case involving a gender-based affirmative-action program. The transportation agency of Santa Clara County, California, in 1978 adopted a temporary affirmative-action program regarding the promotion of qualified applicants of racial and gender minorities in job classifications in which women and members of racial minorities had been traditionally underrepresented. For example, none of the agency's skilled craft workers were women. The program established annual goals in hiring and promoting rather than specific numbers. In 1979 there was a vacancy for the job of road dispatcher, a job that no woman had ever held. Johnson, a male employee, and Joyce, a female employee, applied for the job. Both were rated well-qualified, although Johnson had a slightly higher interview score. Johnson sued and lost in both the district court and the court of appeals. He then appealed to the Supreme Court.

The court upheld the voluntary gender-based affirmative-action program and Joyce's promotion under it as permissible under Title VII of the 1964 Civil Rights Act (*Johnson v. Santa Clara County*). Brennan wrote the court opinion. Blackmun, Marshall, and Powell joined him, and O'Connor and Stevens concurred separately. Brennan stressed the history of past societal discrimination against women and the flexibility of the program and cited *Weber* as a precedent. Under the plan women competed with other qualified applicants, and gender was only one of the factors considered. Scalia, joined by Rehnquist and White, dissented. Scalia argued that Title VII prohibited voluntary workplace discrimination except to remedy actual past discrimination by the county and that *Weber* should be overruled.

Privacy The Rehnquist Court decided several important cases involving restrictions on abortion. In one, several health professionals and private corporations providing abortions and other gynecological services brought suit in a federal district court challenging the constitutionality of a 1986 Missouri statute imposing restrictions. The most controversial restriction required physicians to perform medical tests to determine the viability of the fetus when the doctor judged that the gestational age of the fetus was twenty weeks, which falls within the second trimester of pregnancy as defined in the Roe decision. The district court invalidated seven provisions, and the court of appeals in 1988 affirmed. Missouri appealed the case to the Supreme Court.

In 1989 the court by the narrowest margin reversed the decision of the court of appeals and upheld the restrictions (*Webster v. Reproductive Health Services*). Rehnquist wrote the plurality opinion, in all of which only Kennedy and White joined. On the most controversial restriction, Rehnquist held that the provision could be upheld only if the Roe decision was modified. He acknowledged that abortion was a liberty interest protected by the due process clause, but it could be affected if the state had a sufficient countervailing public interest. He argued that the state's interest in potential human life was present throughout pregnancy, and so the state could require the medical test. O'Connor agreed with the plurality opinion's judgment on the constitutionality of the provision but for a different reason—namely, that the provision was consistent with *Roe*, since the fetus might be in the third trimester of pregnancy. Scalia concurred with the result in the case but argued that Rehnquist and O'Connor had failed to take the decisive step of overruling *Roe*. Blackmun wrote a vigorous dissent, and Brennan, Marshall, and Stevens joined him. Like Rehnquist, Blackmun took the medical-test provision to be a second-trimester regulation that was not designed to protect the health of the mother, and so he deemed its interest in preserving the life of the fetus unconstitutional.

In 1991 the court considered a federal regulation of abortion. Title X of the 1970 Public Health Service Act provided grants to public and private family-planning services and authorized the secretary of the Health and Human Services Department to promulgate regulations. The act provided that none of the funds appropriated may be used in programs where abortion is a method of family planning. In 1988 the secretary set three new conditions on fund grants, two of which prohibited counseling or advocating abortion. Irving Rust and other grantees brought suit on behalf of themselves and their clients in a district court, claiming that Title X did not authorize the regulations and that they violated the rights of clients and especially the First Amendment rights of the health providers. The district court rejected the statutory and constitutional claims, and the court of appeals affirmed. The Supreme Court granted review.

The court by the narrowest margin affirmed the lower court's decision (*Rust v. Sullivan*). Rehnquist wrote the court opinion, and Kennedy, Scalia, Souter, and White joined him. Rehnquist held that the regulation was a permissible interpretation of the statute to which the courts should defer. He rejected the free-speech claim on the grounds that the doctors could continue to advise women about the availability of abortions outside the funded programs. He also held that the rules did not impermissibly burden the clients' right to choose to have an abortion. Blackmun, Marshall, O'Connor, and Stevens dissented. Blackmun stressed that the government could not impose spending conditions that discriminated against a particular point of view.

In 1988 and 1989 Pennsylvania amended its abortion-control act to mandate informed-consent counseling, a twenty-four-hour waiting period, the consent of one parent or judicial approval for minors, and the consent of the husband in the case of married women, with an exception for medical-emergency cases. A local planned-parenthood organization sued in a federal district court to enjoin enforcement of the amendments, and the court did so. The court of appeals reversed except regarding the husband-notification requirement. The case then went to the Supreme Court.

In 1992 the court affirmed the decision of the court of appeals (*Planned Parenthood of Southeastern Pennsylvania v. Casey*). The justices issued five opinions that totaled more than 125 pages in the official reports. Kennedy, O'Connor, and Souter wrote a joint plurality opinion. They affirmed the fundamental right of women to have an abortion and defended *Roe* both in terms of following precedent and maintaining judicial credibility in the face of adverse political pressure. But the joint opinion also held that the right of a woman to have an abortion is subject to the public interest in the potential life of the fetus and rejected the rigid trimester framework of *Roe*. They employed an undue-burden test—namely, whether a restriction put a substantial obstacle in the way of a woman seeking an abortion. Applying that test, they concluded that only the spousal-consent requirement was an undue burden. Blackmun and Stevens agreed with reaffirmation of *Roe* but would strike down all the restrictions (Blackmun) or all but the informed-consent requirement (Stevens). Rehnquist, Scalia, Thomas, and White would have upheld all the requirements and indeed overruled *Roe*.

In 2003 the court reconsidered its decision in *Bowers v. Hardwick*. A Texas statute made it a crime for two persons of the same sex to engage in certain sexual acts (oral and anal sex). Police in Houston, Texas, had gone to a private residence to investigate a reported weapons disturbance. They entered the apartment of John Lawrence and saw him and Tyron Gardner engaged in sodomy. The two were arrested and convicted of violating the statute, over their objection that it was unconstitutional. A Texas court of appeals affirmed the constitutional validity of the Texas statute on the basis of the Bowers decision. Lawrence and Garner appealed to the U.S. Supreme Court.

The court declared the Texas law unconstitutional and expressly overruled *Bowers* (*Lawrence v. Texas*). Kennedy wrote the court opinion, and Breyer, Ginsburg, Souter, and Stevens joined him. Kennedy argued that individuals have a fundamental right to choose personal relationships and that the state has no legitimate interest on the basis of which to intrude on its expression. He pointed out the modern decriminalization of sodomy in other countries (e.g., in the United Kingdom in 1967 and the European Court of Human Rights in 1981) as evidence that Western opinions about homosexuality had changed. O'Connor, who had concurred in *Bowers* and was unwilling to overrule it, concurred in the judgment on equal-protection grounds. She argued that the Texas law, by banning same-sex but not opposite-sex sodomy, indicated that the law was based only on moral disapproval of homosexuality and that that basis lacked minimal rationality. Rehnquist, Scalia, and Thomas dissented. Scalia stressed the role of stare decisis, the ancient roots of criminalizing sodomy, and the legitimate interest in morality. He also charged that the court had signed onto the homosexual agenda and argued that culture wars should be left to legislatures. Thomas thought the law silly but also argued that the matter should be left to legislatures and that there is no general right to privacy in the Constitution.

Criminal The Rehnquist Court, like the Burger Court, generally supported the government in criminal cases. For example, the Rehnquist Court in the 1987 term supported the government in fourteen out of the twenty criminal cases on which the justices divided. The court decided a number of cases involving what constitutes a search by the police and whether a search, if there be one, requires a warrant. In one case police had received information that Greenwood was engaged in drug-trafficking along with a complaint from one of his neighbors about noise. Without a warrant, they collected and opened a sealed opaque bag left with other refuse at a street curb for garbage collection. In the bag were items indicative of drug use. On the basis of that evidence the police obtained a warrant to search his house, where they found quantities of cocaine and hashish. (After his release on bail, this sequence was repeated to the letter.) Greenwood was convicted of possession of illegal drugs, but the California Supreme Court held that the evidence in the bag had been illegally searched, and so the warrant to search the house was invalid. California appealed to the U.S. Supreme Court.

In 1988 the court held that opening the sealed bag involved no search within the meaning of the Fourth Amendment, so that the evidence from it was legally obtained (*California v. Greenwood*). White wrote the court opinion, and Blackmun, O'Connor, Rehnquist, Scalia, and Stevens joined him. White argued that Greenwood had no reasonable expectation of privacy in bags left for garbage removal. In the view of the majority the issue was whether an expectation of privacy in the discarded items was objectively reasonable. It was not, in their view, because the refuse was open to rummaging by humans and animals. Brennan, joined by Marshall, dissented. Brennan argued that Greenwood did have a reasonable expectation that the *police* would not rummage through his garbage. (Newly appointed Kennedy did not participate.) Most of the press and probably many of its readers agreed with Brennan.

Two cases in 1989 concerned the constitutionality of federally mandated drug testing of employees. In one case the Federal Railroad Administration required blood and urine testing of employees involved in railroad accidents and permitted urine tests where employees violated certain safety rules. Railroad unions successfully challenged the regulations in the district court, claiming that they violated the Fourth Amendment, and the government appealed the case to the Supreme Court.

The court upheld the regulations (*Skinner v. National Labor Executives Association*). Kennedy wrote the court opinion. Blackmun, O'Connor, Rehnquist, Scalia, and White joined him, and Stevens concurred in the judgment. Kennedy admitted that the government mandate implicated the Fourth Amendment but held that public safety justified an exception to its usual warrant, probable cause, and individualized suspicion requirements. Brennan and Marshall dissented vigorously. They found the court's special-needs test unprincipled, dangerous, and a cavalier disregard for the constitutional text.

The companion case involved the constitutionality of the program of the United States Customs Service that required urine drug testing of employees who sought promotion to positions involving the interdiction of drugs. A union of employees sued to enjoin the program, and a district court granted the injunction. The government appealed to the Supreme Court.

The court by the narrowest margin upheld the program (*National Treasury Employees Union v. Von Raab*). Kennedy wrote the court opinion, and Blackmun, O'Connor, Rehnquist, and White joined him. Kennedy held that the Fourth Amendment applied to the program but argued that the government's special needs justified a departure from the amendment's warrant, probable cause, and individualized suspicion requirements. He thought that service personnel using drugs could be bribed and misuse their arms. He held that the government had a compelling public interest in protecting the borders against drug trafficking and that the public-safety interest was sufficient to outweigh the privacy expectations of employees. Brennan, Marshall, Scalia, and Stevens dissented. Brennan and Marshall complained, as they had in *Skinner,* that the decision's elimination of probable cause was unprincipled and unjustifiable. Scalia and Stevens complained that the decision was based solely on speculation about actual or possible harm.

Drug testing of students in public schools also raised a Fourth Amendment issue. A school district in Veronia, a small Oregon town, adopted a program of random drug testing of middle- and high-school athletes. James Acton, a twelve-year-old seventh-grader, wanted to try out for the football team, but his parents refused to sign the urinalysis form and sued in a federal district court to enjoin the program. The district court dismissed the suit, but the court of appeals reversed. Because another court of appeals had permitted random drug testing, the Supreme Court reviewed the two cases.

The court upheld the Veronia program (*Veronia School District v. Acton*). Scalia wrote the court opinion, and Breyer, Ginsburg, Kennedy, Rehnquist, and Thomas joined him. Scalia held that school officials have more authority over students than other officials have over free adults, that the urine samples were taken in relative privacy, that the school board had an important interest in attacking drug use in the schools, and that its program for campus leaders was likely to be an effective means. Ginsburg in a concurring opinion argued that the decision was limited to random testing of student athletes. O'Connor, joined by Souter and Stevens, dissented. She supported the idea of random drug testing but thought the testing should be limited to students who were disciplinary problems. She objected to what she described as a mass search without individualized suspicion of those tested.

In a related area of administrative searches, the court decided a case involving a Michigan program establishing highway checkpoints to test drivers' sobriety, with specific guidelines about the location of the points and their operation as well as well-publicized information about them. Some drivers sued, claiming that the checkpoint operations violated the Fourth Amendment requirement of probable cause and a warrant. The drivers won their case in the state courts, and Michigan appealed the case to the U.S. Supreme Court.

In 1990 the Supreme Court reversed and held that the state courts had misinterpreted the balancing test for administrative searches (*Michigan Department of State Police v. Sitz*). Rehnquist wrote the court opinion, and Blackmun, Kennedy, O'Connor, Scalia, and White joined him. The fear to be balanced against the substantial public interest in restricting drunken driving was that of law-abiding drivers undergoing an administrative search, not that of drunken drivers. Brennan, Marshall, and Stevens dissented.

In the same year the court considered the level of justification that the Fourth Amendment requires before police can without a warrant conduct a protective sweep of the premises of a home in the course of lawfully arresting a suspect. In the course of arresting Jerome Buie in his home, a protective sweep without a warrant produced incriminating evidence used in his trial. The state courts ruled against Buie's claim that the evidence had been illegally obtained because of the lack of a search warrant. Buie appealed to the U.S. Supreme Court.

The court upheld the legality of the protective search and laid down the principles governing such searches (*Maryland v. Buie*). White wrote the court opinion, and Blackmun, Kennedy, O'Connor, Rehnquist, and Scalia joined him. White held that police may always search closets and spaces immediately in the area of the arrest from which an attack could be launched and that police may conduct a search of other places if the circumstances would lead an officer reasonably to believe that the area to be searched harbors an individual posing a danger to the officer. Brennan and Marshall dissented on the latter point.

In 1991 the court returned to the question of when a warrant is required for police to open a closed container in a lawfully stopped automobile when they have probable cause to believe that it contains contraband. Police in Santa Ana, California, knew that several wrapped marijuana packages had been delivered to the apartment of Charles Acevado. Later in the day they observed him leave his apartment carrying a large paper bag that was the size of one of the marijuana packages. He placed the bag in the trunk of his car and drove away. Police stopped the car, opened the trunk and the bag, and found marijuana. The contents of the bag were admitted into evidence at his trial, and Acevado was convicted of possession of marijuana with the intent to sell it, but the appellate state court reversed the conviction, holding that the police needed to obtain a warrant to open the bag. California appealed to the U.S. Supreme Court.

The court held that the police, having probable cause, had no need to obtain a warrant before they opened a closed container in a lawfully stopped automobile (*California v. Acevado*). Blackmun wrote the court opinion, and Kennedy, O'Connor, Rehnquist, Scalia, and Souter joined him. There were two precedents to go by. One was that of *Arkansas v. Sanders*, which held that police need a warrant to search a container that they have probable cause, even certainty, to believe contains contraband but no probable cause to search the motor vehicle itself. The other was *U.S. v. Ross*, which held that, if the police had probable cause to search an entire vehicle for contraband and came across a closed container, they could open the container without a warrant. Blackmun adopted a uniform rule for searches of containers found in an automobile—namely, that that there was no difference between whether the search of a vehicle incidentally turns up contraband in a container or the search of a container probably containing contraband incidentally turns up in a vehicle. Scalia in a separate concurrence in the judgment went further. He would allow searches of closed containers on probable cause without a warrant anywhere but homes. Stevens, who wrote the Ross opinion, and White wrote dissenting opinions, and Marshall joined Stevens's opinion.

In the same year the court considered a case concerning what constitutes the seizure of a person within the context of the Fourth Amendment. Under a random program to interdict drugs, the Broward County, Florida, police boarded a bus about to leave on which Terrance Bostick was a passenger, The police asked him for identification, questioned him, and got his permission to search his luggage. In the luggage were contraband drugs, and Bostick was convicted of possession of illegal drugs. On appeal, Bostick contended that he had been illegally seized and that his consent to the search was coerced, since a reasonable person would not feel free to leave the bus. The Florida Supreme Court agreed, and Florida took the case to the U.S. Supreme Court.

The court held that the Florida court erred when it adopted an absolute rule prohibiting police from boarding buses and approaching passengers at random to interdict drugs and remanded the case to the Florida court for reconsideration in light of the court opinion (*Florida v. Bostick*). O'Connor wrote the court opinion, and Kennedy, Rehnquist, Scalia, Souter, and White joined her. O'Connor admitted that the movement of Bostick as a passenger was limited and that, if he left the bus, he risked being stranded and losing his luggage. But she held that the appropriate legal question was whether a reasonable person would feel free to terminate the encounter, not whether a reasonable person would feel free to leave the bus. Marshall, joined by Blackmun and Stevens, strongly dissented. Marshall thought the whole program involved the seizure of individuals without any individualized probable cause.

In 1995 the court held unanimously that the Fourth Amendment requires the common-law rule that police knock and announce themselves before they execute a search warrant (*Wilson v. Arkansas*). Arkansas was one of the few states that did not require police executing a warrant to knock and announce themselves. On New Year's Eve 1992 state police without knocking burst into the home of Sharlene Wilson of Malvern. They had a valid search warrant to search for narcotics. They found a large quantity of narcotics, a gun, and ammunition and stopped Wilson from flushing narcotics down the toilet. She was arrested, convicted, and sentenced to thirty-one years in prison. The Arkansas Supreme Court upheld the conviction, holding that the Fourth

Amendment did not include the knock-and-announce rule. Because of different rulings on the issue by lower federal courts, the U.S. Supreme Court granted review.

Thomas wrote the court opinion, which all the justices joined. He relied on the history of the Fourth Amendment but also found that the framers did not intend that the police must always knock and announce themselves before executing a search warrant. He held that the framers wanted the police to have discretion to do so when necessary to prevent the destruction of evidence, harm to the officers, or the escape of suspects. He remanded the case to the state courts to apply the decision to the facts of the case, which seemed to indicate that the police had good reason to fear the destruction of evidence. The ruling was a rare victory for criminal defendants in the Rehnquist Court and a rare instance of a signed court decision without concurring opinions or dissent.

The Burger Court heard arguments on the use of peremptory challenges in December 1985 in one of the last cases it decided. Batson, a black man, was tried for burglary and receiving stolen goods. The trial judge permitted the prosecutor to exercise his customary right to peremptorily—that is, without explanation—oppose the sitting of a prospective juror. The prosecutor's peremptory challenges removed all four black persons from the panel. Batson moved to discharge the jury, claiming that the removal of all the black panelists violated his Sixth Amendment right to be tried by a cross-section of his peers. The trial judge denied the motion, and Batson was convicted on both counts. The Supreme Court of Kentucky affirmed the convictions, and Batson appealed to the U.S. Supreme Court.

The court in 1986 ruled that prosecutorial use of peremptory changes on the basis of race was unconstitutional (*Batson v. Kentucky*). Powell wrote the court opinion, and Blackmun, Brennan, Marshall, O'Connor, Stevens, and White joined him. Burger and Rehnquist dissented. In effect, the court held that the public interest in a jury being representative trumped the public interest in putative jury impartiality. Traditionalists strongly criticized the decision.

The Rehnquist Court extended the reach of the Batson decision. In 1991 the court held that potential jurors could not be peremptorily excluded from a jury on the basis of race in civil cases any more than in criminal cases (*Edmonson v. Leesville Concrete Co.*). Kennedy wrote the court opinion, and Brennan, Marshall, Souter, Stevens, and White joined him. Kennedy held that a civil litigant has third-party standing to raise the excluded juror's right in behalf of the litigant and that the state sanctioning a private party's exercise of peremptory challenges on the basis of race constitutes state action subject to the equal protection clause. O'Connor, Rehnquist, and Scalia dissented. They argued that not everything that happens in a courtroom is state action and that peremptory exclusion of jurors is a matter of private choice not subject to the equal protection clause.

In the following year, 1992, the court extended the Batson principle to include defense attorneys in criminal cases. The case involved three white owners of a dry-cleaning establishment in Albany, Georgia. They had been indicted and tried for assaulting two black customers, and the state attorney general, at the instigation of leaders of the black community, asked the trial judge to order the defense counsel not to use his peremptory challenges to exclude blacks from the jury. The trial judge refused, and the Georgia Supreme Court affirmed. Georgia took the case to the U.S. Supreme Court.

The court held that defense attorneys, just like prosecutors, could not use peremptory challenges against prospective jurors on the basis of race (*Georgia v. McCollum*). Blackmun wrote the court opinion, and Kennedy, Souter, Stevens, and White joined him. Blackmun held that the Constitution prohibits a criminal defendant from engaging in deliberate racial discrimination in the exercise of peremptory challenges. The fact that defense attorneys in criminal cases were essentially acting as agents of the state in selecting a jury made their use of peremptory challenges on the basis of race state actions. Rehnquist and Thomas agreed with the judgment but only because of the court decision the previous year in *Edmonson*. O'Connor and Scalia dissented. They objected to limiting peremptory challenges and thought that the ruling would make it harder for minority defendants to place on the jury persons who might be sympathetic to them because of race or ethnicity.

In 1990 the court decided a case involving the confrontation clause of the Sixth Amendment. Sandra Craig was tried in Maryland and convicted of child abuse. At the trial, the victim, as permitted by statute, testified by one-way closed-circuit television to the courtroom. The judge, jury, and defendant remained in the courtroom while the prosecutor examined and the defense attorney cross-examined the witness. The state appellate court reversed, saying that Craig was denied the right to confront the witness as guaranteed by the Sixth Amendment, and the U.S. Supreme Court granted review.

The court by the narrowest margin held that the statute did not violate the confrontation clause and reinstated Craig's conviction (*Maryland v. Craig*).

O'Connor wrote the court opinion, and Blackmun, Kennedy, Rehnquist, and White joined her. O'Connor argued that the closed-circuit television testimony preserved the right of the defense attorney to cross-examine the witness and the jury's observation of the witness's demeanor. Although she accepted the importance of face-to-face confrontation of witnesses in criminal prosecutions, she argued that it was not an essential element of criminal procedure, especially because of the public interest in protecting child witnesses from the trauma of directly confronting the accused. Scalia, joined by Brennan, Marshall, and Stevens, dissented. Scalia argued that face-to-face confrontation of a witness in a criminal trial was categorically guaranteed by the words of the Sixth Amendment. He admitted that society favored the closed-circuit television procedure but insisted that the Constitution did not permit it.

In its last years the Rehnquist Court decided two cases involving whether the death penalty in the cases violated the Eighth Amendment's prohibition of cruel and unusual punishments. In one, Daryl Atkins committed armed robbery, abduction, and capital murder. Atkins was convicted and sentenced to death. One expert testified that Atkins was mildly retarded, but another expert testified that Atkins was not. He scored 59 on a standard I.Q. test. The Virginia Supreme Court upheld the conviction and death sentence. Atkins appealed to the U.S. Supreme Court.

In 2002 the court reversed the death sentence, holding that such a sentence on a mentally retarded criminal violated the Eighth Amendment's prohibition of cruel and unusual punishments (*Atkins v. Virginia*). Stevens wrote the court opinion, and Breyer, Ginsburg, Kennedy, O'Connor, and Souter joined him. The decision overturned *Penry v. Lynaugh*, a 1989 decision authored by O'Connor. Stevens argued that death sentences of mentally retarded persons violated contemporary standards of decency. They were also excessive because they did not serve the deterrent and retributive purposes of a death sentence. Rehnquist, Scalia, and Thomas dissented. Scalia argued that the court was basing its decision on the justices' personal opinions rather than a proper interpretation of the amendment or an accurate assessment of current social attitudes. Rehnquist criticized the court for invoking foreign laws, professional and religious organizations, and opinion polls.

The second case involved the death sentence of a minor. Christopher Simmons, seventeen years old at the time, took a woman from her home, bound and gagged her, and threw her from a bridge into a river, where she drowned. He was tried as an adult, convicted, and sentenced to death. After the Atkins decision by the U.S. Supreme Court, the Missouri Supreme Court overturned the death sentence, and Roper, the superintendent of the correctional institution in which Simmons was incarcerated, appealed to the U.S. Supreme Court.

In 2005 the court by the narrowest margin affirmed the decision of the Missouri Supreme Court overturning Simmons's death sentence (*Roper v. Simmons*). Kennedy wrote the court opinion, and Breyer, Ginsburg, Souter, and Stevens joined him. Reversing its prior decision in *Stanford v. Kentucky* (1989), the court held that imposing the death sentence on a minor violated the Eighth Amendment's prohibition of cruel and unusual punishment. Kennedy cited evolving standards of decency and noted that the United States was only one of seven countries that had executed juveniles since 1990. He did not think that either deterrence or retribution could justify executing juveniles. O'Connor, Rehnquist, Scalia, and Thomas dissented. Scalia thought that the majority reached an implausible result by invoking subjective views about capital punishment to interpret the Eighth Amendment. One might ask why the age difference of one year between seventeen and eighteen should be so critical to the question of the propriety of imposing the death sentence on a particularly brutal murderer. Perhaps a better argument could be made against the death penalty itself.

Prisoners' habeas corpus petitions for Supreme Court review of their convictions or sentences formed a large part of the docket of the Warren Court in the 1960s. The Burger Court began the process of cutting back on the availability of the writ to convicted prisoners, and the Rehnquist Court in the late 1980s and early 1990s further narrowed their right to the writ. One important case was *Keeney v. Tamayo-Reyes*. José Tamayo-Reyes was an Oregon inmate whose lawyer, in appealing the inmate's conviction, had failed to present a crucial piece of evidence. That concerned the Spanish translation of his confession, which misrepresented the content of what Tamayo-Reyes was signing. The federal court of appeals of the ninth circuit ordered a habeas corpus hearing against Keeney, the prison warden, but Oregon appealed to the Supreme Court.

In 1992 the court by the narrowest margin held that Tamayo-Reyes was not allowed to file a habeas corpus petition. White, who had dissented from the 1963 precedent that he now overturned (*Townsend v. Swain*), wrote the court opinion, and Rehnquist, Scalia, Souter, and Thomas joined him. The standard in the precedent was that a state prisoner could seek a writ of habeas corpus in federal court if the material facts were not adequately presented at the state-court hearing. White replaced that rule with one that required the prisoner to demonstrate cause—that is, newly discovered facts that cast serious doubt on the conviction. O'Connor, joined by Blackmun, Kennedy, and Stevens, dissented. She argued that the petition was proper and should be heard. (Note the difference that the appointments of Souter and Thomas to replace Brennan and Marshall, respectively, made.)

In 1993 the court denied a habeas corpus petition on the grounds of harmless error. Todd Brecht was convicted in Wisconsin of killing his brother-in-law. The prosecutor, contrary to the holding of the court in *Griffin v. California* (1965), commented several times to the jury that Brecht had refused to say anything after having been read his Miranda rights. Brecht later sought a writ of habeas corpus against Abrahamson, a corrections official, on the grounds that the trial should not have been permitted to go forward after the prosecutor's comments. The Wisconsin Supreme Court affirmed the conviction despite the prosecutor's comments. On Brecht's petition for a writ of habeas corpus, the district court overturned his conviction, but the court of appeals reversed. Brecht then appealed to the Supreme Court.

The court by the narrowest margin ruled against Brecht (*Brecht v. Abrahamson*). Rehnquist wrote the court opinion, and Kennedy, Scalia, Stevens, and Thomas joined him. Rehnquist held that a conviction should not be overturned if there was harmless error beyond reasonable doubt and added that the conviction should not be overturned unless the error had a substantial and injurious effect or influence on the jury's verdict. In the instant case, Rehnquist found that the error was harmless and Brecht's guilt beyond reasonable doubt. Blackmun, O'Connor, Souter, and White dissented, arguing that the prosecutor's comment might have influenced the jury.

A few months before the Brecht decision the court decided a case that began as a petition for habeas corpus and later involved a stay of execution. Leonel Torres Herrera was a death-row inmate convicted of the murder of two state police officers. He claimed that newly discovered evidence established his innocence. A nephew, Raul Herrera Jr., claimed that his father, Raul Herrera Sr., had told him in 1983 that he, Raul Sr., had committed the murders. (Raul Sr. had died the following year.) Leonel also presented statements from three others to corroborate the nephew's story. Texas law provided that newly discovered evidence must be presented within thirty days of conviction, a time period that had long elapsed. Herrera petitioned for a writ of habeas corpus in a federal district court against Collins, a corrections official. The district court denied the writ but stayed Herrera's execution to give the state authorities time to process his claim. The court of appeals lifted the stay, and Herrera appealed to the Supreme Court. The Supreme Court agreed to hear the case on the merits without staying the execution, but a Texas court granted a stay.

The court rejected Herrera's claim that the thirty-day time limit violated the due process clause (*Herrera v. Collins*). Rehnquist wrote the court opinion, and Kennedy, O'Connor, Scalia, Thomas, and White agreed with him in whole or in part. Rehnquist concluded that the evidence provided by Herrera fell far short of the level of proof required to secure a new trial. A death-row inmate is not ordinarily entitled to a new trial, although truly persuasive evidence might lead the court to order a hearing. Kennedy, O'Connor, and White agreed with the judgment but argued that the Constitution might still provide relief and that the court should never permit the execution of an innocent person. Blackmun, joined by Stevens and Souter, dissented, arguing that the new evidence was plausible enough to require a new trial. Herrera was subsequently executed, proclaiming his innocence until the end.

In 1995 the court rendered a decision that made it difficult for prisoners alleging lack of due process in disciplinary actions to sue prison officials. DeMont Conner, a convicted murderer, was serving a thirty-year-to-life sentence in a maximum-security prison in Hawaii. He brought suit against Cinda Sandin, the manager of the prison, seeking injunctive relief and damages. He claimed that Sandin refused to allow him to call witnesses before being placed in solitary confinement for thirty days as punishment for violating prison rules and that this violated his constitutional right to due process. Connor lost in the district court but won in the court of appeals. Hawaii, in the person of Sandin, then appealed to the Supreme Court.

The court by the narrowest margin ruled against Connor (*Sandin v. Connor*). Rehnquist wrote the court opinion, and Kennedy, O'Connor, Scalia, and Thomas joined him. Previous court decisions had attempted to draw a line between matters that involved a substantial liberty interest and matters that did not. Rehnquist set a standard that required a showing that prison authorities had imposed an atypical and significant hardship rather than a case of the routine business of the prison. Breyer, Ginsburg, Souter, and Stevens dissented. They thought Rehnquist's opinion went too far and left lower federal courts with little indication of how to separate significant prisoner complaints from trivial ones. (One of the ironies in the case is that, after Connor had served thirty days in solitary confinement and before the court decision, appellate prison authorities dropped the only serious charge against him, physical obstruction of prison officials.)

In 1997 the court decided a case involving a Kansas law that required the indeterminate civil confinement in mental hospitals of violent sex offenders suffering from a mental abnormality that incapacitated them from controlling their sexual conduct and made them a menace to others. Leroy Hendricks had a forty-year record of molesting children and was convicted in 1984 of molesting two boys. When his sentence for that crime expired, Kansas acted to commit him under the act. Hendricks argued that the commitment was tantamount to being punished twice for the same crime. The Kansas Supreme Court sided with Hendricks, arguing that a person could be committed to a mental hospital only if he had a mental illness, not just a mental abnormality. Kansas appealed the case to the U.S. Supreme Court.

The court by the narrowest margin reversed the decision of the Kansas Supreme Court (*Kansas v. Hendricks*). Thomas wrote the court opinion, and Kennedy, O'Connor, Rehnquist, and Scalia joined him. Thomas held that, in involuntary civil commitments, the state had only to establish an individual's dangerousness and mental incapacity, whether that incapacity was the result of mental illness or mental abnormality. Moreover, he rejected Hendricks's claim that he was being punished twice, since confinement to a mental hospital was a form of treatment. There was no known cure for Hendricks's condition, but that did not entitle him to live in the community. Breyer, joined by Ginsburg, Souter, and Stevens, dissented. Breyer found the law unacceptable because it offered no treatment, and so one could only understand the decision to commit Hendricks as a form of punishment.

After the destruction of the World Trade Center in New York City on September 11, 2001, Congress authorized President Bush II to use force against those responsible for the attack. He committed forces to action in Afghanistan, and they took thousands of prisoners. The prisoners were designated unlawful enemy combatants, and Bush set up a facility at the U.S. naval base in Guantanamo Bay for their detention, where they began to arrive in January 2002. Bush claimed the right to detain them there until the conclusion of hostilities, although it is difficult to imagine when, or even if, that threshold could be met. Questions were raised about the applicability of the Geneva Conventions, since the conflict was not between sovereign states, and the enemy combatants were not in uniform. Rasul, acting through a close friend, and other detainees sought to obtain a writ of habeas corpus in a district court of the District of Columbia, claiming that they (two Australians and twelve Kuwaiti) were not enemy combatants. (Many detainees claimed to be bystanders or relief workers on the battlefield and so outside the laws of war.) The district court denied the writ on the grounds that Guantanamo Bay was not a territory of the United States. Rasul and the others appealed to the Supreme Court.

The court in 2004 ruled in favor of the petitioners (*Rasul v. Bush*). Stevens wrote the court opinion, and Breyer, Ginsburg, O'Connor, and Souter joined him. Kennedy joined only in the judgment. Stevens held that the habeas corpus statute applied to the detainees at Guantanamo, since the United States exercised complete jurisdiction and control over the naval base, even though the base was outside the jurisdiction of any federal civilian court. Scalia, joined by Rehnquist and Thomas, dissented. Soon almost every detainee at Guantanamo filed a habeas corpus petition in the district court of the District of Columbia.

On the same day as the Rasul decision, the court decided the case of another detainee. Yaser Hamdi was a native-born American citizen who was seized on an Afghan battlefield allegedly in possession of an assault rifle and held in the naval brig in Charleston, South Carolina. His father petitioned in the district court in Charleston for a writ of habeas corpus to obtain his release. The district court asked the government to provide material for the court to decide whether to issue the writ, but the court of appeals reversed. Hamdi then appealed to the Supreme Court.

The court held that the military could not detain an American citizen without holding a minimal hearing to decide whether the detainee was an enemy combatant (*Hamdi v. Rumsfeld*). O'Connor wrote the plurality opinion, in which Breyer, Kennedy, and Rehnquist joined. O'Connor held that the detention was properly authorized, but that Hamdi, as an American citizen held in the United States, was entitled to unspecified due process to contest his detention. Souter, joined by Ginsburg, concurred in the judgment requiring a formal hearing on Hamdi's detention but thought the detention itself unauthorized. Scalia, joined by Stevens, dissented. Scalia argued that there were only two legal choices regarding detention of U.S. citizens: the ordinary civilian criminal process or suspension of the writ of habeas corpus by Congress. (Scalia's dissent was thus actually more radical than O'Connor's plurality position.) Thomas dissented from O'Connor's opinion as an intrusion on presidential powers.

Religion The Rehnquist Court decided a large number of cases involving religion. In 1987, the end of its first year, the court decided a case involving a Louisiana statute requiring the teaching of what was described as creation science whenever evolution was taught in public-school science courses. The statute did not explain what creation science meant beyond equating it with scientific evidences for creation, nor did it explain what the legislature intended by the word *creation*. The statute probably concerned teaching the scientific evidence for the discrete appearance of different forms of matter and life—that is, the discreteness, speed, and relative recentness of the origins of things. The lower courts interpreted the statute as mandating the teaching of creation, the origin of things from God, and so held that the statutory mandate to teach it an establishment of religion. Louisiana, in the name of the governor, Edwards, took the case to the Supreme Court.

The court agreed that the statute violated the establishment clause (*Edwards v. Aguillard*). Brennan wrote the court opinion, and Blackmun, Marshall, O'Connor, Powell, and Stevens joined him. (White concurred in the judgment but not the opinion.) Brennan held that the statute had a religious purpose—namely, to promote the idea that a supernatural being created human beings—and not a secular purpose—namely, to promote academic freedom.

Scalia, joined by Rehnquist, dissented. Since the Louisiana Supreme Court never had an opportunity to resolve the question of what creation science was, Scalia was willing at this stage to accept at face value that creation science meant scientific evidence that the universe appeared suddenly. To justify constitutionally the inclusion of that subject in the public-school curriculum, he argued, it was only necessary to find a secular purpose. Moreover, the free exercise clause sometimes requires or permits the government to do so. Examining the legislative history, he cited the fact that legislators asserted that they had a secular motive and thought that their statements should be accepted at face value. Their concern was with the origins of life—that students have the opportunity to examine evidence that forms of life appeared suddenly and relatively recently and changed little. Their purpose was academic freedom, here meaning the freedom of students not to be indoctrinated in a theory of evolution that excluded the possibility of quantum leaps in the origin of living things, and the people of Louisiana were entitled, as a secular matter, to have presented in their schools whatever scientific evidence there may be for quantum leaps.

In 1992 the court ruled on the constitutionality of prayers at public-school graduations. Such prayers were common at those ceremonies and a sensitive point of conflict between civic culture and legal precedents on the establishment clause. It was the practice of a Providence, Rhode Island, middle school to invite members of the clergy to offer an invocation and benediction. A student at the school, Deborah Weisman, and her father filed a suit in 1989 after a rabbi offered a prayer at graduation that thanked God for the liberty that Americans enjoyed and asked for God's blessing on teachers, students, and administrators at the school. The district court and the court of appeals found the practice unconstitutional. The school and city took the case to the Supreme Court.

The court by the narrowest margin agreed with the lower courts (*Lee v. Weisman*). Kennedy wrote the court opinion, and Blackmun, O'Connor, Souter, and Stevens joined him. Kennedy held, without reexamining court precedents, that any state-sponsored prayer in the public schools violated the establishment clause. He carefully indicated that the decision did not necessarily apply to cases involving adults. Scalia, joined by Rehnquist, Thomas, and White, dissented. Scalia argued that prayer was an accepted practice to unite groups when they meet, and he saw no reason the government and school boards should be unable to do so.

On questions relating to various forms of governmental financial aid to church-related primary and secondary schools, the Rehnquist Court was generally less restrictive, and it in one case spectacularly reversed a Burger Court decision. In 1993 the Rehnquist Court decided a case involving the eligibility of a deaf student attending a church-related school to have the aid of a publicly employed sign-language interpreter. James Zobrest, a student deaf since birth, attended an accredited sectarian school and asked the Tucson, Arizona, school district to provide an interpreter for him at the school pursuant to a federally assisted program for disabled students. The school district declined, Zobrest took his case to the federal courts, and both the district court and the court of appeals ruled against him, holding that the primary effect of providing a sign-language interpreter for a deaf student attending a sectarian school would be to advance religion. Zobrest pursued his case to the Supreme Court.

The court by the narrowest margin ruled in favor of Zobrest (*Zobrest v. Catalina Foothills School District*). Rehnquist wrote the court opinion, and Kennedy, Scalia, Thomas, and White joined him. Rehnquist gave several arguments for so holding. First, provision of a sign-language interpreter for a deaf student in a sectarian school is part of a general governmental program to handicapped children. Second, the aid is provided to pupils and their parents, not to the sectarian school. Third, the task of a sign-language interpreter is different from that of a teacher or counselor in that the interpreter merely transmits in signs what the instructor is saying. Blackmun, with Souter, and O'Connor, with Stevens, dissented. Blackmun stressed that the government, by providing a sign-language interpreter, facilitated the transmission of a religious message. The case obviously hinges on whether the primary effect of providing the sign-language interpreter is the benefit to the student, and the benefit to religion incidental, or the converse.

As has been noted, the Burger Court in the 1985 Aguilar decision held that New York City school authorities could not use federal funds to provide public-school teachers in parochial schools for remedial instruction of needy students. The school authorities then rented private property and invested in mobile vans parked on streets near the parochial schools, on both of which federally funded public-school teachers provided remedial instruction to more than 20,000 needy parochial-school pupils at a cost of more than $100,000 in 1986–87. (That expenditure reduced the net funds for the pupils.) The 1993 Zobrest decision just discussed threw the continued validity of the Aguilar decision in doubt, and five justices in a 1994 decision indicated a willingness to reconsider *Aguilar*. The city's school authorities took up the invitation and petitioned the district court to lift the court order mandated by the Aguilar decision on the grounds that changed circumstances (namely, *Zobrest*, other decisions, and costs) had made the original order inequitable. The district court refused to do so, and the court of appeals affirmed. The city authorities took the case to the Supreme Court for review.

In 1997 the court by the narrowest margin ruled for the city (*Agostini v. Felton*). O'Connor wrote the court opinion, and Kennedy, Rehnquist, Scalia, and Thomas joined her. O'Connor insisted that the court had already effectively overruled *Aguilar*. She rejected the arguments of the court opinion in *Aguilar* and cited the fact that the costs of mobile vans lessened the money available for the remedial program. Breyer, Ginsburg, Souter, and Stevens dissented in two opinions. Souter objected on the merits and Ginsburg to the extraordinary way in which the case came to the court.

In 2002 the court considered a case involving tuition aid to inner-city parents choosing to send their children to suburban public or private schools. In order to improve the educational opportunities for children in Cleveland, whose public schools had been held to be deficient, Ohio provided remedial tutorial aid to students in the city's public schools and tuition aid to low-income parents to send their children to participating suburban public schools and private schools. In the 1999–2000 school year, no suburban public school participated, 82 percent of the participating schools were religious, and 96 percent of the students participating in the program attended church-related schools, most of which were Catholic. Simmons-Harris and other Ohio taxpayers sued in a federal district court to enjoin Zelman, the Ohio superintendent of public instruction, from implementing the tuition program, claiming that it violated the religious establishment clause. The district court did so, and the court of appeals affirmed. The state, in the person of Zelman, took the case to the Supreme Court.

The court by the narrowest margin reversed the court of appeals and upheld the program (*Zelman v. Simmons-Harris*). Rehnquist wrote the court opinion, and Kennedy, O'Connor, Scalia, and Thomas joined him. Rehnquist stressed the distinction between programs that provide direct aid to religiously affiliated schools and programs that provide aid dependent on private choice, in which case the aid comes to such schools only as a result of the independent choice of private individuals. He argued that the program was facially neutral in all respects toward religion. Breyer, Ginsburg, Souter, and Stevens dissented. They argued that, despite the element of parental choice, the program had the primary effect of advancing religion. They also noted that two-thirds of the parents participating in the program sent their children to schools that proselytized in a religion other than their own. (Arguably, that fact indicates that the parents sent their children to those schools for secular educational benefits.) This case is important because of its implication for the validity of a system of vouchers to attend nonpublic schools, including religiously affiliated schools.

In 1989 the court decided a case involving two Christmas displays on public property. Alleghany County, Pennsylvania, in the Christmas season had a privately owned crèche with figures of Jesus and Mary in the county courthouse of Pittsburgh, which was adorned with the banner "Gloria in excelsis Deo." The county also had a display on the steps of the city-council building that had an eighteen-foot menorah and a forty-five-foot tree decorated with ornaments. The ACLU sought and obtained an injunction against both. The case then went to the Supreme Court.

The court disallowed the first display and upheld the second (*Allegheny County v. American Civil Liberties Union*). Kennedy, Rehnquist, Scalia, and White would have approved both displays, and Brennan, Marshall, and Stevens would have disapproved both. Blackmun, joined by O'Connor, wrote what was in effect the court opinion. Blackmun struck down the first display and upheld the second. He argued that it was unconstitutional to display a crèche unadorned with secular objects in the county courthouse, but that it was constitutional to display a menorah, as long as it was surrounded by secular symbols, on public property.

On the same day in 2005 the court decided two cases involving the display of the Ten Commandments on public property, striking down one and approving the other. In one case, two counties in Kentucky set up large framed copies of the Ten Commandments in their courthouses, which McCreary County had installed at the behest of its legislature, and which Pulaski County had installed in a ceremony including statements of a religious character, some by a clergyman. The ACLU filed suit in a federal district court to prohibit the displays. After instigation of the suit, the legislatures of both counties ordered new displays that included eight government documents with religious statements. The district court entered preliminary injunctions against the displays, and the counties added more government documents with religious statements. The district court extended the injunctions to those displays. The counties then took the case to the Supreme Court.

The court by the narrowest margin held that the displays, even as modified, violated the religious establishment clause (*McCreary County v. American Civil Liberties Union*). Souter wrote the court opinion, and Breyer, Ginsburg, O'Connor, and Stevens joined him. Souter interpreted the purpose prong of the Shempp-Lemon test in an objective sense—namely, whether an observer would perceive that the displays conveyed a predominantly religious message. He thought that an observer would. The newest displays were too selective and excluded too many other documents of a purely secular nature. O'Connor, concurring, stressed that the displays endorsed a religious message. Scalia, with Rehnquist, Thomas, and Kennedy in part, dissented. Scalia argued that the establishment clause does not preclude public acknowledgement of God, that no observer would find the displays unusual, and that the counties' earlier religious motivations were irrelevant.

The second case involved monuments and memorials on the grounds of the capitol of Texas, among which was a six-foot monument inscribed with the Ten Commandments. The monument also included nonreligious symbols, such as an eagle with an American flag. A fraternal organization donated the monument in 1961. Thomas Van Orden, a citizen of Texas, sued Rick Perry, the governor, to have the monument removed from the capitol grounds. He lost in the district court and appealed to the Supreme Court at the same time as the McCreary case.

The court by the narrowest margin ruled that the monument did not violate the establishment clause (*Van Orden v. Perry*). Rehnquist wrote the court opinion, and Breyer, Kennedy, Scalia, and Thomas joined him. Rehnquist noted that acknowledgments of the role of religion, including the Ten Commandments, are common in the nation's history. He did not discount the religious message but found its presence insufficient to violate the establishment clause, since the Ten Commandments also have a historical significance, the monument serving both a religious and a historical function. Scalia, concurring, argued that the establishment clause should allow a state to favor religion in general. Thomas, concurring, maintained that the establishment clause should not apply to the states at all. Breyer, who had provided the swing vote in both the McCreary and Van Orden cases, argued that the monument did not use the text of the Ten Commandments to endorse religion, whereas the Kentucky displays had a religious objective. Ginsburg, O'Connor, Souter, and Stevens dissented, arguing that the monument conveyed a religious message. Given the more serious issues on which the court is called upon to judge, one wonders whether its effort in these two cases was worth it. As Roman jurists said, *de minimis non curat praetor* (the magistrate doesn't worry about minimal things).

In 1992 the court considered restriction of Hare Krishna activities at airports. The religious group routinely used airports to solicit money and distribute literature. In the 1970s the Port Authority of New York and New Jersey banned those activities. The group sued in a district court to enjoin Walter Lee, the superintendent of the Port Authority, from enforcing the bans, claiming that they violated its right of religious exercise. The district court enjoined the authority, and the federal court of appeals sustained the ban on soliciting money but overturned the ban on the distribution of literature. Both sides took the case to the Supreme Court.

The court upheld the ban on soliciting funds (*International Society of Krishna Consciousness v. Lee*). Rehnquist wrote the court opinion, and O'Connor, Scalia, Thomas, and White joined him. (Kennedy concurred in the judgment.) Rehnquist argued that airports were not public forums, where the authority would need to demonstrate a compelling public interest for regulating speech and religious exercise. Airports were subject to special security requirements, and their terminals were established to serve travelers and employees. The authority had power to make any reasonable regulations to avoid congestion and disruption to passengers seeking to board planes, claim baggage, or purchase tickets. Souter, joined by Blackmun and Stevens, dissented. Souter argued that airports were public forums and that there was no compelling public interest to justify banning solicitations inside or outside the airports.

In an unsigned opinion, the justices by the narrowest margin upheld the court of appeals decision striking down the ban on the distribution of literature in airports (*Lee v. International Society of Krishna Consciousness*). Kennedy and O'Connor joined the dissenters in the prior case in this decision. O'Connor in a concurrence argued that, while airports were not public forums, the ban on distributing literature failed to pass the test of minimal rationality. Rehnquist, joined by Scalia, Thomas, and White, dissented. Rehnquist argued that there was no practical difference whether someone soliciting money was delaying a traveler or someone distributing literature was.

In 1995 the court decided a case involving a conflict between a free-speech claim and the religious establishment clause or, arguably, a conflict between a free-exercise claim and the establishment clause. Ronald Rosenberger, a student in 1990 at the University of Virginia and editor of *Wide Awake,* a publication with an editorial policy calling on Christians to live according to the faith and including Christian symbols on each page, requested $6,000 from the student activity fund. The student advisory group and the university denied the request on the grounds that the publication proselytized religion and violated existing guidelines that prohibited the funding of religious groups. At the same time, the fund granted funds to Jewish and Muslim associations. The district court ruled summarily against Rosenberger, and the court of appeals affirmed on the basis of the establishment clause. Rosenberger appealed to the Supreme Court.

The court by the narrowest margin ruled in favor of Rosenberger (*Rosenberger v. University of Virginia*). Kennedy wrote the court opinion. Rehnquist and Scalia joined the opinion, and O'Connor and Thomas concurred separately. Kennedy held that the university, by denying funds to subsidize the printing of *Wide Awake,* had discriminated against a viewpoint and so violated the free-speech right of students to express a viewpoint. When the establishment and speech clauses came into conflict, the balance should be tipped in favor of the latter. Souter, joined by Breyer, Ginsburg, and Stevens, dissented. Souter accused the court opinion of approving the direct funding of core religious activities by an arm of the government. (Note that the funds were student funds, and the student advisory group, not the university, made the decision to exclude Rosenberger's project, although this distinction did not feature in the case.)

In 2001 the court considered another case involving a free-speech/free-exercise claim and the requirements of the establishment clause, this time involving a public-school facility. A school district in Milford, New York, adopted a community-use policy that authorized the after-school use of public-school buildings by residents for instruction, social and recreational meetings, and other uses pertaining to the welfare of the community. The school district refused to allow the Good News Club, a private Christian organization, to use a public-school building for singing songs, hosting a Bible lesson, and memorizing Scripture, on the ground that the proposed use was the equivalent of religious worship. The club sued in federal court to force the district to allow it to use the facility. The club lost in the district court and the court of appeals and appealed the case to the Supreme Court.

The court ruled in favor of the club (*Good News Club v. Milford Central School*). Thomas wrote the court opinion, and Kennedy, O'Connor, Rehnquist, and Scalia joined him. Thomas held that speech could not be excluded from a limited public forum on the ground that the subject is discussed from a religious viewpoint. The exclusion of the club constituted viewpoint discrimination—that is, religious uses were excluded precisely because they were religious. But the court remanded the case to the lower court to decide the case in its factual context. Ginsburg, Souter, and Stevens dissented. Stevens argued that, although the free speech clause protects speech about a particular topic from a religious viewpoint, expression amounting to religious worship or proselytizing is different, and that the establishment clause prohibits the use of public buildings for it. Souter, with Ginsburg, in addition argued that the lower court needed to consider the factual context before deciding the case. Breyer dissented from the court opinion in principle but agreed that the case should be remanded to the lower court to adjudicate the case.

The Rehnquist Court decided a number of cases involving what accommodations the religious exercise clause required governments to make for persons with religious beliefs contrary to regulations. In the first case the court in 1987, using the compelling-public-interest test, held that a convert to the Seventh Day Adventist religion had a right to receive unemployment benefits, even though he was unwilling to accept work on Saturday (*Hobbie v. Unemploy-*

ment Appeals Commission). Only Rehnquist dissented. The decision mirrored the 1963 Sherbert decision.

The following year, 1988, the court decided a case involving the construction of a paved road through government land used by Indians for religious purposes. An Indian group sought an injunction to prevent the forest service from constructing the road, but the district court ruled against the group. The case went to the Supreme Court.

The court affirmed the lower-court decision (*Lyng v. Northwest Indian Cemetery Protective Association*). O'Connor wrote the court opinion, and Rehnquist, Scalia, Stevens, and White joined her. (Newly appointed Kennedy did not participate.) O'Connor held that the free exercise clause did not require the government to conduct its own affairs in ways that comport with particular religious beliefs. She thought the Burger Court decision in *Bowen v. Roy* directly apposite. When, as here, it is a question of the indirect effects of governmental action that make the practice of religion difficult, but which neither coerce action contrary to religious belief nor penalize the exercise of religion, the religious exercise clause does not apply, and so the government does not need to demonstrate a compelling public interest for its action. In short, the government had a right to use its own land without regard to the religious effects on the Indians. She pointed out and endorsed the government's efforts to accommodate the Indians' religious beliefs and practices.

Brennan, joined by Blackmun and Marshall, dissented. Brennan thought that the free exercise clause is directed against any form of governmental action that frustrates or inhibits a religious practice, which the road did. He argued further that the free exercise clause should protect Indian use of land central and indispensable to their religious practices and that the government had no compelling interest in the road, indeed no need for it at all. Indians themselves could make clear what land was central to their religious practices and what land was not. (O'Connor thought that any attempt to do that would involve the courts in determining religious belief itself.)

In 1990 the court drew a line in the sand against claims of religious objectors to the applicability of otherwise valid criminal laws to them (*Employment Division v. Smith*). Oregon prohibited the knowing possession of a variety of drugs, including peyote. A private drug-rehabilitation clinic fired Alfred Smith and Galen Black because they had ingested peyote while at work and as part of a ritual of the Native American Church. They applied for unemployment compensation, but Oregon officials ruled them ineligible because they had been dismissed for work-related misconduct. The state courts ruled that the denial of benefits violated their rights under the free exercise clause. After the Oregon Supreme Court, on remand from the U.S. Supreme Court, ruled that Oregon law provided no exception from the drug law for the religious use of peyote and reaffirmed its decision that the denial of unemployment-compensation benefits violated the free exercise clause, the case returned to the U.S. Supreme Court.

The court ruled that Smith and Black had no rights under the free exercise clause to exemption from a generally applicable criminal law. Scalia wrote the court opinion, and Kennedy, Rehnquist, Stevens, and White joined him. Scalia argued that the Oregon drug law was a general law and not one that was aimed directly at religious use and that the prior unemployment-compensation cases (*Sherbert, Hobbie,* and *Thomas*) had nothing to do with an across-the-board criminal prohibition of a particular form of conduct. Moreover, if the compelling-public-interest test were adopted for religious exemptions, many laws would fail to meet that test. He concluded that, because Oregon prohibited ingestion of peyote and because that law was constitutional, the state might consistently with the free exercise clause deny religiously motivated peyote-users unemployment compensation when their dismissal results from use of the drug. O'Connor concurred in the judgment but thought the court should have used the compelling-public-interest test, which she thought would lead to the same conclusion. Blackmun, joined by Brennan and Marshall, dissented. Blackmun argued that the religious peyote users had a valid claim under the free exercise clause and that Oregon had no compelling public interest in denying exemption to them. (As a footnote to the case, Oregon one year later passed a law permitting the sacramental use of peyote by Native American Indians.)

Religious groups and much of the press criticized the Smith decision, and Congress responded in 1993 by passing the Religious Freedom Restoration Act (RFRA) to restore the compelling-public-interest test of claims to exemptions for religious reasons from laws of general applicability. The RFRA required that a law substantially burdening a religious practice have a compelling public interest and use the least restrictive means to achieve that interest.

P. F. Flores, Catholic archbishop of San Antonio, applied for a permit to enlarge a church in Boerne, Texas. The permit was denied on the grounds that the existing church, built in 1823, was a historical monument protected by a local ordinance. Flores then sued in reliance on the RFRA. He won in the district court, and the city appealed to the Supreme Court.

In 1997 the court ruled for the city, holding that the RFRA provision was unconstitutional because Congress has no power under section 5 of the Fourteenth Amendment to define or enlarge the substance of civil rights (*Boerne v. Flores*). Kennedy wrote the court opinion, and Ginsburg, Rehnquist, Scalia, Stevens, and Thomas joined him. Kennedy argued from the legislative history of the Fourteenth Amendment and the Civil Rights Cases that the power granted to Congress to enforce section 1 extends only to preventive or remedial measures. That said, he endorsed the Smith holding and ruled for the city. Scalia concurred except regarding the reach of the Fourteenth Amendment and directed his attention to rebutting O'Connor's dissent. Breyer, O'Connor, and Souter dissented. They did not defend the law but argued that the case should be reargued regarding the Smith decision. O'Connor wrote a long disquisition on the history of the free exercise clause and claimed that it reached religious claims to exemption from laws of general applicability unless the government could demonstrate a compelling public interest. Berger joined O'Connor except with regard to her agreement with the court on Congress's limited power to enforce the guarantees of the Fourteenth Amendment.

Congress in response passed the Religious Land Use and Institutionalized Persons Act (RLUIPA). The act put rezoning on a list of prohibited land use affecting religion. There have been only a few lower-court federal decisions on the constitutionality of the law, and it is likely that the court would limit its applicability to putting churches on the same footing with nonreligious assembly uses.

Property The Rehnquist Court considered and vindicated the most property claims against local governments since the heyday of the Lochner era. In its first year, 1987, the court considered the taking clause of the Fifth Amendment and a decision of the California Coastal Commission. In 1982 the commission granted a permit to James and Marilyn Nollan to build a larger house in place of their small bungalow on their beachfront but required that the Nollans give the public an easement to pass across their beach, which was located between two public beaches. The affected property was a stretch of beach between the mean high-tide line, which marks the point above which the land is private, and their seawall. (Note that many of those passing through the Nollans's beach were likely to settle down.) The lower state court granted the Nollans a writ of mandamus against the easement requirement, but the state appellate court reversed. The Nollans took their case to the U.S. Supreme Court.

The court by the narrowest margin ruled for the Nollans and held that the condition was a taking of property (*Nollan v. California Coastal Commission*). Scalia wrote the court opinion, and O'Connor, Powell, Rehnquist, and White joined him. Scalia recognized the legitimacy of prohibiting construction on beachfront property in order to protect the public's view of the beach as well as the government's power to condition construction on concession of property rights. But the easement would have only benefited persons already on the beaches. And so the lack of nexus between the easement condition and the avowed purpose of protecting the public's view of the beach converted the condition into a taking of private property without the payment of just compensation. Blackman, Brennan, Marshall, and Stevens dissented. The dissenters stressed the legitimacy and importance of protecting public access to the beach and thought the nexus between the easement and that public interest rational.

In the same year the court held that a land-use regulation could amount to a taking of property. The First Evangelical Lutheran Church in Glendale, California, owned buildings that were destroyed by a flood. After the flood a Los Angeles County ordinance prohibited all construction in a flood plain area that included the church's land. When the church sued in state courts, the courts held that the church could seek compensatory damages for alleged taking only if the ordinance were first declared a taking and if the county then chose not to rescind the ordinance. The church then appealed the second condition to the U.S. Supreme Court.

The court ruled that a land-use regulation can amount to a taking of property and that, if it does, compensation is due to the owner even if the regulation is later rescinded as a result of a successful judicial challenge (*First Evangelical Lutheran Church of Glendale v. County of Los Angeles*). Rehnquist wrote the court opinion, and Brennan, Marshall, Powell, Scalia, and White joined him. Rehnquist held that compensation is due for temporary takings of property and remanded the case to the California courts for reconsideration in the light of the court decision. He did not indicate when regulation becomes a taking. Nor did he indicate how damages should be calculated. He did indicate that normal administrative delays in obtaining building permits, changes in zoning regulations, variances, and the like do not involve the taking of property. Stevens, joined by Blackmun and O'Connor, dissented. Stevens argued that the ruling would unduly inhibit land-use regulatory processes, since regulators would fear liability. On remand, the California courts held that the ordinance did not involve a taking.

Also in the same year the court decided a case involving a Pennsylvania statute that prohibited underground mining that would cause subsistence damage to surface structures and required that mining companies leave in place at least half of the coal beneath the structures. The Keystone Bituminous Coal Association sued in a federal district court against enforcement of the statute, claiming that it involved a taking of property without just compensation. The district court and the court of appeals ruled against the association, and it appealed to the Supreme Court.

The court by the narrowest margin held that the statute was a valid exercise of the state's police powers to protect the public's health, safety, and welfare and did not prevent companies from profitable mining (*Keystone Bituminous Coal Association v. De Benedictis*). Stevens wrote the court opinion, and Blackmun, Brennan, Marshall, and White joined him. Stevens denied that the relatively small amount of coal that the statute required to be left in place for surface support was a discrete property interest that the state had taken without compensation. Rehnquist, joined by O'Connor, Powell, and Scalia, dissented. The facts in the Keystone case were almost identical to those in *Pennsylvania Coal Co. v. Mahon* (1922), and the dissenters relied on it. In the Mahon case a statute prohibited an owner from engaging in underground mining if the mining would cause structural subsistence, and the court, per Holmes, held that the statute constituted a taking of property without compensation.

In 1992 the court ruled that a regulation governing land use constituted a taking of property. In 1986 David Lucas paid $975,000 for two residential lots on the Isle of Palms near Charleston, South Carolina, on which he hoped to build two family homes. In 1988 the South Carolina legislature enacted a beachfront management act that effectively banned him from erecting any permanent habitable structure. A trial state court found that this prohibition rendered Lucas's property valueless and constituted a taking of property, but the state appellate court reversed. Lucas appealed the case to the U.S. Supreme Court.

The court ruled in favor of Lucas, holding that the law deprived Lucas of all economically beneficial or productive use of the land and that South Carolina must demonstrate principles of nuisance and property law that would justify the prohibition of such use (*Lucas v. South Carolina Coastal Commission*). Scalia wrote the court opinion, and O'Connor, Rehnquist, Thomas, and White joined him. Kennedy concurred separately. Scalia admitted that the general principles of nuisance and property law may limit owners' use of their property, but the council must demonstrate the applicability of those principles when, on its face, the law, unlike a zoning law, deprives Lucas of *all* beneficial use. Blackmun, joined by Stevens, dissented. Blackmun doubted that the property had lost all beneficial use and argued that the court had repeatedly recognized that the government might in certain circumstances regulate property without compensation, no matter how adverse the financial effect on the owner may be. Souter also filled a statement that was in effect a dissent.

In 1994 the court by the narrowest margin added another nexus beyond the one annunciated in *Nollan (Dolan v. Tigard)*. Florence Dolan owned an electrical and plumbing supply store in the central business area of Tigard, Oregon. Dolan proposed to double the size of her store on her land and pave over a gravel parking lot. The city planning commission agreed to the expansion on two conditions. First, she was required to give the city property in a flood plain in order to improve drainage and minimize flooding that might result from paving over the gravel lot. Second, the commission required that she give the city a strip of land for use of pedestrians and bicyclists in order to relieve congestion in the business district created by the store's expansion. Dolan objected to both requirements on the grounds that they were unrelated to expansion of the store and so constituted an unconstitutional taking of property without compensation. The trial court and the Oregon Supreme Court ruled in favor of the city, and she appealed to the U.S. Supreme Court.

The court by the narrowest margin reversed and remanded the case to the Oregon courts for reconsideration in the light of the court's decision. Rehnquist wrote the court opinion, and Kennedy, O'Connor, Scalia, and Thomas joined him. Rehnquist admitted that there was a nexus between the land-use conditions and the permission to enlarge Dolan's store but that the city could not impose the requirements unless there was a rough proportionality between the two. There thus needs to be a second nexus between the degree of land-use required of Dolan and the impact of Dolan's expansion, which the city had not sufficiently demonstrated. Stevens and Souter, joined by Blackmun and Ginsburg, dissented. Both dissents would have put the burden on the developer to prove the conditions unwarranted and thought the court's decision a striking departure from previous decisions granting broad authority to local governments to regulate land use.

In 2002 the court reviewed a case involving a temporary moratorium on all development of land in the Lake Tahoe Basin, California. The Tahoe Regional Planning Agency had imposed a thirty-two-month moratorium on development until the regulatory agency adopted a land-use plan. Landowners, represented by the Tahoe-Sierra Preservation Council, brought suit for compensation, claiming that the temporary moratorium deprived them of all viable economic use of their property and so, under the holding in the Lucas case, constituted a taking and required compensation. The district court ruled in favor of the council, but the court of appeals reversed. The landowners then appealed to the Supreme Court.

The court ruled in favor of the agency (*Tahoe-Sierra Preservation Council v. Tahoe Regional Planning Agency*). Stevens wrote the court opinion, and Breyer, Ginsburg, Kennedy, O'Connor, and Souter joined him. Stevens argued that, when considering the impact of a land-use regulation, all future value of the land, not merely the thirty-two-month moratorium at issue, had to be considered. Since there would always be remaining value if a regulation were temporary, he held that the Lucas rule was inapplicable to temporary moratoria, although a temporary moratorium could amount to a taking of property. Rehnquist, Scalia, and Thomas dissented, arguing that any temporary moratorium involved a taking of property and so required commensurate compensation.

In the last year of the Rehnquist Court, 2005, it ruled on whether a redevelopment project satisfied the requirement that power of eminent domain be exercised for a public purpose. Connecticut had declared the city of New London a distressed municipality. Under an integrated development plan, a public agency condemned parcels of residential land, including homes overlooking the water, for use to facilitate the revitalization of the downtown area. Much of the land would be used to create private stores, hotels, and offices to complement a new Pfizer complex. Susette Kelo, the owner of a parcel of waterfront land destined for condemnation in the project, and eight other residential landowners sued in a state court to enjoin the city from doing so, claiming that the condemnation would not be for a public purpose. Since the residential land was not blighted and the planned project would benefit private businesses not obligated to serve the general public, as the railroads were when the government condemned land for their use, Kelo seemed to have a good case. The plaintiffs won a partial victory in the trial court, but the Connecticut court ultimately sustained the entire plan. The plaintiffs took their case to the Supreme Court.

The court by the narrowest margin held that the project served a public purpose (*Kelo v. New London*). Stevens wrote the court opinion, and Breyer, Ginsburg, Kennedy, and Souter joined him. Citing precedents, Stevens argued that public purpose should be broadly interpreted to include any public benefit and that the court should defer to legislative judgments about public benefit. On the other hand, he observed that the use of eminent domain had sometimes been a pretext for private gain and that courts would view with skepticism one-to-one transfers of private property that were not part of an integrated plan. Kennedy, in a concurrence, also stressed the importance of a comprehensive plan. O'Connor, Rehnquist, Scalia, and Thomas dissented. O'Connor's dissent was forceful. She argued that the court's argument that the incidental public benefits from the subsequent ordinary use of private property render the use of eminent domain for economic development takings for a public purpose conflates public and private use. She said that, under the court's broad view of eminent domain, nothing would prevent a state from replacing a Motel 6 with a hotel.

The Kelo decision was controversial and unpopular with most Americans, especially property owners. Property owners would presumably receive fair compensation, but they would lose the spot where they preferred to live or even the place where they did business. The court opinion acknowledged that states could limit the power of eminent domain, and that is exactly what more than half of them did after the decision. Many states now forbid takings by eminent domain for economic development except for the alleviation of blight.

In 1996 the court decided a case related to property—namely, the size of punitive damages. Common law and state laws provide for juries awarding punitive damages in addition to compensatory damages when they determine that the defendant's actions deserve punishment. The case involved Dr. Ira Gore, a doctor in Birmingham, Alabama. He bought a BMW car but later discovered that it had been damaged in transit and repainted. Gore claimed that BMW had breached its contract with him and committed a fraud. A trial jury awarded Gore $4,000 in compensatory damages and $4 million in punitive damages. The Alabama Supreme Court upheld the verdict but cut the punitive damages in half. BMW appealed to the U.S. Supreme Court, arguing that the punitive damages violated the due process clause.

The court by the narrowest margin and an unusual division of the justices ruled for BMW (*BMW v. Gore*). Stevens wrote the court opinion, and Kennedy, O'Connor, and Souter joined him. Breyer concurred separately. Stevens argued that the punitive damages were grossly excessive but did not determine when such damages became excessive. Ginsburg, Rehnquist, Scalia, and Thomas dissented. The dissenters stressed the historical role of the states in determining the limits of punitive damages, and Scalia argued that the court's opinion gave no guidance to legislatures about what punitive damages would be constitutionally acceptable and threw the whole tort-reform effort into chaos.

Equal Protection In 1994 the court passed judgment on gender-based peremptory challenges. In 1991 Alabama in the interest of Teresia Bible (T. B.), the mother of a son, Rhett, filed a paternity complaint in Scottsboro, Alabama, against James E. Bowman (J. E. B.). The state attorney for Alabama used nine out of his ten peremptory challenges to exclude men from the jury, and the jury as a result comprised twelve women. The counsel for Bowman used the same number of challenges to exclude women from the jury. Both attorneys apparently believed that women would be more favorable to women's paternity claims. The verdict of the all-female jury was for Bible and against Bowman. His counsel appealed the verdict, claiming that the Batson decision precluded the use of gender-based peremptory challenges. The Alabama Court of Appeals rejected the argument and sustained the trial court's verdict, including an order that Bowman pay child support. Bowman appealed to the U.S. Supreme Court.

The court overturned the verdict (*J. E. B. v. Alabama ex rel. T. B.*). Blackmun wrote the court opinion, and Ginsburg, O'Connor, Souter, and Stevens joined him. Blackmun bluntly argued that there was no legitimate rationale for excluding potential jurors based on what he described as invidious, archaic, and overbroad stereotypes. He concluded that, whether a trial is criminal or civil, potential jurors and litigants have an equal-protection right to jury selection procedures free of gender discrimination. O'Connor, concurring, agreed but argued that the rule should apply only to the government, not the defense. Kennedy concurred only in the judgment, noting his belief that the equal protection clause protected only individual, not group, rights. Rehnquist, Scalia, and Thomas dissented. Rehnquist argued that gender categories, as distinguished from race categories, were governed by heightened rather than strict scrutiny. Scalia's dissent was sharper, arguing that the majority opinion was a politically correct decision totally divorced from the real issues in the case.

In 2000 the court ruled on the right of gay males to be members of the Boy Scouts. In 1990 the Boy Scouts rescinded the membership of an assistant scoutmaster and Eagle Scout, James Dale, for violating an organization rule forbidding membership to homosexuals. Dale, aided by a gay organization, sued the organization in a New Jersey superior court, claiming that the organization's decision to exclude him violated a state statute regarding public accommodations. The trial court ruled for the Boy Scouts, but the appellate division of the superior court reversed. That court held that, since the state had a compelling public interest to end discrimination in public accommodations, application of the statute to the Boy Scouts did not violate the First Amendment. The Boy Scouts then appealed to the U.S. Supreme Court.

The court by the narrowest margin ruled against Dale and upheld the Boy Scouts (*Boy Scouts of America v. Dale*). Rehnquist wrote the court opinion, and Kennedy, O'Connor, Scalia, and Thomas joined him. Rehnquist held that court-mandated inclusion of homosexuals in the Boy Scouts would substantially alter the Boy Scouts' message and so impair its First Amendment right of protected association. He accepted that the organization was a private association and that it taught that homosexual conduct is morally wrong. The Boy Scouts could not be compelled to send a message that it did not want to send. He also noted that expansive definitions of public accommodation in state statutes threatened First Amendment values. Breyer, Ginsburg, Souter, and Stevens dissented. Stevens contended that Dale's membership by itself could not be construed as the Boy Scout's own message. In the light of relatively recent cases of sexual abuse of minors by the clergy and coaches, one might question the suitability of male homosexuals for the role of assistant scoutmaster of young boys, although there was no question about the correct behavior of Dale himself as a scout and assistant scoutmaster.

Speech The court decided two cases involving desecration of the flag and symbolic speech. In the first Gregory Johnson had, in the course of protesting the policies of President Reagan, burned a flag outside a building during the 1984 Republican National Convention in Dallas, Texas. Texas police arrested him for violating a state statute that made it a crime intentionally or knowingly to desecrate a national or state flag. He was convicted and sentenced to a year in prison and fined $2,000. The Texas Court of Criminal Appeals reversed, holding that Johnson's actions were symbolic speech protected by the First Amendment. Texas took the case to the U.S. Supreme Court.

The court in 1989 by the narrowest margin upheld the Texas Court of Criminal Appeals (*Texas v. Johnson*). Brennan wrote the court opinion, and Blackmun, Kennedy, Marshall, and Scalia joined him. Brennan ruled that the desecration was expressive conduct, since it attempted to convey a special message. He argued that there was no evidence that Johnson's symbolic act would imminently incite a disturbance of the peace and that the statute's protection of the flag's integrity as a symbol improperly infringed on the communication of a message. O'Connor, Rehnquist, Stevens, and White dissented. Rehnquist, joined by O'Connor and White, gave a rhetorical citation of song and verse praising the flag. Stevens stressed the special nature of the flag as a symbol not only of the nation but also of its fundamental principles.

The Johnson decision aroused a political storm, and Congress after the decision rapidly passed the 1989 Flag Protection Act, which President Bush I signed. That act prohibited the knowing mutilation, defacement, physical defilement, burning, or trampling on an American flag without reference to desecration of it. The federal government sought to prosecute Eichman, who had burned flags on the steps of the capitol, and another man, who had burned a flag in Seattle, Washington. The defendants sought and obtained desist orders from two district courts, both of which held the act unconstitutional. The United States, as authorized by the act, immediately appealed to the Supreme Court.

The court in 1990 by the narrowest margin affirmed the decisions of the district courts and declared the 1989 law unconstitutional (*U.S. v. Eichman*). Brennan again wrote the court opinion, and the same justices as in *Johnson* joined him. Brennan argued that, although the act contained no explicit content-based limitation on the scope of the prohibited conduct, it was clear that the government's asserted interest is related to the suppression of free expression. The same justices as in *Johnson* dissented. Stevens argued that the law had minimal impact on protesters' freedom of expression, since they had ample alternate means to convey their message, and that the law was neutral regarding the specific content of the speech suppressed along with the prohibited conduct.

Summary The Rehnquist Court was a fractured court. Of the eighty-three cases described above, forty-seven (56.6 percent) involved decisions in which the justices divided five to four. That is the margin by which the court decided nine of the eleven cases involving claims of states' rights in relation to federal laws or the Constitution (85 percent), ten of the twelve cases involving race (83 percent), six and a half of the eight cases involving religious-establishment questions (81 percent), and five of the eight cases involving property (62 percent). In two areas the court was less sharply divided. Only six of the twenty-one criminal cases (28 percent) and two and a half of the seven cases (36 percent) on religious exercise resulted in five-to-four decisions. One should note that the eighty-three cases represent only a small sample of the court's full-opinion decisions during the nineteen years of the Rehnquist Court. Moreover, the cases represent only an infinitesimal fraction of the court's decisions if one includes the many thousands of petitions for review, most of which were unanimously rejected.

At the inception of the Rehnquist Court there were three conservative justices (O'Connor, Rehnquist, and Scalia), three liberal justices (Brennan, Marshall, and Stevens), two justices liberal on many issues (Blackmun and White) and one swing justice (Powell). With the appointment of Kennedy to replace Powell, the conservative bloc increased to four, and with the appointment of Thomas to replace Marshall, the bloc became a majority. The appointments of Souter, Breyer, and Ginsburg to replace Brennan, White, and Blackmun, respectively, did not alter the balance. After Thomas became a justice (1991), the liberal justices could only win if O'Connor and/or Kennedy voted with them.

In the two cases on separation of powers (*Morrison, Mistretta*), the Rehnquist Court was more flexible than the Burger Court. The Rehnquist Court supported states' rights in nine of the eleven cases (85 percent). Those decisions revived the Tenth Amendment as a source of state power and expanded the reach of the Eleventh Amendment beyond its wording. The Rehnquist Court opposed racial gerrymandering in all seven cases by a five-to-four vote, ultimately turned its back on affirmative-action set-aside provisions, and split on affirmative-action admissions programs. It approved some restrictions on abortion but reaffirmed the Roe decision, and it ruled an anti-sodomy law unconstitutional. It affirmed the government in fourteen out of twenty-one criminal decisions (67 percent). It split its decisions in religion cases almost evenly, eight pro-religious individuals or institutions and eight against. It rendered five out of eight decisions (62.5 percent) in favor of property interests. (The states' rights and property decisions were the most innovative features of the court.) It invalidated gender-based peremptory challenges under an intermediate-scrutiny test. It held that the Boy Scouts were permitted to exclude homosexuals. It invalidated a state statute banning desecration of the American flag and a federal statute banning its mutilation.

12

THE ROBERTS COURT

(2005–)

The Justices

John Roberts Jr. On July 1, 2005, O'Connor announced that she would retire when a new justice was sworn in, and President Bush II on July 19 nominated John Roberts Jr. to succeed her. When Rehnquist died on September
3, Bush, three days later, September 6, withdrew Roberts's nomination for
O'Connor's seat and instead nominated him to succeed Rehnquist as chief
justice. The Senate confirmed Roberts on September 29. Roberts, a Republican and a Catholic, was born in Buffalo, New York, on January 27, 1955, but
the family moved to Indiana when he was nine years old. His father, John,
was an executive of Bethlehem Steel. Roberts married Jane Sullivan in 1996,
and they adopted two children. Roberts attended private schools, including a
Catholic boarding school. He graduated summa cum laude from Harvard College in 1976 and magna cum laude from Harvard Law School in 1979, where
was managing editor of the *Harvard Law Review.*

After graduation from law school Roberts clerked with Judge Friendly
of the Second Circuit Court of Appeals from 1979 to 1980 and with Justice
Rehnquist from 1980 to 1981. He worked in the Reagan administration from
1981 to 1986. He was in private practice from 1986 to 1989. He returned to
government service in 1989 under Kenneth Starr, the solicitor general, until

the end of 1992. He was again in private practice from 1993 to 2003, when Bush II appointed him to the Court of Appeals for the District of Columbia.

Samuel Alito Jr. For the vacancy created by O'Connor's prospective retirement, Bush, after shifting the Roberts appointment to replacement of Rehnquist as chief justice, nominated Harriet Miers. That nomination ran into objections, and she withdrew. Then, on November 19, Bush nominated Samuel Alito Jr., and the Senate confirmed Alito on January 31, 2006. Alito was born in Trenton, New Jersey, on April 1, 1950. Alito's father, Samuel, was a teacher, as was his mother. Alito, a Republican and a Catholic, graduated from Princeton College in 1972 and was elected to Phi Beta Kappa. He graduated from Yale Law School in 1975.

Alito clerked with a judge of a federal court of appeals from 1976 to 1977. He was an assistant U.S. district attorney from 1977 to 1981 and U.S. district attorney from 1987 to 1990. He was an assistant to the solicitor general from 1981 to 1985 and an assistant in the White House Office of Legal Counsel from 1985 to 1987. He was a judge on the Third Circuit Court of Appeals from 1990 to 2006.

Sonia Sotomayor Souter indicated his intention to retire from the court on June 29, 2009, and President Obama on May 26 nominated Sonia Sotomayor to replace him; the Senate confirmed her on August 7. Sotomayor, a Democrat and a Catholic, was born in New York City on January 25, 1954. Her father was a laborer and union leader. She married Kevin Noonan in 1976, but they were divorced in 1983. She attended a Catholic high school, graduated summa cum laude from Princeton College in 1976, and graduated from Yale Law School in 1979.

She was assistant district attorney of the borough of Manhattan from 1979 to 1984, a federal district judge from 1992 to 1998, and a judge on the Second Circuit Court of Appeals from 1998 to 2009.

Elena Kagan Stevens effectively retired from the court on June 30, 2010, and Obama on May 10 nominated Elena Kagan to replace Stevens; the Senate confirmed her on September 13. (She had already taken her seat as a temporary appointee on August 7.) Kagan, a Democrat and a Jew, was born in New York City in 1960. Her father was a labor leader. She graduated summa cum laude from Princeton College in 1981, received a master's degree from Worchester College, Oxford, in 1983, and graduated magna cum laude from Harvard Law School in 1986.

She clerked with a judge of the federal court of appeals from 1986 to 1987 and with Justice Marshall from 1987 to 1988. She was in private practice from 1989 to 1991 and taught at the University of Chicago Law School from 1991 to 1999. She was also associate counsel to the Clinton administration from 1995 to 1999 and taught at Harvard Law School from 1999 to 2003, serving as its dean in 2003.

Summary A Republican president (Bush II) appointed two Republicans (Alito and Roberts), and a Democratic president (Obama) two Democrats (Kagan and Sotomayor). Three (Alito, Roberts, and Sotomayor) were Catholics, and one (Kagan) a Jew. Thus, in 2010, there were six Catholics, three Jews, and no Protestant on the court, although all the justices until Taney, and after Taney's death until Edward White, were Protestants. Sotomayor and Kagan are women, and so, with Ginsburg, three women currently sit on the court. Sotomayor is the first Hispanic justice. The father of one Republican (Roberts) was a business executive, and the father as well as the mother of the other (Alito) a teacher. All graduated from elite colleges, Alito, Kagan, and Sotomayor from Princeton College and Roberts from Harvard College. All graduated from elite law schools, Kagan and Roberts from Harvard Law School and Alito and Sotomayor from Yale Law School; in addition, Kagan has a master's degree from Worcester College, Oxford University. All had executive governmental experience, and three (Alito, Roberts, and Sotomayor) had judicial experience; in contrast to nineteenth-century justices, none had legislative experience. Kagan was an academician. All were from the northeastern quadrant of the United States: Roberts from Indiana, Alito from New Jersey, and Sotomayor and Kagan from New York.

Leading Decisions

Regime On June 28, 2012, the Roberts Court handed down its most important and much awaited decision to date, the decision on the constitutionality of key provisions of the 2010 Affordable Care Act (Obamacare). Twenty-six states were challenging a provision that expanded the Medicaid program to cover all those whose income was up to 133 percent of the poverty level and threatened to cut off all Medicaid funds to states choosing not to do so. The National Federation of Independent Business was challenging a provision mandating that individuals not covered by third-party insurance buy private insurance and that those who did not would be obliged in 2014 to pay a percentage of their income up to $695 per year to the federal government. The two groups of plaintiffs brought suit in a federal district court against Kathleen Sibelius, secretary of health and human services, to enjoin those provisions and indeed to strike down the entire law. The district court ruled for the government on the expansion of Medicaid and against the government on the individual mandate. The court of appeals affirmed both holdings but held the individual-mandate provision separable from the rest of the act. The plaintiffs took the case to the Supreme Court. The court, having heard three days of oral argument, upheld the mandate and invalidated the provision on state participation in the expanded Medicaid program in 900 pages of opinions (*National Federation of Business v. Sibelius*).

Roberts wrote the court opinion, supported by different blocs of justices. He, supported by the joint opinion of four justices (Alito, Kennedy, Scalia, and Thomas) held that the individual mandate was not valid under the commerce clause. Roberts argued that the commerce clause empowered Congress to regulate commerce-related activities, including noncommercial activities with a substantial effect on interstate commerce, but not the inactivity of individuals in order to force them to do what the federal government wants them to do (e.g., to follow a specific diet). (Thomas in his separate opinion would not include activity with a substantial effect on interstate commerce in the regulatory power of Congress under the commerce clause.) Against the government argument that sickness is unavoidable and that the mandate makes individuals to do what they will inevitably do and pay for, Roberts argued that the individuals mandated to buy insurance were not currently active in the health market. Nor did he think that the government could rely on the necessary and proper clause without the governmental action being related to an enumerated power.

Roberts did, however, uphold the individual mandate under the tax power, and Breyer, Ginsburg, Kagan, and Sotomayor joined him. Roberts admitted that the tax looked like a penalty, but the law did not make nonpayment of the tax unlawful, and many would pay the tax rather than comply with the mandate to buy insurance. Moreover, individuals cannot avoid the tax by inactivity, and the tax is only an incentive to activity—namely, buying insurance. Alito, Kennedy, Scalia, and Thomas in their joint opinion dissented, arguing that the tax was on its face a penalty for noncompliance. Note that Roberts's validation of the individual mandate under the tax power meant that his preceding argument against invalidating it under the commerce power was simply obiter.

Roberts further held that the law's threat to eliminate all funding for Medicaid unless a state expanded its Medicaid program to cover more recipients was effectively compulsion. On this holding Breyer and Kagan, as well as Alito, Kennedy, Scalia, and Thomas, joined him.

Last, Roberts held that the provision on states expanding their Medicaid coverage was separable from other provisions of the law, and Breyer, Ginsburg, Kagan, and Sotomayor joined him. (Ginsburg and Sotomayor joined reluctantly, since they would have upheld the whole expansion program.) Roberts argued that Congress would not have wanted the whole Medicaid expansion to fail if one provision was invalidated. Alito, Kennedy, Scalia, and Thomas in their joint opinion dissented, arguing the provision "compelling" the states to participate in the expansion was an essential part of the expansion.

In her opinion, Ginsburg, joined by Sotomayor, defended the commerce power as a basis for the individual mandate, citing precedents, especially those in and after 1937, and defended the necessary and proper clause as a basis for the mandate, citing John Marshall in *McCulloch v. Maryland*. As to the Medicaid expansion's alleged coercion of the states, she pointed out that Congress could have simply abolished the existing program and created a new one with expanded coverage for the states to accept or reject.

A few days before the decision on Obamacare, the court ruled on a 2010 Arizona law dealing with illegal aliens in the state. (Illegal aliens comprised an estimated 6 percent of the state's population.) Four provisions of the law were at issue. One made it a misdemeanor for an alien not to carry an alien registration document, which federal law already required. A second made it a misdemeanor for an illegal alien to work in the state. A third authorized a state officer to arrest any illegal alien that an officer had probable cause to believe was guilty of a crime that made the alien deportable. A fourth required police officers to make a reasonable effort to determine the immigration status of persons stopped, detained, or arrested if they had reasonable suspicion that the person was an illegal alien, but persons were to be presumed to be legally in the country if they had a driver's license or its equivalent. The federal government sued to enjoin enforcement of the law, claiming that the immigration laws of the federal government preempted state action in the field. The district court did so, and the court of appeals affirmed. Arizona took the case to the Supreme Court.

The Supreme Court held that federal law preempted the first three provisions but reserved judgment on the fourth until the Arizona court construed it (*Arizona v. U.S.*). Kennedy wrote the court opinion, and Breyer, Ginsburg, Roberts, and Sotomayor joined him. Scalia and Thomas dissented, arguing that none of the provisions were in conflict with federal law. (Scalia also claimed that the federal government's lack of enforcement of its laws was the source of the problem for Arizona.) Alito agreed with the court on the first and fourth provisions but dissented on the second and third. He agreed on the first because of precedent, the single alien registration system, and the incompetence of states to enforce it. Kagan did not participate in the decision.

Earlier in the same year the court considered a case involving sovereign state immunity and federal regulation of family and medical leave for state employees. The federal Family and Medical Leave Act required employers, including state employers, to grant unpaid self-care leave of twelve weeks to employees. The act was principally designed to remedy gender discrimination against women but included male employees to make the act more politically palatable. Daniel Coleman sued his employer, the Maryland Court of Appeals, for violating the act. When Coleman applied for leave under the act, the state told him to resign or else he would be terminated. The district court ruled for the state on the grounds of its sovereign immunity, and the court of appeals affirmed. Coleman appealed to the Supreme Court.

The court by the narrowest margin affirmed (*Coleman v. Court of Appeals of Maryland*). Kennedy wrote the plurality opinion, and Alito, Roberts, and Thomas joined him. Kennedy argued that the statute purported to abrogate the state's sovereign immunity, that the state was Coleman's employer, but that the act regarding the state as employer lacked congruence and proportion between the injury to be prevented (gender discrimination) and the means chosen. Scalia concurred only in the judgment, arguing that the power of Congress under section 5 of the Fourteenth Amendment was limited to conduct prohibited by the amendment. Ginsburg, joined by Breyer, Kagan, and Sotomayor, dissented. She argued that Congress had the power to enforce the right to be free from gender discrimination in pregnancy and child-care leave and that the safe-care provision for male and female state employees was a valid means to achieve that end.

The issue of federal preemption featured in earlier decisions of the Roberts Court. In 2006 the court ruled on the compatibility of an Oregon law permitting the use of drugs by physicians to assist suicide with the Federal

Controlled Substances Act. In 2001 Albert Gonzales, the attorney general, ruled that the use of controlled drugs to assist suicide was not a legitimate medical practice permitted under the act. The state sought an injunction against enforcement of the ruling, and the district court ordered a permanent injunction. The court of appeals affirmed, and Gonzales appealed to the Supreme Court.

The court affirmed (*Gonzales v. Oregon*). Kennedy wrote the court opinion, and Breyer, Ginsburg, O'Connor, Souter, and Stevens joined him. Kennedy argued as a matter of statutory construction that the act concerned only illicit drug dealing and opined that to interpret the act to permit the federal government to define standards of medical practice would constitute a radical shift of authority from the states to the federal government. Roberts, Scalia, and Thomas dissented. Scalia, with Roberts, argued that the attorney general's interpretation of the act was valid, since the act was concerned with public health and safety. Thomas made the point that, if the decision in favor of states' rights were to have involved a constitutional question, it would be contrary to the decision in *Raich* (the marijuana case), in which he was a dissenter.

In the same year the court decided a case involving preferential transfers to state agencies in bankruptcy proceedings. Bernard Katz, the trustee in charge of liquidating a company, sued in a federal court to recover preferential transfers of the company's funds to a state agency, as Virginia law required. Over the agency's claim to sovereign state immunity, Katz won in the district court, and the court of appeals affirmed, on the grounds that Congress had abrogated the state's immunity in bankruptcy proceedings. The state agency took the case to the Supreme Court.

The court by the narrowest margin upheld the decision of the lower courts in favor of Katz (*Central Virginia Community College v. Katz*). Stevens wrote the court opinion, and Breyer, Ginsburg, O'Connor, and Souter joined him. Stevens argued that Article I, section 8, clause 5 of the Constitution gave Congress the power to establish uniform laws on bankruptcy and exclusive jurisdiction over the property in bankruptcy liquidations and so authorized limited subordination of states to the federal government. Thomas, joined by Kennedy, Roberts, and Scalia, dissented. Thomas argued from precedent—namely, the states' rights decisions of the Rehnquist Court—and that the suit really represented a suit by private individuals (other creditors) against the state.

In 2011 the court reviewed an Arizona law that required employers to check the legal status of their employees—namely, whether the employees were citizens or authorized aliens. The local Chamber of Commerce challenged the constitutionality of the law, claiming that federal immigration laws preempted state action. Both the district court and the court of appeals upheld the Arizona law, and the Supreme Court affirmed (*Chamber of Commerce v. Whitney*). Roberts wrote the plurality opinion, and Alito, Kennedy, and Scalia joined him. Roberts found the law a licensing requirement and so not preempted by federal immigration laws. Thomas concurred in the judgment. Breyer, joined by Ginsburg, dissented, arguing that the law, because of its heavy penalties, was not a licensing requirement and that mandatory vetting seriously risked error. Sotomayor also dissented, arguing that federal law preempted state action. Kagan took no part in the decision.

In 2007 the court returned to a troublesome issue since the days of the Taney Court, the so-called dormant power of the commerce clause by itself in the absence of federal laws to negate state actions affecting interstate commerce. New York State had established an authority to manage solid waste in two counties, Oneida and Herkimer. Private haulers could pick up trash, but the authority would process it and charge fees to the haulers. A haulers association sought declaratory and injunctive relief in a federal district court, claiming that they could dispose of the waste at out-of-state facilities at far less cost, so requiring disposal at authority facilities discriminated against interstate commerce. The district court ruled in their favor, but the court of appeals reversed. On appeal, the Supreme Court ruled in favor of the authority (*United Haulers Association v. Oneida-Herkimer Solid Waste Management Authority*).

Roberts wrote the plurality opinion, and Breyer, Ginsburg, and Souter joined him. Roberts argued that the discrimination was for the public benefit and that the benefit outweighed the financial effect on the haulers. Scalia and Thomas concurred in the judgment but only because they did not believe in any dormant power (Thomas) or only anti-protectionist dormant power (Scalia). Alito, joined by Kennedy and Stevens, dissented. Alito argued that discrimination in favor of a local public utility was no different from discrimination in favor of a local private business and that the commerce clause prohibited discriminatory legislation unless it was the only means to achieve the legislative goal. Note that seven justices, the Roberts bloc and the dissenters, agreed that there is a broad dormant commerce power, although they disagreed about its application to this case.

In 2008 the court decided another case involving the dormant commerce power (*Department of Revenue v. Davis*). Kentucky, like many states, taxed the income on out-of-state bonds but exempted the income from its own bonds from taxation. A badly fractured court upheld the tax in four opinions. Souter wrote the plurality opinion, in which only Breyer and Stevens fully joined. Souter argued that the dormant commerce power did not affect a state's issuance of bonds, since the bonds served a public purpose, and that the state entered the bond market as a participant. Stevens in a separate opinion argued that Kentucky had the right to make the interest on its own bonds tax-exempt. Scalia, in a concurring opinion, argued that the reach of the dormant commerce should not be extended beyond existing precedents, and Thomas would entirely discard the dormant commerce power and leave the matter to Congress. Alito and Kennedy dissented. Alito argued that precedents covered the case, and Kennedy argued that Kentucky's tax policy discriminated against out-of-state bondholders.

The court in June 2010 rendered a decision on the delegation of power to a federal agency. It by the narrowest margin declared a provision of the 2002 Sarbanes-Oxley Act unconstitutional (*Free Enterprise Fund v. Public Accounting Board*). That act established the board, whose five members the Securities Exchange Commission would appoint, and the board was empowered to regulate accounting firms. Roberts, joined by Alito, Kennedy, Scalia, and Thomas, wrote the court opinion. Roberts held that the provision violated the constitutional separation of powers. He argued that the board was twice removed from presidential control. The commission presumably could remove members of the board only for good cause, such as malfeasance, and the president could remove members of the commission only for good cause, so the board was too insulated from presidential control. Breyer, joined by Ginsburg, Sotomayor, and Stevens, dissented. Breyer argued that the separation-of-powers doctrine is a functional—that is, practical—concept, that the court should defer to Congress, and that the commission had control over the board's policies.

In 2006 the court decided a third case involving detainees at Guantanamo Bay charged with being enemy combatants. In November 2001 local militia forces fighting the Taliban government in Afghanistan captured Salim Hamdan, a Yemeni national, and handed him over to the U.S. military. In June 2002 he was transferred to Guantanamo Bay. In 2003 he was declared eligible for military trial. In 2004 he was charged with one count of conspiracy to commit offenses liable to trial by a military court. He filed in a federal district court a petition for habeas corpus against Donald Rumsfeld, the secretary of defense, claiming that he should be tried according to the Uniform Code of Military Justice (UCMJ), that conspiracy is not a war crime, and that the procedures in place at Guantanamo were not according to the laws of war and international law. The trial court granted the writ in 2004, but the court of appeals reversed in 2005. The Supreme Court granted review in the same year.

In the meantime, after the 2004 Rasul decision, the administration established a Combatant Status Review Tribunal (CSRT) to hear challenges to the military's claim that detainees were enemy combatants, and Congress passed the Detainee Treatment Act (DTA), which became effective on December 30, 2005. The act provided that no court shall have jurisdiction over habeas corpus petitions by detainees at Guantanamo and that the Court of Appeals of the District of Columbia should have exclusive jurisdiction to hear appeals from decisions of the CSRT.

The court reversed the decision of the court of appeals (*Hamdan v. Rumsfeld*). Stevens wrote the court opinion, and Breyer, Ginsburg, Kennedy, and Souter joined him. Stevens held that the DTA did not apply to cases pending before December 30, 2005. On the merits, he held that the presidential military commissions under the CSRT violated the UCMJ and the Geneva Conventions, and so Hamdan was entitled to the writ of habeas corpus. Kennedy wrote a concurring opinion. Alito, Scalia, and Thomas dissented. Scalia, joined by Alito and Thomas, argued on the jurisdictional question that the DTA specifically said that *no* court had jurisdiction over habeas corpus petitions by the detainees. Thomas, joined in part by Alito and Scalia, argued that military necessity and the authority of the president as commander-in-chief legitimated the detentions at Guantanamo. Alito, joined in part by Scalia and Thomas, argued that the military commissions established by Bush II were the regularly constituted courts required by Article 3 of the 1949 Geneva Conventions. (Arguably, the detainees at Guantanamo did not fall under the Geneva Conventions because the war was unconventional and because the prisoners were captured out of uniform.) Roberts did not participate.

In 2008 the court delivered its fourth and most radical decision regarding detainees at Guantanamo as enemy combatants. In 2006 Congress passed the Military Commission Act (MCA), which denied the jurisdiction of civilian federal courts to hear habeas corpus petitions by detainees. Two aliens held as enemy combatants at Guantanamo petitioned for habeas corpus. The district court in one case granted jurisdiction, and the district court in the other denied it. The court of appeals, on the basis of the MCA, dismissed both cases. The Supreme Court by the narrowest margin reversed, holding that the petitioners were entitled to a habeas corpus hearing and that the MCA's denial of jurisdiction was unconstitutional (*Boumedienne v. Bush*).

Kennedy wrote the court opinion, and Breyer, Ginsburg, Souter, and Stevens joined him. Kennedy argued that the habeas corpus suspension clause (Article I, section 9, clause 2) protects the petitioners from the provision of the MCA, that the United States has de facto sovereignty at Guantanamo, and that the procedures provided in the DTA, including review by the Court of Appeals of the District of Columbia, were no equivalent substitute for habeas corpus. Moreover, the petitioners did not need to exhaust their military appeals before seeking the writ. There were two strong dissents. Roberts, joined by Alito, Scalia, and Thomas, argued that Congress had provided for review by the court of appeals. Scalia, joined by the other dissenters, argued that the writ never ran in favor of aliens abroad, that the decision warped the Constitution, that the suspension clause had no application to the case, and that the decision benefited radical Islamists.

In 2008 the court heard a case involving the rights of defendants to invoke violations of international conventions as the basis for a new trial. Jose Medellin, a Mexican citizen, was convicted and sentenced for murder without being allowed to consult with a representative of his government. The International Court of Justice had after his conviction rendered a decision in another case mandating such consultation, and President Bush II had issued a memorandum calling for adherence to it. Medellin petitioned for a writ of habeas corpus, but the Texas court of criminal appeals dismissed the petition because he had failed to raise the issue at the proper time. Medellin appealed to the U.S. Supreme Court.

The court affirmed the denial of habeas corpus (*Medellin v. Texas*). Roberts wrote the court opinion, and Alito, Kennedy, Scalia, and Thomas joined him. Roberts argued that the decision of the International Court of Justice was not enforceable as federal law over state limitations on habeas corpus. Stevens concurred only in the judgment, arguing that the relevant treaties did not authorize federal courts to enforce their provisions on the states. Breyer, joined by Ginsburg and Souter, dissented. Breyer argued that the treaties were self-executing and that the supremacy clause governed the case. He also appealed to the president's plenary power over foreign affairs.

The Roberts Court decided several cases involving districting. In 2006 the court decided a case involving political gerrymandering of Texas congressional districts. After the 2000 census, Texas gained two new representatives.

After the 2002 state elections, the Republicans, who already occupied the governor's chair, gained control of both houses of the legislature. They then reapportioned the congressional districts in their favor. The result in 2004 was that the Republicans won twenty-one seats and the Democrats eleven, a distribution grossly out of proportion to the overall division of votes in the state. A group of Latino citizens sued in federal district court for injunctive and declaratory relief against Rick Perry, the governor. The district court rejected the plaintiffs' suit, and they appealed to the Supreme Court.

A badly fractured court rendered a split decision, basically affirming the holding on one disputed district (no. 24) and reversing the holding on another (no. 23) (*League of United Latin-American Citizens v. Perry*). Kennedy, supported by different coalitions of justices, relied on the 1965 Voting Rights Act, not the equal protection clause. Stevens, joined by Breyer, thought the patently political gerrymandering invalidated the whole districting plan. Souter, joined by Ginsburg, would also have held the whole districting plan invalid but because of its resulting disproportionate party representation, not because of the motives of the legislators. Roberts, joined by Alito, would have upheld the whole districting plan. Scalia, joined by Thomas, saw nothing wrong with political gerrymandering and so would likewise have upheld the whole districting plan. Stevens, on the one hand, and Scalia and Thomas, on the other, held diametrically contrary views on the constitutionality of political gerrymandering, and the other justices could not agree on whether the issue was statutory or constitutional or whether the standard was subjective (the legislators' motives) or objective (the disproportionate results). The court's jurisprudence on political gerrymandering is, as Stevens pointed out, a cacophony.

In 2009 the court by the narrowest margin rejected the contention that the 1965 Voting Rights Act required officials to draw district lines to maximize the proportion of racial minorities to a majority of white voters (*Bartlett v. Strickland*). A state subject to the act had done so, splitting a county to maximize the number of minority voters in white majority districts. Kennedy, joined by Alito and Roberts, wrote the plurality opinion, holding that the act did not require that. Thomas, joined by Scalia, concurred separately, arguing that the act did not touch the question of voter dilution. Souter, joined by Breyer, Ginsburg, and Stevens, dissented, and Breyer wrote a separate dissenting opinion.

In 2008 the court considered the constitutionality of an unusual primary system. An initiative in Washington State provided that primary candidates should be identified on a primary ballot by self-designated party preference.

Voters were permitted to vote for any candidate, and the two top contestants, regardless of their party self-designation, ran against each other in the general election. The Republican Party in the state sought an injunction against the system, claiming that it violated the party's freedom of association. The district court granted summary judgment against the system, and the court of appeals affirmed. The Washington State Grange Association appealed the case to the Supreme Court.

The court reversed and upheld the system (*Washington State Grange Association v. Washington State Republican Party*). Thomas wrote the court opinion, and Alito, Breyer, Ginsburg, Roberts, Souter, and Stevens joined him. The lower courts thought that the Washington system was governed by the court decision in *California Democratic Party v. Jones*, which invalidated a primary system in which voters could vote in the primary of any party. Thomas distinguished the Washington system from the California system. He argued that the Washington system, unlike the California system, did not choose party nominees, found no severe burden on a party's freedom of association, and thought fears about voter confusion purely speculative. In a separate concurrence, Roberts stressed that the court was only upholding the constitutionality of the system on its face. Scalia, joined by Kennedy, dissented. Scalia argued that there was a serious risk that a political party would be misrepresented and compelled to be associated with an undesirable candidate. Moreover, he found no public interest, compelling or otherwise, in the system.

In 2008 the court upheld an Indiana law requiring that persons voting on election day provide valid government-issued photo identification (*Crawford v. Marion County Election Board*). William Crawford and others sought an injunction against the law on its face, claiming that it imposed a substantial burden on the right to vote. The district court ruled for the defendant, and the court of appeals affirmed. The Supreme Court affirmed. Stevens, joined by Kennedy and Roberts, argued that the law imposed no severe burden and that the state had a legitimate interest in validating the credentials of voters. Scalia, joined by Alito and Thomas, argued that the law required everyone to produce the identification, and so the burden on voters was equal. Souter, joined by Ginsburg, dissented, arguing that the law imposed the burden of travel costs and photo fees on some (e.g., those without drivers' licenses). Breyer also dissented, arguing that the burden was disproportionate.

In 2011 the court by the narrowest margin upheld a three-judge district-court decision ordering a radical reduction of the inmates in the California prison system (*Brown v. Plata*). The system had almost double the 80,000 prisoners that it was designed to hold. The district court adopted a master's report and ordered a reduction of the number of prisoners within two years to 135 percent of the number that the prisons were designed to hold, and the court of appeals affirmed. The governor appealed, but the Supreme Court by the narrowest margin affirmed.

Kennedy wrote the court opinion, and Breyer, Ginsburg, Kagan, and Sotomayor joined him. Kennedy argued that the order was reasonable and necessary, but that the lower court could consider a time extension for its implementation. Scalia and Alito wrote dissenting opinions. Scalia, joined by Thomas, argued that the order would result in the release of 46,000 convicted criminals, that only a small number of prisoners were affected by poor medical conditions, and that judges shouldn't run penal systems. Alito, joined by Roberts, argued that federal judges had no authority to run prisons and that release of the prisoners would pose a grave risk to public safety.

In 2009 the court by the narrowest margin invalidated a New York law that removed prisoners' federal civil rights' damage suits against state prison officials from the jurisdiction of the state courts of general jurisdiction (*Haywood v. Drown*). Instead, the state required prisoners to sue in the state court of claims, in which there would be no payment of the prisoner's attorney fees, no punitive damages, and no power to issue injunctions. When a prisoner, Haywood, attempted to sue Drown, a corrections official, under a federal civil rights statute in a New York court of general jurisdiction, that court dismissed the suit, and the New York Court of Appeals, its highest court, affirmed. Stevens wrote the court opinion, and Breyer, Ginsburg, Kennedy, and Souter joined him. Stevens argued that federal law established the civil rights at issue and that the supremacy clause empowers state courts to hear cases involving claims to those rights. Thomas, joined by Alito, Roberts, and Scalia, dissented, arguing that neither the Constitution nor precedent required New York to open its courts to suits by claimants of federal rights.

In 1999 private organizations petitioned the Environmental Protection Agency (EPA) to begin regulating the emission of so-called greenhouse gases, principally carbon dioxide, under the Clean Air Act. In 2003 the agency denied the petition, claiming that the act did not authorize it to do so, and that action now, in the context of uncertain scientific knowledge, would be unwise. Massachusetts joined the petitioners and sought review of the EPA decision in the district court of the District of Columbia. The district court denied review, and the court of appeals affirmed. The Supreme Court accepted the case to consider two questions. First, did Massachusetts have standing to sue? Second, were the agency's stated reasons for denying the petition consistent with the act?

In 2007 the court by the narrowest margin supported Massachusetts on both issues (*Massachusetts v. Environmental Protection Agency*). Stevens wrote the court opinion, and Breyer, Ginsburg, Kennedy, and Souter joined him. On the standing issue, Stevens argued that the state had\ a concrete interest in the air its citizens breathe. On the merits, he argued that the emissions caused real injury and that there were remedies to cure it. Alito, Roberts, Scalia, and Thomas dissented. Roberts, joined by the other dissenters, argued that the substantive issues were not justiciable, since decisions regarding them belong to the legislative and executive branches of the federal government. The state would have standing if it could demonstrate concrete injury, but it cannot in the present state of the evidence. Nor is there an easy remedy, since 80 percent of the emissions come from outside the United States. Scalia argued that the act gives the EPA discretion to act or not to act.

Campaign Financing The Roberts Court handed down a number of decisions on campaign financing laws, including a very big one (*Citizens United*). In 2006 the court considered a 1997 Vermont law that limited campaign contributions and campaign expenditures over a two-year election cycle, ranging from $300,000 for gubernatorial campaigns to $2,000 for legislative campaigns. Former candidates for state office, voters, campaign contributors, and political parties challenged the law in federal court. The district court ruled that all the expenditure limits violated the First Amendment and that some of the contribution limits also did. The court of appeals upheld all the contribution limits and remanded the case to the district court to determine whether the expenditure limits were narrowly enough tailored to the public interest in controlling the corrosive influence of money on the political process. The plaintiffs appealed to the Supreme Court.

A fractured court struck down the law (*Randall v. Sorrell*). Breyer wrote the plurality opinion, and only Roberts fully and Alito for the most part joined him. Breyer relied on the 1976 Buckley decision, which, as we have seen, invalidated federal limits on campaign expenditures but upheld limits on campaign contributions. On the contribution limits, Breyer argued that the law was not sufficiently tailored (i.e., proportional) to the state's interest in insulating the political process from the corrosive influence of money. He noted that the Vermont contribution limits were only a fraction of those approved in *Buckley*. Alito left the Buckley decision for a later review. Kennedy, expressing exasperation with the court's jurisprudence, concurred only in the judgment. Thomas, joined by Scalia, also concurred only in the judgment and explicitly called on the court to overrule *Buckley*. Ginsburg, Souter, and Stevens dissented. Stevens would have overruled *Buckley* on expenditure limits and upheld them as well as the contribution limits in the Vermont law. Souter, joined in full by Ginsburg and in part by Stevens, would have upheld the contribution limits and remanded the case to the lower court to reinterpret *Buckley* and determine whether the expenditure limits were sufficiently tailored, as the court of appeals had done.

The 2002 Bipartisan Campaign Reform [McCain-Feingold] Act (BCRA) made it a federal crime for corporations to use general funds to pay for any electioneering commercials referring to candidates for federal office within thirty days of a primary election or sixty days of a general election. On July 26, 2004, the Wisconsin Right to Life (WRTL) organization, which was incorporated, filed suit against the Federal Elections Commission (FEC) for declaratory and injunctive relief before the blackout period began on August 15. The district court denied relief, but the Supreme Court reversed and remanded. On remand but after the 2004 elections, the district court gave summary judgment for the WRTL organization, holding that the proposed commercials were issue, not express advocacy, ads. The Supreme Court granted review and identified two issues. First, since the 2004 elections were over, was there now a case or controversy? Second, if there was, was the WRTL organization entitled to declaratory and injunctive relief?

In 2007 the court by the narrowest margin ruled in favor of the WRTL organization on both questions (*Federal Elections Commission v. Wisconsin Right to Life*). Roberts wrote the court opinion, and Alito, Kennedy, Scalia, and Thomas joined him on the jurisdictional question. On that issue Roberts argued that the case was not moot, since the issue could occur in a subsequent election. On the merits he, joined only by Alito, argued that ads would be electioneering if and only if they could be interpreted as advocacy and that the ads at issue could not be so interpreted. Scalia, joined by Kennedy and Thomas, concurred only in Roberts's judgment that the WRTL organization was entitled to declaratory and injunctive relief and argued that the statute's time limits on ads were unconstitutional. Souter, joined by Breyer, Ginsburg, and Stevens, dissented on the merits. Souter cited what he perceived to be the paramount danger of money corrupting the political process and argued that, since the distinction between issue and advocacy ads was a fiction, it was wise to stick with the blackout time. Note that six justices (Roberts, Alito, and dissenters) accepted the constitutionality of the provision.

In 2008 the court ruled on an amendment to the BCRA. The amendment provided that if a self-financed candidate for federal office spent more than $350,000 on the candidate's campaign, the limits on contributions to a publicly financed candidate were relaxed threefold, while the limits remained intact for the self-financed candidate. Jack Davis, who was twice (2004 and 2006) an unsuccessful candidate for a congressional seat in New York, filed a suit challenging the amendment, and the district court, while granting him standing, ruled against him on the merits. As provided for by the act, the case went to the Supreme Court on direct appeal. The court accepted his standing and ruled in his favor (*Davis v. Federal Elections Commission*).

Alito wrote the court opinion, and Kennedy, Roberts, Scalia, and Thomas joined him. Alito argued that raising the limits on contributions for publicly funded candidates when the self-financed candidate spent more than the specified amount imposed an unconstitutional burden on free speech. Stevens, joined in full by Souter and in the main part by Breyer and Ginsburg, dissented. Stevens both rejected the Buckley decision's permission of unlimited campaign expenditures by candidates from their own and their families' pockets and approved limits on campaign contributions and relaxing the limits on publicly financed candidates if the expenditures of a self-financed candidate exceeded a specified amount. The prevention of money corrupting the political process justified this encumbrance on free speech. Ginsburg, joined by Breyer, noted that they would affirm the Buckley decision on expenditures by private individuals.

On January 21, 2010, the court handed down its landmark decision on independent election activity by corporations and unions. The BCRA prohibited corporations and unions from campaign advertisements within certain dates before elections, as well as requiring disclaimers and disclosures. Citizens United, a political action group, wanted to distribute the film *Hillary* (a derogatory film on Hillary Clinton) within the prohibited time, but the FEC ruled that the film constituted electioneering and so could not be distributed in the specified timeframe. The Union then filed suit in a district court challenging the constitutionality of the law's provision, and the court ruled them facially valid. The case then went directly to the Supreme Court, and fifty-four amici filed briefs. The court, with two days of oral arguments, upheld the disclaimer and disclosure provisions but held that the ban on corporation and union ads within the specified times was invalid on its face (*Citizens United v. Federal Elections Commission*).

Kennedy wrote the plurality opinion, and Alito, Roberts, and Scalia joined him. Kennedy argued that the advertising ban on the electioneering film violated the exercise of free speech and that it could not survive the strict scrutiny that infringement of speech requires. Thomas provided the fifth vote against the advertisement ban but would have also invalidated the other requirements. Stevens, joined by Breyer, Ginsburg, and Sotomayor, dissented. Stevens cited the long tradition of limiting campaign expenditures by corporations and unions and the history of the First Amendment in relation to political speech. Scalia, joined by Alito and Thomas, wrote a separate opinion to answer Stevens. Alito's replacement of O'Connor was probably the key factor in the different result in this case from that in the 2003 McConnell decision.

On June 27, 2011, the last day of the court's term that year, the court decided a case on an Arizona campaign-finance law. The law provided additional funding to publicly funded candidates if the expenditures of privately funded candidates and groups supporting them exceeded the initial allotment of all publicly funded candidates, roughly dollar for dollar up to the amount of the original grant. A political-action committee brought suit against the secretary of state, Kay Bennett. The district court ruled for the plaintiffs, but the court of appeals reversed. The Supreme Court by the narrowest margin reversed again and ruled for the plaintiffs (*Arizona Free Enterprise Club's Freedom Club Political Action Committee v. Bennett*).

Roberts wrote the court opinion, and Alito, Kennedy, Scalia, and Thomas joined him. Roberts argued that the escalating matching funds for publicly funded candidates substantially burdened political speech—namely, of the privately funded candidates—and that the alleged compelling public interests—namely, to prevent the corruption of the political process and to level the playing field—did not justify it. He did not think that independent expenditures amounted to corruption. Kagan, joined by Breyer, Ginsburg, and Sotomayor, dissented. Kagan argued that the law promoted a healthy political system and prevented corruption.

Criminal The largest number of cases decided by the Roberts Court, as has been so since the landmark Warren Court decisions, was in the area of criminal law. The court reached several decisions on the Fourth Amendment and police searches.

In 2006 the court considered a case involving the knock-and-announce rule. Police in Detroit, Michigan, obtained a warrant to search the home of Booker Hudson for drugs and firearms, and the officer executing the warrant knocked and announced himself but waited only three to five seconds before forcibly entering the residence. He found Hudson with a loaded gun lodged between the cushion and the armchair on which Hudson was seated, as well as a quantity of crack cocaine. The officer arrested Hudson for possession of drugs and firearms. At the trial, the evidence discovered after the entry was admitted, and Hudson was convicted. The Michigan Supreme Court affirmed, holding that the exclusionary rule did not require exclusion of the evidence, even though the police had violated the time required before entry. Hudson appealed to the U.S. Supreme Court.

The court by the narrowest margin upheld the conviction (*Hudson v. Michigan*). Scalia wrote the court opinion, and Alito, Kennedy, Roberts, and Thomas joined him. Scalia assumed that the waiting time before entering after the officer knocked and announced his purpose was too short, since the prosecution had conceded the point. He concluded, however, that the exclusionary rule did not require that the evidence obtained pursuant to a valid search warrant should be excluded because of a partial violation of the knock-and-announce rule. To exclude the evidence would amount to giving the criminal a get-out-of-jail-free card. Breyer, joined by Ginsburg, Souter, and Stevens, dissented. Breyer argued that the decision undermined the legal incentive for the police to follow the full knock-and-announce rule, which the court had unanimously affirmed in the 1995 Wilson decision.

In the same year the court decided a case involving a domestic dispute that culminated in the search of a home with the consent of the wife but not of the husband. The wife, Janet, separated from her husband, Scott, in late May 2001 and went to Canada with her son. She and the son returned in July. On July 6 she complained to the police that her husband had taken her son away. When officers came to the home, she told them that Scott was a cocaine user. Janet said that there were items of drug use in the house. An officer asked Scott for permission to search the house, but he refused. The officer then asked Janet for permission, and she gave it. Janet led the officer to a bedroom. The officer found a drinking straw with a powdery residue, which proved to be cocaine. The police then obtained a search warrant for the house and found more evidence. Scott was indicted for drug possession. The trial court did not exclude the evidence, but the Georgia Supreme Court did, ruling that one occupant cannot give consent to a search if the other expressly objects. Georgia appealed to the U.S. Supreme Court.

The court affirmed (*Georgia v. Randolph*). Souter wrote the court opinion, and Breyer, Ginsburg, Kennedy, and Stevens joined him. Souter argued that contemporary social customs would not deem that one occupant has the authority to consent to the search of a home over the objection of the other occupant, although he admitted that this represented a fine distinction from a precedent that allowed one occupant to do so in the absence of the other. Breyer and Stevens wrote concurring opinions. Stevens used his opinion to criticize the so-called originalists, who hold that the text of the Constitution should be interpreted according to the original intent of its authors. He argued that, at the time of the drafting of the Fourth Amendment, the husband would have had the sole authority to consent to a police search. Roberts, Scalia, and Thomas dissented. Roberts, joined by Scalia, argued that the distinction from the precedent was too fine and that each occupant had the authority to consent. Scalia rebutted Stevens with the argument that the Fourth Amendment was based on the notion of trespass and that anyone with authority over the premises can consent to a police search. Thomas argued that there was no general search, and that Janet, who took the officer to the bedroom, was not a police agent. Newly appointed Alito did not participate.

Also in that year, the court decided a case involving the application of the Fourth Amendment to searches of parolees. In California, a parolee on release from prison agreed to a search or seizure at any time, with or without probable cause. A policeman on patrol stopped and searched a parolee, Donald Samson, without probable cause and found methamphetamine. The trial court admitted the methamphetamine into evidence, and Samson was convicted of possession of a controlled substance. The state court of appeals affirmed, and Samson appealed to the U.S. Supreme Court.

The court affirmed (*Samson v. California*). Thomas wrote the court opinion, and Alito, Ginsburg, Kennedy, Roberts, and Scalia joined him. Thomas argued that the California rule on searches of parolees served an important governmental interest and that parolees have less liberty and expectation of privacy than ordinary citizens. Stevens, joined by Breyer and Souter, dissented. Stevens argued that parolees have a higher expectation of privacy than prisoners and should not be subject to searches without reasonable suspicion.

In 2009 the court by the narrowest margin upheld the conviction of a previously convicted felon in possession of a gun and amphetamine (*Herring v. U.S.*). Bernie Herring was arrested for failing to answer a filing charge. The police discovered the gun and the drugs during a search of Herring. The investigating officer had made a routine effort to obtain verification of the reported failure from the county clerk but received no timely reply. In fact, the police report was erroneous. The court of appeals affirmed the conviction, and Herring appealed to the Supreme Court.

Roberts wrote the court opinion, and Alito, Kennedy, Scalia, and Thomas joined him. Roberts argued that the record-keeping error was not the result of grave negligence, and so the arrest and subsequent search were in good faith. Ginsburg, joined by Breyer, Souter, and Stevens, dissented. She called the recording error inexcusable. Breyer, joined by Souter, argued in a separate dissent that there was a difference between police error, which is not excusable, and judicial error, which is.

In the same year the court returned to the Belton decision on the police search of the passenger compartment of a stopped automobile after the valid arrest of its driver or a passenger. Police officials and legal commentators had interpreted *Belton* to mean that the police in the course of such an arrest were permitted to search the entire passenger compartment and anything in it without a warrant or probable cause. Arizona police arrested Rodney Gant for driving with a suspended license. He was handcuffed and locked in the patrol car. The officer then searched the car and found a jacket, in the pocket of which was cocaine. Gant was convicted of drug possession, but the Arizona Supreme Court reversed, holding that *Belton* did not apply, since the police had already secured Gant. The U.S. Supreme Court by the narrowest margin affirmed (*Arizona v. Gant*).

Stevens wrote the court opinion, and Ginsburg, Scalia, Souter, and Thomas joined him. Stevens held that the Chimel decision controlled *Belton*. The Chimel decision allowed police making an arrest in a home to search only the area within the immediate control of the arrestee in order to prevent the acquisition of a weapon or the destruction of evidence before a search warrant could be obtained. Applying *Chimel* to the instant case, Stevens argued that Gant, already secured, was not within reaching distance of the automobile and that there was no reason to believe that the vehicle contained evidence of a crime by Gant. Scalia in a concurring opinion indicated that he would abandon the Chimel approach to automobile searches incidental to an arrest. He would hold that, when an arrestee has been secured, automobile searches are reasonable only when their object is to obtain evidence of the crime for which the arrestee has been arrested or other criminal evidence that the officer has reason to believe is in the car. Alito, joined by Breyer, Kennedy, and Roberts, dissented, arguing that the police acted in good faith when they made the search and that the decision in effect overruled *Belton.* Breyer dissented separately to argue for the principle of *stare decisis* regarding the Belton decision.

In 2012 the court invoked the pre-Katz trespass doctrine to invalidate what it called an unconstitutional search. The District of Columbia police obtained a search warrant to install a GPS tracking system on the automobile of a suspected drug dealer, Antoine Jones, but the device was installed on the wrong day and in the wrong place (Maryland). The evidence from the device was used in the trial of Jones for conspiracy to distribute cocaine and crack. Jones was convicted, but the court of appeals overturned it, holding that the information was obtained from the vehicle while it was traveling on public streets and that this violated Jones's reasonable expectation of privacy. The Supreme Court by the narrowest margin held that the search was illegal for a different reason (*U.S. v. Jones*).

Scalia wrote the court opinion, and Kennedy, Roberts, Sotomayor, and Thomas joined him. Scalia argued that the Fourth Amendment prohibits obtaining information by trespass on a person's property and that the illegal installation of the device committed a trespass on Jones's property. He interpreted the Katz decision as supplementary to the trespass doctrine. Alito, joined by Breyer, Ginsburg, and Kagan, dissented. Alito objected to the trespass analysis of the case. He argued that the installation of the device was a seizure, not a search, and that it was the use of the device that raised the search question—namely, whether Jones had a reasonable expectation of privacy against the government obtaining information from the device.

In 2012 the court reviewed the constitutionality of strip-searching an arrestee for a minor, nonindictable offense before being entered into the general prison population. Albert Florence was arrested for failing to pay a fine and strip-searched before his imprisonment in the absence of reasonable suspicion that he was carrying weapons or drugs. Police did not touch him during the search. He sued the county, claiming that his civil rights were violated. He lost the case in the local courts and appealed to the Supreme Court. The court by the narrowest margin upheld the search (*Florence v. Board of Freeholders*). Kennedy wrote the court opinion, and Alito, Roberts, Scalia, and Thomas joined him. Kennedy held that the balance between prison security and individual freedom made the search reasonable. Breyer, joined by Ginsburg, Kagan, and Sotomayor, dissented, arguing that the search involved close observation of the arrestee's private areas and that the search was unnecessary.

The Roberts Court handed down a few decisions on the Sixth Amendment and the right to counsel. In 2006 the court ruled on an involved case on the Sixth Amendment right to the assistance of hired counsel. A federal district attorney in Missouri had Cuauhtemoc Gonzalez-Lopez indicted for conspiracy to distribute more than 100 kilograms of marijuana. Gonzalez-Lopez had a Missouri lawyer but contacted and met with a California lawyer, Joseph Low, after arraignment. Gonzalez-Lopez wanted Low to be his only counsel at his trial, but the district court denied Low's application to represent Gonzalez-Lopez because the lawyer had violated a technical court rule. Gonzalez-Lopez then obtained another, local lawyer to represent him. Gonzalez-Lopez was convicted, but the court of appeals vacated the conviction, holding that the court rule was misinterpreted and that Gonzalez-Lopez had a constitutional right to paid counsel. On appeal to the Supreme Court, the government conceded the right to paid counsel but claimed that the error was harmless, since there was no evidence that the substitute counsel was ineffective.

The court by the narrowest margin upheld the court of appeals (*U.S. v. Gonzalez-Lopez*). Scalia wrote the court opinion, and Breyer, Ginsburg, Souter, and Stevens joined him. Scalia argued that the Sixth Amendment absolutely guaranteed the defendant a right to paid counsel and that the error was not harmless, since the chosen counsel might have made a better defense than the substitute counsel. Alito, joined by Kennedy, Roberts, and Thomas, dissented. Alito pointed out that the Sixth Amendment guarantees the right of assistance of counsel, but that there was harmless error because the substitute counsel was effective. Note that the justices were unanimous on the right of defendants to paid counsel.

Jeffrey Landrigan was convicted of murder in 1982. He escaped from prison in 1989 and murdered a woman in Arizona. He stopped his ex-wife and birth mother from giving evidence on mitigating circumstances in the death-sentence phase of his trial. Landrigan later brought a habeas corpus action in the trial court, claiming that his counsel had failed to present the evidence from his ex-wife and birth mother. The trial court rejected the petition, and the Arizona Supreme Court affirmed. Landrigan then went to a federal district court for a writ of habeas corpus against Schriro, his corrections official. The district court denied the petition, but the court of appeals reversed, holding that Landrigan's counsel failed to do his duty, that the Arizona trial court failed to do its duty, and that Landrigan was entitled to an evidentiary hearing on his petition for habeas corpus.

In 2007 the court by the narrowest margin reversed again and upheld denial of the petition (*Schriro v. Landrigan*). Thomas wrote the court opinion, and Alito, Kennedy, Roberts, and Scalia joined him. Thomas argued that the court of appeals was in error because the district court had discretion and that Landrigan himself would not allow his counsel to present any evidence on mitigating circumstances. Stevens, joined by Breyer, Ginsburg, and Souter, dissented, arguing that Landrigan was at least entitled to an evidentiary hearing.

In 2009 the court overruled the 1986 precedent of *Michigan v. Jackson.* The Jackson decision forbade police from initiating interrogation once the suspect had invoked his right to counsel. In the instant case, Jesse Montejo was charged with murder, and the judge assigned a counsel for him. Later, after police had read Montejo the Miranda warnings, he wrote an incriminating letter of apology to the widow, and the letter was introduced into evidence at the trial. He was convicted and sentenced to death. The Louisiana Supreme Court affirmed, arguing that the Jackson precedent was inapplicable, since Montejo himself had not invoked his right to counsel. Rather, the state had assigned the counsel.

The U.S. Supreme Court by the narrowest margin affirmed (*Montejo v. Louisiana*). The court chose to overrule rather than distinguish the Jackson precedent but remanded the case to Louisiana to consider Miranda questions. Scalia wrote the court opinion, and Alito, Kennedy, Roberts, and Thomas joined him. Stevens, joined by Breyer, Ginsburg, and Souter, dissented, arguing principally on the basis of stare decisis. (Alito wrote a concurring opinion to rebut Stevens on that point).

The Roberts Court also handed down three decisions on the Sixth Amendment and the right of a defendant to confront the witnesses against him. The first case was in 2009. Police had seized drugs in the possession of Luis Melendez-Diaz. The drugs were submitted to laboratory analysis and the report was admitted into evidence at his trial. He was convicted, and the state appellate court affirmed. The U.S. Supreme Court by the narrowest margin reversed (*Melendez-Diaz v. Massachusetts*). Scalia wrote the court opinion, and

Ginsburg, Souter, Stevens, and Thomas joined him. Scalia held that the Sixth Amendment requires that the author of the lab report testify in court, so that the defendant had an opportunity to confront the witness. He nonetheless remanded the case to the state courts to consider whether the failure to have the witness testify constituted harmless error. Kennedy, joined by Alito, Breyer, and Roberts, dissented, arguing that the admission of scientific evidence without the personal testimony of its author was traditional.

In 2011 the court decided another case involving the confrontation clause. Donald Bullcoming was convicted in New Mexico of aggravated drunken driving. At his trial the lab report on his blood-alcohol content at the time of his arrest was submitted into evidence, and the supervisor of the laboratory, not the analyst, testified. The New Mexico Supreme Court affirmed. The U.S. Supreme Court by the narrowest margin reversed (*Bullcoming v. New Mexico*). Ginsburg wrote the court opinion, in which Scalia fully joined, and in which Kagan, Sotomayor, and Thomas joined for the most part. Ginsburg argued that the Sixth Amendment requires that the primary analyst testify in front of the defendant. Sotomayor wrote to stress that the decision was limited to holding that the supervisor had little connection with the test. Kennedy, joined by Alito, Breyer, and Roberts, dissented. Kennedy argued that the supervisor who testified at the trial was a knowledgeable representative of the lab, that the testimony was on scientific findings, and that the decision turned the court into a national tribunal on the admissibility of evidence in criminal trials.

In 2012 the court considered a case involving the admission of testimony by another expert who had not made the lab report about which the expert was testifying. Sandy Williams was tried and convicted of rape, robbery, and kidnapping, and the Illinois Supreme Court affirmed. A forensic police expert testified at the trial that she matched a DNA profile by an outside lab to a profile that the state lab produced from a sample of Williams's blood. The Supreme Court by the narrowest margin affirmed (*Williams v. Illinois*). Alito wrote the plurality opinion, and Breyer, Kennedy, and Roberts joined him. Alito argued that the expert's testimony referred to the outside DNA profile without claiming to verify it, and so the testimony did not violate the confrontation clause. Breyer concurred in the opinion but urged a broader resolution, arguing that lab reports are not testimonial, and pointed out that the defense could call lab witnesses if it wished. (If it did, of course, it would have to pay them for testifying.) Thomas concurred only in the judgment and, like Breyer, argued that lab reports were not formally testimonial. Kagan, joined by Ginsburg, Scalia, and Sotomayor, dissented, arguing that there are often errors in lab reports and that the outside analyst should be called to testify.

In 2007 the court reviewed a case involving the prosecutor's peremptory challenge of a potential juror. The defendant, Cal Brown, had murdered one woman in California and another woman in Washington two days later. A Washington trial court convicted Brown of the second murder and sentenced him to death, and the Washington Supreme Court affirmed. A federal district court denied Brown's petition for a writ of habeas corpus, but the court of appeals reversed, holding that one potential juror had been unconstitutionally excluded. Washington State, in the name of Brown's warden, appealed to the U.S. Supreme Court.

The court by the narrowest margin reversed again (*Uttecht v. Brown*). Kennedy wrote the court opinion, and Alito, Roberts, Scalia, and Thomas joined him. Kennedy argued that precedent favored deference to the decision of the trial judge on the impartiality of potential jurors. He further argued that the defense counsel in the case had raised no objection at the time of impaneling the jury. Breyer, Ginsburg, Souter, and Stevens dissented. Stevens, joined by the other dissenters, argued that precedent favored Brown. Breyer, joined by Souter, additionally argued that the absence of objection by the defense attorney was irrelevant.

The Roberts Court handed down three decisions extending the Eighth Amendment prohibition of cruel and unusual punishment to new areas. In 2007 the court ruled on the competent mental state required for executing a convict. In 1992 Scott Panetti drove to the home of his estranged wife's parents, broke in, and killed them in front of his wife and daughter. Found competent to stand trial, he was convicted and sentenced to death by a Texas court. Later, post-conviction, he claimed insanity. Experts testified that his post-conviction behavior was a deliberate effort to look insane, and the trial court rejected his claim. He then petitioned in a federal district court for a writ of habeas corpus against Quarterman, the corrections official. The district court and the court of appeals rejected it. Panetti appealed to the Supreme Court.

In 2007 the court by the narrowest margin reversed and ruled for Panetti (*Panetti v. Quarterman*). Kennedy wrote the court opinion, and Breyer, Ginsburg, Souter, and Stevens joined him. Kennedy held that the state court had failed to abide by *Ford v. Wainwright*, which applied the Eighth Amendment to the states and prohibited them from imposing death sentences on the insane, even those sane at the time they committed the capital crime. Kennedy argued that a convict before execution must be aware of the reason he was being executed and not merely of the fact that he was. Thomas, joined by Alito, Roberts, and Scalia, dissented. Thomas complained that the majority was not deferring to the state court and that the court should not reject the decision of the court of appeals without a constitutional argument.

In 2008 the court by the narrowest margin ruled that a death sentence for rape was unconstitutional (*Kennedy v. Louisiana*). Patrick Kennedy was convicted of aggravated rape of his stepdaughter and sentenced to death, and the Louisiana Supreme Court affirmed. Justice Kennedy wrote the court opinion, and Breyer, Ginsburg, Souter, and Stevens joined him. Kennedy held that a death sentence for a crime that involved no death was contrary to the Eighth Amendment. He argued that standards of decency had evolved and that there was now a national consensus against the death sentence in cases involving no victim's death. Moreover, he pointed out that there was a risk of wrongful execution because the child-victim's testimony might be false. Alito strongly dissented, and Roberts, Scalia, and Thomas joined him. Alito argued that the framers did not consider the death penalty for rape a cruel and unusual punishment, that no precedent supported the decision, that there was no objective proof of a national consensus on the issue, that child rapists were the most depraved criminals, and that the victim had suffered most serious harm.

Four years later, in 2012, the court decided a pair of cases involving life sentences for juveniles. Evan Miller, a juvenile adolescent, was convicted of felony murder during a robbery and sentenced to life in prison without the possibility of parole. The Alabama Supreme Court affirmed. Kendrell Jackson, also a juvenile adolescent, received a life sentence without parole for being a coconspirator in the killing of a store clerk during a robbery in Arkansas, and he petitioned for a writ of habeas corpus against Hobbs, his corrections officer. The U.S. Supreme Court by the narrowest margin held that mandatory life sentences without parole for juveniles violated the Eighth Amendment (*Miller v. Alabama; Jackson v. Hobbs*).

Kagan wrote the court opinion, and Breyer, Ginsburg, Kennedy, and Sotomayor joined her. Kagan held that the punishment was disproportionate to the offense and the offenders. She cited evolving standards of decency and argued that children were different from adults and that their sentences should be individualized. Moreover, she pointed out that Jackson lacked the intention to kill and that Miller had been high on drugs and alcohol at the time of the murder he committed. She remanded the cases to the lower courts to determine whether there were mitigating circumstances. Four justices (Alito, Roberts, Scalia, and Thomas) dissented in three opinions. Roberts and Thomas argued that the Eighth Amendment was not intended to prohibit life sentences for juvenile murderers. Alito pointed out that seventeen-year-olds commit many murders each year.

The Roberts Court rendered decisions in many other cases on various aspects of criminal due process. In 2006 the court considered whether a district-court judge had discretionary power on his own initiative to correct the calculation of the time between a prisoner's conviction and his habeas corpus petition. Florida had convicted Patrick Day of murder, and the state appellate court affirmed. In 2003 Day filed a petition for habeas corpus against McDonough, his corrections official. The state conceded that Day was within the prescribed time limit for filing after conviction. A federal magistrate noticed that the state had miscalculated the time, and a district-court judge accordingly dismissed the petition. The court of appeals affirmed, and Day appealed to the Supreme Court. The court by the narrowest margin affirmed (*Day v. McDonough*). Ginsburg wrote the court opinion, and Alito, Kennedy, Roberts, and Souter joined her. Breyer, Scalia, Stevens, and Thomas dissented on procedural grounds.

In the same year the court considered a case involving a habeas corpus petition twenty years after a murder conviction. Paul House was convicted of murdering Carolyn Muncey in rural Tennessee, but recent revelations cast doubt on House's guilt. The district court denied relief as untimely, and the court of appeals affirmed. On House's appeal the court reversed and remanded the case with instruction to consider the petition (*House v. Bell*). Kennedy wrote the court opinion, and Breyer, Ginsburg, Souter, and Stevens joined him. Kennedy reviewed in detail the evidence and claimed that House had made stringent but not conclusive showing of innocence. Roberts, joined by Scalia and Thomas, concurred only in the judgment. Newly appointed Alito did not participate.

In 2009 the court considered whether a voluntary confession was admissible if the defendant was not arraigned before a magistrate within six hours, as federal law mandated, or whether the defendant was in fact questioned for six hours before arraignment. Federal officers intermittently questioned the defendant over six hours, which was interrupted by the defendant's visit to a hospital for treatment, and he confessed orally and in writing to a bank robbery in the course of the questioning. The district court denied a motion to suppress the confessions, and Johnnie Corley, the defendant, was convicted. The court of appeals affirmed. On appeal, the Supreme Court by the narrowest margin reversed and remanded to the trial court to consider whether the net amount of time that Corley was questioned before arraignment was within the mandated six hours (*Corley v. U.S.*). Souter wrote the court opinion, and Breyer, Ginsburg, Kennedy, and Stevens joined him. Alito, joined by Roberts, Scalia, and Thomas, dissented. Alito argued that voluntary confessions should be admitted even if the accused is not brought before a magistrate within six hours, that Corley's confession was voluntary, and that the convictions should be affirmed.

In the same year the court, by the narrowest margin and an unusual coalition of justices in the majority and minority, allowed a judge to determine the facts necessary for the imposition of consecutive rather than concurrent sentences (*Oregon v. Ice*). Thomas Ice was convicted of the crimes of burglary and sex abuse. As permitted by Oregon law, the trial judge determined facts that necessitated consecutive sentences, but the Oregon Supreme Court reversed. Ginsburg wrote the court opinion, and Alito, Breyer, Kennedy, and Stevens joined her. Ginsburg based the decision on the fact that common law allowed judges to impose consecutive sentences. Scalia, joined by Roberts, Souter, and Thomas, dissented. Scalia argued that the Sixth Amendment requires that juries determine facts that increase punishment of crime.

Also in that year the court by the narrowest margin ruled against William Osborne's right to have the state provide him access to the DNA evidence used to convict him of a sex-abuse case (*District Attorney's Office v. Osborne*). Osborne claimed that he had a civil right to it, and both the district court and the court of appeals agreed with him. On appeal, the Supreme Court reversed. Roberts wrote the court opinion, and Alito, Kennedy, Scalia, and Thomas joined him. Roberts argued that the states were free to decide whether to provide the evidence after his trial. Alito, joined by Thomas, argued in a concurring opinion that Osborne had not asked for the DNA evidence at his trial, when he would have had a right to it. Stevens, joined by Breyer, Ginsburg, and Souter, dissented.

In 2010 the court upheld the permanent civil commitment of Grayson Comstock, a sexually dangerous federal prisoner about to be released (*U.S. v. Comstock*). The district court and the court of appeals had ruled against his commitment, but the court reversed. Breyer wrote the court opinion, and Ginsburg, Roberts, Sotomayor, and Stevens joined him. Breyer argued that the commitment was a necessary and proper means of managing federal prisoners. Alito and Kennedy concurred in the judgment. Thomas, joined by Scalia, dissented, arguing that the commitment relied on no enumerated federal power. Note that state commitment would be the only alternative to federal commitment and that this might leave Comstock on the loose before some state did so.

In the same year the court decided a Michigan case involving the question of whether a murder suspect had waived his right to remain silent when police officers questioned him. The officers questioned the suspect, Van Tompkins, for three hours, in the course of which he made inculpatory statements. The statements were admitted into evidence at his trial, and he was convicted. On his habeas corpus petition objecting to their admission into evidence, the federal court of appeals ruled in his favor. The Supreme Court by the narrowest margin reversed (*Berghuis v. Tompkins*). Kennedy wrote the court opinion, and Alito, Roberts, Scalia, and Thomas joined him. Kennedy argued that the police had given Tompkins the Miranda warnings and that he, by responding to questions, implicitly indicated waiver of his rights. Moreover, Tompkins's counsel didn't object to the judge's instruction to the jury. Sotomayor, joined by Breyer, Ginsburg, and Stevens, dissented, arguing that Tompkins had not explicitly waived his rights, whether or not he had invoked them, and that he had been unresponsive during the three-hour interrogation up to the inculpatory statements.

In 2011, at the end of the court's term that year, it decided a case involving the question of whether the police were obliged to give the Miranda warnings to a juvenile interviewed at his school. Police in North Carolina suspected J. D. B. of being responsible for two break-ins and visited his school. A school official brought him from the classroom to a closed-door conference room, where the police and school authorities questioned him without giving him the Miranda warnings or an opportunity to call his grandmother. After he confessed orally and in writing, he was allowed to go home. He was later arrested and convicted in juvenile court of felonious breaking-and-entering and larceny. His oral and written confessions were admitted into evidence at the trial. The North Carolina Supreme Court affirmed, but the U.S. Supreme Court by the narrowest margin overturned the conviction (*J. D. B. v. North Carolina*).

Sotomayor wrote the court opinion, and Breyer, Ginsburg, Kagan, and Kennedy joined her. Sotomayor argued that the age of the person interviewed affects the question of whether interrogation is custodial and that the questioning of the juvenile in the school conference room was custodial, and so the confessions should not have been admitted. Alito, joined by Roberts, Scalia, and Thomas dissented, arguing that objective facts about the interrogation, not characteristics of the subject, should determine whether the interrogation was custodial.

In a pair of cases in 2012 the court ruled on the responsibility of counsel regarding plea bargains for the defendants. In *Lafler v. Cooper*, the court by the narrowest margin ruled that counsel improperly prejudiced Anthony Cooper by advising him to reject the plea bargain. Kennedy wrote the court opinion, and Breyer, Ginsburg, Kagan, and Sotomayor joined him. Scalia, joined by Roberts and Thomas, and Alito dissented. In *Missouri v. Frye*, the court by the narrowest margin and with the same division of justices held that a defense counsel has the duty to communicate a formal plea-bargain offer to the defendant.

In its first three years the Roberts Court handed down several decisions in death-sentence cases. In 2006 the court reviewed the death sentence of Robert Sanders. He was convicted of the first-degree murder of a woman in her home, which he had invaded, and the jury sentenced him to death on the basis of four special circumstances. The California Supreme Court ruled out two of the circumstances but upheld the conviction and sentence. Sanders sought a writ of habeas corpus in a federal district court on the grounds that invalidating the two circumstances invalidated his death sentence. The district court denied the petition, but the court of appeals reversed. California, in the name of Brown, the warden of Sanders's prison, appealed to the Supreme Court.

The court by the narrowest margin reversed and ruled in favor of California (*Brown v. Sanders*). Scalia wrote the court opinion, and Kennedy, O'Connor, Roberts, and Thomas joined him. Scalia argued that invalidation of two special circumstances constituted harmless error and that the presence of a single special circumstance was enough to justify the death sentence. Breyer, Ginsburg, Souter, and Stevens dissented. Stevens, joined by Souter, argued that California allowed the jury to consider whether mitigating circumstances outweighed the aggravating circumstances and that four aggravating circumstances would tilt the jury more to a death sentence than only two would. Breyer, joined by Ginsburg, argued that, irrespective of the weighing question, the jury's death-sentence decision in the absence of the two invalidated aggravating circumstances was not beyond reasonable doubt.

In the same year the court considered another death-sentence case. Michael Marsh had broken into the home of a woman to await her return. When she and her nineteen-month-old daughter returned, he killed the woman and set the home on fire, which killed the daughter. Marsh was convicted of both murders and sentenced to death for the murder of the daughter. Kansas required that a jury impose the death sentence in a capital case if the mitigating circumstances did not outweigh the aggravating circumstances. Marsh appealed the death sentence, arguing that imposing a death sentence when there was an equipoise between the two sets of circumstances weighted the jury's decision in favor of the death sentence. The Kansas Supreme Court agreed and ordered a new trial on the death sentence. On appeal, the U.S. Supreme Court by the narrowest margin remanded and reinstated the death sentence (*Kansas v. Marsh*).

Thomas wrote the court opinion, and Alito, Kennedy, Roberts, and Scalia joined him. Thomas found the statute rational because it was a means to channel the jury to a decision in the case of equally balanced factors for and against the death sentence. Scalia wrote a long concurring opinion to respond to Stevens and Souter. Against Stevens, he argued that there was a need to clarify the law on the point at issue. Against Souter, he argued strongly that death-sentence policy should rest with state legislatures. Breyer, Ginsburg, Souter, and Stevens dissented. Stevens argued that the court should have deferred to a state-court decision that made a death sentence more difficult and should never have agreed to review the Kansas decision in the first place. Souter, joined by Breyer, Ginsburg, and Stevens, argued that death sentences result in many innocents being put to death, that equipoise means doubt about a death sentence, and that the doubt should be resolved in favor of the defendant.

In 2007 the court considered another death-sentence case involving mitigating circumstances. Fernando Belmontes was convicted of killing a woman that he encountered while burglarizing a home in California. The judge instructed the jury to consider any mitigating circumstance in its death-sentencing deliberations. The defense counsel argued that Belmontes would do good works in prison, but the jury imposed the death sentence. Belmontes objected to the jury instruction because it failed to specify good behavior as a mitigating circumstance. On direct appeal, California upheld the conviction and the death sentence. Belmontes then sought a writ of habeas corpus in a federal district court. The district court denied relief, but the court of appeals reversed. California then, in the name of Ayers, the prison warden, appealed to the Supreme Court.

The court by the narrowest margin reversed the decision of the court of appeals and reinstated the death sentence (*Ayers v. Belmontes*). Kennedy wrote the court opinion, and Alito, Roberts, Scalia, and Thomas joined him. Kennedy argued that the instruction to the jury allowed it to consider any mitigating circumstance, including prospective good behavior. Scalia, joined by Thomas, added in a concurring opinion that he would go further and allow state-imposed limits on the mitigating circumstances for the jury to consider. Stevens, joined by Breyer, Ginsburg, and Souter dissented, arguing that the prosecutor's closing address to the jury assumed that prospective good behavior could not be a mitigating circumstance, and so did the judge in his instruction.

In the same year the court considered another death-sentence case, one in which the judge had given no specific instructions on mitigating circumstances. Jalil Abdul-Kabir, whose legal name was Ted Cole, strangled his step-mother-in-law's grandfather in 1987 in order to get cash. He was convicted of murder, and the trial judge in his instruction to the jury on the death-sentence phase made no mention of mitigating circumstances, after which the jury sentenced him to death. On direct appeal the Texas appellate court affirmed, and the Texas courts denied his petition of habeas corpus. Cole then went to a federal district court for the writ of habeas corpus against Quarterman, the corrections official, and that court denied it.

On appeal, the Supreme Court by the narrowest margin reversed and remanded the case for a new trial on the death sentence (*Abdul-Kabir v. Quarterman*). Stevens wrote the court opinion, and Breyer, Ginsburg, Kennedy, and Souter joined him. Stevens argued that specific instructions on mitigating circumstances were necessary for the jury to make its death-sentence decision. Alito, Roberts, Scalia, and Thomas dissented. Roberts, joined by Alito, Scalia, and Thomas, argued that the judge had made it sufficiently clear about mitigating circumstances without specific instructions. Scalia, joined in part by Alito and Thomas, argued that it was not against the Eighth Amendment to limit the jury's discretion on mitigating circumstances and that the state court's decision on the requested instructions was reasonable.

In a companion case, also from Texas, *Brewer v. Quarterman*, the court reached the same result, the justices divided in the same way, and the same justices wrote opinions. In still another Texas death-sentence case but one involving the timeliness of defense objection to jury instructions (*Smith v. Texas*), the court reached the same result, and the justices divided in the same way, but Kennedy wrote the court opinion and Alito the dissenting opinion.

In 2008 the court reviewed a mode of carrying out death sentences. Ralph Baze and others were convicted of a murder and sentenced to death. The Kentucky appellate court affirmed, but the convicts filed a habeas corpus petition against the mode of execution, contending that the protocol of lethal injection practiced in Kentucky risked significant unnecessary pain. The court affirmed denial of the petition (*Baze v. Rees*). Roberts wrote the plurality opinion, and Alito and Kennedy joined him. Roberts argued that the petitioners had failed to satisfy their burden of proof. Alito in a concurring opinion argued that the petitioners had failed to show that modification of the protocol would significantly reduce a substantial risk of severe pain. Breyer, Scalia, Stevens, and Thomas concurred separately. Ginsburg, joined by Souter, dissented. She argued that the protocol had an untoward risk of pain and that the state should determine the state of consciousness of the one to be executed before admission of the lethal dose of the drug in controversy.

The Roberts Court considered a number of federal sentencing cases. In 2007 the court heard a case involving a mandatory sentence if the defendant had committed prior violent felony crimes. Alphonso James pled guilty to the federal crime of illegally possessing a firearm. Federal law required a mandatory fifteen-year sentence if the defendant had committed three prior violent felony crimes, which the trial judge imposed on James, and the court of appeals affirmed. James appealed to the Supreme Court, claiming that one of his prior crimes, an attempted burglary, was not a violent crime.

The court by the narrowest margin ruled for the government (*James v. U.S.*). Alito wrote the court opinion, and Breyer, Kennedy, Roberts, and Souter joined him. Alito argued that burglary involved a threat to use force. Ginsburg, Scalia, Stevens, and Thomas dissented. Scalia, joined by Ginsburg and Stevens, argued that the sentencing mandate was vague regarding the definition of violent felony crimes and that it could not be imposed on the defendant by inclusion of burglary as a violent felony crime. Thomas argued that the jury, not the judge, should have determined the sentence.

In the same year the court decided a case involving the discretionary power of judges in sentencing persons convicted of violating federal laws. In 2000, Brian Gall, a college student at the University of Iowa, participated in a group distributing methamphetamine (ecstasy) on the campus. He dropped out of the group four months later, became self-rehabilitated, and graduated in 2002. He was indicted in 2004, pled guilty, and the district judge sentenced him to thirty-six months' probation, although the presentencing report, following the judicial sentencing guidelines, recommended thirty to thirty-seven months' imprisonment. The court of appeals reversed and remanded for resentencing according to the guidelines. The Supreme Court restored the original sentence (*Gall v. U.S.*). Stevens wrote the court opinion, and Breyer, Ginsburg, Kennedy, Roberts, Scalia, and Souter joined him. Stevens argued that the district judge acted reasonably in view of Gall's subsequent good behavior. Alito and Thomas dissented. Alito argued that the judge must give some weight to the guidelines. Thomas argued that it was statutory error for the judge to have departed from the guidelines.

In a companion case that term, the court rendered another decision in favor of the discretionary power of judges sentencing persons convicted of a federal felony. In 2004 Derrial Kimbaugh was indicted for various drug-related crimes, including the distribution of crack cocaine. He pled guilty, and the district court sentenced him to fifteen years' imprisonment, which was the least sentence possible under the guidelines. The court of appeals reversed and remanded for sentencing strictly according to the guidelines. The Supreme Court reversed and upheld the decision of the district judge (*Kimbaugh v. U.S.*). Ginsburg wrote the court opinion, and the same justices as in the Gall case joined her. Alito and Thomas dissented for the same reasons that they gave in *Gall.*

In 2008 the court reviewed the sentence imposed on Larry Begay. He had three prior state convictions of driving while intoxicated, each of which was punishable by more than a year in prison—technically a felony—but the state designated the crime a misdemeanor. He had threatened his sister and aunt with a rifle and was convicted of violating the federal law that prohibited previously convicted felons from possessing a firearm. The court of appeals affirmed the sentence, but the Supreme Court reversed (*Begay v. U.S.*). Breyer wrote the court opinion, and Ginsburg, Kennedy, Roberts, and Stevens joined him. Breyer argued that driving while intoxicated might not risk harm to anyone and was not an aggressive crime. Scalia concurred in the judgment, arguing that drunken driving, unlike the violent felonies enumerated in the statute, did not necessarily involve risk to others. Alito, joined by Souter and Thomas, dissented, arguing that Begay had twelve prior convictions of drunken driving and was dangerous to others.

In 2011 the court considered the applicability of the sentencing guidelines to a felon convicted before their adoption. William Freeman had agreed to enter a guilty plea in a cocaine case and accept a specified sentence. After adoption of the guidelines, he petitioned for the lower sentence recommended by the guidelines. He lost in the district court and the court of appeals, but the Supreme Court by the narrowest margin reversed (*Freeman v. U.S.*). Kennedy wrote the plurality opinion, and Breyer, Ginsburg, and Kagan joined him. Sotomayor concurred in the judgment. Roberts, joined by Alito, Scalia, and Thomas, dissented.

In 2012 the court by the narrowest margin held that the sentencing guidelines could be applied to a felon convicted of possession of crack before the guidelines were adopted (*Dorsey v. U.S.*). The justices divided as they had in *Freeman*, but Breyer wrote the court opinion and Scalia the dissenting opinion.

In 2007 the court ruled on the related area of punitive damages in civil cases, this time in connection with a suit in Oregon against a tobacco company. Jesse Williams, a smoker, died of lung cancer, and his wife brought a wrongful-death suit against Philip Morris Tobacco Company. The jury awarded her $821,000 in compensatory damages and 75.5 million dollars in punitive damages. The trial court reduced the punitive damages, but the Oregon Supreme Court restored them and rejected the argument that the jury could not punish the company for the harm putatively caused to other smokers. The company appealed to the U.S. Supreme Court.

The court by the narrowest margin ruled for the company (*Philip Morris Co. v. Williams*). Breyer wrote the court opinion, and Alito, Kennedy, Roberts, and Souter joined him. Breyer argued that imposing punitive damages for the harm caused to others besides the plaintiff constituted a taking of property but remanded the case to Oregon to determine the appropriate punitive damages for the harm to her. Ginsburg, Scalia, Stevens, and Thomas dissented. Stevens argued that it was permissible to punish the offender for harm to others not parties to the case. Thomas argued that the Constitution set no limits on punitive damages. Ginsburg, joined by Scalia and Thomas, argued that Philip Morris did not make a timely objection to the jury instructions.

Religion The Roberts Court decided several cases on the religious establishment clause. Two of these involved the standing required of taxpayers challenging governmental actions under the clause. In 2001 President Bush II created the White House Office of Faith-Based Community Initiatives with executive-department centers that funded conferences. The office and centers were financed from funds appropriated by Congress to the executive departments without special appropriations. The Freedom-from-Religion Foundation sought declaratory and injunctive relief against Hein, the director of the

White House office, and directors of the executive-department centers. The foundation claimed that the programs violated the religious establishment clause. The district court dismissed the suit, holding that the foundation lacked standing because the initiatives were executive, not congressional, programs. The court of appeals reversed, holding that the foundation had standing because there were congressional appropriations. The government appealed to the Supreme Court. At issue was the breath of the Flast exception to the general rule against taxpayers having standing to sue in federal courts against governmental actions.

In 2007 the court by the narrowest margin ruled against standing for the foundation (*Hein v. Freedom-from-Religion Foundation*). Alito wrote the plurality opinion, and Kennedy and Roberts joined him. Alito argued that the foundation failed to satisfy the second nexus of the Flast decision—namely, that the contested programs be exercises of congressional power under the tax and spending clauses. Alito did not overrule *Flast,* but he declined to expand it to cover programs established by executive action. Kennedy also concurred separately to argue from the separate powers of the president and Congress. Scalia, joined by Thomas, concurred only in the judgment. Scalia thought that the plaintiffs in the case, like those in *Flast,* were complaining about psychic rather than tangible injury and that *Flast* itself should be overruled. Souter, joined by Breyer, Ginsburg, and Stevens, dissented. Souter saw no difference between the instant case and *Flast* and argued that the use of taxpayer money for religious purposes was a paramount concern of the framers of the establishment clause.

In 2011 the court invoked standing to deny review of a state program of tax credits for contributions to an organization that provided funds to private, including church-related, schools. Arizona granted a tax credit of up to $500 to individuals who contributed to a student-tuition organization. Kathleen Winn, a taxpayer, sued in a federal court to enjoin the tax credits, and the student-tuition organization intervened to defend the credits. The district court dismissed the suit, but the court of appeals reversed. The Supreme Court by the narrowest margin reversed again, holding that the taxpayer lacked standing (*Arizona Christian School-Tuition Organization v. Winn*). Kennedy wrote the court opinion, and Alito, Roberts, Scalia, and Thomas joined him. Kennedy distinguished the *Flast* decision, arguing that the latter case related to governmental expenditures and that tax credits were not expenditures from money collected in taxes. Scalia, joined by Thomas, concurred in the opinion but would repudiate *Flast* altogether. Kagan, joined by Breyer, Ginsburg, and Sotomayor, dissented. Kagan observed that the tax-credit program had cost 350 million dollars of revenue since its inception and ridiculed the court's distinction of tax credits from appropriations.

The court decided a case involving a city's refusal to put a monument with a religious message on public land. In 2009 the court upheld the right of a city government in Utah to decide whether to accept the donation of a monument with a religious message to a city park (*Pleasant Grove City v. Summum*). The city had ten monuments in the park, including one with the Ten Commandments, but rejected the request of Summum, a group that described itself as Gnostic Christian, to erect a monument to the Seven Aphorisms of Summum. Summum sued the city, claiming that the rejection infringed its right of free speech. The district court rejected the claim, but the court of appeals reversed, ruling against the city and ordering it to allow the monument to be erected. On appeal the Supreme Court again reversed and ruled in favor of the city. Alito wrote the court opinion, in which every justice but Souter joined. Alito argued that the acceptance or rejection of a monument represents government speech and is immune from a private free-speech claim. Souter concurred only in the judgment and worried about the implications of immune government speech for the establishment clause. Scalia, joined by Thomas, pointed out that the establishment clause was in the shadows of the case, although the case came to the court on the issue of free speech.

In 2010 the court decided a case involving a religious symbol erected in a national park. In 1934 the Veterans of Foreign Wars placed a cross on Sunrise Rock in the Mojave National Preserve to honor soldiers killed in World War I. Frank Buono, a retired employee of the National Park Service, brought suit to enjoin the service from maintaining the cross on park land, claiming that its presence violated the religious establishment clause. The district court issued the injunction, and the court of appeals affirmed. Congress then passed a statute authorizing the transfer of the land on which the cross was erected to the veterans organization in exchange for a nearby parcel of land owned by the organization. Buono returned to the district court to seek an injunction against the transfer. Again, the district court issued an injunction to that effect, and the court of appeals affirmed. Ken Salazar, secretary of the interior, appealed to the Supreme Court. The court by the narrowest margin reversed (*Salazar v. Buono*).

Kennedy wrote the plurality opinion, and Alito and Roberts joined him,

Alito in large part and Roberts fully. Kennedy held that Buono had standing but deferred to Congress in its resolution of the conflict between violating the initial injunction and disrespecting the dead if the government removed the cross. Transfer of the land seemed to him an expedient solution, but he remanded the case to the lower courts to determine whether there was a continued need for an injunction. Roberts wrote separately to echo Kennedy's theme. Alito wrote separately to say that he would hold outright that the statute may be implemented. Scalia, joined by Thomas, concurred only in the judgment, arguing that Buono's distaste for the religious symbol on public land was not enough to give him legal standing to object to its presence there. Stevens, joined by Ginsburg and Sotomayor, dissented, arguing principally that the transferred land would still seem to the ordinary observer to belong to the government. Breyer also dissented, arguing that the matter should be left in the hands of the trial-court judge and that the court review was improvidently granted. Thus six justices wrote opinions in the case, which seems more attention than the case deserved. Although contemporary religious-establishment jurisprudence would not permit such a cross to be erected on government land, its long tenure on the land should militate against removing it now.

The Roberts Court also reached decisions on several cases touching on religious exercise. In 2006 the court heard one such case. The UDV Church in its religious rites uses a tea made from Amazon plants with hallucinogen content, and custom inspectors seized a shipment of the tea from Brazil. The church sought declaratory and injunctive relief on the grounds that use of the tea was an exercise of religion. The district court granted the relief, finding no compelling public interest against such use, and the court of appeals affirmed. Albert Gonzales, the attorney general, took the case to the Supreme Court. The court unanimously reversed (*Gonzales v. UDV Church*). Roberts wrote the court opinion, and all the justices but Kagan, who did not participate, joined him. Roberts decided the case on statutory grounds. He cited a provision of the Religious Freedom and Restoration Act (a different one than that struck down in *Boerne v. Flores*) that prohibited the federal government from substantially burdening religion.

In 2010 the court decided a controversial case involving the putative rights of student organizations in public universities with religious and moral orientations to reject students without those commitments. The Hastings College of Law, part of the public University of California, required recognized student organizations to comply with a nondiscriminatory admissions policy. An unrecognized student organization would receive no funds from the school and could be excluded from use of the school facilities. The Christian Legal Society of students at Hastings required members to sign a statement professing the Christian faith and the traditional code of sexual morality. It brought a federal suit to enjoin the school from carrying out the admissions policy regarding the society, claiming that the policy infringed on the society's rights of free speech and association. The district court ruled against the society, and the court of appeals affirmed. The Supreme Court by the narrowest margin affirmed (*Christian Legal Society v. Martinez*).

Ginsburg wrote the court opinion, and Breyer, Kennedy, Sotomayor, and Stevens joined her. Ginsburg argued that the policy did not prohibit any activity of the society but rather denied the benefit of a subsidy. In fact, according to Ginsburg, the college had not denied the society use of the school facilities. (After the decision, however, the school would presumably be free to do so.) She further argued that the policy served a public interest—namely, no discrimination—and so was religiously neutral. Moreover, recognized student organizations may condition membership on attendance and payment of dues. Kennedy and Stevens also wrote concurring opinions, Kennedy to contend that the case involved only a limited forum of speech and Stevens to stress that the policy was viewpoint-neutral.

Alito, joined by Roberts, Scalia, and Thomas, dissented. Alito pointed out that the society was the only disqualified group and that the policy would require the society to admit atheists. The policy allowed Republican and Democratic student clubs to exclude nonparty members but not religious student organizations to exclude nonreligious members. Moreover, he found the policy irrational, since it limited the expression of viewpoints. Maybe it was viewpoint-neutral on its face, he conceded, but it seemed to him to be a pretext to target the society for its religious and moral views.

In 2012 the court considered a conflict between a church-related school and the Economic Employment Opportunity Commission (EEOC). Cheryl Perich taught secular subjects and a religion class at a Missouri Synod Lutheran school in Redford, Michigan. She was a "called" teacher with a diploma certifying her vocation and was a commissioned minister. She developed narcolepsy and went on disability leave in the 2004–5 academic year. When she wanted to return to her teaching post in 2005, the school told her that the post was already filled. She was asked to resign and was offered help with her medical insurance. She threatened to take legal action, and the church rescinded her "call" and terminated her employment. Perich filed a charge against the school with EEOC under the Americans with Disability Act. The EEOC brought suit against the school. The church school claimed that it enjoyed a ministerial exception regarding employment of its teachers. The district court ruled for the church school, but the court of appeals reversed, holding that Perich was not a minister.

The Supreme Court reversed again and ruled in favor the church school (*Hosanna-Tabor Evangelical Lutheran Church and School v. Equal Economic Opportunity Commission*). Roberts wrote the opinion for a unanimous court. He argued that the church had freedom to choose its ministers, that the church had "called" Perich, and that she was performing religious duties. Thomas wrote separately to argue that a church itself decides who are its ministers and that Perich would have to rely on the church's internal dispute-resolution forum. Alito, joined by Kagan, wrote separately to indicate that function rather than title determines whether someone is a minister and that one who conducts religious services and teaches religious doctrine is a minister.

Gun Possession In 2008 the Roberts Court delivered a landmark ruling that the Second Amendment guaranteed the right of individual citizens to keep handguns in their homes (*District of Columbia v. Heller*). The District of Columbia banned individuals' possession of handguns. Dick Heller, a special police officer, and others sought permission to keep a gun in their homes, and the District refused permission. They then sought to enjoin enforcement of the law. The district court dismissed the suit, but the court of appeals reversed. The Supreme Court by the narrowest margin affirmed the court of appeals. Scalia wrote the court opinion, and Alito, Kennedy, Roberts, and Thomas joined him.

Scalia argued that the language of the amendment guaranteed the right of individual persons to retain and carry weapons, that the word *militia* in the text referred to all able-bodied men, and that the initial phrase about a well-regulated militia being necessary to the security of a free state indicated only the purpose of the amendment, not its scope. He also reviewed the history of the amendment in subsequent legislation and cases and admitted that the right was not unlimited and that licenses can be required. Breyer, Ginsburg, Souter, and Stevens dissented. Stevens, joined by the other dissenters, argued contrariwise that the text and the historical context favored restricting the amendment to the right to have state militias and that a 1939 precedent

(*U.S. v. Miller*) was contrary to the present decision. Breyer, also joined by the other dissenters, argued that, even if the amendment applied to the right of individuals to possess handguns, it permits reasonable regulation of their possession, and that the District regulation was reasonable.

In 2010 the court by the narrowest margin held that the Fourteenth Amendment required that its interpretation of the Second Amendment in the Heller case should be applied to state gun-control laws (*McDonald v. Chicago*). The same five justices as in *Heller* (Alito, Kennedy, Roberts, Scalia, and Thomas) voted to overturn a Chicago law prohibiting the possession of guns in one's home. Alito wrote the plurality opinion, in which Kennedy, Roberts, and Scalia joined, and rested the decision on the due process clause. Thomas concurred in the judgment but would rest the decision on the privileges and immunities clause. Scalia wrote a concurring opinion stressing his interpretation of the history of the Second Amendment. Breyer, Ginsburg, Sotomayor, and Stevens dissented. Stevens wrote a long opinion, mainly arguing against Scalia's historical interpretation. Breyer, joined by Ginsburg and Sotomayor, argued that the Second Amendment was not fundamental to a free society and that *Heller*'s historical interpretation was wrong.

Speech In 2006 the Roberts Court decided a case involving the right of public employees to express their views about official business publicly. Richard Caballos, a deputy district attorney of Los Angeles County, California, stated in a memo to Garcetti, the district attorney, that he perceived inaccuracies in an affidavit and testified to that effect in a defendant's trial. Caballos filed suit against Garcetti in federal district court for damages allegedly resulting from retaliation. The county denied retaliation and claimed that the First Amendment did not protect the speech of public employees on official business. The district court ruled for the county on the constitutional issue, but the court of appeals reversed. The county appealed to the Supreme Court on that issue.

The court by the narrowest margin ruled for the county (*Garcetti v. Caballos*). Kennedy wrote the court opinion, and Alito, Roberts, Scalia, and Thomas joined him. Kennedy argued that public employees have no First Amendment rights to speech about their official duties. Breyer, Ginsburg, Souter, and Stevens dissented. Souter, joined by Ginsburg and Stevens, argued that public employees are citizens and as such have free-speech rights. Breyer argued for a balancing test in which governmental personnel rules would prevail against speech rights on important policy matters but not on unimportant matters.

When the Olympic torch was being carried through Juneau, Alaska, on January 24, 2002, while on route to the winter games at Salt Lake City, Utah, the students at Juneau-Douglas High School were permitted to go out to the street to greet it. One student, Joseph Frederick, displayed a banner reading, "BONG HiTS 4 JESUS." The message of the words on the banner was not clear, but the principal, Deborah Morse, interpreted it to refer to smoking marijuana. Since the school board had a policy against drug advocacy in the schools, she confiscated the banner and suspended Frederick. The school superintendent supported her decision. Frederick then brought suit against her in federal court. The district court ruled for Morse, but the court of appeals reversed, since it found no threat of potential disruption. The Supreme Court granted review on two questions. First, did Frederick have a right to unfurl the banner? Second, if he had such a right, is it so clearly established that Morse is liable for damages?

In 2007 the court ruled for Morse (*Morse v. Frederick*). Roberts wrote the court opinion, and Alito, Kennedy, Scalia, and Thomas joined him. Roberts argued that the students were in a school event, that student rights were not coextensive with adult rights, that controlled drugs were harmful, and that schools had a right to prohibit drug advocacy, which he thought the principal could reasonably interpret the words on the banner to mean. Since he answered the first question in the negative, he had no need to address the second. Alito, joined by Kennedy, concurred separately only to say that schools may not impose restrictions on speech potentially relating to political or social issues, such as advocacy of legalization of drugs. Thomas concurred separately to indicate his view that the Constitution gives no basis for minors to claim rights to speech. Breyer concurred only in the judgment, saying that Morse enjoyed a qualified immunity from suits for damages. Stevens, joined by Ginsburg and Souter, dissented. Stevens argued that Frederick only wanted to get on television, and that, although pulling down the banner was permissible, the punishment administered to him was not.

The Federal Communications Commission (FCC) in 2004 announced a change of policy that made actionable even one use of the *F*-word or *S*-word by radio and television media and fined a network for doing so. The network objected that the new rule violated the Administrative Procedures Act. The court of appeals set aside the fine, but the Supreme Court by the narrowest margin reversed in 2009 (*Federal Communications Commission v. Fox Television Stations*). Scalia wrote the plurality opinion, and Alito, Roberts, and Thomas joined him.

Scalia argued that a court should not substitute its judgment for that of the commission. Kennedy concurred in the judgment. Breyer, joined by Ginsburg, Souter, and Stevens, dissented, arguing that the commission needed to explain its change of policy.

In 2011 the court rendered an unpopular decision involving the picketing of the funeral of Matthew Snyder, a marine killed in Iraq, in Maryland. Fred Phelps of Kansas, founder of the Westboro Baptist Church, and six others picketed on public land 1,000 feet from the church where the funeral took place. They peacefully displayed signs denouncing homosexuals and pedophile priests for a half-hour before the funeral. Albert Snyder, Mathew's father, filed suit against Phelps in federal court for damages to compensate for the emotional distress caused by the picketing. The jury awarded the father millions of dollars in compensatory and punitive damages, which the judge reduced. The court of appeals reversed on the basis of Phelps's right of free speech, and the Supreme Court affirmed (*Snyder v. Phelps*).

Roberts wrote the court opinion, and every justice but Alito joined him. Roberts argued that the views expressed by Phelps were matters of public concern distinct from the funeral service but thought that future laws could protect funeral services. Breyer concurred to observe that the decision did not touch broadcasting of the picketing, which had not taken place. Alito dissented, arguing that the signs constituted a vicious verbal assault on the fallen soldier, falsely implying that he was homosexual, that Snyder was not a public figure, and that Phelps had other means to manifest his views.

In 2012 the court considered the constitutionality of fees for a union's political activities that it assessed on nonmembers. The court held that this violated nonmembers' First Amendment rights (*Knox v. Service Employees Union*). Alito wrote the court opinion, and Kennedy, Roberts, Scalia, and Thomas joined him. In addition, Alito ruled that the union could not exact any funds from nonmembers without their affirmative consent—that is, that they must opt in. Sotomayor, joined by Ginsburg, concurred in the judgment but held that the union need only give nonmembers the opportunity to opt out. Breyer, joined by Kagan, dissented, arguing that the fees were collected only to pay last year's expenses.

In 2005 Congress passed the Stolen Valor Act, which criminalized falsely claiming military decorations or medals. Xavier Alvarez falsely claimed that he had received the Congressional Medal of Honor, and the government prosecuted him for doing so. He was convicted, but the court of appeals reversed on First Amendment grounds. In 2012 the Supreme Court affirmed (*U.S. v. Alvarez*). Kennedy wrote the plurality opinion, and Ginsburg, Roberts, and Sotomayor joined him. Kennedy held that the First Amendment protected false speech and that criminalizing it was disproportionate to the offense. Breyer, joined by Kagan, concurred in the judgment, arguing that the law abridged freedom of speech and that its objective could be achieved in other ways. Alito, joined by Scalia and Thomas, dissented, arguing that such lies caused substantial harm to other veterans applying for security jobs and that false statements have no intrinsic value.

Property In 2006 the Roberts Court considered a case involving the right of landowners to develop their property on wetlands, the climax of twelve years of civil and criminal litigation. The 1972 Clean Waters Act required landowners to obtain a permit from the Army Corps of Engineers to discharge fill material into the navigable waters of the United States. The corps defined navigable waters to include tributaries and wetlands neighboring the waters. John Rapanos, a landowner and would-be developer, backfilled three areas of Michigan wetlands without a permit, and the federal government brought a civil enforcement action against him. The nearest navigable water to the areas was eleven to twenty miles away. The district court ruled for the government, and the court of appeals affirmed. Rapanos appealed to the Supreme Court.

The court ruled in his favor (*Rapanos v. U.S.*). Scalia wrote the scathing plurality opinion, and Alito, Roberts, and Thomas joined him. Scalia cited the dictionary definition of *waters* as streams, rivers, and lakes, described them as relatively permanent bodies, and claimed that the act so defined them. (He also charged that the corps exercised the discretion of an enlightened despot!) Roberts concurred separately to argue that the corps had failed to develop rules. Kennedy concurred only in the judgment, allowing the possibility of a significant nexus of wetlands with navigable waters but holding that the corps had not developed such an argument. Stevens, joined by Breyer, Ginsburg, and Souter, dissented. Stevens would have affirmed the decision of the lower courts, arguing that the corps had determined that the wetlands were adjacent to, or tributaries of, navigable waters. Breyer wrote to urge that the corps write new regulations.

Labor Relations In 2009 the Roberts Court by the narrowest margin ruled that unions with contracts committing them to submit disputes with employers to arbitration are not allowed the recourse to courts authorized by federal statute (*Fourteen Penn Plaza v. Pyett*). The district court and the court of appeals had allowed a union to do so, but the Supreme Court reversed. Thomas wrote the court opinion, and Alito, Kennedy, Roberts, and Scalia joined him. Thomas held that unions could bargain away their otherwise legal remedies. Souter, joined by Breyer, Ginsburg, and Stevens, wrote the principal dissent. Stevens wrote a separate dissent.

In 2010 the court heard another case involving a contract that committed employees to arbitrate disputes with employers, this time regarding the putative right of individuals to bring a civil-rights action. Antonio Jackson brought a federal suit against his employer, Rent-a-Car West, alleging racial discrimination. The district court ruled for the company, but the court of appeals reversed, holding compulsory arbitration of civil-rights claims unconscionable. The Supreme Court reversed (*Rent-a-Car West v. Jackson*). Scalia wrote the court opinion, and Alito, Kennedy, Roberts, and Thomas joined him. Scalia argued that the employee was bound by the contract. Stevens, joined by Breyer, Ginsburg, and Sotomayor, dissented, arguing that Jackson was challenging the contract itself.

Racial Discrimination In 2007 the Roberts Court returned to the question of state-imposed racial integration of public schools. Seattle, Washington, and Jefferson County, Kentucky, had voluntary student-assignment plans in which race was used as a tiebreaker to achieve more racial balance in oversubscribed schools proportional to the district-wide racial division, Seattle in its high schools and Jefferson County in its grade schools. (Seattle had never had a mandatory segregated school system, and Jefferson County had desegregated its schools.) Seattle divided potential students into white and nonwhite, and Jefferson County divided them into black and nonblack. A group of disaffected parents in Seattle and the mother of Joshua McDonald in Jefferson County brought suits in federal district courts in Washington State and Kentucky, claiming that assignment of students on a racial basis violated the equal protection clause. (Joshua had been assigned to a school ten miles away from his home, while there was another school only one mile away.) Seattle and Jefferson County won in both the district courts and the courts of appeals. The plaintiffs appealed to the Supreme Court.

The court by the narrowest margin ruled for the plaintiffs in both cases (*Parents v. Seattle School District*; *Meredith v. Jefferson County Board of Education*). Roberts wrote the plurality opinion, and Alito, Scalia, and Thomas joined him. First, Roberts argued that the racially discriminatory policies could not be justified as remedies for past segregation, since Seattle had never segregated its schools, and Jefferson County had by the year 2000 eliminated the vestiges of its past segregation. Second, he argued that, assuming that racial diversity could be a compelling public interest, the use of race could be upheld only if narrowly tailored to be part of a wholly individualized review of other factors (e.g., personal achievement). Third, he argued that no other purpose could be a compelling public interest. Thomas wrote a separate concurring opinion to argue that racial imbalance was not itself unconstitutional and that, contrary to Breyer, there was no evidence that schools in Louisville, Kentucky, were moving back to, or schools in Seattle moving into, segregation. Kennedy, who provided the fifth vote, concurred only in the judgment. He was willing to accept that some race-conscious measures to achieve racial balance (e.g., attendance zones on the basis of neighborhood demographics) might be a compelling public interest, but programs like the ones at issue, which distinguished between individuals on the basis of race, were unacceptable. Breyer, Ginsburg, Souter, and Stevens dissented. Stevens argued that beneficial race-conscious measures were valid if they did not impose burdens on only one race. Breyer, joined by the other dissenters, argued that the programs were remedial in a broader sense and that they prevented new segregation.

In 2009 the court ruled on the action of New Haven, Connecticut, canceling the results of an examination for promoting personnel in its fire department. White candidates had higher scores on the exam, and no black candidate qualified for promotion. The city threw out the results, claiming that the exam was not a valid test of the candidates' qualifications. Frank Ricci and the white and Hispanic candidates who had qualified for promotion on the exam sued De Stephano, the New Haven official, in the federal district court for declaratory and injunctive relief, claiming that the city was discriminating against them. The district court gave summary judgment for the city, and the plaintiffs appealed to the Supreme Court.

The court by the narrowest margin ruled in favor of the qualifying candidates (*Ricci v. De Stephano*). Kennedy wrote the court opinion, and Alito, Roberts, Scalia, and Thomas joined him. Kennedy argued on statutory grounds that the city's action nullifying the results of the examination violated Title VII of the 1964 Civil Rights Act and that the city had no rational basis to fear liability to black candidates because of the disparate impact of the exam, as the city had argued. Scalia in a separate concurrence voiced his view that awarding damages solely on the basis of disparate racial impacts was unconstitutional. Alito, joined by Scalia and Thomas, claimed that the city was using fear of liability as a pretext for its discriminatory action. Ginsburg, joined by Breyer, Souter, and Stevens, dissented, arguing that the plaintiffs had no vested right to promotion and that the history of past racial discrimination against blacks in the city fire department should justify the city's action as remedial.

Gender Discrimination In 2007 the Roberts Court ruled on a gender-discrimination case, a ruling that much of the press and public thought harsh. Lilly Ledbetter was a salaried employee at the Goodyear plant in Gadsden, Alabama, from 1979 to 1998. In July 1998 she filed charges with the EEOC against Goodyear for acts of discrimination. After her retirement in November of that year, she filed suit in the district court. The jury brought in a verdict for Ledbetter, but the court of appeals reversed, holding that she had not met the statutory time limit for bring the suit.

On appeal, the court by the narrowest margin affirmed (*Ledbetter v. Goodyear Tire and Rubber Co.*). Alito wrote the court opinion, and Kennedy, Roberts, Scalia, and Thomas joined him. Alito stressed the importance of rigid time limits on suits and cited precedents. Ginsburg, joined by Breyer, Souter, and Stevens, dissented. She pointed out the difficulties that a victim faced in discovering that there had been discrimination (e.g., the pay differences may seem small before they accumulate, and comparable pay scales may be hard or impossible to obtain).

Abortion In 2003 Congress passed the Partial-Birth Abortion Ban Act. The usual abortion involves simple dilation and extraction. The doctor dilates the woman's cervix and then uses surgical instruments to extract the fetus, which is often ripped apart as it is extracted. In intact dilation and extraction, a doctor dilates the cervix, extracts the fetus with the head intact, and then crushes the head. The act banned doctors from knowingly performing destructive acts on the partially extracted fetus. Dr. Leroy Carhart, a Nebraska physician, challenged the act on its face in a district court, and the court permanently enjoined Alberto Gonzales, the attorney general, from enforcing the act except when the fetus was viable. That court argued that the act made no exception for when partial-birth abortions are necessary for the health of the mother and that the act could cover other dilations and extractions. The court of appeals affirmed. In a companion case initiated in California by the state Planned Parenthood Association there, the district court and the court of appeals had done the same. The government, in the name of Gonzales, appealed both cases to the Supreme Court.

The court by the narrowest margin reversed both courts of appeals (*Gonzales v. Carhart*). Kennedy wrote the court opinion, and Alito, Roberts, Scalia, and Thomas joined him. Kennedy argued that the plaintiffs had not demonstrated that the act on its face was vague or that it overburdened a woman's right to an abortion. The act banned intact abortion but not other abortions by dilation and extraction, and he did not think that partial-birth abortions were necessary to protect the mother's health. Thomas, joined by Scalia, wrote separately to argue against the constitutionality of *Roe v. Wade* itself. Ginsburg, joined by Breyer, Souter, and Stevens, dissented, arguing that intact dilation and extraction were safer for the mother's health.

Summary The two leading regime cases, exclusive of campaign financing cases, were *Boumedienne v. Bush* (2008) and *National Federation of Business v. Sibelius* (2012). In the first decision the court narrowly struck down the provision of a federal law barring civilian courts from hearing habeas corpus petitions by detainees at Guantanamo. Kennedy, the swing vote, wrote the court opinion with the support of the liberal bloc (Breyer, Ginsburg, Souter, and Stevens) and over the dissent of the conservative bloc (Alito, Roberts, Scalia, and Thomas). In the second decision the court upheld the individual mandate and most of Obamacare but invalidated a Medicaid provision that a supermajority (six justices) thought coerced states to participate. Roberts was the swing vote on validating the mandate and most of the law, but he had to rely on different coalitions. On validating the mandate and most of Obamacare, he had the support of the liberal bloc, and on invalidating the expansion of Medicaid, he had the support of the conservative bloc plus Breyer, Kagan, and Kennedy.

Kennedy was also the swing vote in other narrowly decided regime cases, sometimes with the liberals and sometimes with the conservatives. In *Massachusetts v. Environmental Protection Agency* (2007), he voted with the liberal bloc to allow a state to sue the federal agency. In *Haywood v. Drown* (2009), he voted with the liberal bloc to invalidate a state law that removed civil-rights suits from its courts of general jurisdiction. In *Bartlett v. Strickland* (2009), he voted with the conservative bloc to hold that the 1965 Voting Rights Act did not require that states subject to the act in decennial redistricting maximize minority voters in districts with a white majority. In *Free Enterprise Fund v. Public Accounting Board* (2010), he voted with the conservative bloc to strike down the provision of a federal law delegating power to an accounting board. In *Brown v. Plata* (2011), he voted with the liberal bloc to uphold a decision mandating a radical reduction of the prison population in California. In *Coleman v. Court of Appeal of Maryland* (2012), he voted with the conservative bloc to overturn a federal law that applied to state employees. And in *Arizona v. U.S.* (2012), he and Roberts voted with Breyer, Ginsburg, and Sotomayor to invalidate several state regulations affecting immigrants and uphold one other.

On campaign financing laws, both federal and state, the court ruled uniformly against limitations or disincentives on expenditures by individual candidates or groups. In *Randall v. Sorrell* (2006), Breyer and Kennedy joined the conservative bloc to strike down a Vermont law that stringently restricted campaign expenditures by candidates. In *Federal Elections Commission v. Wisconsin Right to Life* (2007), five justices upheld the right of an organization to run ads within the blackout period required by the BCRA, two (Alito and Roberts) holding that they were not advocacy ads falling under the BCRA blackout and three (Kennedy, Scalia, and Thomas) holding that the blackout period itself was unconstitutional. (Note that Kennedy here indicated that he was not a swing vote on independent campaign expenditures.) In *Citizens United v. Federal Elections Commission* (2010), the court narrowly upheld unlimited independent campaign expenditures by corporations and unions, with Kennedy and the conservative bloc prevailing. In *Arizona Free Enterprise Club's Freedom Club Political Action Committee v. Bennett* (2010), the court with the same division of justices struck down a state law that expanded funds for a publicly funded candidate if privately funded candidates spent more than all publicly funded candidates.

The list of forty full-opinion criminal decisions includes fourteen habeas corpus actions, eight death-sentence cases, and six cases involving federal sentencing on lesser counts. Defendants or convicts won twenty-three of the cases, and federal and state governments won seventeen. Thirty-three of the decisions were five to four. In two-thirds of these (twenty-two), Kennedy was the swing vote, thirteen times with the liberal bloc and nine times with the conservative bloc. Most pro-defendant and pro-convict decisions fine-tuned precedents, although one decision (*Montejo v. Louisiana*) expressly overruled one. Two involved expansion of the Eighth Amendment ban on cruel and unusual punishments, one to ban mandatory death sentences for juvenile adolescents and the other to ban mandatory life sentences without parole for rape. Three cases involved the confrontation clause of the Sixth Amendment, which the narrowly divided court in two cases interpreted to require the testimony of the technicians responsible for laboratory analyses.

Two cases (*Hein v. Freedom-from-Religion Foundation; Arizona Christian School-Tuition Organization v. Winn*) narrowly denied standing to taxpayers to challenge governmental actions on the basis of the religious establishment clause, with Kennedy and the conservative bloc prevailing in both cases. In *Pleasant Grove City v. Summum* the court unanimously permitted a city to reject the erection of a monument with a religious message in its park. In another case (*Salazar v. Buono*), the court narrowly accepted congressional legislation permitting government land on which a monument with a religious symbol was located to be transferred to a private organization, with Kennedy and the conservative bloc prevailing.

The court in one case on religious exercise (*Gonzales v. UDV Church*) almost unanimously upheld customs' seizure of a shipment of hallucinogenic tea for use in a church's religious rites. In a second case touching on religious exercise (*Christian Legal Society v. Martinez*), the court narrowly upheld a public law school's requirement that a religiously oriented student organization comply with the school's nondiscriminatory admissions policy if it wished to use school facilities and receive a financial subsidy, with Kennedy and the liberal bloc prevailing. In a third case (*Hosanna-Tabor Evangelical Lutheran Church and School v. Equal Economic Opportunity Commission*), the court unanimously upheld the right of a church school to hire and fire teachers.

The court, for better or worse, gave new vitality to the Second Amendment. It narrowly held that the amendment guaranteed the right of individuals to keep guns in their homes and struck down a federal law that prohibited them from doing so (*District of Columbia v. Heller*). Two years later the court narrowly applied this interpretation of the Second Amendment to the states (*McDonald v. Chicago*). In both cases Kennedy and the conservative bloc were the majority and the liberal bloc the minority.

In one case on speech (*Garcetti v. Caballos*), the court narrowly held that public employees have no rights to speech about their official duties, with Kennedy and the conservative bloc prevailing. In a second case (*Morse v. Frederick*), the court held that a student at a school event had no right to unfurl a banner interpreted to advocate the use of drugs, with the same majority prevailing. In a third case (*Federal Communications Commission v. Fox Television Stations*), the court narrowly upheld the FCC policy against the use of the *F*-word or *S*-word by radio and television media, with the same majority prevailing. In a fourth case (*Snyder v. Phelps*), the court almost unanimously ruled that the free speech clause protected picketers at a funeral from suits for emotional distress. In a fifth case (*Knox v. Service Employees Union*), the court narrowly held that a union could not exact funds for political activities from nonmembers without their affirmative consent, with Kennedy and the conservative bloc prevailing. In a sixth case (*U.S. v. Alvarez*), the court held, with Alito, Scalia, and Thomas dissenting, that the government could not prosecute a person claiming false military honors. Note that Kennedy in these cases always voted with the majority.

In *Rapanos v. U.S.* (2006), with Rehnquist barely buried, the court continued his legacy on property rights. The court narrowly ruled in favor of a would-be developer of his property in the face of opposition from the Army Corps of Engineers, with Kennedy and the conservative bloc prevailing.

In one labor-relations case (*Fourteen Penn Plaza v. Pyett*), the court narrowly ruled that unions with contracts committing them to arbitrate with employers might not resort to courts for adjudication, with Kennedy and the conservative bloc prevailing. In another (*Rent-a-Car West v. Jackson*), the court narrowly ruled that an employee who had committed himself to arbitrate disputes with his employer could not bring a civil-rights action against the employer, with Kennedy and the conservative bloc again prevailing.

The court narrowly struck down two voluntary state school student assignment plans in which race was used as a tiebreaker to achieve more racial balance in oversubscribed schools (*Parents v. Seattle School District; Meredith v. Jefferson County Board of Education*), with Kennedy and the conservative bloc prevailing. In a second case (*Ricci v. De Stephano*), the court narrowly held that a city's action nullifying the results of a promotion exam for firemen in which no blacks qualified violated the 1964 Civil Rights Act, with Kennedy and the conservative bloc again prevailing.

Kennedy and the conservative bloc also narrowly prevailed in upholding the federal Partial-Birth Abortion Ban Act (*Gonzales v. Carhart*).

Postscript

(2012–14)

The court held that President Obama had no constitutional power to make the recess appointments he made to the National Labor Relations Board in 2012 (*National Labor Relations Board v. Noel Canning Co.*). The Senate was at the time of the appointments effectively adjourned but was meeting in pro-forma sessions every three days without conducting any business. The company brought suit after it lost a ruling under the newly constituted board and won in the court of appeals. The board then appealed to the Supreme Court. The court decision was unanimous, but the justices differed sharply on the rationale. Breyer, joined by Ginsburg, Kagan, Kennedy, and Sotomayor, held that the three-day breaks were too small to constitute recesses, but that ten-day breaks had historically sufficed to allow presidents to make recess appointments and could continue to do so. Scalia, joined by Alito, Roberts, and Thomas, objected to the ten-day rule as judicial legislation and argued that recess appointments should be restricted to the times between formal congressional sessions.

Shaun McCutcheon, an Alabama businessman, and the Republican National Committee challenged the cap on the aggregate total that individuals could contribute to federal candidates and political parties in a two-year electoral cycle. They lost in the lower federal courts, but the Supreme Court by the narrowest margin ruled in their favor (*McCutcheon and the Republican National Committee v. Federal Elections Committee*). Roberts, joined by Alito, Kennedy, and Scalia, wrote the plurality opinion, holding that the free-speech clause of the First Amendment guaranteed the right of individuals to unlimited aggregate contributions to candidates and political parties. Thomas concurred separately to indicate that he thought limits on contributions to individual candidates were unconstitutional. Breyer, joined by Ginsburg, Kagan, and Sotomayor, dissented, arguing that the aggregate limits were justified as barriers to money corrupting the political process.

The court, over the dissents of Alito and Roberts, held that the Environmental Protection Agency can regulate sources of greenhouse gases as long as those sources (e.g., power plants and oil refineries) are required to obtain permits for the emission of conventional pollutants (*Utility Air Regulatory Group v. Environmental Protection Agency*). But the court by the narrowest margin strongly rejected the agency's principal rationale for the regulations. The agency relied on the Clean Air Act to justify regulation of greenhouse gases and modified the express statutory languasge for practical reasons to restrict its application to big emitters. Scalia, joined by Alito, Kennedy, Roberts, and Thomas, held that the agency had no power to rewrite unambiguous statutory terms. Breyer, joined by Ginsburg, Kagan, and Sotomayor, dissented on this point and argued that the agency had made a sensible attempt to achieve the chief purpose of the Clean Air Act.

The court by the narrowest margin held that the sovereign immunity of an Indian tribe prevented Michigan from suing to close a casino the tribe operated 175 miles from its reservation (*Michigan v. Bay Mills Indian Community*). Kagan, joined by Breyer, Kennedy, Roberts, and Sotomayor, argued that the tribe under existing federal policy enjoyed sovereign immunity unless and until Congress deemed otherwise, and that the state had other means, including lawsuits against individuals violating its laws. Thomas, joined by Alito, Ginsburg, and Scalia, dissented, arguing that the decision rendered the tribe's illegal activities litigation-proof and substantially hindered the state's efforts to halt the casino's operations permanently.

The court by the narrowest margin struck down an Illinois law requiring nonmembers to pay union dues, as applied to partial public employees such as home-care Medicaid workers (*Harris v. Quinn*). Alito, joined by Kennedy, Roberts, Scalia, and Thomas, wrote the court opinion. Distinguishing full-time from partial employees, he argued that, since the state normally determined the wages of partial public employees, the unions conferred little benefit on them, and that they should not be compelled to subsidize a union's political speech that they did not wish to support. Kagan, joined by Breyer, Ginsburg, and Sotomayor, dissented, arguing that Illinois had authority over the partial workers' terms and conditions of employment, and that the state had an interest in protecting unions from free riders.

Same-Sex Marriage The court handed down two decisions on same-sex marriage in 2013. In the first case (*U.S. v. Windsor*), the court by the narrowest margin struck down the federal 1996 Defense of Marriage Act, which denied benefits to legally married same-sex spouses. The case concerned two New York City women, Edith Windsor and Thea Clara Spyer, who were married in Canada in 2007. Spyer died in 2009, and Windsor was her heir. The Internal Revenue Service, following the law, refused to treat Windsor as a surviving spouse, and she faced a tax bill of $360,000, which the surviving spouse of an opposite-sex marriage would not have incurred. Windsor appealed the ruling, and the New York federal court of appeals struck down the law. The Obama administration did not oppose the decision and indeed requested that the Supreme Court review and affirm it. This left no party in the case to defend the law, but Republican leaders in the House of Representatives intervened to do so and appealed the case to the Supreme Court.

Kennedy wrote the court opinion, and the liberal bloc (Breyer, Ginsburg,

Kagan, and Sotomayor) joined him. On the issue of the Republican leaders' standing to bring the appeal, Kennedy argued they represented a sharply adversarial interest, and that the rights of so many same-sex spouses were at issue as to require the Court to render a definitive ruling. On the merits, Kennedy argued that there was no legitimate purpose to justify denying or penalizing the right of same-sex couples to marry, a right the Fifth Amendment guarantees. Four members of the conservative bloc (Alito, Roberts, Scalia, and Thomas) dissented, arguing that the law had a legitimate purpose, and that the legality of same-sex marriage should be decided by democratic vote, not judicial fiat.

The second same-sex marriage case (*Hollingsworth v. Perry*) involved the state of California. California had legalized same-sex marriage in 2008, but a popular initiative later that year adopted Proposition 8, which overturned the law. Two same-sex couples sued in a federal district court to have the ban declared unconstitutional. The district court did so, and the state acquiesced in the decision. Proponents of Proposition 8 then appealed to the court of appeals, but that court affirmed the district court decision. The proponents then appealed to the Supreme Court. By the narrowest margin, the court ruled that the proponents of Proposition 8 lacked standing to appeal the district court ruling, and that the court of appeals should not have heard the appeal. Roberts wrote the court opinion, in which three liberals (Breyer, Ginsburg, and Kagan) and one conservative (Scalia) joined. Alito, Kennedy, Sotomayor, and Thomas dissented but without indicating their views of the merits.

In *Windsor*, the court decided the case on the merits and divided sharply along ideological lines. The majority thought the right of same-sex couples to marry and receive federal benefits available to opposite-sex spouses a constitutional right of personhood. The dissenters thought that the government had a right to favor traditional marriage and deny benefits to same-sex spouses.

The court decided the California case on a threshold question, not the merits. But there seems little or no difference between the adversarial status of the Republican officials to challenge the lower-court invalidation of the Defense of Marriage Act and the adversarial status of the proponents of Proposition 8 to challenge the trial-court invalidation of the California ban on same-sex marriage. In fact, the latter had expended more effort (e.g., soliciting signatures for the initiative and campaigning statewide for its adoption) than the Republican leaders had in organizing the congressional vote on the Defense of Marriage Act. Therefore, the court's decision in the California case was one of deliberate avoidance. The question then is why the same justices who chose to give the court's imprimatur to invalidating the federal law chose not to give an imprimatur to invalidating the California ban on same-sex marriage.

It should be noted that the court, not the defending party, introduced the standing issue into the case. When the court accepted the case for review, it asked the parties to address the standing question in their briefs. The four dissenters thought that the appellants had standing. We may safely assume that Alito and Thomas would have upheld the ban, and that Sotomayor would not have. The strong views on the right to same-sex marriage that Kennedy expressed in the federal case make it unlikely that he would have upheld the California ban, despite his New Federalist principles. Of the majority justices, we may assume that, were the case to be decided on the merits, Breyer, Ginsburg, and Kagan would have voted against the ban, and that Roberts and Scalia would have voted to uphold it. Therefore, it appears on the surface that a majority would have given a court imprimatur against the ban had the case been decided on the merits. Had a majority rendered a decision on the merits against the ban, however, it would have established a binding precedent for every state in the nation. Therefore, it is very reasonable to suppose that Breyer, Ginsburg, and Kagan, although in principle against the constitutionality of state bans of same-sex marriage, thought it wiser policy for now to avoid such a sweeping decision and its potential negative feedback. Roberts and Scalia had a different reason for avoiding a decision on the merits, since, had they agreed to a decision on the merits, there would presumably have been a five-to-four vote to outlaw the ban nationally and not only in California.

Race Relations. The court in 2013 handed down two important decisions involving race relations. In *Shelby County v. Holder*, the court by the narrowest margin struck down section 4 of the Voting Rights Act of 1965, which Congress in 2006 had renewed for twenty-five years. Section 5 required state and localities specified in section 4 to obtain clearance from the Justice Department or a federal court in Washington before making any changes in existing voting procedures. Section 4 specified that nine Southern states and many counties and municipalities in other states required prior clearance, and Congress had not updated the states and localities covered since 1975.

Roberts wrote the court opinion, and Alito, Kennedy, Scalia, and Thomas joined him. Roberts argued that the coverage clause was outdated and so an infringement on the sovereignty of the designated states. He pointed out that the participation of black voters in elections in those states has increased so dramatically since 1965 that it is now often greater than the participation of white voters. (In a separate concurrence, Thomas argued that the court's reasoning should have required it to strike down section 5 itself.) Ginsburg, joined by Breyer, Kagan, and Sotomayor, wrote a passionate dissent, much of which she delivered orally in court. She argued that racial discrimination continues to exist in the designated states, albeit in new forms (e.g. gerrymandered apportionments, voter identification requirements), and that the court should defer to the judgment of Congress. The decision does not affect possible litigation after changes in voting procedures have been instituted, nor does it preclude Congress from revising section 4 to reflect more recent data, although it is most improbable that Congress will do so.

In *Fisher v. University of Texas*, the court returned to the constitutional issue of preferential affirmative action programs for admission of minority students to public colleges and universities, which it had last considered ten years earlier in *Grutter v. Bollinger*. The University of Texas admitted three quarters of its undergraduates by a facially race-neutral program that automatically accepted all Texas high school students who graduated in roughly the top 10 percent of their class. In recent years, about 25 percent of the freshmen admitted under the program were Hispanics, and 6 percent black. (As dissenting Justice Ginsburg pointed out, this result is only superficially race neutral, since school neighborhoods are in fact racially segregated.) The remaining students from Texas schools or elsewhere were selected under criteria that included race and ethnicity as a factor.

Abigail Fisher, a white applicant, narrowly missed admission under the top-of-the-class program, and she sued the university in a federal district court, claiming that the university's affirmative-action program effectively discriminated against her because of her race. Losing in both the district court and the court of appeals, she appealed to the Supreme Court. The court sent the case back to the lower courts with instructions to judge the affirmative-action program strictly.

Kennedy wrote the court opinion, and all the other participating justices except Ginsburg joined him. (Kagan did not participate.) Kennedy admitted that promotion of racial diversity is a compelling public interest but held that strict scrutiny required a close fit between the means chosen and the end. Instead of simply deferring to the judgment of Texas school officials, the lower courts should have made a careful inquiry to verify whether the university could have achieved sufficient diversity without the use of racial classifications. Colleges and universities need to demonstrate that race-neutral alternatives would not suffice. In separate concurring opinions, Scalia and Thomas argued, as they had in *Grutter*, that no racially preferential affirmative action program is constitutional except to remedy specific prior discrimination. Ginsburg vigorously dissented, arguing that governments need not be blind to the lingering effects of their overt past discrimination and can take racially conscious means to remedy it.

After the 2003 Supreme Court decision upholding an affirmative-action program of college admissions to the University of Michigan (*Grutterr v. Bollinger*), the state in 2006 adopted by popular initiative a ban on affirmative-admission programs in public universities. Opponents of the ban brought suit to invaldate it, and a federal court of appeals by the narrowest margin did so in 2012. In 2014, a fractured Supreme Court reversed the lower court and upheld the ban (*Schuette v. Coalition to Defend Affirmative Action*). Kennedy, joined by Alito and Roberts, wrote the plurality opinion, arguing that it was not up to the courts to decide whether there should be affirmative-action programs. Breyer concurred in the decision, arguing that the Constitution permitted but did not require affirmative-action programs in admissions to public universities. Scalia, joined by Thomas, concurred in the decision but adhered to his view that affirmative action programs were unconstitutional. Sotomayor, joined by Ginsberg, dissented passionately, citing her own experience and arguing that minorities now would have to overcome a constitutional barrier before the state could initiate an affirmative-action program. Kagan did not participate.

Gun Control The court by the narrowest margin interpreted a federal law to require gun buyers to disclose that they were making the purchase for someone else, even someone eligible to own guns (*Abramski v. U.S.*). Bruce Abramski, a former police officer in Virginia, bought a handgun for his uncle in Pennsylvania. Abramski attested on a federal form that he was buying the gun for himself. He was convicted of making a false statement and sentenced to probation for five years. Kagan, joined by Breyer, Ginsburg, Kennedy, and Sotomayor, wrote the court opinion, arguing that a true statement about the matter was material to the governmental aim to keep firearms out of the wrong hands and to help solve serious crimes. Scalia, joined by Alito, Roberts, and Thomas, dissented, arguing that the majority made it a federal crime for a lawful gun owner to buy a gun for another lawful gun owner.

Business The court in 2013 handed down several significant decisions favorable to business interests. In *Kiobel v. Royal Dutch Petroleum Co.*, the court unanimously limited lawsuits against corporations for violations of human rights abroad. *In Bowman v. Monsanto*, the court unanimously ruled that a farmer violated patent laws by saving genetically modified seeds for future use.

In *American Express Co. v. Italian Colors Restaurant*, a narrow majority (Alito, Kennedy, Roberts, Scalia, and Thomas), over the dissents of Breyer, Ginsburg, Kagan, and Sotomayor, held that arbitration agreements bar signatories from bringing class-action suits against companies, although that results in higher, perhaps prohibitively higher, litigation costs for individual plaintiffs. In *Vance v. Ball State University*, the same narrow majority limited the definition of supervisor in racial and sexual harassment cases to an employee authorized to take employment actions (e.g., demotion, firing). In *University of Texas Southwestern Medical Center v. Nassar*, the same narrow majority adopted a tougher standard of proof for workers claiming that employers discriminated against them for filling discrimination complaints. In *Mutual Pharmaceutical Co. v, Bartlett*, the same narrow majority ruled that patients claiming that defectively designed generic drugs injured them could not sue the generic drug manufacturer, since federal law required the manufacturer to use the same safety label as the brand-name manufacturer.

In 2014 the court ruled that Aereo, a television service, violated copyright law by capturing broadcast signals on minature antennae and delivering them to subscribers for a fee (*American Broadcasting Co. v. Aereo*). Copyright law requires permission from copyright owners for public performances of their work, including retransmission to the public. Aereo argued that its transmissions were private performances by individual antennae. Breyer, joined by Ginsberg, Kagan, Kennedy, Roberts, and Sotomayor, wrote the court opinion, arguing that the technological differences in transmission did not change the net effect. Scalia, joined by Alito and Thomas, dissented, arguing that Aereo had found a loophole, and that it as up to Congress, not the court, to close it.

Criminal Itext: The court by the narrowest margin held that police may collect DNA samples from arrestees without either a warrant or probable cause to believe that an arrestee is suspected of another crime than the one for which he was arrested (*Maryland v. King*). In this case, however, Breyer and Scalia switched roles, Breyer voting with the conservatives (Alito, Kennedy, Roberts, and Thomas), and Scalia with the liberals (Ginsburg, Kagan, and Sotomayor)

The decision could have a broad impact on law enforcement, since it allows police to use any lawful arrest routinely to investigate whether the arrestee's DNA connects him to another crime.

Los Angeles police visited the home of Walter Fernandez in the course of investigating a robbery that he was suspected of having committed and saw evidence that he had abused his domestic partner, Roseanne Rojas. They arrested Fernandez for domestic abuse and took him to the police station. One hour later, they returned to the home without either Frenandez or a search warrant. They obtained permission from Rojas to search the home and found evidence that linked Fernandez to the robbery. The trial court refused to suppress the evidence, and Fernandez was convicted of the robbery as well as domestic abuse. The U.S. Supreme Court in 2014 upheld admission of the evidence and the robbery conviction (*Fernandez v. California*). Alito, joined by Breyer, Kennedy, Roberts, Scalia, and Thomas, wrote the court opinion, distinguishing the case from *Georgia v. Randolph* in that the defendant here was not physically present to object. Ginsburg, joined by Kagan and Sotomayor, dissented, arguing that the police had time to obtain a search warrant.

In a pair of cases the court in 2014 unanimously held that police need a search warrant to search the contents of cellphones on the person of arrestees (*Riley v. California; U.S. v. Wurie*). David Riley was arrested in San Diego in 2006 for driving with an expired license. A comprehensive search of his cellphone led to information that linked him to a shooting, and he was convicted of attempted murder. Brima Wurie was arrested in Boston in 2007, and evidence obtained from his cellphone without a warrant helped to convict him of gun and drug possession. Roberts wrote the opinion, stressing the pervasive personal data contained on cellphones and minimizing the risk of delay to the safety of the officers or destruction of evidence. Moreover, he pointed out that the officers at the scene could obtain a warrant within fifteen minutes by e-mail. Nonetheless, he conceded that the police could search the contents of an arrestee's cellphone without a warrant in exigent circumstances (e.g., a terrorist attack).

Religion The town of Greece, New York, had a twenty-year-old practice of beginning its town meetings with a prayer by a chaplain, usually a Christian minister, and the prayers were sometimes sectarian. Two residents of Greece, Linda Stephens and Susan Galloway, one Jewish and the other atheist, sued in federal court to enjoin the practice as a violation of the establishment clause.

They won in the lower courts, but the Supreme Court by the narrowest margin reversed the ruling (*Greece v. Galloway*). Kennedy, joined in full by Alito and Roberts, wrote the plurality opinion, arguing chiefly from the tradition of legislative congressional chaplains and that allowing only nonsectarian prayer would make the courts censors determining when a prayer becomes impermissibly sectarian. But Kennedy insisted that, were the prayers consistently to denigrate unbelievers or religious minorities, to proselytize, or endorse sectarian religious views, they would be unconstitutional. Scalia and Thomas concurred in the judgment and most of Kennedy's opinion but would allow state and local governments more freedom to accommodate religion. Kagan, joined by Breyer, Ginsburg, and Sotomayor, dissented. Kagan did not object to a sectarian legislative prayer but argued that a town meeting differed from a legislative session in that citizens as well as legislators participated, that individual citizens of whatever religious belief should participate in their government on equal terms, and that sectarian prayers are contrary to that equality.

The court by the narrowest margin held that the Affordable Care Act's mandate on employers to provide employees with insurance for contraception, as applied to family-owned for-profit companies with religious objections to abortifacient contraception, violated the Religious Freedom Restoration Act (*Burwell v. Hobby Lobby Stores*; *Conestoga Wood Specialties v. Burwell*). The statute prohibited legal imposition of substantial burdens on religious freedom except for a compelling public interest that could not be achieved by less restrictive alternatives. Alito, joined by Kennedy, Roberts, Scalia, and Thomas, conceded for the sake of argument that the government had a compelling public interest but held that application of the mandate to closely held for-profit companies imposed a substantial burden on employers with religious objections, and that there were less restrictive alternatives (e.g., the government paying for the insurance). Note that Alito relied on the statute to decide the case rather than on the religious-exercise clause of the First Amendment. Ginsburg, joined by Sotomayor, dissented, arguing that the decision radically altered corporate law and could be applied to all for-profit corporations and invite religious challenges to many laws. Breyer and Kagan joined most of Ginsburg's dissent but saw no need to hold, as Ginsberg did, that corporations may never bring suit under the religious freedom statute. The dissent did not challenge the majority's claim that the statute's mandate of contraceptive insurance for employees imposed substantial burdens on the religious freedom of employers. This is curious, since the mandate only compelled employers to pay for the insurance, and they would not be involved at all in their employees' decisions whether to use the insurance.

Speech. The court struck down a Massachusetts law that prohibited protests, counseling, or speeches within a 35-foot buffer zone around abortion clinics (*McCullen v. Coakley*). The decision was unanimous, but the justices divided on the reasoning. Roberts, joined by Breyer, Ginsburg, Kagan, and Sotomayor, argued that the public had a right to free speech on public sidewalks, and that public safety and access to the facilities could be preserved in other ways. Scalia, joined by Kennedy and Roberts, thought the majority's approach was too tentative and would have expressly overruled a diametrically contrary precedent (*Hill v. Colorado*), which the majority did not do. Alito concurred separately, arguing that the law patently discriminated on the basis of viewpoint, namely, anti-abortion views.

THE CONSTITUTION OF THE
UNITED STATES OF AMERICA

We the people of the United States, in order to form a more perfect union, establish justice, insure domestic tranquility, provide for the common defense, promote the general welfare, and secure the blessings of liberty to ourselves and our posterity, do ordain and establish this Constitution of the United States of America.

Article I

Section 1. All legislative powers herein granted shall be vested in a Congress of the United States, which shall consist of a Senate and House of Representatives.

Section 2. The House of Representatives shall be composed of members chosen every second year by the people of the several states, and the electors in each state shall have the qualifications requisite for electors of the most numerous branch of the state legislature.

No person shall be a representative who shall not have attained to the age of 25 years and have been seven years a citizen of the United States, and who shall not, when elected, be an inhabitant of that state in which he shall be chosen.

[Representatives and direct taxes shall be apportioned among the several states which may be included within this union, according to their respective numbers, which shall be determined by adding the whole number of free persons, including those bound to service for a term of years and excluding Indians not taxed, and three-fifths of all other persons.][1] The actual enumeration shall be made within three

---

1. Amendment XIV, section 2 replaced the representation provision, and Amendment XVI gave Congress power to levy direct taxes without apportionment. Sentences and phrases in brackets were in the original Constitution.

years after the first meeting of the Congress of the United States and within every subsequent term of ten years, in such manner as they shall by law direct. The number of representatives shall not exceed one of every 30,000, but each state shall have at least one representative, and until such enumeration shall be made, the state of New Hampshire shall be entitled to choose three, Massachusetts eight, Rhode Island and Providence Plantations one, Connecticut five, New York six, New Jersey four, Pennsylvania eight, Delaware one, Maryland six, Virginia ten, North Carolina five, South Carolina five, and Georgia three.

When vacancies happen in the representation from any state, the executive authority thereof shall issue writs of election to fill such vacancies.

The House of Representatives shall choose their Speaker and other officers and shall have the sole power of impeachment.

Section 3. The Senate of the United States shall be composed of two senators from each state [chosen by the legislature thereof][2] for six years, and each senator shall have one vote.

Immediately after they shall be assembled in consequence of the first election, they shall be divided as equally as may be into three classes. The seats of the senators of the first class shall be vacated at the expiration of the second year, of the second class at the expiration of the fourth year, and of the third class at the expiration of the sixth year, so that one-third may be chosen every second year, [and if vacancies happen by resignation or otherwise during the recess of the legislature of any state, the executive therefore may make temporary appointments until the next meeting of the legislature, which shall then fill such vacancies.][3]

No person shall be a senator who shall not have attained to the age of 30 years and have been nine years a citizen of the United States, and who shall not, when elected, be an inhabitant in that state in which he shall be chosen.

The vice president of the United States shall be president of the Senate but shall have no vote unless they be equally divided.

The Senate shall choose their other officers, and also a president pro tempore in the absence of the vice president or when he shall exercise the office of president of the United States.

The Senate shall have the sole power to try all impeachments. When sitting for that purpose, they shall be on oath or affirmation. When the president of the United States is tried, the chief justice of the United States shall preside. And no person shall be convicted without the concurrence of two-thirds of the members present.

Judgment in cases of impeachment shall not extend further than to removal from office and the disqualification to hold and enjoy any office of honor, trust, or profit

2. Replaced by paragraph 1, Amendment XVII.
3. Replaced by paragraph 2, Amendment XVII.

under the United States, but the party convicted shall nevertheless be liable and subject to indictment, trial, judgment, and punishment according to law.

Section 4. The times, places, and manner of holding elections for senators and representatives shall be prescribed in each state by the legislature thereof, but the Congress may at any time by law make or alter such regulations [except as to the places of choosing senators].[4]

The Congress shall assemble at least once in every year [and such meeting shall be on the first Monday in December unless they shall by law appoint a different day].[5]

Section 5. Each house shall be the judge of the elections, returns, and qualifications of its own members, and a majority of each shall constitute a quorum to do business, but a smaller number may adjourn from day to day and may be authorized to compel the attendance of absent members, in such manner and under such penalties as each house may provide.

Each house may determine the rules of its proceedings, punish its members for disorderly behavior, and with the concurrence of two-thirds expel a member.

Each house may keep a journal of its proceedings and from time to time publish the same, excepting such parts as may in their judgment require secrecy, and the yeas and nays of the members of either house on any question shall, at the desire of one-fifth of those present, be entered on the journal.

Neither house during the session of Congress shall without the consent of the other adjourn for more than three days, nor to any other place than that in which the two houses shall be sitting.

Section 6. The senators and representatives shall receive a compensation for their services to be ascertained by law and paid out of the treasury of the United States. They shall in all cases except treason, felony, and breach of peace be privileged from arrest during their attendance at the session of their respective houses, and in going to and from the same, and for any speech or debate in either house, they shall not questioned in any other place.

No senator or representative shall during the time for which he was elected be appointed to any civil office under the authority of the United States which shall have been created or the emoluments whereof shall have been encreased during such time, and no person holding any office under the United States shall be a member of either house during his continuance in office.

Section 7. All bills for raising revenue shall originate in the House of Representatives, but the Senate may propose or concur with amendments, as on other bills.

Every bill which shall have passed the House of Representatives and the Senate

4. Paragraph 1, Amendment XVII, eliminated the election of senators by state legislatures.
5. Amendment XX, section 2, changed the date to January 3.

shall, before it become law, be presented to the president of the United States. If he approve, he shall sign it, but if not, he shall return it with his objections to that house in which it shall have originated, who shall enter the objections at large on their journal, and proceed to reconsider it. If after such reconsideration, two-thirds of that house shall agree to pass the bill, it shall be sent to the other house, by which it shall likewise be reconsidered, and if approved by two-thirds of that house, it shall become a law. But in all such cases, the votes of both houses shall be determined yeas and nays, and the names of the persons voting for and against the bill shall be entered on the journal of each house, respectively. If any bill shall not be returned by the president within ten days (Sundays excepted) after it has been presented to him, the same shall be a law in like manner as if he had signed it, unless Congress by their adjournment prevent its return, in which case it shall not be a law.

Every order, resolution, or vote to which the concurrence of the Senate and House of Representatives may be necessary (except on a question of adjournment) shall be presented to the president of the United States, and before the same shall take effect shall be approved by him, or being disapproved by him, shall be repassed by two-thirds of the Senate and House of Representatives, according to the rules and limitations prescribed in the case of a bill.

Section 8. The Congress shall have power to lay and collect taxes, duties, imposts, and excises, to pay the debts and provide for the common defense and general welfare of the United States, but all duties, imposts, and excises shall be uniform throughout the United States;

To borrow money on the credit of the United States;

To regulate commerce with foreign nations and among the several states, and with the Indian tribes;

To establish an uniform rule of naturalization and uniform laws on the subject of bankruptcies throughout the United States;

To coin money, regulate the value thereof and of foreign coin, and fix the standard of weights and measures;

To provide for the punishment of counterfeiting the securities and current coin of the United States;

To establish post offices and post roads;

To promote the progress of science and useful arts by securing for limited times to authors and inventors the exclusive right to their respective writings and discoveries;

To constitute tribunals inferior to the Supreme Court;

To define and punish piracies and felonies committed on the high seas and offenses against the law of nations;

To declare war, grant letters of marque and reprisal, and make rules concerning captures on land and water;

To raise and support armies, but no appropriation of money to that use shall be for a longer term than two years;

To provide and maintain a navy;

To make rules for the government and regulation of the land and naval forces;

To provide for calling forth the militia to execute the laws of the union, suppress insurrections, and repel invasions;

To provide for organizing, arming, and disciplining the militia, and for governing such part of them as may be employed in the service of the United States, reserving to the states respectively the appointment of the officers, and the authority of training the militia according to the discipline prescribed by Congress;

To exercise exclusive legislation in all cases whatsoever over such District (not exceeding 10 miles square) as may by cession of particular states and the acceptance of Congress become the seat of the government of the United States, and to exercise like authority over all places purchased by the consent of the legislature of the state in which the same shall be, for the erection of forts, magazines, arsenals, dock yards, and other needful buildings; and

To make all laws which shall be necessary and proper for carrying into execution the foregoing powers, and all other powers vested by this Constitution in the government of the United States or in any department or officer thereof.

Section 9. The migration or importation of such persons as any of the states now existing shall think proper to admit shall not be prohibited by the Congress prior to the year 1808, but a tax or duty may be imposed on such importation not exceeding 10 dollars for each person.

The privilege of the writ of habeas corpus shall not be suspended unless, when, in the cases of rebellion or invasion, the public safety may require it.

No bill of attainder or ex-post-facto law shall be passed.

[No capitation or other direct tax shall be laid unless in proportion to the census or enumeration herein before directed to be taken.][6]

No tax or duty shall be laid on articles exported from any state.

No preference shall be given by any regulation of commerce or revenue to the ports of one state over those of another, nor shall vessels bound to or from one state be obliged to enter, clear, or pay duties in another.

No money shall be drawn from the treasury but in consequence of appropriations made by law, and a regular statement and account of the receipts and expenditures of all public money shall be published from time to time.

No title of nobility shall be granted by the United States, and no person holding any office of profit or trust under them shall without the consent of Congress accept of any present, emolument, office, or title of any kind whatever from any king, prince, or foreign state.

---

6. Amendment XVI eliminated this provision.

Section 10. No state shall enter into any treaty, alliance, or confederation, grant letters of marque and reprisal, coin money, emit bills of credit, make anything but gold and silver coin a tender in payment of debts, pass any bill of attainder, ex-post-facto law, or law impairing the obligation of contracts, or grant any title of nobility.

No state shall without the consent of the Congress lay imposts or duties on imports or exports except what may be absolutely necessary for executing its inspection laws, and the net produce of all duties and imposts laid by any state on imports or exports shall be for the use of the treasury of the United States, and all such laws shall be subject to the revision and control of the Congress.

No state shall without the consent of Congress lay any duty of tonnage, keep troops or ships of war in time of peace, enter into any agreement or compact with another state or with a foreign power to engage in war, unless actually invaded or in such imminent danger as will not admit of delay.

Article II

Section 1. The executive power shall be vested in a president of the United States of America. He shall hold his office during the term of four years and together with the vice president chosen for the same term, be elected as follows.

Each state shall appoint, in such manner as the legislature thereof may direct, a number of electors equal to the whole number of senators and representatives to which the state may be entitled in the Congress, but no senator or representative or person holding an office of trust or profit under the United States shall be appointed an elector.

[The electors shall meet in their respective states and vote by ballot for two persons, of whom one at least shall not be an inhabitant of the same state with themselves. And they shall make a list of all the persons voted for and of the number of votes for each, which list they shall sign and certify and transmit sealed to the seat of the government of the United States, directed to the president of the Senate. The president of the Senate shall in the presence of the Senate and House of Representatives open all the certificates, and the votes shall be counted. The person having the greatest number of votes shall be the president if such number be a majority of the whole number of electors appointed, and if there be more than one who have such majority, and have an equal number of votes, then the House of Representatives shall immediately choose by ballot one of them for president, and if no person have a majority, then from the five highest on the list, the said House shall in like manner choose the president, but in choosing the president, the votes shall be taken by states, the representation from each state having one vote. A quorum for this purpose shall consist of a member or members from two-thirds of the states, and a majority of all the states shall be necessary to a choice. In every case, after the choice of the president, the person having the greatest number of votes of the electors shall be the vice president. But if there should remain two or more who have equal votes, the Senate shall choose from them by ballot the vice president.]⁷

The Congress may determine the time of choosing the electors and the day on which they shall give their vote, which day shall be the same throughout the United States.

No person except a natural born citizen or a citizen of the United States at the time of the adoption of the Constitution shall be eligible to the office of president. Neither shall any person be eligible to that office who shall not have attained the age of 35 years and been 14 years a resident within the United States.

In case of the removal of the president from office or his death, resignation, or inability to discharge the powers and duties of the said office, the same shall devolve on the vice president, and the Congress may by law provide for the case of removal, death, resignation or inability both of the president and vice president, declaring what officer shall act as president, and such officer shall act accordingly until the disability be removed or a president shall be elected.

The president shall at stated times receive for his services a compensation which shall neither be encreased nor diminished during the period for which he has been elected, and he shall not receive within that period any other emolument from the United States or any of them.

Before he enters on the execution of his office, he shall take the following oath or affirmation: "I do solemnly swear (or affirm) that I will faithfully execute the office of president of the United States and will to the best of my ability preserve, protect, and defend the Constitution of the United States."

Section 2. The president shall be commander-in-chief of the army and navy of the United States and of the militia of the several states when called into the actual service of the United States. He may require the opinion in writing of the principal officer of each of the executive departments upon any subject relating to the duties of their respective offices, and he shall have power to grant reprieves and pardons for offenses against the United States, except in cases of impeachment.

He shall have the power by and with the consent of the Senate to make treaties, provided that two-thirds of the senators present concur, and he shall nominate and by and with the advice and consent of the Senate shall appoint ambassadors, other public ministers and consuls, judges of the Supreme Court, and all other officers of the United States whose appointments are not herein otherwise provided for, and which shall be established by law, but the Congress may by law vest the appointment of such inferior officers, as they deem proper, in the president alone, in the courts of law, or in the heads of departments.

The president shall have the power to fill up all vacancies that may happen during the recess of the Senate, by granting commissions which shall expire at the end of their next session.

7. Amendment XII replaced this paragraph.

Section 3. He shall from time to time give to the Congress information of the state of the union and recommend to their consideration such measures as he shall judge necessary and expedient. He may on extraordinary occasions convene both houses or either of them, and with respect to the time of adjournment, he may adjourn them to such time as he shall think proper. He shall receive ambassadors and other public ministers. He shall take care that the laws be faithfully executed and shall commission all officers of the United States.

Section 4. The president, vice president, and all civil officers of the United States shall be removed from office on impeachment for, and conviction of, treason, bribery, and other high crimes and misdemeanors.

Article III

Section 1. The judicial power of the United States shall be vested in one Supreme Court and in such inferior courts as the Congress may from time to time ordain and establish. The judges, both of the Supreme and inferior courts, shall hold their offices during good behavior and shall at stated times receive for their services a compensation which shall not be diminished during their continuance in office.

Section 2. The judicial power shall extend to all cases in law or equity arising under the Constitution, the laws of the United States, and the treaties made or which shall be made under their authority: to all cases affecting ambassadors, other public ministers and consuls; to all cases of admiralty and maritime jurisdiction; to controversies to which the United States shall be a party; to controversies between two or more states; between a state and citizens of another state;[8] between citizens of different states; between citizens of the same state claiming lands under grants of different states; between a state, or the citizens thereof, and foreign states, citizens, or subjects.

In all cases affecting ambassadors, other public ministers and consuls, and those in which a state shall be a party, the Supreme Court shall have original jurisdiction. In all other cases before mentioned, the Supreme Court shall have appellate jurisdiction both as to law and fact, with such exceptions and under such regulations as the Congress shall make.

The trial of all crimes, except in cases of impeachment, shall be by a jury, and such trial shall be held in the state where the said crimes have been committed, but when not committed within any state, the trial shall be in such place or places as the Congress may by law have directed.

Section 3. Treason against the United States shall consist only in levying war against them or, in adhering to their enemies, giving them aid and comfort. No person shall

8. Amendment XI expressly restricted this judicial power.

be convicted of treason unless on the testimony of two witnesses to the same overt act or on confession in open court.

The Congress shall have power to declare the punishment of treason, but no attainder of treason will work corruption of blood, or forfeiture, except during the life of the person attainted.

Article IV

Section 1. Full faith and credit shall be given in each state to the public acts, records, and judicial proceedings of every other state. And the Congress may by general laws prescribe the manner in which such acts, records, and proceedings shall be proved, and the effect thereof.

Section 2. The citizens of each state shall be entitled to all privileges and immunities of citizens in the several states.

A person charged in any state with treason, felony, or other crime who shall flee from justice and be found in another state shall on demand of the executive authority of the state from which he fled be delivered up to be removed to the state having jurisdiction of the crime.

No person held to service or labor in one state under the laws thereof, escaping into another, shall in consequence of any law or regulation therein be discharged from such service or labor but shall be delivered up on claim of the party to whom such service or labor may be due.

Section 3. New states may be admitted by the Congress into the union, but no new states may be formed or erected within the jurisdiction of any other state, nor any state be formed by the junction of two or more states, or parts of states, without the consent of the legislatures of the states concerned as well as of the Congress.

The Congress shall have power to dispose of and make all needful rules and regulations respecting the territory or other property belonging to the United States, and nothing in the Constitution shall be so constructed as to prejudice any claims of the United States or of any particular state.

Section 4. The United States shall guarantee to every state in the union a republican form of government and shall protect each of them against invasion and, on application of the legislature or of the executive (when the legislature cannot be convened), against domestic violence.

Article V

The Congress, whenever two-thirds of both houses shall deem it necessary, shall propose amendments to this Constitution or, on the application of the legislatures of two-thirds of the several states, shall call a convention for proposing amendments, which in either case shall be valid to all intents and purposes as part of this Constitution when ratified by the legislatures of three-fourths of the several states or by conventions in three-fourths thereof, as the one or the other mode of ratification may be proposed by Congress; provided that no amendment which may be made prior to the year 1808 shall in any manner affect the first and fourth clauses in the ninth section of the first article, and that no state without its consent shall be deprived of its equal suffrage in the Senate.

Article VI

All debts contracted and engagements entered into before the adoption of this Constitution shall be as valid against the United States under this Constitution as under the Confederation.

This Constitution and the laws of the United States which shall be made in pursuance thereof and all treaties made or which shall be made under the authority of the United States shall be the supreme law of the land. And the judges in every state shall be bound thereby, anything in the constitution or laws of any state to the contrary notwithstanding.

The senators and representatives before mentioned and the members of the several state legislatures and all executive and judicial officers, both of the United States and of the several states, shall be bound by oath or affirmation to support this Constitution, but no religious test shall ever be required as a qualification to any office or public trust under the United States.

Article VII

The ratification of the conventions of nine states shall be sufficient for the establishment of this Constitution between the states so ratifying the same.

Amendment I (1791)

Congress shall make no law respecting an establishment of religion or prohibiting the free exercise thereof or abridging the freedom of speech or of the press, or the right of the people peaceably to assemble and to petition the government for a redress of grievances.

Amendment II (1791)

A well-regulated militia being necessary to the security of the free state, the right of the people to keep and bear arms shall not be infringed.

Amendment III (1791)

No soldier shall in time of peace be quartered in any house without the consent of the owner, nor in time of war but in a manner prescribed by law.

Amendment IV (1791)

The right of the people to be secure in their persons, houses, papers, and effects against unreasonable searches and seizures shall not be violated, and no warrants shall issue but upon probable cause supported by oath or affirmation and particularly describing the place to be searched and the persons or things to be seized.

Amendment V (1791)

No person shall be held to answer for a capital or otherwise infamous crime unless on a presentment or indictment of a grand jury, except in cases arising in the land or naval forces or in the militia when in actual service in time of war or public danger. Nor shall any person be subject for the same offense to be twice put in jeopardy of life or limb, nor shall be compelled in any criminal case to be a witness against himself, nor be deprived of life, liberty, or property without due process of law, nor shall private property be taken for public use without just compensation.

Amendment VI (1791)

In all criminal prosecutions, the accused shall enjoy the right to a speedy and public trial by an impartial jury of the state and district wherein the crime shall have been committed, which district shall have been previously ascertained by law, and to be informed of the nature and cause of the accusation, to be confronted by the witnesses against him, to have compulsory process of obtaining witnesses in his favor, and to have the assistance of counsel for his defense.

Amendment VII (1791)

In suits at common law where the value in controversy shall exceed 20 dollars, the right of trial by jury shall be preserved, and no fact tried by jury shall be otherwise reexamined in any court of the United States than according to the rules of the common law.

Amendment VIII (1791)

Excessive bail shall not be required nor excessive fines imposed, nor cruel and unusual punishments inflicted.

Amendment IX (1791)

The enumeration in the Constitution of certain rights shall not be construed to deny or disparage others retained by the people.

Amendment X (1791)

The powers not delegated to the United States by the Constitution nor prohibited by it to the states are reserved to the states respectively or to the people.

Amendment XI (1795)

The judicial power of the United States shall not be construed to extend to any suit in law or equity commenced or prosecuted against one of the United States by citizens of another state or by citizens or subjects of any foreign states.

Amendment XII (1804)

The electors shall meet in their respective states and vote by ballot for president and vice president, one of whom, at least, shall not be an inhabitant of the same state with themselves. They shall name in their ballots the person voted for as president and in distinct ballots the person voted for as vice president, and of the number of votes for each, which list they shall sign and certify and transmit sealed to the seat of government of the United States, directed to the president of the Senate. The president of the Senate shall in the presence of the Senate and the House of Representatives open all the certificates, and the votes shall then be counted. The person having the greatest number of votes for president shall be the president if such number be a majority of the whole number of electors appointed. And if no person have such majority, then from the persons having the highest numbers, not exceeding three, on the list of those voted for as president, the House of Representatives shall choose immediately by ballot the president. But in choosing the president, the votes shall be taken by states, the representation from each state having one vote. A quorum for this purpose shall consist of a member or members from two-thirds of the states, and a majority of all the states shall be necessary to a choice. [And if the House of Representatives shall not choose a president whenever the right of choice shall devolve upon them, before the fourth day of March next following, then the vice president shall act as president, as in the case of the death or other constitutional disability of the president.][9] The person having the greatest number of votes as vice president shall be the vice president if such number be a majority of the whole number of electors appointed. And if no person have a majority, then from the two highest number on the list, the Senate shall choose the vice president. A quorum for the purpose shall consist of two-thirds of the whole number of senators, and a majority of the whole number shall be necessary to a choice. But no person constitutionally ineligible to the office of the president shall be eligible to that of vice president of the United States.

Amendment XIII (1865)

Section 1. Neither slavery nor involuntary servitude, except as a punishment for crime whereof the party shall have been duly convicted, shall exist within the United States or any place subject to their jurisdiction.

Section 2. Congress shall have the power to enforce this article by appropriate legislation.

9. Replaced by Amendment XX, section 3.

Amendment XIV (1868)

Section 1. All persons born or naturalized in the United States and subject to the jurisdiction thereof are citizens of the United States and of the state in which they reside. No state shall make or enforce any law which shall abridge the privileges and immunities of citizens of the United States, nor shall any state deprive any person of life, liberty, or property without due process of law, nor deny to any person within its jurisdiction the equal protection of the laws.

Section 2. Representatives shall be apportioned among the several states according to their respective numbers, counting the whole persons in each state, excluding Indians not taxed. But when the right to vote at any election for the choice of electors for president and vice president of the United States, representatives in Congress, the executive and judicial officers of a state, or the members of the legislature thereof is denied to any of the male inhabitants of such state, being 21 years of age and citizens of the United States, or in any way abridged, except for participation in rebellion or other crime, the basis of representation therein shall be reduced in the proportion which the number of such male citizens shall bear to the whole number of male citizens 21 years of age in such state.

Section 3. No person shall be a senator or representative in Congress, or elector of president and vice president, or hold any office, civil or military, under the United States or under any state, who, having previously taken an oath as a member of Congress or as an officer of the United States or as a member of any state legislature or as an executive or judicial officer of any state to support the Constitution of the United States, shall have engaged in insurrection or rebellion against the same or given aid and comfort to the enemies thereof. But Congress may by a vote of two-thirds of each house remove such disability.

Section 4. The validity of the public debt of the United States authorized by law, including debts incurred for payment of pensions and bounties for services in suppressing insurrection or rebellion, shall not be questioned. But neither the United States nor any state shall assume or pay any debt or obligation incurred in aid of insurrection or rebellion against the United States, or any claim for the loss or emancipation of any slave, but all such debts, obligations, and claims shall be held illegal and void.

Section 5. The Congress shall have power to enforce by appropriate legislation the provisions of this article.

Amendment XV (1870)

Section 1. The right of citizens of the United States to vote shall not be denied or abridged by the United States or any state on account of race, color, or previous condition of servitude.

Section 2. The Congress shall have power to enforce this article by appropriate legislation.

Amendment XVI (1913)

The Congress shall have power to lay and collect taxes on incomes from whatever source derived without apportionment among the several states and without regard to any census or enumeration.

Amendment XVII (1913)

The Senate of the United States shall be composed of two senators from each state elected by the people thereof for six years, and each senator shall have one vote. The electors in each state shall have the qualifications requisite for electors of the most numerous branch of the state legislatures.

When vacancies happen in the representation of any state in the Senate, the executive authority of such state shall issue writs of election to fill such vacancies: provided that the legislature of any state may empower the executive thereof to make temporary appointments until the people fill the vacancies by election as the legislature may direct.

This amendment shall not be so construed as to affect the election or term of any senator chosen before it becomes a part of the Constitution.

Amendment XVIII (1919)

Section 1. After one year from the ratification of this article, the manufacture, sale, or transportation of intoxicating liquors within, the importation thereof into, or the exportation thereof from, the United States and all territory subject to the jurisdiction thereof for beverage purposes is hereby prohibited.

Section 2. The Congress and the several states shall have concurrent power to enforce this article by appropriate legislation.

Section 3. This article shall be inoperative unless it shall have been ratified as an amendment to the Constitution by the legislatures of the several states, as provided in the Constitution, within seven years from the date of the submission hereof to the states by Congress.

Amendment XIX (1920)

The right of citizens of the United States to vote shall not be denied or abridged by the United States or any state on account of sex.

Congress shall have power to enforce this article by appropriate legislation.

Amendment XX (1933)

Section 1. The terms of the president and vice president shall end at noon on the twentieth day of January, and the terms of senators and representatives at noon of the third day of January, of the years in which such terms would have ended if this article had not been ratified, and the terms of their successors shall then begin.

Section 2. Congress shall assemble at least once in every year, and such meetings shall begin at noon on the third day of January unless they shall appoint a different day.

Section 3. If at the time fixed for the beginning of the term of president, the president-elect shall have died, the vice president-elect shall become president. If a president shall not have been chosen before the time fixed for the beginning of his term, or if the president-elect shall have failed to qualify, then the vice president-elect shall act as president until a president shall have qualified. And the Congress may by law provide for the case wherein neither a president-elect or a vice president-elect shall have qualified, declaring who shall then act as president or the manner in which one who is to act shall be selected, and such person shall act accordingly until a president or a vice president shall have qualified.

Section 4. The Congress may by law provide for the case of the death of any of the persons from whom the House of Representatives may choose a president whenever the right of choice shall have devolved upon them, and for the case of the death of any of the persons from whom the Senate may choose a vice president whenever the right of choice shall have devolved upon them.

Section 5. Sections 1 and 2 shall take effect on the fifteenth day of October following the ratification of this article.

Section 6. This article shall be inoperative unless it shall have been ratified as an amendment to the Constitution by the legislatures of three-fourths of the several states within seven years from the date of its submission.

Amendment XXI (1933)

Section 1. The eighteenth article of amendment to the Constitution of the United States is hereby repealed.

Section 2. The transportation or importation into any state, territory, or possession of the United States for delivery or use of intoxicating liquors in violation of their laws is hereby prohibited.

Section 3. This article shall be inoperative unless it shall have been ratified as an amendment to the Constitution by conventions in the several states, as provided in the Constitution, within seven years from the date of the submission hereof to the states by the Congress.

Amendment XXII (1951)

Section 1. No person shall be elected to the office of the president more than twice, and no person who has held the office of president or acted as president for more than two years of a term to which some other person was elected president shall be elected to the office of president more than once. But this article shall not apply to any person holding the office of president when this article was proposed by the Congress and shall not prevent any person who may be holding the office of president or acting as president during the term within which this article becomes operative from holding the office of president or acting as president during the remainder of such term.

Section 2. This article shall be inoperative unless it shall have been ratified as an amendment to the Constitution by the legislatures of three-fourths of the several states within seven years from the date of its submission to the states by the Congress.

Amendment XXIII (1961)

Section 1. The District constituting the seat of government of the United States shall appoint, in such manner as Congress may direct, a number of electors of president and vice president equal to the whole number of senators and representatives in Congress to which the District would be entitled if it were a state, but in no event more than the least populous state. They shall be in addition to those appointed by the states, but they shall be considered for the purposes of the election of president and vice president to be electors appointed by a state, and they shall meet in the District and perform such duties as provided by the twelfth article of amendment.

Section 2. The Congress shall have power to enforce this article by appropriate legislation.

Amendment XXIV (1964)

Section 1. The right of citizens of the United States to vote in the primary or other election for president or vice president, for electors for president or vice president, or for senator or representative in Congress shall not be denied or abridged by the United States or any state by reason of a failure to pay any poll tax or other tax.

Section 2. The Congress shall have power to enforce this article by appropriate legislation.

Amendment XXV (1967)

Section 1. In case of the removal of the president from office or his death or resignation, the vice president shall become president.

Section 2. Whenever there is a vacancy in the office of the vice president, the president shall nominate a vice president, who shall take office upon confirmation by a majority of both houses of Congress.

Section 3. Whenever the president transmits to the president pro tempore of the Senate and the Speaker of the House of Representatives his written declaration that he is unable to discharge the powers and duties of his office, and until he transmit to them a written declaration to the contrary, such powers and duties shall be discharged by the vice president as acting president.

Section 4. Whenever the vice president and a majority of either the principal officers of the executive department or of such other body as Congress may by law provide transmit to the president pro tempore of the Senate and the Speaker of the House of Representatives their written declaration that the president is unable to discharge the powers and duties of his office, the vice president shall immediately assume the powers and duties of the office as acting president.

Thereafter, when the president transmits to the President pro tempore of the Senate and the Speaker of the House of Representatives his written declaration that no inability exists, he shall resume the powers and duties of his office unless the vice president and a majority of either the principal officers of the executive department or of such other body as Congress may by law provide transmit within four days to the president pro tempore of the Senate and the Speaker of the House of Representatives their written declaration that the president is unable to discharge the powers and duties of his office. Thereupon, Congress shall decide the issue, assembling within 48 hours for that purpose if not in session. If the Congress within 21 days after receipt of the latter written declaration, or if Congress is not in session, within 21 days after Congress is required to assemble, determines by two-thirds vote of both houses that the president is unable to discharge the powers and duties of his office, the vice president shall continue to discharge the same as acting president. Otherwise, the president shall resume the powers and duties of his office.

Amendment XXVI (1971)

Section 1. The right of citizens of the United States who are eighteen years of age or older to vote shall not be denied or abridged by the United States or any state on account of age.

Section 2. The Congress shall have power to enforce this article by appropriate legislation.

Amendment XXVII (1992)

No law varying the compensation for the services of the senators and representatives shall take effect until an election of representatives shall have intervened.

ᗡ Appendix 2 ᗡ

THE SUPREME COURT SYSTEM

The Decision Makers

Litigants Legal actors involve at least two parties or litigants. An individual or corporation may sue another individual or corporation for monetary recompense (damages) alleged to result from wrongful action by the latter (e.g., an assault or breach of contract). Or an individual or corporation may sue another individual or corporation to enjoin the latter from performing actions that the former allege will cause irreparable harm and for which no monetary recompense will be adequate (e.g., an injunction to prevent the construction of a nuclear power plant). Or an individual or corporation may sue another individual or corporation for specific performance of a contract (e.g., a contract for the sale of a Rembrandt). Federal or state governments may bring suits against individuals or corporations, but individuals and corporations may sue governments only if and to the extent that the Constitution or statutes of the respective legislatures so specify. Federal and state officials may in limited circumstances be sued to compel performance of duties prescribed by law or enjoin them from performing unlawful acts. All these suits are civil actions. The party bringing the civil action is the plaintiff, and the party answering the action is the defendant.

Federal and state governments may also bring criminal actions against individuals and corporations. The government bringing the action is the prosecutor, and the party answering the charge is the defendant. Upon conviction, the defendant is liable for financial penalties or imprisonment or both.

The motives of litigants are varied and often complex. The usual motive for civil actions is economic interest. Sometimes individuals have a political motive. Sometimes they have motives of civic virtue, and sometimes motives of personal spite. Even government prosecutors in criminal cases may have motives other than civic duty. Since lawsuits consume a great deal of time and cost a good deal of money, only strongly motivated litigants resort to the law courts. Litigants need even stronger motives to take lawsuits to the U.S. Supreme Court for review. In general, the higher a litigant or the litigant's lawyer deems the stakes and the prospect of victory, the more likely that the litigant will press the case.

Civil litigants may have a choice as to which court to bring the suit. The choice may be between a federal court and a state court or between different federal district courts or between the courts of different states. The choice of forum may significantly affect the prospects for a successful outcome at the trial stage (e.g., lawyers for plaintiffs in medical malpractice suits generally prefer to try their cases in local courts).

Interest Groups Organized interest groups may sponsor or support test cases at their earliest stages in efforts to secure favorable legal decisions. Or they may seek to intervene formally as parties where permissible. Or they may become concerned with pending decisions in the Supreme Court and seek to file amicus curiae (friend of the court) briefs in favor of one of the parties in pending cases. When interest groups sponsor or support litigants, they provide the latter with experienced counsel, continuity of service over the lengthy time of trial and appeal, court costs, and incidental expenses (e.g., printing the record and the briefs). This support, especially the financial, is almost a necessity for individuals belonging to underprivileged minority groups, although federal and state governments are now obliged to provide counsel for indigent criminal defendants at the trial and the first appellate levels. Whether interest groups participate in cases as sponsors, parties, or amici, they communicate the views of their members to the legal process of conflict resolution. They will be permitted to file amicus briefs if both parties in a case, or one party and the court, consent. Interest groups may also influence the court over the long run by promoting favorable legal research and scholarly articles.

In the twentieth century the influence of organized interest groups on the legal process, including that of the Supreme Court, mushroomed. The National Consumers' League hired Louis D. Brandeis, who submitted a fact-laden amicus brief to the court in a successful 1908 case (*Muller v. Oregon*). In 1934 conservative businessmen organized the American Liberty League, which sponsored briefs against the constitutionality of New Deal legislation. The National Association for the Advancement of Colored People played a central role in improving the legal status of blacks, especially since World War II. The American Civil Liberties Union has been active and successful in defending the rights of individuals under the Bill of Rights. More recently, the legal services staff of the Office of Economic Opportunity has assisted the poor in suits against local governments.

The influence of organized interest groups on the legal process can be exaggerated. Organized interest-group activity in litigation was rare before the twentieth century. Moreover, even today, most cases before the court are not sponsored or supported by organized groups themselves, although they do mobilize as amici in important cases. The typical litigant is concerned about the litigant's own interest, not that of a group. But justices on the Supreme Court and judges on other appellate courts are normally aware in a general way of the competing interests at stake in important cases. Thus, even when organized interest-group activity is absent, the interests themselves may be indirectly represented through the justices' consciousness of them.

Federal and state governments may be allowed to submit amici briefs, and they are almost certain to seek to do so if a lower court has invalidated one of their statutes or administrative decisions. Supreme Court rules require no consent of a party when the federal government sponsors an amicus brief, and the rules also favor the federal government over other amici in the grant of special leave to participate in oral argument. Most of the cases in which the federal government participates as an amicus (around ten a year) have broad policy implications, and many of them involve politically active interest groups. In other cases the federal government may have a negative influence by declining to be an amicus. The Department of Justice is the government agency where the decision to intervene as an amicus is made, and the attorney general makes the decision.

Political Parties Party organizations rarely initiate lawsuits, and these are usually connected with allegations of irregularity or discrimination in the electoral process (e.g., suits over contested elections). Only occasionally are party organizations defendants in legal actions brought by members dissatisfied with the rules or practices of the organizations (e.g., suits by blacks to void the whites-only Democratic primary in the pre–Civil Rights South). Indeed, the parties themselves are rarely aligned uniformly with one or another private party in lawsuits. *Marbury v. Madison* is exceptional in this respect, with the Federalists uniformly on the side of Marbury and the Jeffersonians uniformly on the side of Madison. Even in the Dred Scott case, while the Republicans were uniformly on the side of Scott, Northern and Southern Democrats were divided on the right of a territory to exclude slavery.

Although party organizations are only occasionally litigants or uniformly aligned with litigants, they may have large stakes in the outcome of lawsuits, especially in constitutional cases. The fate of the parties is linked to the success or failure of government policies pursued by their elected members. Thus the Democratic and Republican parties had stakes in the Supreme Court decisions on New Deal legislation, despite the fact that some Democrats opposed parts of the New Deal and some Republicans supported parts of it. Moreover, individual units of the parties may be differently affected by decisions on the electoral process. For example, the Reynolds decision requiring legislative districts to represent equal numbers of people hurt both rural Democrats and rural Republicans and helped their respective suburban party organizations in different parts of the country.

The Media Judges, like most Americans, read newspapers, listen to the radio, and view television. The media, including books and periodicals, help to make justices and judges aware of the political, economic, and social environment and of the conflicting interests involved in the rulings of constitutional, statutory, and administrative law that they are called upon to render. Moreover, newspaper editorials and articles in popular periodicals indicate to them the conflicting community values and attitudes at stake in important cases.

Lawyers and the Legal Profession Lawyers representing the litigants and amici are integral to the judicial process. It is they who present their clients' claims to the court in written briefs and oral arguments. Occasionally in the early days of the court, justices relied heavily on the briefs and arguments of counsel in the preparation of opinions, and Marshall himself incorporated whole paragraphs. Usually today, however, justices reflect and refine the briefs and arguments of counsel rather than incorporate them. The more prestigious the lawyer is, the more likely will be his influence on the justices. In any case, the influence of the lawyers representing the litigants and amici has been and is considerable. Before the Civil War oral arguments were not subject to any limitations of time, and lawyers took the time to exercise their forensic abilities, but oral arguments today are generally limited to a half-hour for each side, although more time may allotted for cases deemed important or on which the justices are closely divided. During the period of oral argument, the lawyers spend much of their time answering questions put to them by the justices.

Of all the lawyers who appear before the court, the most influential is the solicitor general of the United States, the chief officer in charge of representing the federal government in cases before the court. The federal government is a party or amicus in about 60 percent of the cases argued in the court, and the solicitor general, with the aid of his staff of lawyers, assigns a lawyer to represent the government in all the cases argued before the court. More importantly, the solicitor general and his staff decide which cases to appeal, except for cases involving a few agencies operating under special statutes (e.g., the Interstate Commerce Commission). In this respect the solicitor general acts not only as an officer of the president, but also as an officer of the court. He holds a tight rein on government appeals, and so the court regards his requests for review more seriously than those of other appealing parties.

A second class of lawyers who affect the decisions of the justices are the judges of the lower courts who have ruled on the cases before they come to the Supreme Court and the justices who decided previous relevant cases. The influence of these judges will be considered later in connection with the materials involved in court decisions.

Another class of lawyers who may influence the decisions of the justices consists of law professors, law experts, and student editors who write articles or notes in legal periodicals. In recent years references in the justices' opinions indicate that they or their clerks have examined such articles or notes and have been influenced by them.

The clerks of the justices, a fourth class of lawyers, are internally involved in the court's decision-making process, and so they will be considered with the justices.

The Decision Makers: The Justices

Selection Unlike with the offices of president, senator, and congressman, the Constitution does not specify any qualifications as necessary for appointment to the court. The Constitution provides only that the president shall appoint justices to the court "by and with the consent of the Senate" (Article II, section 2). Moreover, justices hold their offices "during good behavior" (Article III, section 1) and may be removed only by impeachment and conviction for "high crimes and misdemeanors" (Article II, section 4). Only one justice, Samuel Chase, was impeached by the House of Representatives but acquitted by the Senate in 1804. Presidents have uniformly followed one informal requirement, however, in their appointments to the court— namely, that the justices be lawyers—and this tradition will surely continue.

Many factors influence a president's selection of appointees. Given the modern role of the federal government in managing the economy and social programs, politically conscious presidents have been most anxious to place persons on the court who will be sympathetic to the presidents' policies insofar as the court passes on questions of constitutional, statutory, and administrative law. To a lesser extent presidents may be concerned about the court's decisions regarding the constitutionality of federal or state policies on economic and social issues of the day (e.g., affirmative-action programs and abortion).

Party membership and activity have been important factors in the selection of justices, and exceptions to this factor were extremely rare until the twentieth century (e.g., President Hayes appointed the elder Harlan to the court in part because the latter helped Hayes win the Republican nomination in 1876). There has been no exception since Republican President Nixon appointed Democratic Lewis Powell to the court in 1971.

Other factors have been important. Personal friendship between the president and the appointee, for example, influenced all four of President Truman's appointments. Regional representation was an important consideration until 1891, since the justices were required until then to sit on circuit (district and appellate) courts in different regions. Religion was not a factor in the first hundred years of the court, all the justices except Taney being Protestants, but a tradition developed in the late nineteenth and twentieth centuries in favor of one member of the court being a Catholic. Later, the tradition of a Jewish justice on the court developed, and blacks and women became members of the court. Today, six members of the court are Catholic, three Jewish, and not one Protestant. Republican presidents since Eisenhower (after Warren) have preferred to appoint justices with prior judicial experience. Last, age is a factor since, other things being equal, presidents prefer to appoint relatively young persons to the court because younger justices are likely to live longer than older justices and so extend the time span of the president's influence.

In the light of the political factor, it is not surprising that most justices previously held political positions. Nor is it surprising that most justices come from relatively privileged backgrounds.

Although the president decides whom to appoint to the court, he receives suggestions from many sources and may consult the opinions of his closest advisers in and out of government. The attorney general is by reason of his office usually the most influential adviser in recent times. He is responsible for screening potential nominees, communicating with key senators, and making recommendations to the president. The justices themselves have no official role in the selections of their associates, but occasionally an individual justice can exercise a strong influence, as Chief Justice Taft did with President Harding (including recommending himself to succeed Chief Justice White). The American Bar Association has played an important role in recent years through its reports on the professional qualifications of a nominee.

The Senate must approve the nominee before the appointment can be officially signed and sealed. The Senate Judiciary Committee holds hearings on the qualifications of the nominee and reports to the Senate favoring or opposing the nomination. Twenty-two nominees (one-quarter) were rejected, blocked, or not acted upon in the eighteenth and nineteenth centuries, usually because of personal antagonisms or partisan considerations. In the twentieth century the Senate formally rejected only four nominees. John Parker (Hoover), Clement Haynesworth Jr. (Nixon), and Robert Bork (Reagan) were rejected principally for ideological reasons. The Senate rejected G. Harrold Carswell (Nixon) principally because of negative evaluation of his qualifications, and Bork's judicial temperament was a factor in his rejection. Significant interest groups, such as organized labor against Parker, Haynesworth, and Carswell, the NAACP against Haynesworth and Carswell, and women's organizations against Bork, also mobilized against these nominees. In addition, three nominees, Abe Fortas to be chief justice (Johnson), Douglas Ginsburg (Reagan), and Harriet Miers (Bush II) withdrew their nominations before a Senate vote.

Attitudes and Background The justices bring to their judicial opinions values and attitudes toward society, government, federal-state relations, and the court's role in the American political system. As with every individual, the basic values and attitudes of a justice are formed early. Childhood experience is likely to be the most formative influence on a justice's adult attitudes. Indications of a justice's psychological development can be found in biographical and autobiographical sources. A justice's economic and social background, religious environment, schooling, party affiliation, activity, previous career in government, and personal friendships contribute to a justice's values and attitudes. Of particular importance are the contributions of the legal profession to the formation of a justice's judicial values and attitudes. The justices are lawyers, and they share the values and attitudes of the profession. Law professors who taught the justices and the legal practice the justices engaged in before their appointment to the court may have an influence on their legal values and attitudes.

And many of the justices' closest friends are likely to be other lawyers with whom they have worked. It is noteworthy how many of the recent justices have taught in law schools.

Clerks Each justice is now permitted to have up to four clerks (in addition to seven assistants, two secretaries, and one messenger). The clerks are particularly important in the court's decision-making process. They are recent law-school graduates at the top of their classes, frequently from Ivy League or other prestigious law schools. As such they are in a position to serve as conduits for ideas from experts of the legal profession to the justices. Their tasks include review of petitions asking for review of lower court decisions, identification of the issues in cases accepted for review, analysis of arguments, review of precedents or analogues, and perhaps statements of their own opinion about the issues. They are usually most influential on the initial decisions granting or denying review. Justices write their own opinions, but the sheer volume of cases, the long list of precedents cited and discussed, and the length of the opinion themselves indicate that the justices must rely heavily on their clerks to provide them with the basic materials.

The Legal Materials

The Supreme Court authoritatively interprets federal statutes and treaties and determines whether federal administrative orders conform to statutory requirements. In addition, the court may be called upon to decide whether these statutes, treaties, or administrative orders violate provisions of the U.S. Constitution. The court does not interpret state constitutions or statutes, nor does it determine whether the administrative orders of state and local officials conform to the state's constitution or statutes. For these determinations the court relies on the rulings of the highest courts of the state concerned. The court considers only whether state statutes, constitutions, or administrative orders, as interpreted by the state's highest court, violate provisions of the U.S. Constitution or federal statutes. Thus the legal materials involved in court decisions may be: (1) federal statutes; (2) federal treaties; (3) federal administrative orders; (4) state statutes or local ordinances; (5) state constitutions; (6) state administrative orders. In every case from the state courts and many cases from the lower federal courts, one or more provisions of the U.S. Constitution will be involved.

The overwhelming bulk of cases come to the court after decisions by other courts—that is, as part of its appellate jurisdiction. Trial courts determine facts, and appellate courts do not ordinarily overturn those findings. Trial judges also make legal rulings on the admissibility and relevance of facts and adjudicate the rights and duties of the litigants under the law. These rulings are subject to review by appellate courts, and the court normally undertakes its review only after previous review of the rulings by the highest state courts or the federal courts of appeals.

Intrinsic to the operation of the court are its own previous decisions in related cases. The court rarely overrules one of its previous decisions. Rather, it normally adheres to the principle of stare decisis—namely, it stands by its previous decisions. This is done to aid lawyers in their advice to clients and their conduct of litigation and to give guidelines to lower court judges for their rulings at the trial stage. Adherence to previous decisions is necessary to maintain stability in the legal system. But the court does not always follow the principle of stare decisis. The principal reason the court deviates from the principle, when it does, is that the legal system is only part of the political system, and changes in the political system may lead the court to reverse previous decisions. The influence of previous court decisions on the outcome of present cases will vary with the time span of the precedent, the unanimity of the decisions, and the prestige of the justices who wrote and joined it. Occasionally the court may in subsequent cases adopt the dissenting opinions of prestigious and prophetic justices in previous cases.

The Decision-Making Process

Jurisdiction The Supreme Court hears only those cases or controversies that fall within the judicial power of the United States. Article III, section 2, clause 1 enumerates nine categories of cases and controversies that can be brought in federal courts. Two of these depend on the nature of the subject matter: (1) cases arising under the Constitution, federal laws, and federal treaties; and (2) admiralty and maritime cases. The other seven categories depend on the personality of the parties: (1) cases affecting ambassadors, other public ministers, and consuls; (2) controversies in which the United States is a party; (3) controversies between two or more states; (4) controversies between a state and citizens of another state; (5) controversies between citizens of different states; (6) controversies between citizens of the same state claiming lands under grants from different states; and (7) controversies between a state or citizens of a state and a foreign government or its citizens or subjects. The federal government may sue or be sued by the states in federal courts, and one state may sue another state in the Supreme Court. After ratification of the Eleventh Amendment, however, no state may be sued in federal courts by citizens of another state or by citizens of a foreign nation. Nor, by extension, may foreign governments or a state's own citizens sue a state in federal courts, although federal courts may enjoin state officials from enforcing unconstitutional statutes. In addition, Congress has specified that civil suits between citizens of different states must involve a minimum threshold of money, which since 1969 is $50,000.

This grant of judicial power to the federal courts does not necessarily mean exclusive jurisdiction. Congress has provided that state courts as well may try all cases or controversies in those categories except cases against ambassadors and foreign councils, bankruptcy, copyright, and admiralty cases and prosecutions for violation of federal criminal laws.

The Constitution authorized federal courts for three reasons. First, the framers feared that state courts might favor their own authority, and so federal courts were necessary to protect federal interests. Second, different interpretations of the Constitution and federal laws by state courts might impair the uniformity and effectiveness of federal laws. Third, federal courts provide an impartial forum for adjudicating disputes between the states or between citizens of different states.

Jurisdiction allocates judicial power to specific courts. Article III, section 2, clause 2 distinguishes two classes of jurisdiction of the Supreme Court: "In all cases affecting ambassadors, other public ministers, and consuls, and those in which a state shall be a party, the Supreme Court shall have original jurisdiction. In all other cases, before mentioned [in section 2, clause 1], the Supreme Court shall have appellate jurisdiction, both as to law and fact, with such exceptions and such regulations as the Congress shall make."

Original jurisdiction refers to the power to try cases and appellate jurisdiction to the power to review cases tried by other courts. For all practical purposes, however, the court is an appellate court. First, cases affecting foreign officials and those involving the states are not too numerous. Second, foreign officials are protected against criminal prosecutions by diplomatic immunity. Third, Congress has authorized federal district courts to share the court's original jurisdiction in actions brought by foreign officials, controversies between the United States and the states, and actions brought by states against the citizens of other states and foreign nations. Last, the Eleventh Amendment and its radiations bar lawsuits against the states in federal courts by private parties or foreign governments. Most of the few cases over which the court exercises original jurisdiction involve disputes between two or more states, usually boundary disputes.

In the federal court system most cases originate in the district courts. There is at least one district court in each state, Puerto Rico, and the District of Columbia. Populous states have as many as four district courts (e.g., New York), and many (e.g., the southern district of New York) have many sitting judges. In addition to those district courts, there are territorial courts in Guam, Puerto Rico, and the Virgin Islands. Thirteen courts of appeal, divided into multi-state circuits, and one for the District of Columbia, review decisions of the district courts, the quasi-judicial decisions of the independent regulatory commissions, and federal administrative agencies. There are approximately 175 federal appellate judges, the largest number (twenty-eight) sitting on the Ninth Circuit (the West Coast), and three judges normally sit on each case.

There are also federal courts of specialized jurisdiction. The Court of Claims hears cases by individuals against the federal government (e.g., breaches of contract). The Court of Customs and Patent Appeals hears appeals from the decisions of the Patent Office, the Tariff Commission, and the Customs Court. (The latter decides controversies over duties on imported goods.) The Court of Military Appeals, composed of five civilian judges, hears appeals from military courts-martial. The Tax Court, an administrative agency, hears appeals from tax rulings of the Treasury Department. Consular courts, also administrative agencies, decide cases involving the application of treaties to foreign nations and businesses.

Article III, section 2, clause 2 specifies that Congress may regulate the appellate jurisdiction of the court, and Congress has done so since 1789. There are four ways in which litigants may bring cases to the court for review: (1) by appeal; (2) by certiorari; (3) by certification; (4) by extraordinary writ. The latter two ways of review have always been extremely rare, and now the first also is.

The word *appeal* in the broad sense refers to any method by which a case is brought to the court from a lower court for review. In the narrow, technical sense, however, the word refers to only one method of review by the court. Congress has specified the method of appeal as a matter of right to the losing party in a lower-court decision—that is, the court has a statutory duty to hear the case. In 1988 Congress largely eliminated mandatory review of lower-court decisions. The few remaining cases mandating court review are those in which a lower federal court has held a federal or state statute unconstitutional or where a state court has held a federal statute unconstitutional. Thus almost all cases come to the court for review by the second method of review—namely, certiorari.

The writ of certiorari is an order from the Supreme Court to a lower court to send the entire record of a decided case to the higher court for review. Parties losing in lower courts can petition the court to issue the writ to federal courts of appeal, federal district courts, specialized federal courts (rare), and state courts. The writ is granted only when at least four justices consider the federal questions involved to be sufficiently important.

The third method of review is that of certification. The federal courts of appeal and the Court of Claims may certify questions of law to the Supreme Court for answers. If the court answers the questions submitted, the lower courts may then decide a case in the light of the answers. Only the judges of the lower courts may instigate this method of review.

An extraordinary writ involves a petition from a litigant for the court directly to intervene in a trial. If the court issues the writ, it will order the trial judge to take, or forbid the judge from taking, a specific action.

Other Limitations on Review Article III, section 2, clause 1 enumerates the cases and controversies to which the federal judicial power extends. This means that litigants, not judges, initiate legal actions in the federal courts, and appellate federal courts must await the motion of adversely affected litigants to appeal lower-court decisions. The court has further interpreted the cases or controversies in the grant of federal judicial power to forbid advisory opinions, decisions in moot cases, and collusive suits. An advisory opinion is one given in a proceeding in which no adversaries participate. A case becomes moot when its outcome has ceased to have practical significance for the litigants. A collusive suit is one in which nominally adverse parties actually represent the same interest. Since the court determines when suits are moot or collusive, those limitations are subject to its exclusive control.

In line with the constitutional requirement that there must be a case of controversy for the federal courts to exercise jurisdiction, the court has developed doctrines of standing and ripeness. A litigant has standing to challenge the constitutionality of a law only if the litigant's personal rights are directly affected. Litigants must show that they have sustained or will immediately sustain some direct harm as a result of the enforcement of a statute and not merely an indefinite loss in common with all citizens. Damage alone is not enough; violation of a legal right must be claimed. The main effect of the doctrine of standing has been to bar taxpayers' suits in federal courts, although the court opened the door a wedge to allow such suits based on specific guarantees in the Bill of Rights (*Flast v. Cohen*). In addition, a litigant with standing may raise objections to a statute or practice only at the proper time. Again, since the court determines the requirements for standing and ripeness, these limitations are subject to its exclusive control.

In the course of decision making over more than two hundred years, the court has developed rules of judicial economy to limit its role of arbiter of the Constitution. The principle of stare decisis has already been mentioned. Another rule is that the court will presume the constitutionality of a statute unless the contrary is clearly demonstrated. But this presumption is stronger in some areas of law than in others and has shifted according to the predilections of the justices. Moreover, the court will not generally pass on a constitutional question if the case can be disposed of on other grounds, such as statutory construction or an independent basis for state action. But this rule has also been breached on occasion. The court has likewise maintained that the invalidation of one part of a law will not ordinarily invalidate other parts of the law. But the court itself determines whether different sections of a law are separable. Thus these rules of judicial economy allow the justices wide discretion.

The court has refused to decide what it has called political questions—that is, questions that the Constitution has entrusted to the president and/or Congress, the political branches of the government. But since the court is the arbiter of the Constitution, it may expand or contract the list of political questions at its own discretion. Those questions are also political in the broader sense because attempts to resolve them judicially may lead to direct conflict with the other branches of the federal government. Note that questions do not fall into this category simply because they threaten conflict with state governments or agencies, although such conflicts might raise problems of compliance and adverse reactions at the national level.

The Process The party bringing an original action before the court is called the plaintiff and the opposing party the defendant. The party bringing an action on appeal is called the appellant, and the opposing party the appellee. The party bringing an action on a writ of certiorari is called the petitioner, and the opposing party the respondent.

Cases filed in the Supreme Court are placed in one of three dockets or listings. The first, the least numerous and usually the least important, is the original docket, where cases asserting original jurisdiction are placed. The second and most important is the appellate docket, where cases seeking review of lower-court decisions are placed. The third and most numerous is the miscellaneous docket, created in 1945, where applications for special writs, such as for mandamus, but principally appeals or petitions for certiorari by indigent prisoners (in forma pauperis), are placed.

Approximately 5,000 litigants currently seek Supreme Court review each year. In the appellate docket, the court denies or dismisses most of the petitions for certiorari. In the miscellaneous docket, the court denies or dismisses almost all of the petitions for certiorari. The court renders usually brief per curiam—that is, unsigned—opinions in relatively few cases, often without oral argument. The court delivers between 100 and 150 full, signed opinions in decided cases.

Appellate docket petitions for certiorari are standardized in format. The petitioners submit printed briefs, usually ten to thirty pages long, asserting the basis of the court's jurisdiction and arguing why the court should exercise its discretion in favor of review. To these petitions are appended the decisions of the lower courts, those of any administrative agencies involved, and at least one copy of the record. Respondents file counter briefs arguing why the court should deny certiorari, and petitioners may file supplementary briefs in rebuttal. Copies of all these documents, usually excepting the record, are distributed to each justice. The justices' clerks, mostly in a pool, then prepare memoranda on the applications to assist the justices in their disposition of the cases.

In the miscellaneous docket indigent petitioners usually submit a single typewritten or computer-printed page, prepared without professional assistance and without an accompanying record. The clerks of the chief justice prepare memoranda analyzing the petitions and distribute copies of the memoranda to each justice. The petitions themselves are circulated among the justices only in a capital case or one involving an important or interesting issue. The clerks will consult the solicitor general's office about many of these cases.

Every petition for certiorari is placed on the agenda of a court conference if even only one justice so wishes. Normally, half of the petitions for certiorari in the appellate docket and the overwhelming majority of petitions in the miscellaneous docket receive slight or no conference discussion. Since the time of Chief Justice Hughes, the chief justice draws up a list of petitions that he judges not to merit conference discussion and circulates the list among the justices before each conference. Only rarely does a justice remove a case from the blacklist and insist on its discussion.

The most basic criterion avowed by the court in granting certiorari is whether a case presents a federal question whose resolution will have immediate import beyond the parties directly involved in the case. A second criterion is whether the case involves a conflict between the rules of different lower federal courts. A third criterion is whether there appears to be a grave error or defiance of the court's previous decisions by a lower court. A fourth criterion, rarely avowed, is whether the political climate is favorable to, or at least not risking serious adverse reactions against, a prospective decision. Moreover, an individual justice may have a tactical reason for voting against review—namely, to avoid an authoritative decision contrary to the justice's views. The most successful petitioner for certiorari is the federal government, 50 to 75 percent of whose petitions are granted, as compared with less than 10 percent of other petitions.

After the court has decided to hear a case, the party bringing the action must file another brief, usually within forty-five days after the case has been accepted. The opposing party has thirty days to file an answering brief. Forty copies of these briefs are filed with the clerk of the court. The justices, with the aid of their clerks, study the briefs and other materials, including the lower-court records. The justices then decide whether oral arguments need to be heard and what amount of time is to be allotted to the parties if oral arguments are heard. Each of the opposing parties and sometimes an amicus is usually allotted one half-hour but may be allowed a full hour in cases involving more difficult or far-reaching issues. During the oral arguments, the justices ask questions of the participating lawyers about pertinent points and issues in the case.

The justices meet each Friday of the court's session in completely private conferences to discuss and vote on the cases on which oral arguments have been heard during the week. On the day before the conference, the chief justice sends to each justice a list of the cases to be taken up at the conference and the order in which they will be considered. This list usually includes every case ready for final disposition, including cases argued the day before the conference. The chief justice initiates the discussion of each case at the conference with a brief statement of the facts, the questions of law presented, and suggestions for disposition of the case. He then calls on each justice, in the order of seniority, to express his or her views on the case. After full discussion, the justices vote in reverse order of seniority, beginning with the newest justice and ending with the chief justice. The secrecy of the conference both encourages frank discussion and increases the authority accorded the final decision of the court.

After the conference the chief justice, if he is in the majority, assigns by memorandum the writing of court opinions to individual justices in the majority. Except for per curiam decisions, an official opinion is written and signed by one of the majority justices, giving the legal reasons for the decision. (Sometimes there is no official opinion because the majority justices do not agree on the legal reasons for the decision.) If the chief justice is in the minority, the senior justice in the majority assigns the opinion. Other justices may write concurring opinions, opinions agreeing with the decision but often disagreeing with some or all of the reasoning of the official positions. Justices in the minority may write dissenting opinions, opinions disagreeing with the decisions and the reasoning of the majority. Drafts of all these opinions are printed and circulated among the justices for suggestions of correction and revision.

Since the conference vote is only tentative, the justices writing the official opinion will try to accommodate other justices of the majority and to win over doubtful or dissenting justices. Concurring justices, of course, have no need to accommodate any other opinion, and dissenting justices may have little hope of doing so. A succeeding conference accepts or rejects the assigned opinion, and that opinion, if accepted, becomes official when the court publicly announces its decision, usually on a Monday until the final week or so of decisions. Dissenting opinions weaken the authority of the court's decisions, and concurring opinions weaken the authority of its official opinions.

The chief justice is the most important individual decision maker on the court. Although he has only a single vote equal to that of every other justice, his prestige and administrative duties place him in a central position to influence the work of the court. The degree of his influence depends on his ability, legal and executive, and his personality. As presiding officer, the chief justice schedules the agenda and sets the tempo of the court's work. As moderator of court conferences, he is its discussion leader and has the first opportunity to express views on pending cases. Successful performance of this function requires both skill and tact. In assigning opinions, the chief justice has another source of influence. He will be sensitive to the special competencies of individual justices and the ability of the justices to mobilize the court behind an opinion. In controversial cases he may select a justice to write an opinion who is most likely to mute potential adverse public reaction.

The success of a chief justice depends on two key elements: his ability to carry out the tasks assigned to the court and his ability to maintain social cohesion among the justices despite their personal and ideological differences. The latter ability is particularly important, because personal antagonisms and ideological cleavage, if they were not controlled, would fragment the court and thereby impede its productivity and weaken its authority.

The voting of the justices may reveal the existence of blocs in certain areas of law. These blocs usually arise from ideological affinities, but they also may be strengthened by personal friendships and social contact. Less visible areas of interpersonal relationships involve the law clerks of the justices, who interact with one another and the justices they serve.

Results and Reactions

The Decision A Supreme Court decision finally adjudicates the legal rights of the parties to a case with respect to the subject matter in dispute. In reaching particular decisions, the court uses different types of legal reasoning in constitutional and statutory interpretation. In addition to what the reasoning reveals about the attitudes of individual justices, they are also important for what it portends for future decisions.

The dominant type of reasoning employed by the court today is that of legal analogy. Since the court has existed for over two hundred years, it has established precedents in most areas of constitutional law. And since the court generally follows the principle of stare decisis, it will be concerned to relate a present decision to preceding decisions. A court opinion using legal analogy will cite precedents deemed favorable and attempt to distinguish precedents deemed unfavorable. The court may attempt to distinguish a previous decision by showing that it rests on a different set of facts than the present case or that the rationale of the previous decision is inapplicable to the present case. Or the court may argue that the "real" reason for the previous decision will not support a similar decision in the present case. The latter argument, of course, effectively but only implicitly overturns the previous decision.

In the early years of the court, however, there were few or no precedents, and an activist justice like John Marshall was not disposed to argue by analogy from decisions of the British courts or those of the American states. Today a justice may confront precedents whose applicability to the present case is unclear or, if clear, is opposed to the justice's own views. In such cases forms of legal reasoning other than analogy will be necessary. A favorite alternate form is lexicographical—that is, arguing from the meaning of the words of the Constitution or a statute—and this approach may involve a critical analysis of the meaning of the words at the time they were written. A related form of legal reasoning is that of textual analysis comparing different parts of a text to one another, or the whole text with others that deal with the same or a similar subject.

Another form of legal reasoning is one of logical analysis of the text or of concepts deemed to be fundamental to the text. An activist justice will be inclined toward this form of legal reasoning because it, in contrast to that of legal analogy, allows broad scope to the justice's own conceptual frame of reference.

Another form of interpreting a constitutional text in dispute is to analyze the historical intention of its authors. Madison's notes on the Constitutional Convention, the legislative record of Congress drafting amendments, or that of state legislatures ratifying the Constitution and amendments to it will be relevant to such analysis, as, to a lesser extent, the Federalist Papers may be. This form of legal reasoning is particularly appealing to those justices disposed toward judicial restraint.

Still another form of legal reasoning is pragmatic—namely, to argue for or against a decision on the basis of its anticipated consequences. This form of legal reasoning, except for consideration of strictly logical consequences, is rarely developed in an explicit manner, although extralegal consequences may be indirectly indicated. Almost all the justices are likely to be well aware of the political repercussions of their decisions in important cases, even if they do not express their hopes or fears.

Occasionally justices simply state their value preferences without attempting to justify them by any legal reasoning.

Most judicial opinions make use of more than one line of legal reasoning. One line may not be conclusive, and a justice, like any lawyer, wants to use any argument that will help his cause. In many, if not most, cases, both parties can cite analogous precedents, and the justices will be free to choose between conflicting sets of inconclusive precedents. Lexicographical analyses may not be conclusive because the framers of a constitutional text chose ambiguity in order to mobilize support, or because the application of the text to the circumstances of the case at hand was not foreseen, or because it is difficult to reconstruct contemporary usage of the key words in the text. Textual analysis may not be conclusive because no strong inferences can be drawn from the texts or because inferences conflict. Logical analyses may not be conclusive because alternate assumptions can be made about the text or the concepts underlying it. Historical analyses may be inconclusive because evidence about the intention of the authors of a text may lack specificity or point in conflicting directions. Pragmatic analyses, of course, are exercises in probabilities and prophecies. Thus the justices are most likely to combine different forms of legal reasoning according to the materials available to them and their own predispositions.

Case Law, Compliance, and Impacts One effect of a court decision is restricted to the legal system itself. Each decision is related to previous decisions dealing with the same or a similar subject matter. Case by case, the court constructs a relatively integrated, substantive body of law. This is particularly evident in areas of developing law.

Further effects of court decisions outside the legal system depend in the first place on the compliance of losing parties in the cases and of those individuals or groups who are in the same position as the losing parties and so affected by the decisions. Only the immediate losing parties are subject to contempt citations for failure to comply, but new suits would presumably lead to the same result for other individuals and groups in the same position. Resistant attitudes of state officials, state judges, federal officials, or even federal judges can complicate compliance by losing or affected parties. In the case of conflict with state officials or state judges, the court depends on the president and his administration for enforcement of its decisions. In the case of direct conflict with the federal administration, the court depends on the president's willingness to accept the legitimacy of its decisions and has been generally able since the Civil War to count on such compliance, however grudging.

Decisions, when fully complied with by the principal and the affected parties, may have significant impacts on economic interests, social relations, and/or political parties. The decisions may also create, confirm, or change community values. In constitutional cases, court decisions tend to have the effect of authoritatively validating or invalidating the decisions of other units of the federal political system or state political systems.

Reactions Decisions may also trigger reactions with consequences for the legal system. On the one hand, at the quantitative level decisions that overrule precedents or invalidate federal or state laws or reverse lower-court decisions are likely to encourage appeals in the areas of law affected by the decisions. Decisions carving out exceptions to a precedent likewise encourage actions for new exceptions. On the other hand, decisions that adhere to precedent or validate laws or affirm lower-court decisions are likely to discourage suits or appeals. Thus the principle of stare decisis, when followed, not only determines the outcome of subsequent cases but also by doing so discourages the initiation or prolongation of legal activity. Innovative decisions in the short run stimulate a flurry of legal activity because of the uncertainty introduced, but subsequent decisions over the long run define the limits of those decisions, and so precedents are established to govern the operations of the legal system.

Favorable or unfavorable reactions to decisions may generate inputs that qualitatively affect the court. As members of the legal profession, the justices are sensitive to the reactions of their fellow lawyers, including lower-court judges, and especially of scholars writing in legal periodicals. Favorable reactions by the legal profession will encourage the justices to continue along the paths marked out by their decisions, and unfavorable reactions may lead them to reconsider their position or limit the boundaries of their previous decisions.

The reactions of the public, interest groups, and the media in general have a less direct influence on the justices. The public does not usually notice or react to court decisions, but when it does, the reaction, usually negative, is likely to wane over time. The justices have usually anticipated the reactions of the principal interest groups affected by court decisions, and usually the groups' favorable or unfavorable reactions balance one another out. Much the same can be said about newspaper reactions to court decisions.

But the reactions of the general public, interest groups, and the media can influence the court when they are translated into political demands on the president, Congress, and the bureaucracy. The president may take a completely positive position on a decision—that is, he may vigorously approve, enforce, and implement it—or may take a completely negative position on a decision—that is, he may simply refuse to enforce it. The latter position has been rare in American history and nonexistent or relatively invisible in recent times. But a president who enforces or implements a decision only because he recognizes it to be the law of the land may seek to reverse or limit it. His greatest power over the court lies in the appointment of new justices, and presidents on average have since 1929 appointed a new justice every two years. Thus, if the president reacts negatively to one or more court decisions, he will seek to appoint nominees sympathetic to his point of view. Moreover, Congress, if it shares a president's negative reaction, may increase the size of the court to give the president extra appointments, as it did regularly in the nineteenth century until the Grant presidency. Congress may also enact laws to slow executive implementation of decisions.

In concert with the president or independently of him, Congress may react favorably to a decision. If so, it may implement the decision by statutory legislation or appropriations. If Congress reacts unfavorably to a decision, it may attempt to limit or circumvent it by statutory legislation or control of appropriations. Or Congress may adopt an amendment to the Constitution contravening the decision and submit it to the states for ratification, although the requirements that Congress pass an amendment by a two-thirds vote and that three-fourths of the states ratify it make this approach difficult. Or Congress has the power to impeach and convict justices of "high crimes and misdemeanors" (Article II, section 4), but it is hardly a crime, much less a high one, for a justice to perform his office faithfully, even if a decision is unpopular. Congress also has power over the appellate jurisdiction of the court (Article III, section 2, clause 2), but removal of the court's appellate jurisdiction would not reverse previous decisions or prevent lower courts, federal and state, from ruling adversely to congressional desires.

The bureaucracy may affect the impact of court decisions by administrative orders implementing them, by administrative orders limiting or circumventing them, or by failing to implement them. The action or inaction of the bureaucracy may be at the president's direction and/or due to the bureaucracy's special relationship with affected interest groups. These reactions, although primarily related to impact, will indirectly encourage or discourage the justices in their future decisions.

Political parties rarely react as organized units for or against court decisions. But their presidential and congressional candidates may reflect generalized demands arising from the reactions of interest groups and the general public to decisions, and the president and Congress may influence the court in the ways indicated.

Sources

Case Material Supreme Court decisions are published in three different editions. The official edition is The *United States Reports*, of which the early volumes (1–107) were listed under their individual reporter (e.g., Dallas [Dall.], 1789–1800). Beginning with volume 108, the official reports are listed simply under the title *United States* (U.S.). West Publishing Company publishes a second edition of the decisions in the *Supreme Court Reporter* (cited as S. Ct.), which includes only decisions since 1883. Lawyers' Cooperative Publishing Company publishes a third edition, *United States Supreme Court Reports*, Lawyers' Edition (cited as L. Ed.). Both the *Supreme Court Reporter* and the Lawyers' Edition contain more detailed head notes summarizing the legal content of the cases. The Lawyers' Edition prints excerpts from the briefs of counsel and annotations on the subject matter of important cases. Early volumes of the official reports summarized the oral arguments of counsel. All three editions record the votes and opinions of justices, the names of the counsel for the parties, and the names of amici in the case. The *Supreme Court Reporter* uses numbered keys under which the cases are indexed at the beginning of each volume.

The title of each case includes the names of the two contesting parties. The first name is that of the party bringing the action (plaintiff in original actions, appellant or petitioner in appellate actions). The second name is that of the party answering the action (defendant in original actions and appellee or respondent in appellate actions). The volume number of the edition, the edition, and the initial page number of the case follow the name of the case (e.g., *Edwards v. California*, 314 U.S. 160, 62 S. Ct. 164, 86 L. Ed. 119 [1941])

Printed copies of each decision are available from the clerk of the court at the time of its announcement, and all three publishers issue advance sheets before volumes are published. Important decisions of the court are reported in the *U.S. Law Week*, and excerpts reported in leading newspapers like the *New York Times*.

The court opinion will cite lower-court decisions in the case. Decisions from the highest state courts are published in official reports and in private regional reporting systems (*Atlantic, Northeastern, Northwestern, Pacific, Southern, Southeastern*, and *South-western Reports*, cited as A., N.E., N.W., P, So., S.E., and S.W., respectively). Decisions of the federal courts of appeals are published in the *Federal Reports*, cited as F. until 1924 and as F.2d after 1924.

The subsequent legal history of a case can be traced in *Sheppard's Citations*. Each decision of the court is listed only by its citation (e.g., 314 U.S. 160). Under the citation, subsequent references to the decision are given in an annotated code indicating the quality of the reference (e.g., approving, distinguishing, criticizing, or overruling the decision). The professional reception accorded a decision can be found in annual comments on the court's work in law reviews and periodicals, and scholarly articles are indexed in the *Guide to Legal Periodicals*.

For an explanation of technical legal terms, the reader may consult *Black's* or *Bouvier's Law Dictionary*. For the rules of the court, see the appendix to Title 28 of the U.S. Code.

Historical-Biographical Kermit L. Hall, ed., *The Oxford Companion to the Supreme Court of the United States*, 2nd ed. (New York: Oxford University Press, 2005), provides a comprehensive compilation of data on the court, the justices, and the leading decisions. A shorter companion volume on the decisions alone is Kermit L. Hall and James W. Ely Jr., eds., *The Oxford Guide to United States Supreme Court Decisions*, 2nd ed. (New York: Oxford University Press, 2009). The leading work on the court up to the twentieth century is Charles Warren, *The Supreme Court in United States History* (Boston: Little, Brown, 1926). Comprehensive data on the justices can be found in Melvin I. Urofsky, ed., *Biographical Encyclopedia of the Supreme Court* (Washington, D.C.: Congressional Quarterly, 2006). There are many full-length biographies of individual justices. A number of books deal with individual cases, the classic example being Anthony Lewis, *Gideon's Trumpet* (New York: Random House, 1961).

Process A recent and comprehensive introduction to the Supreme Court process is Lawrence Baum, *The Supreme Court*, 11th ed. (Washington, D.C.: Sage, 2012). There are many analyses of different aspects of the process. Prominent authors of such monographs include David J. Danielski, Sheldon Goldman, Walter F. Murphy, John W. Peltason, G. Herman Pritchett, John R. Schmidhauser, Glendon A. Schubert, and Clement E. Vose.

Appendix 3

THE JUSTICES

The Federalist Court (1789–1800)

Justice	Birth Date	Birth Place	First Year	President	Party	Religion	Prior Post	Last Year
Jay	1745	N.Y.	1789	Washington	Fed	Prot.	Diplomat	1795, r.
Rutledge, J.	1739	S.C.	1789	Washington	Fed	Prot.	S. Legislator	1791, r.
C.J.			1795	Washington			S. Judge	1795
Cushing	1732	Mass.	1789	Washington	Fed	Prot.	S. Judge	1810, d.
Wilson	1742	Scot.	1789	Washington	Fed	Prot.	Lawyer	1798, d.
Blair	1732	Va.	1789	Washington	Fed	Prot.	S. Judge	1796, r.
Iredell	1751	Eng.	1790	Washington	Fed	Prot.	Lawyer	1799, d.
Johnson, T.	1732	Md.	1791	Washington	Fed	Prot.	S. Judge	1793, r.
Paterson	1745	Irel.	1793	Washington	Fed	Prot.	Governor	1806, d.
Chase, Sam.	1741	Md.	1796	Washington	Fed	Prot.	S. Judge	1811, d.
Ellsworth (C. J.)	1745	Conn.	1796	Washington	Fed	Prot.	Senator	1800, r.
Washington	1762	Va.	1798	J. Adams	Fed	Prot.	Lawyer	1829, d.
Moore	1755	N.C.	1799	J. Adams	Fed	Prot.	S. Judge	1804, r.

The Marshall Court (1801–35)

Justice	Birth Date	Birth Place	First Year	President	Party	Religion	Prior Post	Last Year
Marshall, J.	1755	Va.	1801	J. Adams	Fed	Unit.	Sec. of State	1835, d.
Johnson, W.	1771	S.C.	1804	Jefferson	D-Rep	Prot.	S. Judge	1834, d.
Livingston	1757	N.Y.	1806	Jefferson	D-Rep	Prot.	S. Judge	1823, d.
Todd	1765	Va.	1807	Jefferson	D-Rep	Prot.	S. Judge	1826, d.

Justice	Birth Date	Birth Place	First Year	President	Party	Religion	Prior Post	Last Year
Story	1779	Mass	1811	Madison	D-Rep	Unit.	S. Legislator	1845, d.
Duvall	1752	Md.	1811	Madison	D-Rep	Prot.	Comptroller	1835, r.
Thompson	1768	N.Y.	1823	Monroe	D-Rep	Prot.	Navy Sec.	1843, d.
Trimble	1777	Va.	1826	J.Q. Adams	D-Rep	Prot.	Judge	1828, d.
McLean	1785	N.J.	1829	Jackson	Dem	Prot.	Post. Gen.	1861, d.
Baldwin	1780	Conn.	1830	Jackson	Dem	Prot.	Lawyer	1844, d.
Wayne	1790	Ga.	1835	Jackson	Dem	Prot	Rep.	1867, d.

The Taney Court (1836–64)

Justice	Birth Date	Birth Place	First Year	President	Party	Religion	Prior Post	Last Year
Taney	1777	Md.	1836	Jackson	Dem	Cath.	Lawyer	1864, d.
Barbour	1783	Va.	1836	Jackson	Dem	Prot.	Judge	1841, d.
Catron	1776	Va.	1837	Jackson	Dem	Prot.	Lawyer	1865, d.
McKinley	1780	Va.	1837	Van Buren	Dem	Prot.	Senator	1852, d.
Daniel	1784	Va.	1841	Van Buren	Dem	Prot.	Judge	1860, d.
Nelson	1792	N.Y.	1845	Tyler	Dem	Prot.	S. Judge	1872, r.
Woodbury	1789	N.H.	1846	Polk	Dem	Prot.	Senator	1851, d.
Grier	1794	Va.	1846	Polk	Dem	Prot.	S. Judge	1870, r.
Curtis	1809	Mass.	1851	Fillmore	Whig	Prot.	Lawyer	1857, r.
Campbell	1811	Ga.	1853	Pierce	Dem	Prot.	Lawyer	1861, r.
Clifford	1803	N.H.	1858	Buchanan	Dem	Prot .	Lawyer	1881, d.
Swayne	1804	Va.	1862	Lincoln	Rep	Prot .	Lawyer	1881, r.
Miller	1816	Ky.	1862	Lincoln	Rep	Prot.	Lawyer	1890, d.
Davis	1815	Md.	1862	Lincoln	Rep	Prot.	S. Judge	1877, r.
Field	1816	Conn.	1863	Lincoln	Dem	Prot.	S. Judge	1897, r.

The Chase Court (1864–73)

Justice	Birth Date	Birth Place	First Year	President	Party	Religion	Prior Post	Last Year
Chase, Sal.	1808	N.H.	1864	Lincoln	Rep	Prot.	Lawyer	1873, d.
Bradley	1813	N.J.	1870	Grant	Rep	Prot.	Lawyer	1892, d.
Strong	1808	Conn.	1870	Grant	Rep	Prot.	Lawyer	1880, r.
Hunt	1810	N.Y.	1872	Grant	Rep	Prot.	S. Judge	1882, r.

The Waite Court (1874–88)

Justice	Birth Date	Birth Place	First Year	President	Party	Religion	Prior Post	Last Year
Waite	1816	Conn.	1874	Grant	Rep	Prot.	S. Gov't	1888, d.
Harlan I	1833	Ky.	1877	Hayes	Rep	Prot.	Lawyer	1911, d.
Woods	1824	Ohio	1880	Hayes	Rep	Prot.	Judge	1887, d.
Matthews	1824	Ohio	1881	Garfield	Rep	Prot.	Lawyer	1889, d.

Justice	Birth Date	Birth Place	First Year	President	Party	Religion	Prior Post	Last Year
Gray	1828	Mass.	1881	Arthur	Rep	Prot.	S. Judge	1902, d.
Blatchford	1820	N.Y.	1882	Arthur	Rep	Prot.	Judge	1893, d.
Lamar, L.	1825	Ga.	1888	Cleveland	Dem	Prot.	Interior Sec.	1893, d.

The Fuller Court (1888–1910)

Justice	Birth Date	Birth Place	First Year	President	Party	Religion	Prior Post	Last Year
Fuller	1833	Maine	1888	Cleveland	Dem	Prot.	Lawyer	1910, d.
Brewer	1836	Turkey	1889	Harrison	Rep	Prot.	Judge	1910, d.
Brown	1837	Mass.	1890	Harrison	Rep.	Prot.	Judge	1906, r.
Shiras	1832	Pa.	1892	Harrison	Rep	Prot.	Lawyer	1903, r.
Jackson, H.	1832	Tenn.	1893	Harrison	Dem	Prot.	Judge	1895, d.
White, E.	1865	La.	1894	Cleveland	Dem	Cath.	Senator	1910
C. J.			1910	Taft				1921.d.
Peckham	1838	N.Y.	1895	Cleveland	Dem	Prot.	S. Judge	1909, d.
McKenna	1843	Pa.	1898	McKinley	Rep	Cath.	Atty. Gen.	1925, r.
Holmes	1841	Mass.	1902	T. Roosevelt	Rep	None	S. Judge	1932, r.
Day	1849	Ohio	1903	T. Roosevelt	Rep	Prot.	Judge	1922, r.
Moody	1853	Mass.	1906	T. Roosevelt	Rep	Prot.	Atty. Gen.	1910, r.
Lurton	1844	Ky.	1909	Taft	Rep	Prot.	Judge	1914, d.
Hughes	1862	N.Y.	1910	Taft	Rep	Prot.	Governor	1916, r.
C. J.			1930	Hoover			Lawyer	1941, r.

The White Court (1910–21)

Justice	Birth Date	Birth Place	First Year	President	Party	Religion	Prior Post	Last Year
Van Devanter	1853	Ind.	1910	Taft	Rep	Prot.	Judge	1937, r.
Lamar, J.	1857	Ga.	1910	Taft	Dem	Prot.	S. Judge	1916, d.
Pitney	1858	N.J.	1912	Taft	Rep	Prot.	S. Judge	1922, r.
McReynolds	1862	Ky.	1914	Wilson	Dem	Prot.	Atty. Gen.	1941, r.
Brandeis	1856	Ky.	1916	Wilson	Dem	Jew.	Lawyer	1939, r.
Clarke	1857	Ohio	1916	Wilson	Dem	Prot.	Judge	1922, r.

The Taft Court (1921–30)

Justice	Birth Date	Birth Place	First Year	President	Party	Religion	Prior Post	Last Year
Taft	1857	Ohio	1921	Harding	Rep	Unit.	Law Prof.	1930, r.
Sutherland	1862	Eng.	1922	Harding	Rep	Prot. (?)	Lawyer	1938, r.
Butler	1866	Minn.	1922	Harding	Rep	Cath.	Lawyer	1939, d.
Sanford	1865	Tenn.	1923	Harding	Rep	Prot.	Judge	1930, d.
Stone	1872	N.H,	1925	Coolidge	Rep	Prot.	Atty. Gen.	1941
C. J.			1941	F. Roosevelt				1946, d.

The Hughes Court (1930–41)

Justice	Birth Date	Birth Place	First Year	President	Party	Religion	Prior Post	Last Year
Roberts	1875	Pa.	1930	Hoover	Rep	Prot.	Law Prof.	1945, r.
Cardozo	1870	N.Y.	1932	Hoover	Dem	Jew.	S. Judge	1938, d.
Black	1886	Ala.	1937	F. Roosevelt	Dem	Prot.	Senator	1971, r.
Reed	1884	Ky.	1938	F. Roosevelt	Dem	Prot.	Sol. Gen.	1957, r.
Frankfurter	1882	Austria	1939	F. Roosevelt	Ind.	Jew.	Law Prof.	1962, r.
Douglas	1898	Minn.	1939	F. Roosevelt	Dem	Prot.	S. E. Comm.	1975, r.
Murphy	1890	Mich.	1940	F. Roosevelt	Dem	Cath.	Atty. Gen.	1949, d.

The Stone Court (1941–46)

Justice	Birth Date	Birth Place	First Year	President	Party	Religion	Prior Post	Last Year
Byrnes	1879	S.C.	1941	F. Roosevelt	Dem	Prot.	Senator	1942, r.
Jackson, R.	1892	Pa.	1941	F. Roosevelt	Dem	Prot.	Atty. Gen.	1954, d.
Rutledge, W.	1894	Ky.	1943	F. Roosevelt	Dem	Unit.	Judge	1949, d.
Burton	1888	Mass.	1945	Truman	Rep	Unit.	Senator	1958, r.

The Vinson Court (1946–53)

Justice	Birth Date	Birth Place	First Year	President	Party	Religion	Prior Post	Last Year
Vinson	1890	Ky.	1946	Truman	Dem	Prot.	Treas. Sec.	1953, d.
Minton	1890	Ind.	1949	Truman	Dem	Prot.	Judge	1956, r.
Clark	1899	Tex.	1949	Truman	Dem	Prot.	Atty. Gen.	1967, r.

The Warren Court (1953–69)

Justice	Birth Date	Birth Place	First Year	President	Party	Religion	Prior Post	Last Year
Warren	1891	Cal.	1953	Eisenhower	Rep	Prot.	Governor	1969, r.
Harlan II	1899	Ill.	1955	Eisenhower	Rep	Prot.	Judge	1971, r.
Brennan	1905	N.J.	1956	Eisenhower	Dem	Prot,	S. Judge	1990, r.
Whittaker	1901	Kans.	1957	Eisenhower	Rep	Prot.	Judge	1962, r.
Stewart	1915	Ohio	1958	Eisenhower	Rep.	Prot.	Judge	1981, r.
White, B.	1917	Colo.	1962	Kennedy	Dem	Prot.	Dep. A.G.	1993, r.
Goldberg	1908	Ill.	1962	Kennedy	Dem	Jew.	Labor Sec.	1965, r.
Fortas	1910	Tenn.	1965	L. Johnson	Dem	Jew.	Fed Admin.	1969, r.
Marshall, T.	1908	Md.	1967	L. Johnson	Dem	Prot.	Judge	1991, r.

The Burger Court (1969–86)

Justice	Birth Date	Birth Place	First Year	President	Party	Religion	Prior Post	Last Year
Burger	1907	Minn.	1969	Nixon	Rep	Prot.	Judge	1986, r.
Blackmun	1908	Ill.	1970	Nixon	Rep	Prot.	Judge	1994, r.
Powell	1907	Va.	1971	Nixon	Dem	Prot.	Lawyer	1987, r.

Justice	Birth Date	Birth Place	First Year	President	Party	Religion	Prior Post	Last Year
Rehnquist	1924	Wis.	1972	Nixon	Rep	Prot.	Asst. A.G.	1986
C. J.			1986	Reagan				2005, d.
Stevens	1920	Ill.	1975	Ford	Rep	Prot.	Judge	2010, r.
O'Connor	1930	Tex.	1981	Reagan	Rep	Prot.	S. Judge	2005, r.

The Rehnquist Court (1986–2005)

Justice	Birth Date	Birth Place	First Year	President	Party	Religion	Prior Post	Last Year
Scalia	1936	N.J.	1986	Reagan	Rep	Cath.	Judge	
Kennedy	1936	Cal.	1986	Reagan	Rep	Cath.	Judge	
Souter	1939	Mass.	1990	Bush I	Rep	Prot.	Judge	2009, r.
Thomas	1948	Ga.	1991	Bush I	Rep	Cath.	Judge	
Ginsburg	1933	N.Y.	1993	Clinton	Dem	Jew.	Judge	
Breyer	1938	Cal.	1994	Clinton	Dem	Jew.	Judge	

The Roberts Court (2005–)

Justice	Birth Date	Birth Place	First Year	President	Party	Religion	Prior Post	Last Year
Roberts, J.	1955	N.Y.	2005	Bush II	Rep	Cath.	Judge	
Alito	1950	N.J.	2006	Bush II	Rep	Cath.	Judge	
Sotomayor	1954	N.Y.	2009	Obama	Dem	Cath	Judge	
Kagan	1960	N.Y.	2010	Obama	Dem	Jew.	Law Prof.	

Note: Fed signifies the Federalist Party, *D-Rep* the Democrat-Republican Party, *Dem* the Democratic Party, and *Rep* the Republican Party. *Prot.* signifies Protestant religion, *Cath.* Catholic religion, *Unit.* Unitarian religion, and *Jew.* Jewish religion or ethnicity. The letter *S.* indicates that the office is a state office. Prior governmental position, unless otherwise so designated, refers to a federal office. The letter *d.* indicates that the justice died in office, and the letter *r.* indicates that the justice resigned, often because of illness or impending death.

Appendix 4

THE SUPREME COURTS

Jay (1789–95)

1789 Rutledge Cushing Wilson Blair
1790 Rutledge Cushing Wilson Blair Iredell
1791 Johnson Cushing Wilson Blair Iredell
1793 Paterson Cushing Wilson Blair Iredell

Rutledge (1795)

1795 Paterson Cushing Wilson Blair Iredell

Ellsworth (1796–1800)

1796 Paterson Cushing Wilson Chase Iredell
1798 Paterson Cushing Washington Chase Iredell
1799 Paterson Cushing Washington Chase Moore

Marshall (1801–35)

1801 Paterson Cushing Washington Chase Moore
1804 Paterson Cushing Washington Chase Johnson
1806 Livingston Cushing Washington Chase Johnson
1807 Livingston Cushing Washington Chase Johnson Todd
1811 Livingston Story Washington Duvall Johnson Todd
1823 Thompson Story Washington Duvall Johnson Todd
1826 Thompson Story Washington Duvall Johnson Trimble

1829 Thompson Story Washington Duvall Johnson McLean
1830 Thompson Story Baldwin Duvall Johnson McLean
1835 Thompson Story Baldwin Duvall Wayne McLean

Taney (1836–64)

1836 Thompson Story Baldwin Barbour Wayne McLean
1837 Thompson Story Baldwin Barbour Wayne McLean Catron McKinley
1841 Thompson Story Baldwin Daniel Wayne Mclean Catron McKinley
1845 Nelson Woodbury Baldwin Daniel Wayne McLean Catron McKinley
1846 Nelson Woodbury Grier Daniel Wayne Mclean Catron McKinley
1851 Nelson Curtis Grier Daniel Wayne Mclean Catron McKinley
1853 Nelson Curtis Grier Daniel Wayne McLean Catron Campbell
1858 Nelson Clifford Grier Daniel Wayne McLean Catron Campbell
1862 Nelson Clifford Grier Miller Wayne Swayne Catron Davis
1863 Nelson Clifford Grier Miller Wayne Swayne Catron Davis Field

Chase (1864–73)

1864 Nelson Clifford Grier Miller Wayne Swayne Catron Davis Field
1865 Nelson Clifford Grier Miller Wayne Swayne vacant Davis Field
1867 Nelson Clifford Grier Miller vacant Swayne vacant Davis Field
1870 Nelson Clifford Strong Miller Bradley Swayne Davis Field
1872 Hunt Clifford Strong Miller Bradley Swayne Davis Field

Waite (1874–88)

1874 Hunt Clifford Strong Miller Bradley Swayne Davis Field
1877 Hunt Clifford Strong Miller Bradley Swarne Harlan Field
1880 Hunt Clifford Woods Miller Bradley Swayne Harlan Field
1881 Hunt Gray Woods Miller Bradley Matthews Harlan Field
1882 Blatchford Gray Woods Miller Bradley Matthews Harlan Field

Fuller (1888–1910)

1888 Blatchford Gray Lamar Miller Bradley Matthews Harlan Field
1889 Blatchford Gray Lamar Miller Bradley Brewer Harlan Field
1891 Blatchford Gray Lamar Brown Bradley Brewer Harlan Field
1892 Blatchford Gray Lamar Brown Shiras Brewer Harlan Field
1893 Blatchford Gray Jackson Brown Shiras Brewer Harlan Field
1894 White Gray Jackson Brown Shiras Brewer Harlan Field

1895 White Gray Peckham Brown Shiras Brewer Harlan Field
1898 White Gray Peckham Brown Shiras Brewer Harlan McKenna
1902 White Holmes Peckham Brown Shiras Brewer Harlan McKenna
1903 White Holmes Peckham Brown Day Brewer Harlan McKenna
1906 White Holmes Peckham Moody Day Brewer Harlan McKenna
1909 White Holmes Lurton Moody Day Brewer Harlan McKenna

White (1910–21)

1910 Van Devanter Holmes Lurton Lamar Day Hughes Harlan McKenna
1912 Van Devanter Holmes Lurton Lamar Day Hughes Pitney McKenna
1914 Van Devanter Holmes McReynolds Lamar Day Hughes Pitney McKenna
1916 Van Devanter Holmes McReynolds Brandeis Day Clarke Pitney McKenna

Taft (1921–30)

1921 Van Devanter Holmes McReynolds Brandeis Day Clarke Pitney McKenna
1922 Van Devanter Holmes McReynolds Brandeis Butler Sutherland Pitney McKenna
1923 Van Devanter Holmes McReynolds Brandeis Butler Sutherland Sanford McKenna
1925 Van Devanter Holmes McReynolds Brandeis Butler Sutherland Sanford Stone

Hughes (1930–41)

1930 Van Devanter Holmes McReynolds Brandeis Butler Sutherland Roberts Stone
1932 Van Devanter Cardozo McReynolds Brandeis Butler Sutherland Roberts Stone
1937 Black Cardozo McReynolds Brandeis Butler Sutherland Roberts Stone
1938 Black Cardozo McReynolds Brandeis Butler Reed Roberts Stone
1939 Black Frankfurter McReynolds Douglas Butler Reed Roberts Stone
1940 Black Frankfurter McReynolds Douglas Murphy Reed Roberts Stone

Stone (1941–46)

1941 Black Frankfurter Byrnes Douglas Murphy Reed Roberts Jackson
1943 Black Frankfurter Rutledge Douglas Murphy Reed Roberts Jackson
1945 Black Frankfurter Rutledge Douglas Murphy Reed Burton Jackson

Vinson (1946–53)

1946 Black Frankfurter Rutledge Douglas Murphy Reed Burton Jackson
1949 Black Frankfurter Minton Douglas Clark Reed Burton Jackson

Warren (1953–69)

1953 Black Frankfurter Minton Douglas Clark Reed Burton Jackson

1955 Black Frankfurter Minton Douglas Clark Reed Burton Harlan

1956 Black Frankfurter Brennan Douglas Clark Reed Burton Harlan

1957 Black Frankfurter Brennan Douglas Clark Whittaker Burton Harlan

1958 Black Frankfurter Brennan Douglas Clark Whittaker Stewart Harlan

1962 Black Goldberg Brennan Douglas Clark White Stewart Harlan

1965 Black Fortas Brennan Douglas Clark White Stewart Harlan

1967 Black Fortis Brennan Douglas Marshall White Stewart Harlan

Burger (1969–86)

1969 Black Fortis Brennan Douglas Marshall White Stewart Harlan

1970 Black Blackmun Brennan Douglas Marshall White Stewart Harlan

1972 Powell Blackmun Brennan Douglas Marshall White Stewart Rehnquist

1975 Powell Blackmun Brennan Stevens Marshall White Stewart Rehnquist

1981 Powell Blackmun Brennan Stevens Marshall White O'Connor Rehnquist

Rehnquist (1986–2005)

1986 Powell Blackmun Brennan Stevens Marshall White O'Connor Scalia

1988 Kennedy Blackmun Brennan Stevens Marshall White O'Connor Scalia

1990 Kennedy Blackmun Souter Stevens Marshall White O'Connor Scalia

1991 Kennedy Blackmun Souter Stevens Thomas White O'Connor Scalia

1993 Kennedy Blackmun Souter Stevens Thomas Ginsburg O'Connor Scalia

1994 Kennedy Breyer Souter Stevens Thomas Ginsburg O'Connor Scalia

Roberts (2005–)

2005 Kennedy Breyer Souter Stevens Thomas Ginsburg O'Connor Scalia

2006 Kennedy Breyer Souter Stevens Thomas Ginsburg Alito Scalia

2009 Kennedy Breyer Sotomayor Stevens Thomas Ginsburg Alito Scalia

2010 Kennedy Breyer Sotomayor Kagan Thomas Ginsburg Alito Scalia

Note: New justices took their seat, or vacancies occurred, some time during the given year.

INDEX OF CASES

Note: When the United States is the first party, I have listed the case under the name of the second party. I have cross-listed some cases by their more familiar second-party names.

Index of Cases

INDEX OF JUSTICES' BIOGRAPHIES

INDEX OF TOPICS

A Constitutional History of the U.S. Supreme Court was designed in Vendetta and
Hypatia Sans and composed by Kachergis Book Design of Pittsboro, North Carolina.
It was printed on 60-pound Natures Natural and bound by
Thomson-Shore of Dexter, Michigan.